EVOLUTION OF
THE EUROPEAN IDEA,
1914–1932

Evolution of
the European Idea,
1914–1932

by Carl H. Pegg

THE UNIVERSITY OF NORTH CAROLINA PRESS

CHAPEL HILL AND LONDON

Library of Congress Cataloging in Publication Data

Pegg, Carl H. (Carl Hamilton), 1905–
Evolution of the European idea, 1914–1932.

Bibliography: p.
Includes index.
1. Europe—Politics and government—1918–1945.
2. European federation. I. Title.
D727.P43   1983   940.5   82-24796
ISBN 0-8078-1559-4

To
Eleanor Cunningham and Margaret Harrison Smith,
Daughters of Edward Oscar and Elizabeth Gregory Smith
of Newport News, Virginia

CONTENTS

Contents

PREFACE

My active interest in the idea of the unification of Europe goes back to the spring of 1930 when I first went to Europe for a period of study and travel. Although I had read before sailing for Europe that the Quai d'Orsay had sent a Memorandum on the Organization of a System of European Federal Union to the governments of Europe, I was nonetheless greatly surprised during my first days in Paris to find this memorandum one of the principal topics in the press and to hear people in cafes talking about the unification of Europe and a United States of Europe. The thought had scarcely entered my mind that Europe could be anything except a continent of feuding and warring nations. I had trouble believing what I read and heard, and I soon found myself watching the daily press for articles and editorials on the French memorandum, searching bookstalls and shops for items on the European idea, and questioning French students and bookdealers about Aristide Briand, Edouard Herriot, and Alexis Léger, who most of them believed had played the key role in developing the federal project.

And while this experience sank in and remained with me, I never thought seriously of making a study of the European idea until the middle of World War II when Jan Masaryk, in a lecture at the University of North Carolina, mentioned Briand's efforts to forge a European bond and said in my office the next day that the European idea was coming to life in the French underground and that he felt it would become an important element in European politics after the war. I soon had solid evidence that the idea was being discussed in the French resistance, and indeed my first article on the idea dealt with its revival in the European resistance (*Europa Archiv* 7 [Oct. 5, 1952]). In fact it was the writing of this article together with conversations with Henri Bonnet, then French ambassador to the United States, and Robert Marjolin, secretary general of the OEEC, that started me thinking in terms of a study of the European idea across the 1920s. Both men said—and I was already thinking the same way—that it was not possible to understand the revival of the idea in the European underground and its rapid growth after World War II without an understanding of what had gone on during the 1920s. Then after the European Coal and Steel Community came into full operation, I centered my research on the 1920s and early 1930s. And notwithstanding a heavy teaching and administrative load, I was able during the next fifteen years to examine a large additional body of contemporary material of every sort.

Though I have condensed greatly the original draft of the manuscript for this study, I hope it still provides a fairly complete and solid summary of what most of the more ardent and vocal apostles of the European idea said and did during these years. I also hope that it may serve to encourage others to undertake some of the special studies that are so obviously needed for a more definitive synthesis. Some studies of an economic nature are much needed and are becoming increasingly feasible due to the growing availability of the archives of business firms and the personal papers of business leaders.

I would like at this point to express my gratitude to the many men and women who have helped me with this study since the spring of 1930. I could not, of course, name all of them if space allowed, because many have helped me whose names I never knew. My largest debt is undoubtedly to the staffs of some twenty libraries and archives across the United States and Europe. While my debt is largest to the staff of the library of the University of North Carolina, it is also great to the staffs of several others: the Library of Congress; the Hoover Institution on War, Revolution and Peace; the Bibliothèque Nationale (and at Versailles); the Bibliothèque de Documentation Internationale Contemporaine (Nanterre), the British Museum, and the libraries of the universities of Amsterdam and Strasbourg.

I am also indebted to the proprietors and staffs of several dozen bookshops in Paris, Brussels, Amsterdam, Frankfurt a. M., Munich, Geneva, London, and Gregory Lounz in New York. For the proprietors of many of the shops not only made special efforts to locate scarce items for me, but they were also eager to talk about the European idea through the 1920s, and quite a number of them had taken an active interest in the European movement and knew a great deal about it. I also profited greatly from the many interviews and informal conversations that I had over the years with Europeans of varied backgrounds, sometimes in hotel lobbies, cafes, and parks.

I owe a debt of a different sort to three men—Edgar Stern-Rubarth, Herbert von Beckerath, and Erwin Hexner—who participated in the European movement of the 1920s in varying degrees. For they not only talked with me at length many times and gave me valuable material, but they read portions of the first draft of the first part of this volume many years ago and encouraged me to carry on. Several of my colleagues have aided me in getting the manuscript into final form. Josef Anderle read most of the first draft of the manuscript and made valuable suggestions, and Christoph Schweitzer provided help with some of the German titles. Linda Stephenson typed the manuscript, and Gwen Duffey edited it for the press in a helpful and skillful manner.

Finally, I would like to acknowledge a many-sided debt to the scores of graduate students whose programs I directed from 1935 to 1975. A sizable number of them helped me in various ways with this study. Three of those who helped me—John L. Snell, Franklin D. Laurens, and Walter R. Craddock—have crossed the great divide.

EVOLUTION OF
THE EUROPEAN IDEA,
1914–1932

Chapter 1

THE EUROPEAN IDEA ACROSS

THE CENTURIES

The idea of organizing and uniting Europe, which became a central element in European politics shortly after World War II, stretches back across several centuries.[1] Even in something resembling its modern dress, it goes back at least to Pierre Dubois who studied with Saint Thomas Aquinas and saw service with both King Philip the Fair of France and King Edward I of England. This French jurist and diplomat not only sensed that church and papacy were in decline but also that the principle of nationality was growing and that national monarchies as well as national languages were on the march. These trends toward religious and political diversity and disunity led him to the view that Christendom's greatest need was some sort of broad civil authority capable of maintaining law and order. Accordingly, in 1306, Dubois formulated a general scheme of reform that, among other things, called on the sovereign princes of Europe to establish a permanent European council or confederation dedicated to the maintenance of peace throughout Christendom, to the protection of the Holy Land, and to the containment of Turkish power.[2]

Dubois had put his finger on a real problem and a real need, and the idea of a European structure of some sort was never henceforth very long without a well-known spokesman—a King George of Podebrad, an Eméric Crucé, a William Penn, a Duke of Sully, an Abbé de Saint-Pierre, or a Jean J. Rousseau. Still, in spite of a genuine need and an occasional able spokesman, the European idea made little headway across the four and a half centuries from Dubois to Rousseau, and there were good reasons why this was so. During these centuries most Europeans were much attached to their communities, and human relationships were elemental, intimate, and tenacious; even national themes made headway slowly. And, perhaps most important of all, Europe's economic and military power was so great across the world during these centuries that a common danger from the outside, which is the classic condition for common action and a concert of states, could not arise.

Change is with us always, however, and during the eighteenth century the processes of history began very slowly to transform European society in such a way as to alter both the content and the status of the European idea. In these years of "enlightenments and revolutions" there was increasing talk about humanity, natural rights, representative government, and federal principles; at the same time there was growing awareness of the fact that Europe, despite its ethnic and linguistic diversities, possessed a large degree of spiritual and intellectual unity. These diverse currents of thought and feeling, often with European overtones, found expression not only in the writings of Rousseau and Kant but also in the writings of a host of men and women of varying backgrounds and outlooks. Even Baron de Montesquieu sometimes referred to Europe as a state made up of several provinces, and Napoleon Bonaparte talked, at least at Saint Helena, about how he would have organized and united Europe if the Russian campaign had been successful.[3]

Perhaps no one summed up more effectively and significantly what the years of the Enlightenment and the American and French revolutions did to advance the European idea than Count Henri de Saint-Simon. In 1814 this imaginative social philosopher and his pupil Augustin Thierry published a project, which was destined to be widely read and discussed, for a novel European federal system.[4] Departing from the earlier concept of a diet or confederation of sovereign princes, Saint-Simon and Thierry rested their project on peoples, parliaments, and federalist principles. The keystone of their projected structure was to be a bicameral European parliament made up of men who had already demonstrated real ability and leadership in an important occupation or profession. This European parliament was to stand well above national parliaments and was to chart the broad course of European life. They also sensed that the industrial revolution was making rapid headway and would soon beget new forces that would work for the unity of Europe.

Much as the eighteenth century did to advance the European idea, the nineteenth century was to do more. In fact, during the second quarter of the century a number of ideas, tendencies, and forces, some of which were new, began to exert influence on the European idea in either a positive or negative way. The most important of these developments were: (1) the increasing application of technology and science to industry and transportation; (2) an upsurge of the principle of nationality and a sort of glorification of the process of nation-building; (3) the firm grounding of federal principles in both the United States of America and Switzerland and the establishment of the Zollverein in Germany; (4) the emergence of a rather broadly based international peace movement; and (5) the growth of a crusading socialism with stress on a community of interests among the working classes of all countries.

Of these developments the one that had the greatest immediate impact on the European idea was the international peace movement. The European idea and the peace idea had been closely linked across the centuries, and now, as peace societies multiplied and the peace movement grew in breadth and depth, this traditional linkage became more intimate and the two moved forward in ever closer association.[5] Indeed, the European idea entered into nearly all of the numerous international peace conferences and congresses of the second half of the nineteenth century. At the international peace conference held in Paris from 21 to 24 August 1849, Victor Hugo discussed the European idea at length and said in part: "A day will come when France, Russia, Italy, England, and Germany, all of the nations of the continent . . . will merge into a firm and superior unity. . . . A day will come when these two immense groups, the United States of America and the United States of Europe will be seen facing each other, stretching hands above the seas."[6]

At the larger and more imposing international conference in Geneva in 1867, the delegates, inspired by such well-known personalities as Giuseppe Garibaldi, John Stuart Mill, Edgar Quinet, Charles Lemonnier, as well as Hugo, debated the idea and took a step that contributed significantly to its advance. They established the International League for Peace and Freedom (Ligue Internationale de la Paix et de la Liberté), which soon founded the little journal Les Etats-Unis d'Europe. Both the league and the journal were destined to live and remain active into the 1920s.[7]

Even though the peace movement, with its increasing stress on compulsory arbitration and the reduction of armies, was to grow rapidly and remain the most useful single force in the decades just ahead, some of the other forces exerted ever greater influence on the idea, altering its content and supplying it with telling new arguments. Science, technology, and large-scale industry promoted urbanization and interdependence and thus underscored the basic conflict between the new industrialism and the policies of the nation-state.[8] Too, the United States and Russia (Japan to a lesser extent) loomed as serious economic rivals in the not too distant future.

So as the final quarter of the nineteenth century got underway, with nationalism and imperialism adding to the storm and stress of international relations, there was not only growing concern about Europe's time-honored position of economic and moral leadership in the world but also a growing tendency to see Europe's disunity as an economic handicap if not a real danger. For example, a number of Europeans, including both Anatole and Paul Leroy-Beaulieu, had more and more to say about the growing economic power of the United States and Russia and about the need for a greater measure of economic cooperation among the states of Europe. In the late seventies there was a little flurry of talk about a customs union across western and central Europe which would embrace both France and Germany.[9] At the same time, some men with a legal bent of mind, including Swiss jurist Johann Bluntschli, German diplomat Constantin Frantz, and French lawyer and political scientist Louis Le Fur, sought to define the European idea more precisely and to bring it a little closer to the level of practical politics.[10] Even such political stalwarts as Francesco Crispi and Leo Caprivi are known to have toyed with the European idea in their more relaxed and reflective moments.[11]

At the very end of the century, two isolated and very different events—the Spanish-American war and the first Hague Peace Conference—made quite an impression in Europe and added something to the European idea. Some Europeans saw America's thrust across the Pacific as a new indirect challenge to Europe's economic supremacy in the world, and they viewed the Hague Conference, which was the first official conference to discuss at length the limitations of armaments and the idea of universal peace, as a golden opportunity for the governments of Europe to talk about a new concert of Europe.

Of the men who linked these events to the European idea, no one did so more strikingly than William Stead, British journalist and editor of the *Review of Reviews*. After a quick tour of Europe in 1898, Stead wrote: "And now this far-off, unseen event (a United States of Europe), toward which the whole Continent has been moving with a slow but relentless march, has come within the pale of practical politics, and on the threshold of the twentieth century we await this latest and greatest birth of time."[12]

Much as Stead may have exaggerated, the European idea did make gains and become a little more modern in dress in the crisis-laden years from Fashoda to Sarajevo. There was increasing talk about competition from the United States and Japan, a noticeable increase in literature on the idea, and some interesting collective manifestations, including two conferences that were organized to promote the idea. The first, and perhaps the more impressive, of these conferences came at the dawn of the new century. During the first week in June 1900, France's Ecole Libre des Sciences Politiques held a conference in Paris in which the question of a European federation was the first item on the agenda. Several of France's foremost political scientists, including Anatole Leroy-Beaulieu, André Fleury, Gaston Isambert, Henri de Montardy, and Paul Lefebure, gave papers on the subject. Anatole Leroy-Beaulieu supported the idea strongly and explained why he felt the term "European federation," rather than "United States of Europe," should be used to describe the contemplated union. The other speakers centered on matters of organization, geographical scope, and economic integration with special reference to a customs union. Nor did they hesitate to wrestle with such difficult questions as whether England and Russia could be included in the federation and how the colonies of the member states would be handled.[13]

The second conference came nine years later and was largely the work of Sir Max Waechter, a daring and sensitive British industrialist of German birth. Convinced that Europe's national rivalries and antagonisms were fostering a costly and dangerous armament race and undermining Europe's economic and moral position in the world, Waechter sought to persuade the peoples and governments of Europe to move toward a federal system built around England and Germany. He discussed the matter with many of Europe's industrialists and even with some of the most powerful political personalities, including Emperor William II of Germany. In 1908 Waechter turned to Prince de Cassano of Italy, who was also writing and talking about the need for European cooperation, and the two men took the lead in organizing the Congress for European Federation. This congress, which has been called the first of its kind, was held in Rome from 16 to 20 May 1909 with Prince de Cassano presiding and presenting a paper entitled "La federazione Europea." Perhaps Waechter's most impressive effort came in the early weeks of 1914 when he established the European Unity League, with headquarters in London, to work for a "Federation of the States of Europe on an economic basis."[14]

Another development that had significance for the European idea, though not a direct manifestation of it, came in 1908 when the French and German governments established national committees to examine the commercial relations of the two countries. These committees had at least two joint conferences between 1908 and 1914, and some of the men who participated in these meetings, including Lucien Coquet and Jean Hennessy, were destined to labor openly for a European customs union during the 1920s.[15]

There were also in these years some new proposals concerning the form and nature of a European structure.[16] One of the most unusual of the new projects was elaborated by Georges Luttemer of the Netherlands in his little volume *Les Etats-Unis d'Europe*. Luttemer believed that Europe was too large and diverse to form a single federation so he suggested four regional federations—a Germanic federation, an Anglo-Latin federation, an East European federation, and a federation embracing Russia in Europe—as the basis for a European federation or confederation. One of the key elements in this structure was a system of compulsory arbitration that was to operate in all four federations and to have its headquarters at The Hague.

But much as the European idea had grown across the years, it was still in 1914 largely academic, and there was nothing resembling a movement of opinion in its behalf. Nearly all politicians and men of affairs regarded the idea as too visionary, too utopian, and too sharply at variance with Europe's traditions and the central currents of its history to merit their attention much less their support. Indeed, national values had never held a higher position, and perhaps more people than ever before believed that the nation-state represented the culmination and final fruit of man's political experience.

Chapter 2

THE IMPACT OF WORLD WAR I

World War I, which broke across Europe in the early days of August 1914, had a subtle as well as a profound impact on the European idea.[1] Though the full weight of the war's impact as a unifying force was not to be felt for several years, there was nevertheless some positive impact from the first, and the European idea never dropped from sight at any time during the struggle. For while the war divided the peoples of Europe sharply and deeply and fanned national feelings and hatreds to a fever pitch, it also killed and maimed and shocked and sobered. And, perhaps even more important for the immediate fate of the European idea, it became at once "a war to end war" and thus "a war for durable peace."[2] In fact, there were quite a number of writers, journalists, lawyers, and teachers, mostly men of strong pacifist proclivities, who felt from the outset that the war was largely the product of an arrogant and militant nationalism and would work in many ways for the ultimate unity of Europe. There were even a few highly imaginative souls who professed to believe that there was a chance that the sight of blood and broken bodies would soon bring a call for European federation which would reach from the factories and fields to the trenches.

On 6 August, André Gide noted in his *Journal* that there was talk of the possibility of the early collapse of German power and the commencement of a new era that would take the form of "a United States of Europe." In the same early hours, *La Guerre sociale* and *Le Bonnet rouge* were wondering if the war could not be turned into a crusade for democracy in Germany and Austria and thus made to work for a democratic United States of Europe. Both of these journals continued to speculate about a democratic Europe, and Gustave Hervé expressed the view in *La Guerre sociale* for 28 October 1914 that, if the thrones in Germany and Austria-Hungary could be toppled and democratic regimes firmly established, "a republican United States of Europe could be advanced by a full century."[3] At the same time, Jules Romains, who was to become one of the truly great champions of Europe, wrote the first lines of his poem "Europe" and soon began speculating about the possibility of organizing a small "European party" to develop plans for launching a European movement the moment hostilities ended.[4]

Moreover, quite a number of the many "study groups" that sprang up across Europe during the first weeks of the war, the League for a European Federation (De Europeesche Statenbond) in the Netherlands and The League for a New Fatherland (Der Bund neues Vaterland) in Germany and Austria,

showed some interest in the European idea. The former group, which was
organized and directed by the Dutch writer Nico van Suchtelen and modeled
on Max Waechter's League for European Unity, was rather active during the
early months of the war and elaborated its program for Europe in a series of
brochures.[5] The Bund neues Vaterland appeared in October 1914 and was
composed of a small group of rather well-known Austrians and Germans,
including Alfred Fried, Walther Schücking, Ludwig Stein, Wilhelm F.
Foerster, Albert Einstein, and Lujo Brentano, who were quite critical of
Austro-German policy as well as of the war. This little league professed an
interest in the European idea from the beginning, but it never made that idea
the focal point of its program.[6] Although it was to be outlawed by the German
government in 1916, it carried on a fairly active propaganda during the early
months of the war and maintained contact with Romain Rolland, one of the
fiercest and most unrelenting critics of the war and of European nationalism.[7]

But some of the most impressive and optimistic assertions of the European
idea during the early months of the war were in England. The widely read
Review of Reviews and the labor-oriented *Daily Citizen* told their readers that
Europe could not have real stability and peace until the states formed some
sort of federation. In its first issue after the outbreak of the war, *Review of
Reviews* (Sept. 1914, pp. 190–91) carried an article entitled: "The United
States of Europe: The Only Way Out," and every issue of the journal for
many months carried at least one article urging the political organization of
Europe. *The Daily Citizen* made its most dramatic contribution by publicizing
a calendar, which was designed by Walter Crane, that pictured a wounded
soldier surrounded by fallen comrades and broken machinery peering into the
distance and glimpsing a transfiguration whose caption read: "A Vision of the
Future from the Battlefield—The United States of Europe." Underneath the
caption was a plea for a European federal union and the comment that the
calendar would soon "hang in 10,000 British workshops."[8]

But by the late autumn of 1914, this early flare of the European idea was
waning largely because of two related developments. One of these developments was the growing conviction that the war was almost certain to be a
protracted life and death struggle during which national hatreds across Europe
would inevitably deepen and harden. The other development, and it was far
more important for the future of the European idea, was the rapid growth of
the view that the best chance for peace in the years ahead lay not in a
European structure but in some form of universal association or league of
nations grounded in the principles of national self-determination and compulsory arbitration, resting on a strong international police force. Europe's socialist parties, which were strongly wedded ideologically and emotionally to
the search for lasting peace, had much to do with this development. The
leaders of these parties tended to profess adherence to the doctrine that the
only way peace could be achieved and anchored was through a close alliance

of proletarian elements across the world, and they were thus inclined to frown on the idea of regional structures such as a European federation. Moreover, opinion in the United States, where the League to Enforce Peace was now firmly established with William Howard Taft at its head, was running heavily on the side of a universal league of nations.

Yet, strongly as most surface currents were running against the European idea by 1915, it was not altogether without spokesmen. There were those, and they were more numerous in Europe than in the United States, who felt that it would be easier to organize Europe than the world and that the only hope of getting an effective universal league was to first organize a series of regional structures. Prominent among those who wrote and spoke in 1915 and 1916 in support of some sort of a European organization were C. E. Curinier, French bibliographer; Charles Gide, French economist and leading spokesman of the cooperative movement; Alfred Fried, Austro-German pacifist; Christiaan Cornelissen, Dutch political scientist; and Gabriel Hanotaux, French diplomat and historian.[9]

Curinier, in an article in *La Paix par le droit* in the spring of 1915, argued that economic rivalries, jealousies, and ambitions were the principal causes of war and that peace in Europe in the years to come would depend primarily on "the economic organization of Europe."[10] He said that when the war ended a great effort should be made to lay the foundations for a customs union as the first step toward an economic union, and he sketched the broad lines for a trade and tariff union that would pivot on Europe but would be open to economically developed countries across the world. He realized, he said, that many interests would cry out against such a union, but he insisted that it would be a great boon to Europe economically and a great force for peace.

Charles Gide was now asking if the cooperative movement could not be used to broaden and strengthen the foundations of peace and to begin the economic integration of Europe at the grass roots level. Speaking at a conference of the leaders of European minority groups in Paris in late June 1915, Gide speculated about the possibility of creating "une Europe coopératif" after the war and expressed the opinion that such a course of action would both erode the differences between small and large states and multiply contacts in everyday living across frontiers. Gide's idea of a cooperative Europe was in keeping with, and indeed related to, Curinier's idea of a European customs union.[11] In fact, as we shall see, both concepts were to be greatly elaborated in connection with the European idea during the twenties, and Gide was to be one of the foremost expounders of both to the end of his life.

At the same time, Alfred Fried, who had moved to Zurich in the autumn of 1914 and was now publishing *Friedenswarte* under another name in an effort to keep the journal circulating in Germany, was trying to decide whether the peoples of Europe should center their efforts on a European organization or a world organization. And though Fried was more taken with the idea of a universal league than either Curinier or Gide, he nevertheless gave priority to what he called "a cooperative union of Europe," which he explained would be a paneuropean association in which many layers of life would be grouped in practical cooperation. Such a close and intimate union would, he said, exert an enormous influence for peace.[12]

Christiaan Cornelissen, who thought of Europe in much the same manner as did Curinier, speculated about the possibility of a federation of the states of Europe in both a pamphlet and an article in the autumn of 1915. The article attracted far more attention than the pamphlet because it was entitled "The United States of Europe" and because it focused closely on the question of European organization.[13] Although the title suggested a bit more than Cornelissen advocated, the author did express the view that at the end of the war England and her continental allies would join the neutral states in an effort to evolve a European structure with a measure of economic integration which would be capable of maintaining peace across the continent. He said the charter members of the new association should be England, France, Italy, Belgium, Spain, Portugal, the Netherlands, Switzerland, and the states of Scandinavia. Germany would be added at a later date.

Perhaps the most celebrated and widely noticed assertion of the European idea in the middle months of the war came from the pen of Gabriel Hanotaux, historian and diplomat who had served France twice as minister of foreign affairs during the 1890s. In 1916 this elder statesman treated the European idea in a long article on the problem of war and peace.[14] After commenting briefly on the history of the idea and setting it alongside the idea of a universal league, he declared that the whole problem of postwar international organization should be carefully studied in a congress of allied powers. Such a congress, he said, could and should become a veritable "constituent assembly of united European states," capable of devising a government for the peoples of Europe with legislative, executive, and judicial powers and with a European parliament at its center. He also argued, as did most Frenchmen, that the new international structure, whether it be universal or regional in scope or a combination of the two, should have at its disposal an armed force sufficient to enable it to enforce its decisions.[15]

Shortly after the appearance of Hanotaux's articles, there were two developments that were to affect the European idea, though in very different ways and degrees. The first of these was the formation in Germany of the Central Bureau for International Law (Zentralstelle für Voelkerrecht). This new body, which was directed by the well-known jurist and pacifist Hellmuth von Gerlach, made a conscious effort to keep alive the interest in the European idea which the outlawed Bund neues Vaterland had fostered. Indeed, a number of the members of the suppressed Bund, including Ludwig Quidde, Edmond Fischer, and Wilhelm Foerster, were members of the Central Bureau for International Law. The Central Bureau held its first formal session in June 1917 in Leipzig and drafted a resolution that stated that those who were pondering the conditions for peace in Europe should give careful consideration to an association of European states as well as to a universal league of nations.[16]

The second of these developments—and it was to affect the whole course of the war as well as to have a bearing on the European idea—was the geographic expansion of the war in 1917, especially the entrance of the United States. This extension of the war made a universal league all but a certainty and thus shifted the search for peace and security even more from European solutions to those which were worldwide.[17] Moreover, Europeans were impressed and encouraged by the rapid growth of the League to Enforce Peace in the United States and the strong implications of its very name.

Still, even with the geographic expansion of the war and the spectacular growth of the idea of a universal League of Nations, there were a few who continued to talk about the organization of Europe in terms of world peace as well as Europe's peace. More often than not they were men steeped in the theory and philosophy of federalism as expounded by Pierre Joseph Proudhon and Constantin Frantz, men who had come to feel that the world was so diverse and uneven culturally and politically that a firm and effective international authority could only be realized by stages and through a federative process. Proudhon himself had envisioned the peace of Europe much more in terms of a European regional rather than a universal organization. Indeed, just after the United States entered the war, a small group of federalists, led by Jean Hennessy, Charles Brun, Lucien Le Foyer, and Charles Richet, formed La Ligue d'Action Régionaliste, which soon took the name Société Proudhon. These men were not criticizing the concept of a universal League of Nations so much as they were saying that the world was so diverse that federalism and regional federations offered the only possible road to an effective universal league.[18] Of course, the diversity of opinion in the area of international organization was enormous, and there were those in Europe who tended to use the terms "universal League of Nations" and "federation of peoples" as essentially interchangeable, in the sense of a sort of world government with a world parliament and a world police force.

Perhaps the most striking assertion of the European idea and of the principle of federalism in the late months of the war came from two Italians, Attilio Cabiati, professor of economics at the University of Genoa, and Giovanni Agnelli, a prominent industrialist.[19] Shocked and saddened by the war, these two men set out in 1917 to discover why the peoples and nations of Europe were so given to destructive and costly rivalries and conflicts. After much pondering and many exchanges of ideas, they decided that Europe's central weakness stemmed from an arrogant, jealous, and explosive nationalism that was grounded in the doctrine of nationality and fatally tied to particularism, which was a cramping, debilitating, and barren force in a political and economic sense. They rejected the contemplated universal League of Nations on the grounds that it would be nothing more than a loose association of sovereign nations and would probably aggravate the evils of the doctrine of nationality. They concluded that the principle of federalism offered the only means of reconciling the moral demands of nationality and the political, economic, and strategic necessities of the state, and they believed that the federal structure should have at its base a substantial and thoroughly integrated defense force and a European parliament with large powers.

But even though the European idea never dropped from sight at any time during the war, it was certainly at a low ebb during the final months of the war. This was so not only because of the power of nationalism and four years of bitter fighting but also because the search for the bases of a durable peace had become increasingly centered in a League of Nations, which proclaimed at one and the same time the principle of universalism and the right of national self-determination. Even as the war ended, this program was rather firmly embedded in the mainstream of history and had the active support of millions of people across the world, including many of the world's leading statesmen. Its prestige was so great that even the International League for Peace and Freedom,which had published *Les Etats-Unis d'Europe* for nearly a half century, found itself in a quandary and decided to put a universal League of Nations above a European federation in its program. In any event, it would do this until the projected League had become either firmly grounded or had demonstrated it was unable to do the job for which it was created.[20]

At the same time, the doctrine of national self-determination, which was evolving in close association with the league and which was to be one of the most popular and powerful forces at the Paris Peace Conference, worked against the European idea in a very different way. It tended to reinforce nationalism, and most of all perhaps economic nationalism, in many parts of the world, especially in eastern Europe. For in this region of extreme ethnic diversity, the people who had been yearning for complete national self-expression now sought to found new states and to shape them into clearly and sharply defined political and economic entities. Thus the doctrine of self-determination hastened the dissolution of the old Austro-Hungarian Empire with its common market and weakened for the time being the current of opinion that had developed in support of a Danubian federation.[21] In Germany the doctrine not only buoyed the hopes of those who were bent on keeping nationalism strong but it also provided the German people with another moral issue with which to attack the settlement.

When we add to all this the fact that national passions and hatreds had been at a fever pitch across much of Europe for more than four years and the nation-state had proved itself tough and efficient in total war, it is not hard to see why at the war's end most people clung to nationalist policies and programs and why those who dared speak of a unified Europe were generally regarded as visionaries.

Chapter 3

THE IMMEDIATE AFTERMATH

Although the national policies and programs were firmly grounded and the projected League of Nations was widely proclaimed, the European idea had more vitality and a better future than even federalists like Jean Hennessy and Giovanni Agnelli dared believe. And this was true principally because they underestimated the economic and political, as well as the mental and emotional, impacts of the war on Europe and on the European idea. For the war had come close to being for all of Europe the "orgy in self-destruction" that a number of Europeans, including Romain Rolland and Jules Romains, had predicted it would be.[1] Economically the war had not only cost the European belligerents dearly in blood and resources and left them with greatly enlarged national debts, but it had also torn and dislocated the economic structure of the whole continent, shifting the center of economic gravity to Europe's disadvantage in such a way as to enhance the competitive ability of most of Europe's rivals beyond the seas, including the United States and Japan. Politically the war had laid the groundwork for a searching reappraisal of extreme nationalism in Europe and thus of its national divisions and political fragmentation. For even though nearly all still showed great respect for national characteristics and viewed disciplined patriotism as a beneficent force, there was a growing feeling that extreme nationalism bred arrogance, aggression, and war, and some wondered if the nation-state could any longer provide Europe a sound and viable frame for economic and social growth. With the feeling growing that war was Europe's greatest tragedy and curse, Europeans in increasing numbers probed for a way to put an end to this periodic dissipation of their vital energies and resources, and they toyed more and more with the idea of European bonds and a federal system. Some saw the movement for a universal League of Nations as solid evidence that the war had helped root international institutions and had made Europeans more conscious of both Europe and the world.

In fact, one does not have to search very long in the political literature of those weeks, especially in that having to do with preparations for peacemaking, to find the European idea cropping up in a variety of forms. For example, Christian Lange, Norwegian historian and publicist, and Georges Scelle, professor of law at the University of Dijon, had much to say in these months about the growth of internationalism and expressed the view that the greatest task that the Paris Peace Conference would face would be that of working out a sounder and more constructive balance between nationalism and internationalism. Even more to the point, Fridjof Hansen—Norwegian zoologist, explorer, and politician—stated in an open letter to President Wilson: "Lasting peace in Europe will not be possible until all of the states of Europe have been joined together under the banner of the United Republics of Europe."[2] Then on the last day of the year, Professor Archibald C. Coolidge, whom the newly created American Commission to Negotiate Peace had asked to head a fact-finding mission to various regions of the old Austro-Hungarian empire, reported from Bern, Switzerland, that he had already come upon sentiment for a Danubian confederation as well as for the Anschluss.[3] A month later Professor Coolidge discussed at some length the matter of a Danubian confederation, explaining that there were quite a number of Austrians who thought of such a creation not only as a "sort of reconstruction of the dual empire" but also as a loose federal structure that would greatly benefit the whole region by providing it substantial economic unity and by toning down jealousies and rivalries among the various nationalities. Though well aware of the obstacles to such a union, Coolidge was so enamored with the idea that he argued that even a loose union would go far to solve the Austrian problem and could become a very substantial force for peace across the whole world.[4]

Then, too, the Paris Peace Conference itself made two decisions within the first month of its existence which were to have quite a bearing on the European idea in the months and years ahead. The first of these came on 9 February when the conference decided to set up the Supreme Economic Council to assist with pressing economic problems and with the formulation of broad economic policies. As we shall see, this council was not only to call attention to the need for some sort of an all-European program for rehabilitation and reconstruction, but several of its members and technical assistants— including Louis Loucheur, Daniel Serruys, Jacques Seydoux, Etienne Clémentel, and Arthur Salter—were to become active champions of the European idea.

The second of the conference decisions came on 14 February in the form of the preliminary draft of the Covenant of the League of Nations and had much the greater immediate influence on the European idea. The great majority of those in Europe who had envisioned Europe's peace in terms of a world organization were deeply disappointed with the covenant. For example, Théodore Ruyssen, who was fairly representative of those across Europe who had advocated a strong League of Nations, wrote: "A League of Nations, such as is conceived in this document, will not amount to so much as a confederation of states much less a federal state of the type of Switzerland or the United States."[5] It would be, he said, much too weak to maintain peace.

Indeed, during the ten weeks from the release of the preliminary draft of the covenant until 28 April when the covenant was approved by the full conference, there was quite a campaign, especially in France and Belgium, for a league with authority to regulate and control national armaments and to maintain a substantial military force of its own. For example, on 18 April the Action Committee of the Bureau for International Peace addressed an appeal to the Peace Conference urging it to recast the covenant so as to make the league a "real federation of nations" with an international force "sufficient to guarantee nations against the violations of their rights."[6] Even the famous speech of Léon Bourgeois before the plenary session of the Peace Conference on the occasion of the formal ratification of the covenant on 28 April 1919, was an attack on the concept of absolute sovereignty as well as an open plea for an all-out effort to create a strong league.

The failure of the Peace Conference to provide for a strong League not only increased criticism of extreme nationalism and the concept of national sovereignty, but it also encouraged probing outside and beyond national frames and patterns. Certainly in the late spring and early summer, as the first steps were taken to set up the machinery of the league, expressions with European overtones, such as "European solidarity" and "the European community," became more widespread.[7] These expressions, which were of the same broad ideological pattern as the European idea, appeared most frequently in periodicals of a moderate Left orientation, and the two that were probably most European in spirit at this time were *Le Progrès civique*, a new French biweekly, and *Wissen und Leben*, a well-established Swiss monthly. Each of these journals carried a number of articles during the spring and summer of 1919 that were at least mildly European in flavor. For example, *Le Progrès civique* published within the first two months of its existence articles by Jean Hennessy, Charles Gide, Georges Renard, Alphonse Aulard, and Francis Delaisi, all of whom were toying with the European idea and were soon to be championing it openly. Hennessy, in the first issue of the journal, called for a supreme effort to ground the League of Nations and point it more and more toward a "federation of peoples" pivoting on Europe and geared to deal freely with economic and social as well as political problems. He said further that the League should not concern itself with the safeguarding of national sovereignties but with the coordination and direction of these sovereignties toward broad international goals.[8] Meantime in *Wissen und Leben*, Hans Fischer and Karl Welter reviewed the principal writings of Constantin Frantz and Edwin Hauser and pointed out that both writers had concluded that a federal system with a full-fledged custom union would promote peace and benefit Europe in many ways.[9]

Then in the late summer and early autumn, with signs appearing that the United States might not sign the Treaty of Versailles, anxieties mounted and the world approach to the problem of peace lost a little of its attraction across most of Europe. For just as the entrance of the United States into the war in 1917 had boosted the world approach to many problems, including peace, the prospect of an American retreat from Europe tended to reverse the process and point to a European approach for the peoples of Europe. Georges Clemenceau, who had tried desperately to ground the settlement and the peace in a solid American-British-French alignment, was so disturbed that he wrote Colonel House on 4 September 1919 suggesting that the first session of the Assembly of the League of Nations be held in Washington with President Wilson presiding.[10] Jean Hennessy, among others, began speculating about the feasibility of a new peace conference to rewrite the Treaty of Versailles more in terms of "a European equilibrium and a durable peace." The French were ever mindful of Germany's economic and military potential.

Moreover, isolationist sentiment across the Atlantic aggravated many of Europe's problems and strengthened the feeling that some sort of a common effort at the economic reconstruction of Europe was much needed. Few supported this feeling in the summer and early autumn of 1919 more forcefully than the German journalist Ludwig Quessel and Alfred Capus, the widely known editor of *Le Figaro*. Pointing to the fact that the economies of the European states had been rather highly interdependent before the war, Quessel wrote: "The war shattered Europe's continental economy and left the peoples of Europe, victors as well as vanquished, in danger of being enslaved by the two great Anglo-Saxon world powers. . . . The reconstruction of Europe is not possible on any base other than that of a continental economy. . . . So long as Europe remains fragmented and full of hate, so long as its economy lies in ruins, so long as the channels of trade remain choked, the peoples of Europe will lack the means of a healthy existence."[11] Capus made his principal contribution to the restoration of economic and cultural contacts among the former continental belligerents by tactfully arguing for it in editorials in *Le Figaro* and by publishing articles supporting it by such well-known Europeans as Gabriel Hanotaux, Edmond Théry, Guglielmo Ferrero, and Julien Benda, author to be of *Discours à la nation européenne*.

Perhaps the most noteworthy effort to generate some sort of a common program of economic reconstruction came from the Supreme Economic Council and was thus collective and semiofficial in nature. By the early autumn of 1919 there was a feeling both inside and outside the council that it should be made a permanent part of the emerging League of Nations, and at a meeting in Rome on 24 November 1919, Sir Arthur Salter, with encouragement from Louis Loucheur and Jean Monnet, formally proposed that the council be made a permanent body of the league to deal with European economic problems. But Salter's proposal soon dropped from sight, partly because the United States government frowned on the whole idea.[12]

Even though the Supreme Economic Council was not to become a permanent body, its final report, which was drafted in the early weeks of 1920, was one of the more important economic documents of the early aftermath. The report stated that the war had left nearly all of the states of Europe impoverished and weakened; suggested ways in which a common, systematic effort would help the states achieve strength and stability; and recommended that a general economic conference be convened at once to X-ray Europe's problems and to explore the possibilities of a concerted approach. The International Chamber of Commerce, which was founded in June 1920 with headquarters in Paris, endorsed the report and took an interest in the European idea from the first.

The British, French, Belgian, and Italian governments took to heart this suggestion for an international economic conference and on 24 September 1920, nine weeks after the stormy meeting at Spa, the conference met in Brussels with delegates from thirty-nine countries, including Germany, Austria, Hungary, and Bulgaria, in attendance. Though the conference achieved little in the sense of concerted action, it did serve to underline the fact that most of the problems and issues with which the European states were wrestling were European in scope. Herman Fernau, in commenting on the conference said that it had served to convince many of Europe's political leaders that "the drift toward economic decline cannot be checked and the work of true reconstruction begun without European solidarity."[13]

Moreover, in these months of 1920, there were a few voices speaking rather clearly for the economic and political organization of Europe. In the front ranks, but still representative, were Jean Hennessy, French deputy and delegate to Geneva; Alphonse Aulard, distinguished historian of the French Revolution; Ernest Bovet, Swiss professor of philosophy and editor of *Wissen und Leben*; Albert Demangeon, professor of geography at the Sorbonne, and August Müller, German Social Democratic politician and publicist.

Hennessy and Aulard were already thinking and speaking of the organization of Europe in so nearly the same terms that they can be treated together. Both held that what France, Europe, and the world needed above all else was an authority capable of establishing law and order and of maintaining peace. Though both were ardent supporters of the league, they felt that the league had slight chance of developing into such an authority unless the states of Europe were federated, and they began calling for an all-out effort to organize Europe.[14] Unsure of the precise direction that this organizational effort should take, they talked in terms of both a European federation and a European section within the framework of the emerging League of Nations. As the months passed they leaned more and more toward a strong European section within the League of Nations, arguing that it would not only do much to ground and anchor the league but would be a stepping-stone toward a European federation. This idea of a European section was attractive to most of those who wanted to support the European idea but feared that a European structure would collide with the league.

Bovet, like many other Swiss including his colleague Herman Fernau, wanted to remake the whole of Europe in the image of Switzerland, and he kept this idea before the readers of his journal *Wissen und Leben*. With an eye on Europe's past, he argued that nationalism as well as democracy and industrialism had been working for the unity of Europe for more than a century and that the great war had made that unity a possibility because it had ended

Prussian militarism and made Europeans much more conscious of Europe than they had ever been. In an editorial in his journal, he challenged the leaders of Europe: "What we need do, above all, is to make Europe. The spiritually sensitive heroes of the great war died for this ideal . . . Europe is the logical end of a thousand years of development—Though scattered, all of the ingredients for this Europe are there; it can be seen by the soul; it has become a necessity. Where are the builders?"[15]

Demangeon's chief contribution to the European idea came in his *Le Déclin de l'Europe*, which was one of the most penetrating analyses of Europe's position in the world to appear during the first half of the twenties. The theme of the book was that the war had shifted the center of economic gravity away from Europe and thus had diminished Europe's economic base and its place in the world. He predicted that this process of de-Europeanization would be accelerated in the years ahead and that the states of Europe would be increasingly confronted with problems of adjustment the like of which they had never faced. Though Demangeon did not openly advocate the unification of Europe as the way out, his book was a powerful argument for some sort of massive common effort on the economic front, and he was to be much quoted during the second half of the decade.[16]

August Müller is included here not only because he was saying that the economic destinies of the European states were interwoven but also because he was a member of the German government and an influential voice in the Social Democratic party. In fact Müller was in many ways an excellent representative of a growing group of moderate Left politicians and publicists in Germany, such as Ludwig Quessel, Ludwig Stein, Georg Bernhard, and Erwin Steinitzer, who were suggesting that the German government should make a greater effort to work with France and to develop a program of economic solidarity. Erwin Steinitzer, for example, said that Walther Rathenau, nominal head of Allgemeine-Elektrizitäts Gesellschaft (AEG), had urged this in his new book *Was Wird Werden* and added: "The slogan of European solidarity is on many lips."[17]

Moreover, in the autumn of 1920 and the early months of 1921, there were two developments within the mainstream of political and economic events which had European overtones and which helped the European idea. First, the commodity boom that had set in over most of Europe soon after the Armistice, spent itself at this time, and an economic recession followed which was to hang unevenly over Europe for more than two years, slowly hammering home the fact that the war had dealt Europe a much heavier blow economically than was generally realized. Secondly, the final phase of the Allied effort to get an acceptable reparations plan through direct negotiations with Germany, even though it was to fail in the London conferences of March and May 1921, served nonetheless to maintain and even quicken contacts among the former belligerents and to strengthen the view that Germany would not be able to pay large sums in reparations unless she were allowed to export heavily—a thing that gave pause in Britain and the United States as well as in France.

These developments, which underlined anew the fact that the economies of the European states were very interdependent and that narrow nationalist policies were laden with dangers, spurred the search for some sort of European program. Addressing a peace rally on 2 April, Charles Gide stated that national debts across Europe were so massive and burdensome that they could not be effectively handled by traditional methods and expedients, and he argued that the states of Europe would have to join together to expand production and trade if Europe was to get on the road to sound recovery.[18] Jacques Rivière, who had spent three years in Germany as a prisoner of war and was now editor of *Revue nouvelle française*, had reached much the same conclusion but insisted that the Franco-German difference was near the heart of Europe's troubles. Believing that the Franco-German problem was essentially mental and emotional and using freely such phrases as ''the two mentalities'' and ''the two worlds of thought,'' Rivière called on both sides to make supreme efforts at bridging the political and psychological gulf that divided them. There would have to be on both sides of the Rhine, he said, great modesty and honesty and a sober and mature willingness to make mental and emotional readjustments.[19]

Then, during the second week in June 1921, soon after the Reparation Commission's new plan (London Payments Plan) went into operation, Louis Loucheur and Walther Rathenau conferred at length in Wiesbaden. These two men, who were prominent in both the political and economic affairs of their countries, not only discussed reparations and ways and means of dealing with American economic competition but explored the possibility of some sort of a consortium for the reconstruction of Europe which would have as one of its principal objectives the integration of Russia into the mainstream of European economic life.[20]

A few days later, on 1 July 1921, Johannes Bell, German economist and member of the Center party, said in the Reichstag that all the states of Europe were suffering economically, that what the peoples of Europe needed to do was ''to bury their hatreds,'' and that they must work toward a program of permanent peace. Indeed, he raised the question of a United States of Europe: ''A mere half century has passed since one of the greatest writers of his time [Victor Hugo] spoke out in the French Chamber for a United States of Europe. At that time this idea was brushed aside as sheer utopia. But the thought of the *solidarity of the peoples of Europe*, in which national characteristics and qualities are safeguarded, can no longer be excluded from the agenda. Indeed, this solidarity must come in some form of flesh and blood, if Europe is to regain its health.''[21]

Meantime, as Bell was reminding the Reichstag of Hugo's vision of a united Europe, Aulard was telling the readers of *Le Progrès civique* that the time had come for Germany to enter the League of Nations; André Gide was

calling for the immediate resumption of full intellectual and cultural relations between France and Germany; Thomas Mann was taking his first steps toward Europe; and the idea of some sort of a program of economic reconstruction at the European level, such as Loucheur and Rathenau had speculated about in Wiesbaden, was becoming much more widely discussed, especially in governmental circles.[22] In late August, with preparations for the Washington Naval Conference getting underway, Loucheur and Rathenau met again in Wiesbaden and initialed the document known as the Wiesbaden Agreement. And though this document was never ratified, the fact that it was even signed was a source of encouragement, especially in British circles. Lloyd George was much impressed, and in a series of high level discussions in London, the groundwork was laid for the conferences at Cannes and Genoa, and a tentative consortium scheme was formulated with Lloyd George, Briand, Rathenau and Loucheur taking the lead. Many hoped, and perhaps no one more than Lloyd George, that these projected conferences at Cannes and Genoa could fashion a general European security pact, reknit the economic ties between Russia and the European states, and arrive at agreements that would produce an economic upswing and defuse the problem of reparations.[23]

But the consortium project was difficult and delicate at best, and with many powerful Germans—including Hans von Seeckt, Otto Wolff, Ago Maltzan, and even Hugo Stinnes—pressing for direct German action in Russia, the Treaty of Rapallo was roughed out even before the Genoa Conference opened. While Rapallo wrecked the Genoa Conference and halted the effort at a consortium, it, like the failure at Geneva, had a positive side as far as the European idea was concerned. Indeed the weakness of the League of Nations may have had greater significance than the failure at Genoa. For had the league succeeded in mounting an effective program of economic cooperation in Europe, it would certainly have enhanced its prestige and it might have largely smothered the European idea.

As it was, both the weakness at Geneva and the failure at Genoa helped to stimulate the peace movement and the search for a solid peace structure. In addition the leaders of the peace movement in Europe came more and more to think of durable peace in terms of Europe, and this was a real boon to the European idea.[24]

Perhaps the most striking sign that the peace movement was thinking more in European terms came from the members of the Société Proudhon. In the late autumn of 1921, with the Washington Naval Conference in session and plans for the Cannes and Genoa conferences underway, Jean Hennessy took the lead in organizing a series of lectures on international federalism. He invited Professor Jean Charles Brun to give the first lecture and Professor Georges Renard to introduce the series and preside. On 15 December, with the Amphitheater of the Law Faculty of the University of Paris filled to overflowing, these two able students of Proudhon managed to inject the

European idea into the discussions at the outset. Renard, in his introductory remarks, reminded the group that Proudhon had envisioned the peace of Europe not in terms of a universal organization, such as the league, but in terms of a European federation, and he added that federalist ideas had been making good headway since 1848 and were little by little preparing the way for a United States of Europe. Charles Brun, though obviously a bit embarrassed, stressed this point even more and made it clear that the members of the Proudhon Society did not regard the League of Nations as the last word in the organization of peace. He said in part: "The Proudhon Society gives its loyal support to the League. It is working for it and not against it. . . . Nevertheless Proudhon's federalist ideas are alone able to provide practical results."

At the time the leaders of the Proudhon Society were stressing the fact that the master himself had envisioned Europe's peace largely in terms of a European federal system, the French League of the Rights of Man invited the members of Der Bund neues Vaterland to a joint meeting to be held in Paris in January 1922. Although only Hellmuth von Gerlach, Georg Nicolai, and Otto Lehrmann-Russbueldt made the trip to Paris, the meeting served nonetheless to relate the growing aversion to war to the European idea. For not only had the three Germans who made the trip to Paris already written and spoken about the unity of Europe, but Anatole France, who had just won the Nobel Prize for literature, participated in the meeting and assured a joint session that the peoples of Europe had enough in common to forge a union of the states, insisting that the time had come to move toward such a union. The joint meeting also laid the foundation for the transformation of the Bund into the German Liga für Menschenrechte and produced a joint declaration calling on all Europeans to wage "war on war."[25]

Thus, by the beginning of 1922, the European idea was reviving and even showing faint signs of growth. And though, as we have seen, a number of ideas, forces, and circumstances were contributing to this, perhaps the most telling were: (1) a growing aversion for war coupled with the failure of the League of Nations to measure up to the expectations of its supporters; (2) increasing awareness of the gravity of Europe's economic plight and of the economic power and potential of the United States, Russia, and Japan; and (3) a growing feeling that the peoples of Europe had much in common in an intellectual and spiritual sense and indeed that there was a community of interests that not only transcended the states but could also provide a sense of mission and become a liberating and creative force. There were even some, including Romain Rolland and Walter Schücking, who were saying that the world had become so interdependent that even regional federations were outmoded.

Chapter 4

REVIVAL AND GROWTH

Although the sixteen months that lay between the Genoa Conference and the chancellorship of Gustav Stresemann were full of storm and stress and rocked by the occupation of the Ruhr, this heightened strife and turmoil cut two ways and may have helped the European idea more than it hurt it. For while it intensified national passions a bit and ruled out for the time being any sort of concerted program for the economic reconstruction of Europe, it nonetheless deepened concern about Europe's future and had a sobering impact on millions of people.

In fact, in the summer and autumn of 1922 as tensions mounted and tempers flared in Paris and Berlin, there were those who came to feel that meaningful negotiations would not be possible until there was a confrontation sharp enough to produce a severe mental and emotional shock. Perhaps no one expressed this view more forcefully than Jacques Rivière, who for months had been picturing the Franco-German difference largely in terms of deepseated psychological disparities. Rivière now began to hint that an occupation of the Ruhr might be the surest and quickest way to end the Franco-German deadlock and get serious and constructive negotiations underway. Soon after the occupation of the Ruhr, Rivière wrote: "I have always thought that we [French] must, in order to insure our own recovery, create an attraction for Germany: that of her own recovery. And however parodoxical it may seem, the occupation of the Ruhr is, when viewed from a certain angle, a gesture in that sense; it is, apart from all ideology, a slightly brutal but very clear invitation to Germany to collaborate with us."[1] And Rivière proceeded to challenge his own government as well as the German government to turn the occupation into an economic collaboration dedicated to the creation of new wealth and the forging of new bonds for peace at the grass roots level. He seemed convinced that the surest way to erode mental and emotional barriers was to multiply contacts on the economic plane—a view expressed with increasing frequency during these years.

But whatever may have been the exact impact of the occupation of the Ruhr on the European idea, it is clear that during 1922–23 the idea gained ground and became more respectable, more closely linked both to Europe's economic wellbeing and to the building of a durable peace structure. *Hochland*, Munich's famous Catholic monthly, said in its January issue for 1923 (p. 430) that European thought was coming to life and that the Swiss press was in the forefront of the revival. Among those who spoke during these months with

something of the fervor of the Aulards and the Hennessys but who have not
as yet been mentioned in this study, were Pierre Drieu la Rochelle, Joseph
Caillaux, and René Arcos in France; Wilhelm Heile, Heinrich Mann, and
Richard Baerwald in Germany; Emmanuel Malynski in Poland: and Richard
Riedl and Richard N. Coudenhove-Kalergi in Austria. Though these nine men
came from many different avenues of life and represented a rather wide range
of approaches to the European idea, they had quite a bit in common. They
were, in the main, intellectuals with strong international and humanitarian
impulses, and they were deeply preoccupied with the problem of war and
peace. With few exceptions they were strong supporters of the League of
Nations but in most instances quite aware of its limitations. The broad substance of what they were saying was that the time had come for the peoples of
Europe to curb their nationalisms, to end their wars, and to work for a strong
and united continent.

Drieu la Rochelle was a young man of letters who had served with the
French army in the great war and who sometimes said that life in the trenches
had made him much more conscious of Europe. Now in his late twenties and
searching desperately for solid ground and a cause, he was unsure as to
whether he wanted most to be a novelist, a political analyst, or a social
philosopher. In the early months of 1922, while vacationing in the Austrian
Tyrol, he completed the manuscript for *Mesure de la France*, which was his
first political work. Looking first at France's position in relation to the other
European states, he noted that France had failed to keep step with Germany in
population as well as in the production of goods, and this distressed him
deeply. Turning then to the great empires of the world—the British, the
Russian, the American, the Japanese, and the Indian with their vast spaces
and economic potentialities—he decided that the future belonged to them and
sadly confessed that he could not see how France, or indeed any European
nation, could hold its own in competition with them. Predicting that the
United States and Russia would be the great powers of the next generation, he
asked what the little peninsula of Europe was to do with its politically and
economically fragmented self. His answer was clear and firm: "Europe must
federalize itself or it will be devoured. This is not a matter for cosmopolitan
musing or armchair theorizing. It is a pressing necessity, a miserable question
of life or death."[2] He offered no organizational formula for Europe, but he
warned that each nation would have to sacrifice some of its identity and he
wrote much about a new faith and a new church in the sense of a moral and
intellectual regeneration at the European level.

Caillaux, who had been a member of five prewar ministeries in France and
a warm advocate of European economic cooperation for years, was found
guilty in 1918 of correspondence with the enemy and imprisoned just before
the war ended. Though he was not to regain his full political rights until 1923,
he was released from prison in April 1920 and began at once to argue that the

war had made European cooperation and collaboration more necessary than ever, thus vindicating his economic philosophy. In *Où va la France? Où va l'Europe?* written largely in 1921, he took a close look at the economic problems that beset France and Europe, and he found much that troubled and pained him. Above all, he found the nations of Europe fettered by national debts and "senseless customs barriers" and the Old Continent losing its high position in the world. Asserting that "economic nationalism had been tried in Europe and found ruinous," he attacked it viciously. He urged the peoples of Europe to prepare themselves for "a massive effort at economic rapprochement" and the political leaders of Europe to schedule a conference committed to the drafting of a code that would bind the whole continent into a unified economic entity. He wrote: "United around the democratic idea, organized politically and economically, bound together in equality, the states of Europe will be able not only to live but to recapture the substance of their past grandeur."[3]

Arcos was another French writer who, like so many other writers of the day including Jules Romains and Georges Duhamel, saw Europe as an intellectual and cultural community whose national divisions were not only artificial but were doing great damage. What gave uniqueness to Arcos's work for Europe in these months was that he founded a new literary journal, *L'Europe*, which he dedicated to the promotion of the European spirit and "to the dissipation of the tragic misunderstandings which divide the peoples of Europe." In the first issue of the journal, which appeared on 15 February 1923, Arcos set its European tone with an article entitled "Patrie européenne." He said that Europe's essence was in its culture, that the continent had been "artificially morseled into states," and that the resulting fragmentation could not be defended and was indeed stifling Europe's "creative energies."

Although *L'Europe* was a literary rather than a political journal and was never in the forefront of the European movement, it nevertheless made a contribution to the movement through its title as well as through an occasional article. In the issue of 15 May 1923 (p. 500), René Lalou promised that France, "the intellectual motherland of all Europeans," would produce works in increasing numbers that were truly European in spirit. Within a period of months several other distinguished writers with strong European sympathies, including Georges Duhamel, Romain Rolland, Charles Vildrac, Paul Valéry, and Heinrich Mann, joined Arcos and Lalou in speaking through the pages of this journal.[4]

The three Germans, Heile, Mann, and Baerwald, were quite different types and arrived at the European idea by different routes. Heile, former associate of Friedrich Naumann and now Reichstag deputy, was one of the best representatives of that group of Germans who arrived at a united Europe largely by way of the Anschluss and Mitteleuropa concepts. From the moment the war ended, Heile worried about the future of his country and speculated constantly about the direction that it should take. But he was already deeply attached to Naumann's Mitteleuropa, and he never strayed too far from it. Indeed, he cast about for ways and means of shielding it while his country recovered its strength. He soon decided to link Mitteleuropa with the idea of a united Europe and to present the concept of Middle Europe as a step toward "a United States of Europe." Accordingly in a series of articles and editorials in *Die Hilfe*, which had been founded by Naumann and of which he himself was now coeditor, Heile began in the spring of 1922 to write about "a United States of Middle Europe" as a prerequisite to "a United States of Europe."[5] Few writers in 1922 used the expression "United States of Europe" as frequently as did Heile; and even though he saw it in part as a means of enhancing Germany's influence and power in Middle Europe, he did much to plant the idea of a united Europe in Germany. Too, quite a number of Germans, including Erich Koch-Weser and Paul Löbe, were to follow Heile to Europe by way of the Anschluss and Mitteleuropa concepts, and both concepts, as we shall see, were to be related to the European idea in a variety of ways.

Heinrich Mann, novelist, poet, and politician, had as a young man read Nietzsche, Hugo, Renan, and Zola and had encountered the European idea in some form in all of them. He had reacted to the great war in much the manner of Jules Romains and had found himself at odds with his family, especially with his younger brother Thomas Mann who had remained an ardent defender of the German cause. In 1916 Heinrich had written an article, "Der Europäer," in which he had argued that the peoples of Europe had many common qualities and traits and that the languages of western and central Europe came much closer to being sisters than was generally realized.[6] In the months after the war, his democratic Europeanism slowly grew; he denounced the stab-in-the-back and urged his countrymen to conquer their defeat by rising above it and demonstrating to the world that they were capable of great moral and spiritual leadership. Then, in the early weeks and months of 1923, stirred by the writings of Drieu la Rochelle and Jacques Rivière and heartened by kinder words from his brother Thomas, Heinrich wrote a series of articles insisting that there were two sides to the crisis across the Ruhr and challenging the German and French peoples to reconcile their differences and to begin the unification of Europe.[7] With obvious satisfaction, he reminded his readers that Victor Hugo had said to the French National Assembly in 1871: "Down with frontiers. The Rhine for everyone! Let us create a Republic, let us form the United States of Europe." Having now taken his stand for Europe as his fatherland, he declared: "The European idea has entered a state (Zustand) of scientific demonstration."

Baerwald, a physiologist and psychiatrist, had been attached to an army hospital during the war, and he had been so pained at the sight of mangled bodies and the ravages of war that he had resolved to do all within his power to prevent another bloodletting. Viewing Europe's state relations as essentially irrational, he called for a union of the states (Staatenfusion) and undertook to chart the most promising approaches to "a United States of Europe." Searching for a striking title that would suggest something of the turmoil and violence of the relations of the European states, Baerwald hit upon *Ladokka's Malstrom*. Though the book was theoretical and visionary, it nonetheless helped to plant the idea of "a United States of Europe" in Germany.[8]

Count Malynski, a Pole who had lived and studied in several European countries, presented the most unusual scheme of the day for uniting Europe. Believing that a Prussian-dominated Germany and a Communist-dominated Russia stood at the crux of the European problem, Malynski contended that the peacemakers should have dismembered and weakened Prussia, strengthened the position of the South German states, and laid the groundwork for a Danubian federation to serve as a bulwark to both Germany and Russia.[9] But since they chose rather to further unify and consolidate Germany and to provide her with the possibility of linking up with Russia, the best course left open to the states of Western Europe was to move toward a federation that would include Germany, and then with Germany's help to slice Russia into spheres of influence. If the later enterprise did not succeed in ending the German danger altogether, it would in any event eliminate the Russian menace and provide both the occasion and the cement for "a Paneuropean federation or a United States of Europe," which would be the most powerful political unit in the world. In elaborating on the broad effects of his plan, Malynski wrote (p. 190): "Europe thus united and pacified, with its vast colonial possessions mutually and solidly guaranteed, will form an entity sufficiently homogeneous and unified to live unto itself. . . . This European Union will be able to play the role of stabilizer and pacifier of the world."

Riedl and Coudenhove-Kalergi, the two Austrians, also presented an interesting contrast, including their contributions. Riedl, economist and diplomat, had long wrestled with the Anschluss and Mitteleuropa concepts and had during the great war helped formulate the Salzburg Plan for an Austro-German customs union. Now Austrian ambassador to Germany, he became quite disturbed by the tension that came with the occupation of the Ruhr. Feeling, as he later said, that a federation of the states of Europe was the only alternative to a "new edition of the Thirty Years' War," he decided to suggest to the German government that it work toward this alternative. Accordingly, Riedl drafted a rather detailed memorandum on European federation and sent a copy to Frederic Hans von Rosenberg, the German foreign minister, on 27 April 1923.[10] Although Rosenberg was not impressed and told the ambassador that the time was not ripe for such an idea and that it would be a waste of time to consider it, the document nonetheless made the German government more conscious of the fact that there were prominent and responsible Austrians, including Chancellor Ignaz Seipel, who were thinking about European federation, as well as Anschluss and Mitteleuropa. Indeed, several ministers in Berlin and Vienna doubtless knew this, and it is highly probable that it prompted the report that Maximilian Pfeiffer, German ambassador in Vienna, sent his government on 28 May 1923 concerning the status of the European idea in Vienna.[11] Had Riedl's memorandum been published at this time, it would undoubtedly have caused comment and might have given the European idea a sizable boost.

Lastly, we come to the young Austrian count, Richard N. Coudenhove-Kalergi, who perhaps did more at this time than anyone else to popularize the European idea. By early 1922 this idealistic and cosmopolitan youth, whose father was Austrian and his mother Japanese, had become convinced that the states of Europe should work for a federal union. During the year 1922 he wrote a number of short articles in support of European union, or Paneurope as he preferred to call it, and decided to try to persuade some well-known European personality "with vision and authority" to sponsor his Paneuropean idea.[12] He turned first to Thomas Masaryk and found the Czech president sympathetic to the European idea but unwilling to associate himself with a crusade for Paneurope. Then, on 22 February 1923, Coudenhove addressed an open letter to Benito Mussolini which closed with this daring but prophetic exhortation: "Throw yourself boldly into Europe's chaos and lay the foundations for a United States of Europe! Then your memory shall be blessed and your name shall live forever." But the Italian Fascist leader did not respond to this letter and Coudenhove, with the occupation of the Ruhr in full course, settled down to develop his ideas in a full-length book.

The young count stuck close to his writing desk and by the late spring of 1923 the manuscript of his new book was finished. In the early autumn of that year, *Paneuropa* came from the press. Written in clear and simple German, *Paneuropa* was a passionate plea for a European federation. Coudenhove wrote as the bearer of the great truth that the peoples of Europe could never have peace, prosperity, and ethnic harmony until they fashioned their national states into a firm union. If the author added little by way of new arguments, he summarized in concise and dramatic fashion the standard ones. Displaying courage and conviction, Coudenhove proposed that both Britain and Russia be excluded from the projected union and that the League of Nations be recast along regional lines, with the new European Union to form one of five regional groups.[13] Copies of *Paneuropa* were immediately mailed to scores of politicians, businessmen, journalists, and professors throughout Europe, and each copy contained a card inviting the recipient to give his moral and financial support to the Paneuropean program. The book attracted considerable attention at once, and the *Neue Freie Presse*, Vienna's best known daily, placed Hans Müller's review of it on its front page on 2 December 1923. By the end of the year a goodly number of newspapers and periodicals had reviewed it, especially in the German-speaking world.

Now that Coudenhove had set out his program in detail, he was more determined than ever to find a European statesman of "vision and authority" willing to support it and to help him establish an organization to promote it. Believing that Chancellor Seipel of Austria, who had been struggling with the question of Austria's future for many years, was becoming more interested in the European idea, he turned first to him. And indeed the great Catholic Prelate responded affirmatively and offered Coudenhove space for his projected organization in the Hofburg Palace.[14] Coudenhove was, of course, overjoyed, not only because of the attractiveness of the space, but even more because the Hofburg Palace was the seat of the Austrian government. In a sense Coudenhove had found an official sponsor, and he quickly announced the establishment of the Paneuropean Union and a Paneuropean press with headquarters in the Hofburg Palace. Money for operating the organization and the press was, of course, a problem, but Coudenhove had valuable properties and in addition was soon getting modest sums from various sources.[15]

But as much as these nine men contributed to the revival and growth of the European idea in 1922 and 1923, their efforts were by no means the whole story even at the level of open support. Not only did the Aulards, the Hennessys, and the Bovets work as hard as ever, but there were a goodly number of other men who spoke openly for the idea and there were some instances of collective support. Early in 1922 a group of French youth, led by Jean Luchaire, issued a lengthy manifesto in which they announced that they were planning a new periodical that would bear the title of *La jeune Europe* and that would strive to create among European youth a strong devotion to peace and to Europe. The new journal would, they said, set Europe above the states and endeavor to blur frontiers.[16]

Then in the autumn of 1923, as the debacle over the Ruhr drew to an end and Coudenhove was launching his Paneuropean Union, a group of French writers, professors, lawyers, economists, and journalists—led by Anatole France, Charles Gide, Georges Duhamel, Louis Le Foyer, Gustave Tery, and Victor Basch—got together to discuss the idea of a European federation as a unit in a world confederation. In the closing weeks of 1923 the group, which numbered about fifty, established a loose organization with headquarters at 47 Rue Geoffroy in Paris and issued a manifesto setting forth their program. This manifesto said that Victor Hugo's vision of "a United States of Europe" had now become a necessity because science, technology, and industry had integrated the material framework of much of the world to the point at which "a world organism was needed to unify and direct the political actions of all peoples." The manifesto concluded: "A United States of Europe has now become the order of the day in Europe and the League of Nations has become its foundation stone. A World Republic should be the final step."[17]

Finally, it is evident that most of the forces that had been generating potential for the idea gained some momentum in these years. The failure of the League of Nations to show real strength caused the leaders of the peace movements in Europe to think more in terms of a solution at the European level. More important still, Europe's share in world production and trade continued to shrink, and there was a growing tendency to see Europe's economic ills in terms of economic nationalism and political fragmentation.[18] For example, the Twenty-Second World Peace Congress in London in the summer of 1922 gave much attention to Europe's economic plight and, in spite of the fact that the delegates were from all over the world, adopted a resolution that stated that "the economic reconstruction of Europe is not possible unless it is envisaged by peoples, parliaments, and statesmen in terms of world economic unity." At the World Economic Congress for Overseas Week in Hamburg in the spring of 1923, Bernhard Harms of Germany and G. W. Bruins of the Netherlands joined those who were saying that "a European economic community" was the great need of the time.[19] Too, there was, in the spring and summer of 1923, a noticeable increase in articles dealing with Europe's economic condition and pointing out that Europe's share in world production and trade was still declining. *La Journée industrielle*, which had been founded in 1918 and was now one of Europe's most respected economic journals, warned in its issue of 2 August 1923 that Europe's economic plight could become much worse if the nations continued "to travel the road of political and economic conflict."

Also of considerable significance for the European idea, especially in the sense of building potential, was the steady increase in contacts between business leaders especially across France, Germany, Luxembourg, and Belgium. Hugo Stinnes, Otto Wolff, Paul Silverberg, Albert Voegler, and others maneuvered feverishly and kept in touch with Emil Mayrisch, Luxembourg's leading industrialist and president of ARBED, who was doing his best to get French and German businessmen together for the purpose of initiating meaningful and promising negotiations. Louis Loucheur and Otto Wolff had extensive economic interests in Luxembourg, and by early summer those interests seemed to be working rather smoothly together.[20] In early August, Otto Wolff made contact with General Joseph Denvignes, a key figure in the French occupation force in the Ruhr, and assured him that many German industrialists were anxious to reknit economic relations in the Rhineland area. Then when Gustav Stresemann became chancellor in mid-August, most French industrialists were more inclined to negotiate because they believed, and Von Hoesch was encouraging them in this belief, that Stresemann was prepared to move to a policy of fulfillment. And, of course, Stresemann did understand as fully as Stinnes, Wolff, and Voegler that passive resistance could not be continued for long, but he resisted their pressures for another month, hoping to maneuver the French into making some special concessions in exchange for the formal abandonment of passive resistance. For Stresemann also knew that, in some respects, France had suffered even more than

Germany from the war, that war pensions and reconstruction work in the eastern provinces were eating deeply into French revenues, and that Poincaré knew he might have to appeal to London and Washington for loans at any time.

Thus Rivière had not been altogether wrong in predicting that the occupation of the Ruhr would loosen the Franco-German log jam and open the way for serious negotiations at many points—a development that was sure to have significance for the European idea. Indeed, in the closing weeks of 1923 and the early weeks of 1924, one encounters fairly frequently in the writings of Aulard, Caillaux, Heinrich Mann, Francis Delaisi, Count Wladimir d'Ormesson, and others the idea of a Franco-German committee to work for economic and cultural cooperation.[21]

Chapter 5

THE CLIMATE IMPROVES

As we have seen, the future of the European idea was not quite as bleak at the end of 1923 as the harsher forces of history seemed to indicate. For, as a number of people including Jacques Rivière had anticipated, the occupation of the Ruhr had cut two ways and had generally sobered both sides. The Germans, who had found the French and Belgians more determined than they had expected and had seen their national unity threatened, had turned to Stresemann and begun moving toward a policy of limited fulfillment. The French, yearning for security, faced with mounting national debts, perplexed if not frightened by criticism and pressure from London and Washington, and ever mindful that Germany's economic potential was greater than theirs, were increasingly disposed to moderate the foreign policies of the Poincaré government and to work harder for grounds for constructive agreements. There were signs in business circles on both sides of the Rhine of a growing willingness to face up to the fact that the great industrial region of the Rhine basin, pivoting on Lorraine and the Ruhr, was a natural economic unit and needed to be treated as such. Men like Jacques Seydoux and Louis Loucheur in France and Paul Silverberg and Otto Wolff in Germany were tactfully working to further economic contacts and create new economic bonds, and they were sometimes thinking about a European customs union.[1]

Indeed, in the winter and early spring of 1924 the European idea was getting considerably more attention than ever before in the European press, especially in the Paris daily press. For example, on 3 January 1924, *L'Ere nouvelle*, which was close to the leadership of the Radical Socialist party and a favorite in intellectual circles in Paris, told its readers about the group that had formed around Charles Gide and Anatole France in the autumn of 1923 with headquarters at 47 Rue Geoffroy to work for "a United States of Europe as the first step toward a world federation." Then on 27 January, *Le Temps*, the most respected daily in Paris, carried an editorial by Jean Herbette, in which this foreign affairs expert argued that the larger forces of history were relentlessly propelling Europe toward a federal system. Herbette wrote: "As the relations between nations become more intense and states become more interdependent, Europe must and will develop institutions and habits which provide her the advantages of a federal system." Two days later *L'Oeuvre*, one of France's most prosperous and influential dailies, carried on its front page an article by Jean Hennessy entitled "A European Federation Will Insure World Peace." The French senator warmly complimented Herbette and reaffirmed his own contention that the League of Nations could not be firmly anchored unless the nations of Europe formed a community.[2] Also, *Le Quotidien*, which Henri Dumay with financial assistance from Jean Hennessy had founded in 1923, had become a widely circulating daily and was showing real interest in the European idea.

At the same time, the French section of the International Association for Peace through Law, which had decided in the autumn of 1918 to put the League of Nations ahead of a United States of Europe in its program, was now in the process of restoring the European idea to the center of its program because most members now felt that the League of Nations had been greatly overrated.[3] Even more important in terms of publicity, Coudenhove-Kalergi, who had just been assigned space in the Habsburg Palace for his Paneuropean Union, was preparing to launch a new journal, *Paneuropa*, which would be, he said, "a weapon in the struggle for a European federation" as well as a news medium. The first issue of *Paneuropa* appeared in April 1924, and though it was a small journal, it was dramatic and fiery and attracted considerable attention across Europe.[4]

Then in April 1924, as the Dawes and McKenna committees hammered out the details of a new reparations plan, the idea of a European customs union got a substantial boost. French economist Charles Gide, with Edgar Stern-Rubarth, influential German journalist with access to Stresemann, and Ernö Bleier, Hungarian economist, organized an International Committee for a European Customs Union, consisting of twelve men from five different countries. In a manifesto addressed "To All Europeans," they asserted that a European customs union would, among other things, raise living standards, promote security and peace, and check the drift toward economic anarchy. The manifesto concluded: "Unless you want to see your Europe engulfed in anarchy, and the world about you turned into chaos . . . rally behind a European Customs Union."[5]

Just as the Committee for a European Customs Union was formed, a conference on international trade was held at Lyon which had European overtones. Edouard Herriot, deputy and one of the key figures in the Radical Socialist party, and Etienne Fougère, businessman and soon to be the director of France's Association Nationale d'Expansion Economique, both addressed the conference, stressing interdependence and arguing that peace and prosperity were closely linked and that economic collaboration would promote peace as well as economic growth.[6]

Then on 11 May the French voters, ignoring the tenor of the Reichstag election of the previous week, took power from Poincaré and the Chamber of Blue Horizon and put it in the hands of Herriot and the newly organized Left Bloc (Cartel des gauches).[7] Numerous and varied as were the issues that brought the change, it was clear that the stage had been set for a turn in French foreign policy which would give new impetus to the European idea, at least in

France. In its first issue after the election, *L'Europe nouvelle*, France's most influential and cosmopolitan weekly, declared that the French voters had spoken "decisively for peace—and international cooperation."[8] On 13 May, *L'Oeuvre* said that the "Left Bloc means peace and a greater effort at European cooperation," and *L'Ere nouvelle*, on the same day, declared editorially that France was ready to invite Germany along with all of the states of Europe to join her in an all-out effort "to build a strong League of Nations as a step toward a United States of Europe and even a United States of the World."

Nor was the significance of this election missed across the Rhine. If most of the Rightist press in Germany calmly announced that the Left Bloc would continue the policies of the Poincaré government, most Socialist and Democratic papers, led by *Vorwärts* and the *Vossische Zeitung* (Berlin's oldest daily), admitted their surprise and asked if the election had not provided solid proof that France was ready for a policy of conciliation and pacification.[9]

Moreover Edouard Herriot, who formed the new Left Bloc ministry, maneuvered from the outset to strengthen this anticipation. Herriot was a man of strong European impulses. He argued that the victory of the Left Bloc demonstrated that France had no illusions of grandeur in a power sense and insisted that the central aim of her foreign policy was a pacified and prosperous Europe. Labeling himself "a pacifist patriot," he tackled the problems confronting France and Europe with energy as well as a certain idealism, and he worked closely with Stresemann as well as Ramsay MacDonald in hammering out the Dawes Plan. Coudenhove-Kalergi was so impressed by the turn of events in France that he addressed an open letter to the French Chamber of Deputies praising the deputies for their breadth of outlook and urging them to work openly for Paneurope.[10]

At the same time the European idea had achieved a stronger and clearer echo in the moderate Left press across Europe, especially in France. *L'Oeuvre* (18 June 1924) carried an editorial entitled "Tradition française et patriotisme européen," arguing that France had a tradition of looking at Europe as a whole and that French patriotism had for a long time exhibited European overtones. The writer pointed to Saint-Simon's *De la Réorganisation de la société européenne* as evidence of this and expressed the belief that Herriot would, as he moved forward, keep in mind Saint-Simon's idea of a European community. *L'Ere nouvelle* carried a number of articles and editorials in the late spring and early summer dealing with the European idea and arguing that its time was coming. In a long editorial in this journal on 6 July, Lucien Le Foyer said that Herriot and the Left Bloc were not only inspiring confidence in the democratic process throughout Europe but were also preparing the way for "a European federation" and even of "a United States of the World."[11]

While no other country could match France in the number of dailies that were showing real interest in the European idea, several other countries, including Germany, Austria, and Switzerland, had at least one daily that was not far behind. In Germany the *Vossische Zeitung*, which was edited by Georg Bernhard, gave its readers the substance of the open letter that Coudenhove-Kalergi had addressed to the French Chamber, agreeing with him that the French Chamber was quite conscious of Europe and that the European idea was making headway. On 9 August the *Vossische Zeitung* reported that the French delegation to the International Congress of Transport Workers, then in session in Hamburg, had raised the question of "a United States of Europe," and in the autumn this journal invited its readers to use its pages to debate the Paneuropean concept.

Meanwhile, in midsummer, Coudenhove-Kalergi and some of his supporters made plans to get the Paneuropean program before the Twenty-Third World Peace Congress, which was scheduled to open in Berlin on 4 October 1924. They knew, however, that this would not be easy, for not only were many of Germany's professional pacifists, including Hans Wehberg and Walther Schücking, hostile to the Paneuropean program but they professed to believe that any discussion of the European idea in the congress would offend the delegates from non-European nations. Still Coudenhove pleaded with the agenda committee to put him on the program, and in the end the members of the committee relented and agreed to let him speak.[12]

On 8 October, at the final session of the congress, Coudenhove-Kalergi spoke on "Pan-Europe and the League of Nations." Though he was only in his twenty-ninth year, he was a confident speaker, and he summarized in crisp sparkling sentences the substance of what he had said in his book *Paneuropa*. Some of the German pacifists were hoping to cut short the debate on Paneurope, and Walther Schücking, who was one of them, quickly made a rather acid attack on the Paneuropean idea, arguing that the idea was not only utopian but an artificial and meaningless thing in view of the close economic ties that the major European states had developed with the rest of the world. But Schücking did not succeed in ending the discussion. Indeed, a number of delegates got the floor, and several of them, including Felix Stössinger, Victor Basch, and Georg Bernhard, warmly defended the European idea.[13]

Coudenhove, now that he had got himself and his program before the leading pacifists of Europe and was pleased with the way things were going in France, decided to spend part of the autumn in Germany in an effort to get a group of prominent German political figures to organize a German Paneuropean group. He wanted Wilhelm Heile, who was a deputy and had been writing about a United States of Europe for more than two years, to take the initiative. But Heile had his own plans for a new political organization and also felt that Coudenhove and his program would always be unpopular in Germany. Coudenhove then turned to Social Democrat Paul Löbe who was president of the Reichstag, and Löbe agreed to undertake the organization of a chapter of Paneuropean Union and to serve as its president. Coudenhove and Löbe then got Erich Koch-Weser, chairman of the Democratic party, and

Hugo Lerchenfeld to serve as vice presidents, and a German chapter took shape during the final weeks of the year. But the chapter had serious weaknesses and was never really healthy, for Löbe was an ardent advocate of the Anschluss and a member of the Österreichisch-Deutscher Volksbund, which had been organized in 1919. Coudenhove later said that he realized at the time that most of Germany's political leaders, including Stresemann, lacked "a genuine European outlook and spirit" but that he did not realize the depth of Löbe's Mitteleuropean ambitions. Actually Coudenhove's moves at this time stimulated the effort in Germany to develop new private political organizations, including an organization to work in close alignment with the League of Nations to promote conciliation and understanding. Not only did Heile continue to bestir himself in this sense, but Alfred Nossig, Schücking, and many others became very active.[14]

Then on 24 October, with the Dawes Plan ready to go into operation, the Geneva Protocol already a matter of wide debate, and the French and German governments opening negotiations looking toward a comprehensive commercial treaty, Premier Herriot gave the European idea a tremendous boost with a few carefully chosen words. Speaking on the question of European security before an audience of distinguished politicians and intellectuals at the Sorbonne, the French premier said: "Let us create, if it is possible, a United States of Europe; if that proves to be beyond us, let us at least unite the nations of good will. France is ready for an all-out effort to organize and consolidate the forces of peace." Coming from the man who was both premier and foreign minister of France, this gentle call for an effort "to build a United States of Europe" excited the more ardent apostles of the European idea and moved the idea a little closer to the fringes of politics. Coudenhove-Kalergi, Heinrich Mann, and others quickly hailed Herriot's speech and urged the German people to make a favorable response. In an article that appeared in the *Vossische Zeitung* on 26 October, the young count wrote: "The French Premier has in his most recent speech come out unreservedly for a United States of Europe. . . . As a result of Herriot's declaration, October 24, 1924, can mark a turning point in the history of Europe. Whether or not it does will depend in large measure on the response of the German electorate—Paneurope will become a reality if France and Germany want it. France has called for it, and it is now up to Germany to help create Europe or turn it to ruin."[15]

Even some members of the German government, including Stresemann, felt compelled to make some sort of response. In an interview in early November with a correspondent of the *Frankfurter Generalanzeiger*, Stresemann said that the Dawes Plan had helped the political climate and had even led some people to talk of the possibility of a United States of Europe. He was cautious but he did express the view that there could be something of an "economic flowering" in Europe if national hates were bridled, economic cooperation restored, and Germany freed from the economic restraints of

Versailles.[16] On 2 November, Erich Koch-Weser spoke more directly and positively, stating that a European federation was one of the foreign policy aims of his party.[17] Then a few days later, Stern-Rubarth, whose advice Stresemann sometimes sought, declared that the German foreign minister's remarks to the *Frankfurter Generalanzeiger* were prompted by Herriot's gestures and indeed that a sizable number of the members of the German People's party were toying with the idea of a European customs union.[18] Meantime, the *Sozialistische Monatshefte* began assuring its readers that the victory of the Left Bloc in France had shown that the majority of the French people were ready to work for a reconciled and united Europe and that the time had come for the German government to grasp Herriot's outstretched hand. In fact, each issue of this journal from October through December 1924 contained at least one article praising Herriot and urging its government to join France in laying the foundations for "a European continental union."[19]

This little surge in European thought had become a matter of considerable comment by the second week in November. In an article in the *Vossische Zeitung* on 9 November, Coudenhove-Kalergi said that the Paneuropean idea was being rapidly transformed into a movement and added: "Paneuropean thought has made more progress in the last four weeks than it had made in the previous four years." Five days later Stern-Rubarth wrote that the European idea had made "visible progress since Herriot's speech at the Sorbonne" and contended that many of Europe's political and industrial leaders were beginning to realize that "a customs union offers the only alternative to the economic chaos which threatens to engulf the continent."[20] On 1 December, *L'Ere nouvelle* urged German voters to remember Herriot's words and to cast their ballots for Europe in the approaching Reichstag election.

Actually, in the final weeks of 1924, the idea was doing even better than surface manifestations indicated because both the peace movement and concern about Europe's economic health and strength were building potential at a steady rate. While the growth of the peace movement across Europe was uneven, it was substantial nearly everywhere, and in some countries, most notably France, it was spilling over the frameworks of the formal peace societies and manifesting itself in kindred organizations, such as the League of the Rights of Man. The high point in the peace movement came in the final weeks of the year when a special committee was set up in France to develop plans for the erection of a temple to peace. This committee, which included Premier Herriot, Léon Blum, Paul Painlevé among others, was being much discussed as the year ended, and many Frenchmen were urging the Herriot ministry to take the initiative in organizing a vast crusade for world peace. Even in Germany, where the peace movement had been slow in getting underway, membership in the Deutsche Friedensgesellschaft rose above twenty thousand in 1924, and there was a deepening of peace sentiment in the Democratic and Social Democratic parties.[21]

Meanwhile, on the economic front, facts and figures were now at hand to show that Europe's share in world trade had fallen approximately 25 percent from 1913 to 1924 and that its share in agricultural and industrial production had fallen almost as much. In nearly every field of production, from grains and dairy products to coal and steel, the story was essentially the same—a rather spectacular growth in the United States and several other countries beyond the seas and a rather marked relative decline in Europe. And though economic nationalism remained powerfully rooted and the great majority of economists, business leaders, and economic journals remained overwhelmingly preoccupied with national policies and programs, there was nevertheless increasing talk about Europe's economic ills and an increasing tendency to see Europe's national divisions and rivalries as one of the main sources of those ills.[22] Even Edmond Stinnes, younger son of the late Hugo Stinnes, was pondering the idea of a European customs union more seriously than his father had ever done.

Finally, in order to provide a fairly rounded picture of the growth of the idea in 1924, especially in potential, we must look briefly at its reflection in books and the periodical press, and we must also bear in mind that it entered more and more into the discussion of such problems as European security, the organization of peace, and Europe's economic difficulties.[23]

Of the books and pamphlets to appear in this year dealing directly with the European idea, the ones that seem most worthy of brief review are Albert J. H. Vazeille's *Pour les Etats-Unis d'Europe*: Hermann Kranold's *Vereinigte Staaten von Europa*; and C. F. Heerfordt's *Et Nyt Europa*. These three books approached the idea from different angles and stressed arguments that had been little used.

Vazeille, former French deputy and writer on varied subjects, viewed the European idea against the background of natural law as well as philosophy and history. He believed that the principles of unity and diversity lay at the foundation of all life whether individual or collective and that the principle of federalism was grounded in natural law. He said that in the political realm authority corresponded to unity while liberty corresponded to diversity and that if authority became excessive, the result was tyranny, and if liberty ran to license it was anarchy. Thus, the supreme task of political leadership was to establish and maintain a reasonable harmony and balance between these contending principles. He argued that federalism was the best means that had been devised for doing this and thus for reconciling human differences. He praised the federal systems of Switzerland and the United States and concluded his essay with these words: "Vivent les Etats-Unis d'Europe."

Kranold, a member of the German Social Democratic party and a long-time advocate of Anschluss, approached the problem from the angle of socialist ideology but ended up a firm supporter of a united Europe. Contrary to what most socialists were saying, Kranold argued that federalism would not hamper, much less endanger, the socialization of Europe. So he urged socialists to work for a united Europe because a united Europe would be a much stronger and more exciting thing for socialists to possess.[24]

Heerfordt, the author of *Et Nyt Europa*, was a politically sensitive Danish physician with a burning desire to rid Europe of the scourge of war. Convinced that the world was so diverse politically and culturally that a universal League of Nations could never be more than a loose confederation of essentially sovereign states, he argued that Europe's best chance for peace lay in an "Anglo-European United States" resting on a customs union and a common defense force. He called on the peoples of Scandinavia to take the lead in organizing a massive propaganda campaign across Europe in behalf of such a community and explained that he had already developed a plan for such a campaign, a plan that had been endorsed by many prominent citizens in Norway and Sweden as well as Denmark.

Chapter 6

A EUROPEAN MOVEMENT

EMERGES

If 1924 was a good year in the history of the European idea, 1925 was to be a better year. For nearly every force that had been nourishing the idea was to become intensified, and the idea was to get more attention in books and in the daily and periodical press.[1]

In fact, the new year was full of promise from the outset. On 17 January 1925, Georges Bonnet, prominent French deputy, said in an article in *L'Europe nouvelle*: "When one looks at the United States with its gold and its formidably equipped industry and at Asia, which is in turn arming itself for the economic battle to come, one realizes that the time has come to organize an economic United States of Europe." Eleven days later, on 28 January, Premier Herriot said in a rather hard-hitting speech on European security in the Chamber of Deputies: "Europe is only a small province of the world. . . . Far away on the shores of the Pacific problems are arising which will soon demand concentrated action on the part of a United States of Europe. . . . My great hope is to see a United States of Europe become a reality. And if I have put all of my strength behind the League of Nations, it is because I have seen in this great institution the first step toward a United States of Europe."[2] Thus, for the second time in just over three months, the French premier had openly endorsed the idea of a United States of Europe. The second endorsement was stronger than the first because it stressed Europe's economic position in the world and was made in the Chamber of Deputies in the midst of a debate on foreign policy. Still, it is doubtful that Herriot's primary purpose in injecting this little passage into his speech was to get the European idea as such before Europe in a more formal sense. Rather, it would seem that his principal concern was German power and that he was trying to convince London and Washington as well as Berlin, once and for all, that the aim of French policy was security and not hegemony. Indeed, he was saying that the idea of security was so central to French thought and policy that France, if given firm assurance of security, was prepared to travel the road of European pacification, even to the point of pioneering for a united Europe.

But whatever Herriot's primary purpose, he had given the idea greater vitality and respectability in Europe and made France the unquestioned leader of a budding European movement. In fact, there were some who said at once that Herriot had moved the idea from the realm of speculation to that of practical politics. Coudenhove-Kalergi sought to persuade Chancellor Marx to make a similar statement in the Reichstag. Francesco Nitti, who had been pondering the European idea for years, declared that the premier's words were "full of truth and beauty" and that he himself would henceforth work more diligently for a united Europe.[3] Too, a sizable segment of Europe's daily press, led by *Neue freie Presse*, *Journal de Genève*, and *L'Oeuvre*, called this passage the high point of the speech and some italicized the passage in their reports of the speech. *L'Oeuvre*, for example, said in its 29 January issue that Herriot had not only given clear proof of his attachment to the European idea and to the great ideal of spiritual disarmament but had shown that he was "impatient to get on with the work of organizing Europe."

Most Frenchmen, of course, realized that this rather rapid growth of European thought in France was largely a product of France's fervent search for security, and some said that it had been Herriot's awareness of this that had prompted his dramatic gesture. This feeling had been strengthened on 1 February, when the premier had delivered another stirring speech with strong European overtones before a peace rally in Salle du Trocadéro.[4] Emile Borel, well-known mathematician and member of the Chamber of Deputies, sensed this push toward peace in France and made a special effort to interpret it to the German-speaking world. In an article in the first issue of Prince Karl Anton Rohan's new journal, *Europäische Revue*, Borel said that French opinion had been moving toward a reconciled and united Europe since the election of 11 May 1924 and assured the readers of the new journal that Herriot's foreign policy had the support of the great majority of the French people. Like Coudenhove-Kalergi, Borel urged the German people to make a positive response to Herriot's gesture and added: "The future of Europe is in large measure in the hands of the German people and their government."[5]

Gabriel Chavet, an active member of the League for Peace and Freedom, saw this ferment as a thing of great promise and predicted that it would slowly spread to the whole of Europe, providing a climate more favorable to a solution of the great issues of the hour, which included the Franco-German problem and the problem of economic nationalism. He urged the peoples of Europe to multiply their economic and cultural contacts and to make greater use of the League of Nations as a frame for cooperation. Chavet explained: "In this way the great issues can be simplified and more easily resolved. A network of common interests can be developed to the point where frontiers will be blurred and robbed of their power to divide."[6]

There were those in France, even on the Left, who feared that this ferment, which was obviously fostering moral disarmament and a defensive psychology, might go too far for the good of France. For example, Gustave Rodrigues told his countrymen that their "constant cry of peace, peace, peace" was being interpreted in Germany as a sign of weakness, and he urged them to use the word "security" more and the word "peace" less.[7] Lucien Maury was even more disturbed by this ferment and said in *Babel* that, while arrogant nationalism was an unbearable evil, tempered patriotism was a beautiful and creative force. "We want a Europe free of wars and convulsions, but not shorn of its fires of intensity which spring from its nationalities and different cultures. . . ."[8]

Among those in Austria and Germany who testified to this ferment in French opinion and its significance for the European idea, few did so as eloquently and fervently as Coudenhove-Kalergi, Carl Endres, and Karl Anton Rohan. Coudenhove-Kalergi, who spent the early days of 1925 in France and interviewed a goodly number of French political leaders—including Herriot, Loucheur, Caillaux, and Léon Blum—and studied French opinion at close range, now stated that many Frenchmen had become good Europeans without being aware of it. He later wrote of the French attitude at this time: "In fact, with the exception of the Communists, all of the [French] Left supported the idea of European Union. . . ."[9]

Carl Endres, foreign correspondent for the *Berliner Tageblatt*, in his new book, *Vaterland Europa*, called Herriot's speech of 28 January a declaration "of measureless significance" and asserted that the French Premier had moved the idea of a United States of Europe from "the realm of speculation to that of practical politics." Moreover, Endres assured his readers that the powerful Left Bloc in France was behind Herriot, and he argued that the Left Bloc in France deserved the support of all men of good-will in Europe because it was pointing the way to a peaceful, democratic, and united Europe. More concretely, he reminded his countrymen that nearly all of the school teachers in France supported the Left Bloc and that the League for the Rights of Man in France had approximately 200,000 members while its sister league in Germany numbered just over 1,000.[10]

Karl Anton Rohan, young Austrian journalist and editor of the *Europäische Revue*, testified frequently to this current of opinion in France, saying in the fourth issue of the new journal that France had been very hard hit by the Great War and that she now realized the settlement had not given her the security for which she had so fervently hoped and worked: "France's postwar politics have stressed security at any price because the whole country has wished nothing so much as peace." This desperate search for security was, he said, helping produce the conditions for a federated Europe.[11]

But nothing that was said or done in these weeks provided more striking proof of France's attachment to the European idea than the fall of the Herriot ministry on 10 April. The new ministry formed by Paul Painlevé, a Republican Socialist with a deep understanding of European culture, included Briand, Caillaux, Emile Borel, Anatole de Monzie, and Herriot himself remained in a key position as president of the Chamber of Deputies. Indeed, of the nineteen members of the new cabinet, fourteen belonged to the French League for the Rights of Man.[12]

Perhaps the most compelling reason for the feeling that the Painlevé ministry would pursue the course of European collaboration and pacification with even greater energy than the Herriot ministry had done was the fact that Briand was at the Foreign Office. At the turn of the century, Briand had been a member of the Group de l'Arbitrage International, which had European union in its program, and he was now widely regarded as the most convinced apostle of Europeanism among the statesmen of Europe. In fact, some French nationalists had found fault with his patriotism, and one of his milder critics was soon to say of him that he had let "Europe go to his head."[13]

But Briand's reply to these accusations was that he could be both a good Frenchman and a good European because France could not have security and peace unless Europe had security and peace, and Europe could not have security and peace unless she were better organized and the states were more closely linked. Though he, like most Frenchmen, did not conceal his fear of a resurgence of German power, he insisted that peace was largely a matter of good faith, effort, and organization, that German opinion was fluid and capable of change, and that the best hope of moving it in the direction of European pacification was for France to pursue such a policy. Like Herriot, he felt that German revisionism as well as German power could be best handled in the context of an emerging Europe. Also, he had no illusions concerning French hegemony in Europe, and he placed great emphasis on human contacts and personal diplomacy. Alexis Léger, who became head of Briand's cabinet in 1925 and remained his collaborator to the end, has said of him: "He brought the refinement of the artist to the handling of men."[14]

Though France had now taken the lead in the promotion of the European idea, that idea was nonetheless more alive than ever in Germany. For many Germans had been deeply impressed by the victory of the Left Bloc in France as well as by Herriot's speeches, and the volume of literature on the idea in Germany was now comparable to that in France; and while a much larger proportion of it was hostile to the idea, a considerable portion was in the spirit of Endres's *Vaterland Europa*. The Germans had not made their decision, and there were at least two broad signs of growing support for the European idea.

One of these signs was a new diplomatic offensive launched by the Wilhelmstrasse. For Stresemann, embarrassed by the findings of the Interallied Military Controls Commission and elated at the power of the Left Bloc in France, had already decided that the time had come for some striking gesture on Germany's part in the direction of a general European pacification. Accordingly, after conferring at length with the ever helpful Lord D'Abernon, the British ambassador in Berlin, Stresemann had drafted a memorandum setting out the main lines of a Rhineland pact and a series of arbitration treaties involving the principal powers of Europe. On 20 January 1925, he put this document in the hands of Lord D'Abernon for transmission to the British Foreign Office. Though the wheels of diplomacy moved slowly, by early spring the negotiations, which were to lead to Locarno and to produce a better climate for the growth of the European idea, were out in the open and beginning to move.

The other development in Germany that helped the European idea was a growing effort on the part of sizable segments of the Democratic and Social Democratic parties to mount a peace movement comparable to that in France and to compel some sort of an official response to Herriot's European gestures. In the main these were the Germans who over the years had been urging a forthright effort at collaboration with France and who, more recently, had warmly greeted most of the program of the Left Bloc. In fact, there were some among them, and they were often economists like Paul Göhre and Wladimir Woytinsky, who felt that Paneurope's hour had come and who accordingly urged their countrymen to forsake all ideas of hegemony and to make Paneurope Germany's central mission. For example, Göhre was soon to write: "Germany should now become a fervent champion of Paneurope. A continental European community is now Germany's destiny. Here is her future."[15]

Moreover, there were marked differences within the Social Democratic party on the matter of England's relation to a European structure and the question of the Anschluss as well. The Right wing, like the Democratic party, held that England was essential to a European structure of any sort and that everything possible should be done to enlist England's participation. The Left wing, on the other hand, held that England could not be a party to such a structure because of her adherence to the doctrine of the balance of power on the continent. As Ludwig Quessel put it: "He who desires a United States of Europe must face the fact that it cannot be realized within the framework of the Anglo-Saxon doctrine of the balance of power."[16]

On the question of the Anschluss the difference was perhaps more damaging to the European idea. For the Left wing held that the Anschluss was essentially a Pan-German doctrine and that its pursuit would greatly aggravate tensions and fears across much of Europe and throttle, if not wreck, the Paneuropean movement. On the other hand, most of the members of the Right wing were wedded to the Anschluss and held that it was a legitimate goal of German foreign policy whose realization would reinforce democratic forces in Germany by calming the nationalists. Indeed, some of them, including Paul Löbe, had come to Paneurope by way of the Anschluss, and their attachment to the Anschluss was bringing them perilously close to the main current of nationalist thought and to the position of Democrats like Fritz Nonnenbruch and Willy Hellpach, who saw a German-dominated Middle Europe as the first step toward a European structure and who thus envisioned such a structure largely in terms of German revisionism if not indeed German power.[17]

Still it was not these divisions of opinion in the ranks of the moderate Left, much as they complicated matters, that prevented the emergence of a peace movement with a European thrust comparable to that in France. After all, England would have to make her own decision about her relation to Europe, and even the Anschluss could conceivably have been made a vehicle for union. The decisive fact, put in its simplest terms, was that internationalist, pacifist sentiment was much stronger in France than in Germany, and hard as these Germans tried, they were unable to make much headway in beating down nationalist forces.

In fact, they had been frequently embarrassed over the months by demonstrations of nationalist and antidemocratic sentiments, and the spring of 1925 with its presidential election was no exception. For not only was Paul von Hindenburg elected to the presidency of the Weimar Reich on 26 April, just eleven days after the formation of the Painlevé ministry in France, but throughout the campaign a host of German nationalists, led by such men as Moeller van den Bruck, Oswald Spengler, and Ernst Jünger, poured out their wrath and scorn on parliamentary principles and the whole Weimar system.[18] Indeed, the election not only demonstrated that the German Right was strong and determined to keep a watchful eye on both the policy of fulfillment and parliamentary government, but it brought a sharp and sometimes painful outcry from moderate elements across Europe. Belgium's Le Peuple (30 April 1925) wrote: "The election of Hindenburg is a hard blow to all of those who are working in good faith for the pacification of Europe." Alphonse Aulard called the election "a grave and disturbing event," and François Drotet declared that "it dulls many hopes." Stresemann himself was momentarily shaken, and Vorwärts, deeply embarrassed and no less deeply pained, laid the blame for Hindenburg's election on the Communists and what it called the strand of "mysticism in the German soul," wondering if it meant the restoration of the monarchy.

Still much as Hindenburg's election did to bolster the confidence of nationalist and military circles in Germany, it was soon evident, as L'Europe nouvelle predicted would be the case, that it would not destroy the policy of fulfillment or seriously weaken the European idea. After all, the moderate elements across Europe were capable of great faith. As L'Oeuvre soon put it: "No one can be sure what Hindenburg's election means, but one can be sure that now is not the time to abandon either negotiations or hope."[19]

In fact, moderate elements in Germany, however embarrassed, succeeded in getting the Reichstag to respond to Herriot's European gestures before the spring had passed. The Reichstag's response, which helped to clarify the status of the European idea in Germany, was precipitated by Rudolf Breitscheid of the Social Democratic party on 19 May. On that day, after Stresemann had sketched the main lines of German foreign policy, Breitscheid proceeded in a very cautious way to inject the European idea into the debate. After criticizing the German Right for many things and especially for its contention that there could be no constructive foreign policy without great military power, he said that there was something higher in the life of Europe than military might. There was, he said, a regard for Europe's future and its civilization which was inherent in the idea of a United States of Europe and which could be pursued without great military power. This idea, he said, had real meaning for Europe's economic future and could, if ardently nourished, become realist politics: "What is utopia today may be reality tomorrow."[20]

Although the Reichstag was wary of the European idea, that idea nevertheless received a brief airing in which Count Bernstorff of the Democratic party, Dr. Johannes Bell of the Center party, and Freiherr von Rheinbaben and Counts Lerchenfeld and Brüninghaus of the German People's party participated. While two of these deputies, Rheinbaben and Lerchenfeld, refused to elaborate on the idea on the grounds that it was utopian and should not be allowed to divert attention from the real issues of the day, the other three took the position that Germany should concern herself with it and proceeded to discuss it at some length.

Bernstorff, the first of this latter trio to speak, reminded his colleagues that Herriot had discussed the idea in the Chamber of Deputies early in the year and indicated that he felt that the time had come for the Reichstag to respond to the French premier. After assuring the Reichstag, perhaps not entirely facetiously, that he was well aware of the fact that Napoleon I had also spoken of a United States of Europe on more than one occasion, he said:

> . . . the idea lives on for many reasons and in many forms. I cannot
> accept it in the form that Count Coudenhove presents it, namely without
> England. To me that is impossible. But the idea lives because reasonable
> people in all the states of Europe have come to believe that this Old
> Continent is much too small to withstand the competition of the enor-
> mous economic union which has arisen on the soil of the United States of
> America and one has only to look at Ford to understand this. If Europe
> is to compete with this vast union, it must unite and I am convinced that
> if political union proves impossible a considerable measure of economic
> union will nonetheless develop . . . and if one thinks that this is utopia,
> he must remember that the utopias of today are often the realities of
> tomorrow.[21]

Bernstorff concluded with a plea for an energetic policy of fulfillment and reconciliation which he said could lead to a new renaissance in the culture of Europe.

But the fullest and most positive treatment of the European idea came from Bell, who said at once that he had supported the idea since 1921 and was now more convinced than ever that it was vital to the future of every European state. As he explained the reasons for his having come to this view, he painted a picture that was now quite familiar and quite similar to the one that Demangeon had painted in *Le Déclin d'Europe* in 1920. Bell said that the Great War had struck "Faustian blows" at Europe's economic heart while it stimulated economic growth in many regions beyond the seas. The result was that Europe, still bleeding and economically ill, was steadily losing ground to the United States, Japan, and the Argentine in the battle for markets. This was, he said, the crux of "the European problem," and if it was to be resolved and Europe restored to economic health, the states would have to draw together into an economic union whose frame was "flexible and capable of growth." Such a union, he said, was Europe's supreme need, and he argued that it could be created without weakening the League of Nations or blighting wholesome national qualities. "Here sound *Realpolitik* is required. . . . Only a realistic, practical policy, only an effective economic effort, can save us." Bell spoke sharply to those who would dismiss the European idea as utopian and unattainable: "He who dismisses the idea of a closer union of the states of Europe as utopian and unrealistic, condemns Europe's future. For if the idea is unrealisable, then Europe's revival will be nothing more than sound and smoke."[22]

The last deputy to deal at any length with the European idea was Count Brüninghaus, and he took a stand that was very close to what would come to be the official German position. While admitting that much could be said for some sort of economic union, he insisted that Herriot, Painlevé, and Briand were not to be trusted and that the course that they would have the European states pursue would mean "eternal humiliation and eternal enslavement for Germany, for their aim is to consolidate France's hegemony on the continent for all time." Still, he promised that Germany would be ready to work for a united Europe when she was granted her rights and when France was prepared to accept the fact that "the Rhine is a German River and has been for a thousand years."[23]

So after the formation of the Painlevé ministry, the German presidential election, and the Reichstag debate, it was clear that the European idea was making headway in Germany as well as in France. But there was a difference and that difference, underlined by Count Brüninghaus, was heavily centered in foreign policy considerations. The core fact was that ferment in the direction of peace and moral disarmament had gone further in France than in Germany, and perhaps equally important, the European idea fitted much more naturally and positively into French policy, especially into France's effort to soften German revisionism and to check the Anschluss.[24]

Still, in spite of these differences, there was a feeling among moderate elements in both countries that a large measure of understanding was possible, and nothing was doing so much to feed this feeling as the negotiations between Stresemann, Briand, and Chamberlain anticipating a Rhineland Pact. Although Stresemann steadfastly refused to include the western boundaries of Czechoslovakia and Poland in the projected pact, the proposal was nonetheless being carefully studied in the chancelleries of Europe.[25] Though Briand was trying hard to get at least the proposed arbitration treaties woven in with the Rhineland guarantee and the whole scheme placed within the framework of the League of Nations, he was now too deeply committed emotionally and ideologically to the goal of European pacification to reject any proposal that offered promise of a Franco-German rapprochement.

Moreover, Stresemann, who had been quick to sense the psychology of the Left Bloc, had a strong hand, and he was playing it brilliantly. On the one hand, he was playing to reassure the moderate elements everywhere, but especially in France, and on the other, he was endeavoring to dissuade his own countrymen from words and deeds that might provoke unnecessary anxieties abroad. For example, he tried to keep Paul Löbe, president of the Reichstag, from attending the Anschluss demonstration that the Austrian section of the Volksbund had scheduled for late August in Vienna.[26] Though Löbe defied him and went to Vienna to speak in support of the Anschluss, the foreign minister stated that Löbe did not speak for the German Foreign Office.

Thus, in spite of misgivings in many quarters and occasional embarassing incidents, the negotiations gathered momentum, and by the early summer of 1925, Stresemann, Chamberlain, and Briand were on the road that was to take them to Locarno in October. As they moved forward, the climate improved, and the champions of the European idea worked with greater hope.

Chapter 7

EUROPE'S ECONOMIC ILLS

During the second half of 1925, which was highlighted politically by the Locarno Conference, the search for a cure for Europe's economic ills became more intense and widespread. Quite a number of Europe's economists were arguing with growing conviction that Europe's economic ills were deeply rooted in her national divisions and that economic nationalism was, especially for Europe, a false formula because it based itself on political frontiers rather than economic facts and realities. Indeed, as they discussed the consequences of Europe's political and economic fragmentation and disunity, they often used the economic argument boldly. They argued among other things that economic rivalries and conflicts were the principal causes of war, that economic disarmament was a prerequisite to military disarmament because governments would subsidize industries essential to war as long as there was real fear of war, that security and prosperity were highly interdependent and that there would have to be a much greater degree of security in Europe if there was to be effective economic rationalization, that fragmentation and customs barriers discouraged the spirit of enterprise, and that Europe could not regain its health and strength and hold its place in the world unless all of its political units moved toward the coordination and integration of their economies.[1]

This growing concern about Europe's economic health was not only giving the European idea more of an economic cast and content but it was also noticeably stimulating discussion of it, especially in the daily press where the growth was most quickly and clearly reflected. For example, from 30 July to 30 October 1925, well over a hundred articles and editorials dealing with the European idea appeared in *L'Ere nouvelle*, *L'Oeuvre*, *La Dépêche de Toulouse*, *Le Quotidien*, *L'Information*, *Neue freie Presse*, and *Vossische Zeitung*. Even *Vorwärts*, which was always very cautious about the idea, carried on its front page on 28 July an article by Coudenhove-Kalergi entitled "Paneuropa and Socialism" in which the young count argued that the whole tradition of the working class was Paneuropean and that Europe's workers could save Europe if they would rally in mass to his Paneuropean program.

The European idea also received more attention in the periodical press during these months. Several journals, including *L'Europe nouvelle*, *Le Monde nouveau*, and *Die Gesellschaft*, gave it about as much space as did *Paneuropa*, *La Paix par le droit*, and *Sozialistische Monatshefte*. *L'Europe nouvelle* (1 Aug. 1925) told its readers that interest in the idea was sufficient to justify a special section in each issue of the journal, and it also reviewed

Maury's *Babel* and Filene's *Problème européen et sa solution*.[2] The following issue of the journal reviewed the history of the Paneuropean movement, printed Coudenhove-Kalergi's "European Manifesto" in full, and pointed out that a section of Paneuropean Union was being formed in France (pp. 1061–64). The first autumn issue carried a joint statement by Wolf von Dewall, of the editorial board of the *Frankfurter Zeitung*, and Richard Kuenzer, of the editorial board of *Germania*, supporting the French proposal for a general economic conference, and articles by Louis Loucheur and C. R. Pusta, former foreign minister of Estonia, arguing for economic integration in Europe.[3]

At the same time *Le Monde nouveau*, which had published an article by Lucien Bec in its April issue arguing for a European customs union now warmed to the European idea, and Emile Vandervlugt, the editor, soon made it clear that the journal would henceforth give the idea its energetic support.[4] But perhaps the most striking article to appear in the periodical press in these months came from the pen of the young German economist Wladimir Woytinsky and appeared in *Die Gesellschaft*, a relatively new socialist periodical supposedly dedicated to doctrinal and theoretical questions. Woytinsky marshaled an imposing array of facts and figures in support of a European customs union, and concluded his article: "Without a customs union and indeed without an economic union, the reconstruction of Europe is impossible."[5]

At the same time, many of Europe's political leaders, including Premier Painlevé and Foreign Minister Stresemann, took a closer look at the European idea. Speaking before the International Student Congress at Geneva on 4 September, the French premier said: "Upon youth falls the task of organizing peace. It is you and your generation who must realize the ideal of a European humanity; for Europe is the leader of world civilization and it will perish if it continues to mutilate itself in internal strife." Speaking on the following day before the Fifth Session of the League Assembly, Painlevé said that peace was dependent upon "the interpenetration of nations" and argued that the League should ground itself more deeply in economic and cultural affairs and should work boldly to overcome the forces of disunity in Europe.[6]

Although Stresemann was not speaking of the cultivation of the European spirit in quite the manner of Painlevé, he was apparently convinced that Germany should move away from narrow nationalist policies. He invited Coudenhove-Kalergi to the Foreign Office for a talk, and he said in an article in *Europäische Revue* that all of the states of Europe stood in need of a greater measure of economic cooperation and collaboration as a basis for peace as well as for a program of economic rationalization. "If we are to have peace, we must have a new European economy."[7]

But of all the many men who were writing and speaking at this time for the organization of Europe, few if any were doing so with as much fervor and earnestness as the retired French army officer, General Alexandre Percin. This elderly soldier, who had resolved years before to devote the evening of his life to peace, now seized hold of the European idea with passion and put both his pen and tongue in its service. In late August he sent his publisher a little manuscript in which he called on the peoples of Europe to renounce war and to dedicate themselves wholeheartedly to the promotion of moral disarmament and to the building of "a United States of Europe." The editor of *L'Ere nouvelle* saw the manuscript and asked the author for a summary article for publication in his journal. Percin then wrote a short pithy article in which he said in part: "The Zollverein created the German Empire. A European customs union will create a United States of Europe and put an end to war among the states of Europe."[8]

This article attracted wide attention, and a few days later, when Percin's little volume entitled *Désarmement moral* appeared in the bookshops of Paris, the old soldier found himself a sort of hero, and he was at once overwhelmed with invitations to speak on moral disarmament and European union. The French League for the Rights of Man gave a banquet for him on 4 July 1926, and he continued to speak and to advocate the unification of Europe until his health declined in 1927.

While most of the calls for Europe in the summer and early autumn of 1925 were individual in nature, some were collective. Both the World Federation of Trade Unions and the International Chamber of Commerce raised the question of the economic organization of Europe in their general meetings, even though their memberships spread over much of the world. Each organization drafted a resolution that argued that protectionist policies everywhere, and especially in Europe, were setting nations against one another, fostering a spirit of war, and impairing living standards. Both bodies called on their local groups to work for a reduction of customs barriers and for economic and political cooperation.[9]

While these international bodies were approving resolutions that reflected growing concern about economic nationalism, the Social Democratic party in Germany was in the course of making a more direct and positive gesture in behalf of the European idea. For the German Social Democrats, who had not had a firm and binding platform since the union of the independent and majority wings in 1922, had decided early in the year to draft such a document and had scheduled a party congress for Heidelberg in September. From the first, the Left wing of the party, which had been supporting Coudenhove-Kalergi for many months and had become deeply impressed by the program of the Left Bloc in France, urged the program committee to write European economic union into the new party platform. Though the Right wing of the party was not enthusiastic, it was anxious to avoid fresh dissension within the party and decided to go along.

The program committee then proceeded to insert the following sentence in the new program: "It [the Social Democratic party] demands the formation of a European economic union, which has become a compelling necessity for the consolidation of continental interests and for a United States of Europe."[10] In another article the new program declared that continental economic union was essential to "the growth and protection of the Democratic Republic." On 18 September the party congress at Heidelberg approved the text of the new platform without alterations, and the German Social Democratic party thus apparently became the first political party to endorse formally the idea of a European economic union.

But perhaps no development of the summer of 1925 demonstrated so forcefully the growing concern with Europe's economic plight or touched more deeply the European idea than the call for a general economic conference by Louis Loucheur and the French government. Loucheur, who was to labor unceasingly for a measure of European economic integration until his death in 1931, believed that Europe's economic antagonisms were stunting its growth and sapping its strength, that economic nationalism would have to be understood and controlled if Europe was to have security and prosperity. At the same time, he was keenly aware that Europe's economic life was complex and interest-ridden and that the forces working against economic integration were rugged and powerful. He felt that the wisest course for the time being was to try to unite kindred branches of industry across Europe into cartels under an international authority—perhaps the League of Nations at first. Such cartels, he believed, would help reknit the fabric of economic life, help balance production and consumption, quicken rationalization, and slowly but surely prepare the groundwork for an economic union.[11] Accordingly, on 15 September 1925, Loucheur told the Assembly of the League of Nations that his government felt the time had come for it to organize an international economic conference to diagnose Europe's economic ills and to prescribe ways and means for curing them. He then asked the assembly to invite the Council of the League to set up a committee to begin preparations for such a conference.[12]

Loucheur's proposal created considerable interest across Europe. *L'Information* observed that Loucheur appreciated "the close connection between economic peace and political peace," that German business circles were impressed, and that Count Bernstorff had said that the proposal would further the idea of a United States of Europe.[13] *The Economist*, which was now beginning to take notice of the European idea, said that the proposal was in line with "a considerable movement of opinion on the continent," and warned British leaders that the time had come for them to take steps to adjust the British economy to that current of opinion.[14]

The League of Nations moved rapidly, and on 26 September the assembly asked the council to set up a committee to plan a general economic conference to meet in Geneva which would be composed largely of economic experts rather than diplomats. A few weeks later the council, with Paul Hymans its rapporteur on economic questions taking the lead, set up the

Preparatory Commission, and the projected world economic conference became one of the central themes in the European press and a factor in the European movement.[15]

Meantime, in early October 1925, the Interparliamentary Union held its Twenty-Third Conference in Washington, and despite the fact that nearly half of the delegates were from non-European states, it devoted considerable time to European trade, customs barriers, and the Loucheur proposal. Several of the delegates from European parliaments argued that America's remarkable economic advance was largely a product of her vast, free market and urged their fellow delegates to work for the elimination of Europe's customs barriers. With Hjalmar Procope of Finland, Pierre Flandin of France, and Adolf Braun of Germany taking the lead, the Interparliamentary Union adopted a resolution that called for the creation of a special committee to study Europe's customs and to attempt to assess the impact of their abolition on world economic conditions. This resolution meant that the European idea would be on the agenda of the next conference.[16]

Then on 16 October, the negotiations that Stresemann, Briand, and Chamberlain had spearheaded throughout the summer culminated in the initialing of a series of agreements collectively known as the Locarno Pact. The fact that the new pact had implications for the European idea was obvious, and Briand himself did not hesitate to link the two. During the initialing ceremonies, the French foreign minister talked freely of the significance of the pact and said, among other things, that it represented the first concrete step toward "a United States of Europe."[17] Many others spoke along the same lines. The elderly Joseph Prudhomme praised the pact and referred to these autumn days as the "springtime of the United States of Europe."[18] *Vorwärts* headlined its issue of 17 October "The Victory of Peace" and, in the following issue, reported that Hjalmar Schacht, who had just returned from a trip to the United States, had said that "Europe must be made into a single economic unit."

Perhaps no paper of the day professed to see as much significance in Locarno for the European idea as did *L'Oeuvre*. This journal entitled its first article on the new pact "Toward a United States of Europe" and said editorially on 15 November 1925 that Locarno had made a deep impression across the Atlantic. "Without doubt Locarno signifies that a United States of Europe is no longer pure utopia and that its realization, though perhaps some time off, is possible, and that a Europe in the process of union cannot be treated in the same way as a divided Europe."[19]

Significant as Locarno may have been for the growth of the European idea, its impact was not as great as was initially expected. Not only were two of the powers that signed the pact, Britain and Italy, strongly opposed to any sort of a European structure, but a bitter debate quickly developed over its meaning and significance. For much of the Center and Right in Germany interpreted Locarno to mean a free hand for Germany to the east and as merely the first stage in a round of negotiations that would lead rapidly to the dismanteling of the Versailles Treaty.[20] The large moderate Left elements across France, Belgium, and Czechoslovakia contended that the Franco-German difference could be settled only on the European plane and that Locarno would be of little significance unless it were accepted as an instrument for peace and the beginning of a general pacification in all Europe, east as well as west.[21] Of course, this view found considerable support in moderate circles in the Reich itself. Even the *Sozialistische Monatshefte* warned Luther and Stresemann that, if the Reich government interpreted Locarno as giving it a free hand to the east, the "spirit of Locarno" would wither. It urged the government to come to terms with Poland and Czechoslovakia and to look to the League of Nations as the best means of achieving a peaceful revision of frontiers.[22]

Chapter 8

THE SPIRIT OF LOCARNO

While neither the Locarno treaties nor the league's decision to summon a general economic conference had any direct connection with the European idea, these events nevertheless gave that idea a fresh impulse and strengthened the feeling that some measure of integration might be possible within the foreseeable future. Discussion of the idea became more widespread and animated and, for the first time, a matter of interest, if not concern, in Great Britain. In fact, it is not too much to say that, during the eleven months between the Locarno Conference and Germany's entrance into the League of Nations, discussion of the idea swelled into a veritable debate and came close to reaching its full range and depth. For, in their search for new arguments, the champions of the idea probed into nearly every segment of European life and thought. If they failed to turn up any big new argument, they certainly elaborated and refined every one that had so far been widely used: namely, that federal bonds would undergird Europe's security and advance the cause of peace, provide Europe with the means of strengthening and revitalizing its economic life, ease its territorial and minorities problems by blurring and defusing frontiers, provide additional safeguards against Russian subversion and American economic penetration, and give the peoples of Europe a new sense of mission and thus stimulate their creative energies. Even the contention that natural law was on the side of the unity of Europe was further elaborated by Wilhelm Gutmann and others.[1]

But rich and wide-ranging as was this debate, much of its substance as well as its flavor will come out as our analysis of the European movement proceeds. We shall not, therefore, at this point undertake to do more with the debate than to comment briefly on some of its important peripheral strands and to explore in some detail the customs union idea that was its central and most concrete element. The most important peripheral strands of the debate were the attempt to define federalism in principle and practice and to assess its importance for Europe; to find out why there was a Franco-German problem and how it could best be handled: and to identify and analyze the special problems that would arise from a federal system.

The first of these, the nature and purposes of federalism, received a decided boost right after the Locarno Conference when the Collège Libre des Sciences Sociales announced that it was in the process of organizing a series of fourteen weekly lectures on federalism in Europe.[2] While most of the lectures in this series, which began on 21 November 1925, dealt with federalism in specific countries, including Belgium, Switzerland, and Yugoslavia, the ones that attracted most attention dealt with federalism in theory and its significance for Europe as a whole. Jean Charles Brun, a well-known federalist of Proudhonist persuasion, introduced the series with a lecture entitled "The Principles of Federalism." Brun argued that the federal system was the best political form yet devised for harmonizing human diversities and striking a balance between authority and liberty. He also stated that the growth of nationalism and technology had made federalist principles increasingly relevant to Europe: "The federal system is supple and progressive. It can handle peoples of varying degrees of maturity. . . . Since it calls for the maximum of free consent, it possesses great moral nobility."[3] He concluded that a federal system had become a necessity for the peoples of Europe if they were to achieve stability, peace, and economic well being.

Jean Hennessy, who was then French minister to Switzerland, entitled his lecture "Europe and Federalism." He argued that federalism was on the march because it had demonstrated its worth in an age of growing technology and interdependence, and he insisted that the states of Europe, weakened by war and standing between two massive federal structures—the United States and the Soviet Union—would have to form a federation if they were to live and prosper. "Let us make Locarno a highway over which the federative principle can travel across Europe. . . . Switzerland has already shown us the way to a Europe united in peace by federal bonds."[4]

Francesco Nitti, who spoke on "Federalism and the Future of Europe," said at the outset of his lecture: "Before the war federalism was a political program, today it is both a political program and an economic necessity." Then, after examining briefly the federal structures of Switzerland and the United States, the former Italian premier asserted: "Switzerland offers Europe an example of what it can and should do. Switzerland is the image of what Europe ought to be."[5]

Of the fourteen lectures, perhaps the most scholarly and penetrating was by Paul Szende, who spoke on "Federalism and the Danubian States." This former Hungarian minister took a close look at the problems of the Danubian region and contended that if its peoples were to have peace and prosperity they would have to develop a federal system. He concluded: "May the noble souls in France, who labor with zeal and ardor for the League of Nations and a United States of Europe, remember that a prime condition for the realization of their ideas is a Danubian confederation."[6]

No peripheral strand of this great debate was more interesting and illuminating than that which sought to define Europe or to answer the question: "What is Europe?" While this question had long been asked and debated by poets and novelists as well as geographers, economists, and historians, the literature on it was greatly expanded and enriched during these months. Many felt that an answer to this question was essential to any realistic assessment of the European idea, and most supporters of the idea were convinced that an unbiased answer would itself constitute an argument in support of the idea.

Nor did many of the proponents of the European idea try to gloss over the fact that ethnic, linguistic, political, and cultural diversities existed from one side of Europe to the other. Rather, most of them faced these diversities squarely and agreed that they gave European life much of its beauty, charm, and strength. At the same time, they insisted that there was unity as well as diversity, that there was a great cultural and spiritual unity at the foundation of European life and civilization which derived from a centuries-long fusion of the basic elements in the Greek, Roman, and Hebrew cultures. This vast cultural synthesis was a unity, they argued, that undercut the diversities of race and language as well as the national cultures; it was itself the essence of the European concept. They agreed that in the nineteenth and twentieth centuries the forces of diversity and disunity had grown rampant, but they maintained that a complex of new forces was working to restore the balance, soon to give the victory to the principle of unity. No one expressed this idea better than Lucien Romier, editor of *Le Figaro*, when he wrote: "Geographically, racially, and linguistically Europe is characterized by diversity, but in its intellectual and spiritual tradition it is a unity. The essence of this unity is a fusion of Hebrew religion, Greek intelligence, and Roman law. In our time the Roman element, resting on the doctrine of absolute sovereignty and the new nationalism strengthened by technology and industry, has upset the equilibrium. What Europe needs to do today is to restore the balance in the great tradition and present a united front. . . ."[7]

While most of the proponents of the European idea defined Europe in much the same general ideology as did Romier, there was nevertheless great variety in the language they employed. Coudenhove-Kalergi, whose definition of Europe was almost identical with Romier's, liked to stress the fact that all of the great movements in European history, such as the Renaissance, the Enlightenment, the French Revolution, and the Industrial Revolution, were truly European in scope and ignored national boundaries. Heinrich Rogge, with this great synthesis in mind, wrote that Europe was atomized but that the atomization was on the surface.[8] Paul Painlevé said that Europe's history and the common elements in its culture had created "a sort of brotherhood in the European soul" that, if nurtured and built upon, could develop into a European patriotism. When Paul Valéry spoke of Europe as "a little cape on the Asiatic continent," he was speaking merely in a geographical sense, for Valéry, like Ernest Renan and so many of Europe's literary men, saw Europe's essence not in its geography and politics but in its culture. To him Europe was a great cultural entity, "anterior to and beyond the nations" and something that "the nations tended to conceal" from the peoples of Europe. Julien Benda, Romain Rolland, Heinrich Mann, René Arcos, Charles Vildrac, and many others generally agreed with Valéry, and some of them argued that Europe was a necessity because the nation-state had failed Europe by atomizing it and by fostering national rivalries and conflicts.[9]

Equally animated was the discussion of the Franco-German difference, which nearly everyone agreed lay at the heart of the European problem and would have to be resolved before Europe could be firmly organized. While this problem had been much discussed over the years, it was perhaps explored more widely and intensively at this time than ever before, partly, no doubt, because of the divergence of views between Paris and Berlin on the meaning of Locarno. Many journals gave it space, but few aired it as fully and fervently as Prince Rohan's *Europäische Revue*. Indeed, the first issue of this journal for 1926 contained articles by Anatole de Monzie, August Müller, Professor Klemperer, and Pierre Viénot dealing with it.[10] De Monzie and Müller took fairly similar positions holding that the Franco-German problem was not rooted in differing national characteristics and qualities but in rivalries and fears that could be overcome by proper education and closer contacts. De Monzie, who was a member of the French cabinet, reminded his readers that in 1921 Léon Bourgeois had proposed the creation of a European commission to undertake the rewriting of history texts in terms of greater objectivity.[11] Müller wrote of the possibility of a European economic community in the form of a European Zollverein pivoting on French and German coal and iron ore.

But Klemperer and Viénot took a different position in their much shorter articles, insisting that the Franco-German problem was grounded in contrasting national characteristics and that this fact largely explained why the two peoples tended to see Locarno and Europe differently. They argued that Frenchmen were generally very rational, legalistic, and precise in their thinking, while Germans were more romantic and mystical, more inclined to think in terms of unlimited goals, and thus likely to give more attention to destiny in the formulation of policy.

Although this debate on national characteristics was distasteful to moderate Left circles in both countries, it went on nonetheless. In the April issue of *Europäische Revue*, Herbert Dankworth and Pierre de Lanux squared off. Dankworth stated that the two nationalities were so different in their ways of thinking and feeling that a collaboration was well nigh impossible. While Lanux held with De Monzie that there were no clearly defined mental and emotional differences between the two peoples and that the prevailing hate and distrust would wither away if contacts were multiplied, Lanux wrote: "Realism will go far to cement Europe."[12]

There were many interesting variations of this theme, and perhaps the most interesting of these variations was to put the contrast in terms of "inner power" and "outer power." This was done most strikingly by J. Springer and Fritz Coerper, both of whom argued that territorial imperialism had run its course in Europe, and that Europe would have to look henceforth to its inner resources and power for leadership. Measuring France and Germany in terms of this formula, they found France to be the center of Europe's "outer power" and Germany the center of Europe's "inner power." They concluded that the reconstruction of Europe was a German task. Coerper pressed this point hard, holding that outer power begat a static outlook and a weak policy while inner power engendered a dynamic outlook and a bold policy. Coerper wrote: "If German spirit is strong enough to meet the challenge, this time—this first and last time—Europe and France will follow Germany."[13] Though this debate concerning national qualities continued, it tended to taper off as the moderate Left everywhere frowned on it. Such journals as *La Paix par le droit* and *Sozialistische Monatshefte* shunned it and insisted that proper education and the multiplication of cultural contacts would bring France and Germany to an understanding.[14]

Another interesting aspect of the general debate was the number of men who assumed that a measure of integration was possible and who attempted to anticipate and analyze the major problems that would be involved in the creation of a federal structure. This was especially true of the newer converts who, after much pondering, had come to Europe with strong convictions. They were ready to discuss all sorts of issues, ranging from the geographical limits of a European community to how its common market should be organized, its revenues collected and distributed, and its integrated defense force handled.

But wide as the debate ranged and many as were the peripheral issues, it remained heavily centered on economic factors and economic forms of integration. This was so not only because of the approaching world economic conference and the conviction that the economic problem was the most urgent, but also because Germany's interest in European integration was almost entirely at the economic level. There was also the growing feeling that peace and security could not be substantially advanced until economic rivalries and antagonism were sharply curbed. Even the Locarno pact, though it fell largely in the political and diplomatic realm, tended to stimulate rather than check this emphasis on economic factors, and both Briand and Emile Vandervelde talked about an "economic Locarno." Vandervelde was widely quoted when he said: "Locarno is wonderful, but now we must create a European customs union."[15] *L'Ere nouvelle* said editorially on 2 July 1926: "It is now necessary that the United States of Europe organize and regulate their economies in common accord. If political union is impossible today, economic union is not. Forces stronger than national wills, ambitions, and interests are working for an economic union and without such a union European production will become increasingly anarchic."

Though there was a wide divergence of views as to the form, the extent, and the direction that economic integration should take, thinking nevertheless tended to revolve heavily around a customs union though cartelism was quite a bit in the picture. Europe had had a rich experience with cartels and, even though most labor leaders and doctrinaire socialists denounced them, there was a rather large and influential group that believed cartels were potentially benevolent organizations that could promote economic coordination and union.[16] This group, and it included Louis Loucheur and Paul Silverberg, held that cartels, if properly constructed and publicly supervised, would stimulate trade, increase the productivity of labor, aid the process of economic rationalization, lessen European economic rivalries, and develop moral bonds that would reinforce the bases of peace, thus promoting economic cooperation and union in many ways.

The cartel movement had been slowly gathering strength since the Franco-German Potash Agreement in 1924, and in the spring of 1926, with the able and European-minded director of Aciéries Réunies Burbach-Eich-Dudelange, Emil Mayrisch, in the lead, a steel cartel was looming, and most good Europeans felt that such a cartel would undergird Locarno and strengthen the European idea.

But if many of the supporters of the European movement had mixed feelings about cartels, such was not the case with regard to a customs union. The International Committee for a European Customs Union had been agitating the matter for more than a year, and nearly everyone who pondered the matter of a European community envisioned a customs union as the cornerstone of such a community. In the December issue of *Wirtschaftsdienst*, Felix Deutsch, director of the Electrical Society of Berlin, reviewed Europe's economic position in the world and declared that a multitude of economic facts were pressing for a thorough-going program of rationalization that would include the elimination of customs barriers. He reminded his German readers that a large number of France's most distinguished political and industrial figures, including Briand, Painlevé, and Loucheur, were not only debating this question but were even talking of a European federal structure. He predicted that in the months ahead there would be even more talk of "a unified structure of all the industries of Europe, of the abolition of customs houses, and of a United States of Europe."[17]

In mid-December 1925, as if in response to Deutsch's article, the Reichsverband der Deutschen Industrie issued a memorandum stating that Germany's commercial policy should aim at the lowering of tariff walls and announcing that it would at once appoint a committee from among its members to explore the question of a European customs union. This decision by the members of the Reichsverband stimulated interest in the customs union idea in business circles, especially in Germany and Austria.[18] Two widely known German industrialists—Bruno Bruhn, director of Krupp at Essen, and Albert Zapf, director of Felten-Guilleaume Carlswerk Actien Gesellschaft at Cologne—had short articles in *L'Europe nouvelle* (9 Jan. 1926, pp. 42–45) criticizing economic nationalism and suggesting that the time had come for the governments of Europe to begin the dismanteling of customs barriers across Europe. On 13 February 1926, the same journal published an article (pp. 204–8) by Georges Valensi calling for the establishment of a European telephone system, arguing that such a system would expedite business transactions and help in many ways to unify Europe economically and culturally.

From 26 to 28 February 1926, a group of European socialists, many of whom were prominent labor leaders, met in Brussels and spent considerable time discussing the question of a European customs union. Before adjourning they passed a resolution stating that "the economic interdependence of nations clearly demonstrates the need for commercial accords and for ways and means of familiarizing the peoples of Europe with the meaning of a European customs union" as an element in international policy. The resolution also urged socialists in all European countries to work for the lowering of customs, the suppression of import and export quotas, and the abolition of passports.[19]

The main impulse to the customs union idea did not come, however, from industrial and labor groups but from the writings and speeches of Francis Delaisi, Wladimir Woytinsky, Arpad Török, Paul Göhre, Henri Truchy, and other economists. Of the many contributions that Delaisi made to the customs union idea in these months, the greatest came in November 1925 with the publication of his *Les Contradictions du monde moderne*. This large book was a pungent and powerful plea for a European customs union, and it was widely read in economic circles.[20] Delaisi argued with an amazing richness of illustrative material that a great and stifling contradiction had developed between Europe's political and economic institutions; that economic life, propelled by technology and industrialism, had outgrown the nation-state system; and that the doctrine of absolute sovereignty, "which arose when economic life was basically agrarian and local" had become "a paralyzing and crippling absurdity." Europe he said, must rid itself of its multiplicity of political and economic units and bring its economy abreast of modern technological developments. "Europe must become a single market equal in dimensions to the American market. Then its great industrial potential, liberated from its shackles, will take on new life."[21]

Woytinsky agreed with Delaisi that the states of Europe could not maintain their position in the world unless they went all the way to a firm economic union with a customs union at its base. In *Vereinigte Staaten von Europa*, which was rich in facts and figures, he argued that Europe, though "morseled and murdered by her history," poor in basic resources and raw materials, was still rich in manpower and technical skills. Europe's crisis was not, he said, in the realm of production, but in the realms of marketing and consumption. It was a crisis that had to be faced, because it was "a problem of life and death" for the European economy. A customs union would not do the whole job, but it was the proper place to start and would provide the basis for a common market, the systematic rationalization of economic life, a rational division of labor, the reduction of production costs, more harmonious and effective use of the colonial possessions of the European states, and the expansion of markets at home and abroad. Then, after a customs union was in full operation, Europe could move toward a single monetary sytem, a unified system of social legislation, and a political federation.[22] Though admitting that the obstacles that stood in the way of a customs union were awesome, Woytinsky argued that they were mainly political and psychological in nature and in no sense insurmountable.

Török was about as ardent in his support of a European customs union as Delaisi and Woytinsky, but his approach to such a union was more political and philosophical, and he was more tolerant of nationalism. While Török argued that a customs union was "a precondition to future economic development," he also felt that nationalism had served the cause of national freedom, especially in Eastern Europe and still had much to offer. The best course, he believed, was to restrain and discipline nationalism to the point where it would tolerate a full-fledged customs union, and he felt that this could be done because the peoples of Europe had glimpsed the need for it. The peoples, he said, are beginning to understand that "economic liberalism, with its glorification of the individual will, and nationalism, with its atomization of the political will," must be curbed; that "economic systems are too complex and interdependent to have any future in isolation"; and that "the little organisms of the present must be fastened together into larger organisms."[23]

Göhre was a German socialist and former state secretary who resembled the German geopoliticians in his approach but not in his conclusions. Göhre called for the transformation of all Europe into a single economic sphere so unified that it would function as "a living, organic whole," with North Africa bound firmly to it. He urged his countrymen to forsake all thought of hegemony in Europe and concentrate on the building of a customs union. The facts, he said, spoke so convincingly and overwhelmingly for a customs union that the arguments arrayed against it were not worthy of refutation.[24]

Henri Truchy, distinguished French economist, is a good example of the sizable group of economists who came slowly and painfully to a customs union but in the end embraced it with deep conviction. During the first half of the twenties, Truchy talked and wrote much about the economic impact of the war on Europe, especially about the nine customs units and the fourteen monetary systems that the war spawned and the boost that the war gave to American economic power. He worried about what he sometimes called "the drift toward economic anarchy" and about Europe's inability to rationalize its production. Then shortly after the Locarno Conference, he decided that a "limited customs union" was possible, and in a lecture at the University of Neuchâtel on 26 February 1926, he urged the governments of Europe to rationalize and integrate their economic programs. By the end of the year he was working with the likes of Charles Gide, Francis Delaisi, and Lucien

Coquet, whom he had previously called "the bolder thinkers" and saying to the peoples of Europe: "Fix your eyes on it [a European customs union] and work toward it with patience and determination."[25]

One of the most interesting and effective techniques that the proponents of a customs union used to promote the idea was to paint a glowing picture of the American economic system and to attribute the country's success to its vast, free market. For the United States with its rapidly growing economy and its high standard of living not only inspired fear in Europe but also aroused admiration and envy. Even Coudenhove-Kalergi almost invariably pointed to the United States as the economic model for Europe and said many times that Europe could become as peaceful as Switzerland and as prosperous as the United States if it would unite.

In fact, ever since the war, European economists and businessmen in growing numbers had been probing for the secrets of America's economic power in the hope of discovering practices and techniques that might prove useful to their countries. Some of them had even tried to figure out whether economic unity or political unity came first in the evolution of the American system. Moreover, a goodly number of Europeans who visited the United States in the mid-twenties returned home singing the praises of the American union with its vast, open market. For example, Bronislaw Hubermann wrote in the autumn of 1925 that he had spent considerable time in the United States and that it was there that he had "conceived the idea of a United States of Europe as a possibility and a necessity."[26] Delaisi, in his *Les Contradictions du monde moderne*, pointed to the glories of the vast American market but predicted that the United States would have had a "history as glorious and bloody as that of the Old Continent" if each state had remained politically and economically sovereign.[27]

Of course, the customs union idea had bitter critics as well as staunch supporters. Of those who spoke out against it, few did so with greater conviction and vehemence than Gustav Stolper, Franz Eulenburg, Fritz Coerper, and Hans Hohlfeld. Each of these men attacked the idea from a slightly different angle, and together they summed up rather fully the arguments of the opposition.

Stolper, a vigorous champion of the Anschluss who had moved from Austria to Germany in 1923 and founded the Deutscher Volkswirt, treated the customs union idea in a rather high-handed fashion from a political point of view. In fact, this Austro-German economist hardly came to grips with the customs union idea at the economic level. He argued that the concept of national sovereignty was far too deeply anchored in the complex fabric of European life to permit the establishment of a supranational organization with the extensive authority that a customs union would require. Accordingly, he concluded that for the foreseeable future, in any event, the whole question was utopian and unworthy of serious discussion.[28]

Eulenburg, in contrast to Stolper, based his opposition to a customs union largely on economic considerations. He argued that a customs union and a common market in Europe would depress rather than stimulate economic life because they would lead inevitably to a high tariff wall and to a damaging and enervating trade war with Britain and the United States. What Europe needed was greater production and greater purchasing power, and these needs, he said, lay beyond the reach of a customs union whose concern was with the distribution rather than the production of goods. Europe's needs, he said, could only be met through the rationalization of economic processes, great boldness and daring on the part of entrepreneurs, the intensive exploitation of agricultural and mineral resources, and the creation of new industries.[29]

Coerper was even more outspoken in his rejection of a customs union, holding that such a union would do irreparable damage to European culture. It would, he said, centralize and standardize the economies of the European states to the point where their "innate dynamisms" would be stifled and all but obliterated. He called Coudenhove-Kalergi an enemy of Europe and labeled Göhre "the German Coudenhove" whose thinking resembled that of Karl Marx. Europe's salvation, he concluded, did not lie in a customs union but in the free and unfettered development of the economies of the individual states, especially that of Germany. For "Germany constitutes the core of Europe's inner strength, and she needs freedom not constraint."[30]

Hohlfeld wrote extensively about a customs union and made a substantial contribution to the debate by drawing together all the arguments and examining them as a body. In fact that was what he did in *Zur Frage einer europäischen Zollunion*, and he did a superb job of at least summarizing the arguments. He quoted Stolper and Eulenburg frequently and concluded his little book with the confident assertion that "the creation of a customs union can never provide Europe the means of recovering its former position of well-being."[31]

In addition to staunch proponents and opponents of a customs union, there were many who were unable to come to a firm decision one way or the other. Of this group two of the most interesting and influential were Emil Mayrisch, the great Luxembourg steel magnate, and Walter Layton, editor of *The Economist*.

Mayrisch, like most of the more European-minded industrialists of the day, felt that closer collaboration among the states of Europe was very much needed and said that the Rhine Basin could never reach its full economic potential unless it were treated as an economic unit. But he felt that the obstacles to a customs union were so great that they could not be surmounted unless "all men of good will" in Europe worked patiently to improve the political climate, to extend the European spirit, and to spell out the benefits that would flow from such a union. Like Loucheur, he believed that the proper place to start was with cartels and trade agreements.[32]

Layton's position was colored by the fact that he was an influential English journalist. While he apparently felt that a customs union would be of great benefit to the peoples of the continent, he realized that most of his countrymen feared it, and this realization remained in the forefront of his thinking. Though convinced that nationalism ruled out an integrated Europe for the forseeable future, he believed that a customs union was a distinct possibility, mainly because the bulk of German industrialists felt that Germany was about to recover her former economic predominance and that a free market in Europe would be a distinct advantage to them in a new drive for world markets. In any event, Layton kept telling his government to face up to the possibility of a European customs union.[33]

Moreover, the growing debate over a customs union had its influence on many of the older private international organizations that had been toying with the European idea and created in some of them a stronger desire to try to come to a firm decision about it. The most notable effort in this direction at this time was made by the Leagues of the Rights of Man, which now existed in many European countries and were loosely linked across frontiers.

This was a natural move on the part of the leagues because they drew their memberships largely from those elements of the population that were most inclined to support the European idea, and a sizable percentage of their members were ardent Europeans especially in those countries where the European idea was strongest. For example, the French league, which now had hundreds of local chapters and was headed by Alphonse Aulard, enrolled nearly all of the leading figures of the country who were active in the European movement. Indeed, it is almost certain that the French league, and perhaps others, would have tried to come squarely to grips with the European idea before this time if its leading members had not feared that in so doing they would create dissensions at the international level and thus blunt the effectiveness of the leagues in dealing with established and accepted objectives.

Nevertheless, strong as these fears were, they were gradually giving way to the growing desire to try to face up to the European idea. Accordingly, the Third International Congress, which was scheduled to meet on 26 June 1926 in Brussels, made "A United States of Europe" the first and main item of discussion. The committee then quickly signed up a panel of speakers. Aulard was to discuss the history of the European idea; Goldscheid of Austria was to examine the idea in terms of Europe's general economic situation; Picard of Belgium was to discuss the idea in relation to Europe's financial and monetary problems; Kuczinski of Germany was to explore the matter of a European customs union; and Willmotte of Belgium, who was to serve as president of the congress, was to deal with European intellectual cooperation and the unity of Europe. Each paper was to be followed by a period of discussion from the floor.

When the Third International Congress of the Leagues of the Rights of Man met, it quickly moved through the formalities to the first item on its agenda.[34] Aulard, in setting the stage for the specialized papers, centered on the evolution of the European idea and its increasing relevance and vitality for Europe. He said that Saint-Simon and Victor Hugo, who had taken the lead in propounding the idea in the nineteenth century, should not be thought of as "lost souls spawning a utopia in the clouds" but rather as men of remarkable foresight who sensed the drift of history and realized that the states of Europe would have to unite or face an eternity of decline and misery. It was the Great War, he said, that really brought home to millions of people the urgent need for a European community, especially at the economic level. He argued that such a community would undergird security and prosperity in Europe and facilitate the work of the League of Nations. He concluded by urging his fellow leaguers to keep "the idea of the United States of Europe" before them in their daily work and to take the lead in their respective countries in accelerating and guiding public opinion toward this ideal.[35]

Goldscheid, in dealing with the economic aspects of integration, pictured the United States as an economic giant and warned that, if the states of Europe were to compete on anything like even terms with the American colossus, they would have to strike down their trade barriers and move toward a customs union. He argued that Europe's great wealth lay in the abilities and skills of its peoples and insisted that these gifts and skills could not reach their full potential without an economic union among the states. Labeling nationalism the chief obstacle to such a union, he added: "For us the doctrine of absolute sovereignty is a threat alike to democracy, prosperity, and peace."[36]

Kuczinski argued that a European customs union would add immensely to Europe's economic well-being and strength, and he saw the main obstacles to such a union as psychological rather than economic in nature and "rooted in prejudices rather than in facts." Picard, in his paper on monetary problems, argued that currency matters were so bound up with industry, banking, trade, and budgets that fragmentary solutions could not be effective. What was needed, he said, was common action at the European level. Willmotte, in his paper on the role that the press and school could play in creating a European outlook, urged the governments of the European states to set up departments for cultural and intellectual affairs in their foreign offices.

The discussion from the floor, which was interspersed between the papers, revolved heavily around the questions of how a European community would affect the League of Nations and how England would be related to it. Both questions came up during the initial discussion and revealed, among other things, that the overwhelming majority of the delegates to the Congress supported the European idea. The dominant view concerning the League of Nations was that the league could work with a European union and would itself be strengthened by such a union. Robert Deel of England, who was attending the congress as an observer, asked how his country would be related to a federated Europe. And after some delicate exchanges, Bouglé of France put the matter back to him by observing that England, not Europe, would have to make this decision. "It is not a question as to whether we want England; it is, on the contrary, a question as to whether England wants us."[37]

Such was the nature of the initial effort of the leaders of the Leagues of the Rights of Man to face up to the European idea. While nearly all of those who spoke had supported the idea warmly, this did not mean that the several national chapters across Europe were ready to support the idea actively and openly. This was so not only because the chapters varied greatly in the measure of their support but also because they had numerous well-established programs to consume their energies and, perhaps most important of all, because all of those who were interested in the European idea had other avenues and opportunities for promoting it. As a result of these things, the members of the Leagues of the Rights of Man in their formal meetings in the months ahead rarely discussed the idea. Now and then, however, a local chapter did face up to the idea. For example, the chapter at Tannay, France, debated the idea at length in the early weeks of 1927 and passed a resolution at its meeting on 1 May 1927 calling for "the creation of a United States of Europe."[38]

Chapter 9

A CLUSTER OF FAVORABLE

EVENTS

Meantime in the late summer and early autumn, as the debate gathered force and as Thomas Mann joined the Paneuropean Union, Europe experienced a series of events that taken together had a significant bearing on the European movement and augmented noticeably the hopes of its champions. The most important of these events, taken in sequence, were the founding of two new organizations—the Franco-German Committee for Information and Documentation and the League for European Cooperation; Germany's entrance into the League of Nations; the signing of the International Steel Agreement; and the First Congress of the Paneuropean Union.

Though quite a number of influential Europeans, including Pierre Viénot, Emile Borel, Wilhelm Heile, Wladimir d'Ormesson, Bruno Bruhns, Paul Silverberg, Henri Lichtenberger, Alfred Nossig, and Thomas Mann, had been thinking and talking in terms of one or more private organizations that would work for greater understanding and cooperation among the peoples of Europe, it was Emil Mayrisch who took the decisive step toward the creation of the first of these two new organizations.[1] At Mayrisch's invitation, some two dozen prominent Frenchmen and Germans gathered in Luxembourg on 29 and 30 May 1926 and founded the Franco-German Committee for Information and Documentation. The new body, which was to be made up of some three score French and German business and professional leaders had its headquarters in Luxembourg, but it soon established centers with libraries and conference rooms in Berlin and Paris.[2] Then, in Geneva, on 2 September 1926, with many of Europe's leading political personalities, including Briand and Stresemann, gathered for the opening of the Sixth Regular Session of the Assembly of the League of Nations, the League for European Cooperation was instituted with Borel as president and Heile as secretary.[3] And while neither of these new bodies openly professed support for the European idea, Borel and Heile were warm supporters of the idea, and Briand said to the press only a few minutes after the decision was taken to set up the League for European Cooperation: "A union of the states of Europe, working hand in hand with the League of Nations and the United States of America, offers the way to the security of Europe and the stability of the world."[4] In any event, it was not long until Borel and Heile were working to put the new body in the service of the European movement.

The second in this cluster of events, Germany's entrance into the League of Nations, came on 10 September 1926 and tended to reinforce all other events in the cluster, for it not only brought to Geneva the nation that was the focus of European diplomacy, but it brought the Locarno Pact into operation. Moderate Left elements everywhere sought to convince themselves that here at long last was solid evidence that Germany was "settling down" and was about ready to work energetically for the pacification of Europe. The champions of the European idea were pleased, and some of them agreed with Aulard's optimistic assertion that Germany's entrance was "another step toward the restoration of real peace and toward the grounding of a United States of Europe within the broad framework of the League."

Then, on 26 September 1926, the third in this cluster of events took place. On that day the negotiations, which had been under way for many months among the steel interests of Germany, France, Belgium, Luxembourg, and the Saar, culminated in the signing of the International Steel Agreement (Entente International de l'Acier), which became more nearly European in scope on 4 February 1927 when the steel producers of Austria, Hungary, and Czechoslovakia joined.[5] While the steel pact embraced both the domestic and export markets of the signatory states, it was designed primarily to control Europe's export market, which amounted to about 70 percent of the world's steel exports. The new body was to have its headquarters in Luxembourg, and Emil Mayrisch was to serve as chairman of its board of directors.

Though the steel agreement, which had most of the attributes of a cartel, worried many socialists and labor leaders and was roundly denounced by communists, most good Europeans praised it and some expressed the view that it would have greater significance for the European idea than Germany's entrance into the League of Nations. They liked to say that there was, as Swiss journalist William Martin put it, "a profound natural unity between the metallurgical industries of France and Germany" and that the steel agreement was a manifestation of this unity.[6] Neue freie Presse (1 Oct. 1926) called the new pact "the first step toward Paneuropa," and Louis Loucheur argued that it would help arrest the drift toward economic anarchy in Europe by assisting the states in rationalizing and coordinating their economies and in meeting competition from across the Atlantic.[7] Roger Auboin wrote that many economists saw the steel pact as a possible step toward a European economic union and expressed his own feeling by saying, "The Europe of tomorrow is rising before our eyes." Kurt Singer, of the editorial board of Wirtschaftsdienst, remarked that it was possible that the steel pact would have "an effect on the political structure of Europe similar to that which the Zollverein had on the political structure of Germany." Much would depend, he said, on whether or not the extremes of Right and Left in Germany were capable of compromising their differences and whether the peoples of Europe were capable of moving toward a European spirit.[8]

Moreover the pact made a decided impression across the channel. *The Economist*, in its issues of 2 and 9 October 1926, warned the leaders of industry and government that it could be a step toward a continental economic union. On 8 October a group of prominent English and German industrialists gathered at Ramsey and spent the next two days discussing the steel pact and England's relation to both the pact and the continent.[9] *L'Information* (13 Oct. 1926) observed that the British were speculating on "the possibilities of an economic federation of the United States of Europe" and noted that London's *Daily Telegraph* had said that some German industrialists had succumbed to "the Paneuropean myth."

The last of the big events in this cluster, and a striking epilogue to the first three, was the First Congress of the Paneuropean Union, which was held in Vienna from 3 to 6 October 1926. It was the fruit of long and careful planning on the part of Coudenhove-Kalergi and a group of his most ardent supporters. Indeed, the young count had been dreaming of such a congress ever since he founded the Paneuropean Union, and in January 1926, shortly after his return from the United States, he had set the place and date for the first congress.[10] From that time on, plans for the gathering went forward without interruption. Above all Coudenhove hoped to persuade a sizable number of Europe's leading political personalities to attend the projected congress and thus to give it something of an official cast. In this hope he was encouraged by some Austrian political leaders. Seipel agreed to take an active part, and Chancellor Ramek, even though he was known to look kindly upon the Anschluss, agreed to welcome the delegates.

But the men whom Coudenhove was most anxious to have at the congress were Briand, Herriot, and Painlevé of France and Marx and Stresemann of Germany. While none of these men prepared to attend the congress, the three Frenchmen did agree to send greetings, and Briand instructed Beaumarchais, French minister in Vienna, to represent the French government at the congress. Marx and Stresemann were reserved and less cooperative. In late August, when Coudenhove appealed to Marx to attend the congress, the German chancellor asked the Foreign Office to decide what the government's attitude should be. Stresemann left the matter to undersecretary Bernhard von Bülow, and he, being quite cool to the European idea and determined that the government should do nothing that would encourage Coudenhove, suggested that the best procedure would be for the chancellor to send Coudenhove a polite and friendly telegram in advance of the congress. Marx took this advice, and on 15 September, he sent the young count a short telegram wishing him success in his work and assuring him that the "Reich chancellor will follow the course of the congress with great interest."[11]

Coudenhove received his worst embarrassment when the executive body of the Österreichisch-Deutscher Volksbund, of which Löbe was a member, decided to press hard for the inclusion of the Anschluss question on the agenda of the congress. Keenly aware that a debate on this explosive issue would create divisions and tensions and stir national feelings, Coudenhove took a strong stand against the Volksbund, arguing that territorial problems had no place on the agenda. Though Coudenhove kept the Anschluss off the agenda, many members of the Volksbund sulked about it and some charged that Paneurope was an organization of the victors.

But Coudenhove was not without some success in Germany. Thomas Mann joined the Paneuropean Union on the eve of the congress, and Löbe agreed to serve as an honorary president of the congress, along with Beneš, Caillaux, Politis, Nitti, and Seipel. Too, the *Vossische Zeitung* carried an article on the congress in its issue of 2 October 1926, and the *Neue freie Presse*, which was rather widely read in some sections of Germany, carried an editorial on Coudenhove and articles on the European idea by Siegfried Strakosch, Emil Ludwig, Bronislaw Hubermann, just as the congress opened. Ludwig's article was entitled "Pan-Europe the New Fatherland."[12]

On the morning of 3 October, when Chancellor Ramek of Austria rose to welcome the delegates to the First Paneuropean Congress, Vienna's concert hall was overflowing, and along the sides of the stage were large portraits of Saint-Pierre, Kant, Hugo, Napoleon, and Nietzsche, men who had in their day spoken out in different ways for a union of the states of Europe. Directly behind the speaker's stand was a large flag with a red cross over a golden sun: the official symbol of the Paneuropean movement. Among the more than two thousand men and women before the chancellor, were a number of Europe's most distinguished economists, journalists, and literary figures.[13]

After Ramek's words of welcome, Seipel, Austria's most distinguished statesman, formally opened the congress, declaring that its central aim was "to ground and foster the view that Europe should be and could be economically and politically integrated." Calling Aristide Briand the foremost apostle of the European idea among Europe's statesmen, he said: "We must, as Briand has said, learn to think European, speak European, and feel European."[14]

The remainder of the opening session was set aside for brief comments by the chairmen of the various national delegations. Nearly all chairmen stated at some point that the Paneuropean Union was not interested in forming a bloc against any nation or continent but at ending political and economic fragmentation in Europe. Delaisi of France, Von der Ghinst of Belgium, Nils Nilsen of Norway, and Váslav Schuster of Czechoslovakia were perhaps warmest in their support of the European idea, stressing above all the point that their peoples were deeply animated by considerations of security and peace and that the European idea came easily and naturally to them. After the chairmen of each national delegation had had his turn, Coudenhove-Kalergi, who served as president of the congress, spoke on the nature and aims of Pan-europe. Europe, he said, had long been the political and cultural heart of the world, but it had now arrived at the point where it would have to unite or face the possibility of sharp decline. But he was hopeful: "Yesterday Europe was a battlefield: today it is an anachronism; tomorrow it will be a federation."[15] After the adjournment of the opening session, the chairmen of the national delegations set up a number of committees to take quick looks at some of the more important aspects of the European problem and report back to the full congress.

With the formalities over, and the committees in existence, the congress settled down to a fairly systematic discussion of four much discussed issues: the Paneuropean idea and the League of Nations, a European customs union, Europe's minorities, and European intellectual and cultural coopera-tion. Nicholas Politis led the discussion on Europe and the league. Speaking with obvious conviction and deep earnestness, he told the congress that he was well aware that some of the league's best friends were fearful that a European structure would diminish the league's prestige and authority, under-mine its universalism, and increase the likelihood of war by creating inter-continental tensions. He had, he said, examined all of these matters with great care and had become convinced that a European structure would strengthen the league: "Paneurope will not only facilitate the work of the league in Europe but will enhance its influence and prestige throughout the world."[16]

Delaisi gave the main paper on Europe's economic position, and his paper was a ringing plea for action in the direction of economic integration. The French economist insisted that modern life, especially in its economic mani-festations, negated the assumptions on which national sovereignty was based; that Europe's economic and political fragmentation stood in sharp contradic-tion to the great fact of the interdependence of her peoples; and that the fragmentation was shackling Europe's trade and industry and lowering its standard of life. Europe's greatest need was, he said, a common market, and he argued that such a market could be realized if the leaders of Europe's 250,000,000 people would make up their minds to it. He urged the dele-gates from the European states to press their governments to reduce progres-sively their customs and move on toward a full-fledged customs union and a European currency.[17]

Delaisi's speech made a deep impression on the congress, and several delegates, including Julius Wolf, seconded his plea for a European currency. Elemér Hantos told the congress that the peoples of Europe would benefit enormously from the coordination and unification of their communication and transport facilities; Karl Uhleg argued that Europe was depressed economi-cally and would remain so unless the states reduced their customs barriers and moved toward a system of free trade. Dr. Mittelmann, member of the German Reichstag and chairman of the congress's committee on minorities, gave the key speech on the minorities problem, and argued that the Paneuropean movement could not hope to achieve its goals unless it provided a solution to this key problem. Several of the delegates, including Coudenhove-Kalergi, argued that the solution to the minorities problem lay in relentless blunting and blurring of frontiers.[18]

The final session of the congress was given over primarily to speeches by three leaders of European youth: Jean Luchaire of France, Walter Engesser of Germany, and Waldyslav Landau of Poland. Jean Luchaire, who spoke first, assured the congress that the great majority of French youth was enthusiastic in its support of Paneurope. He expressed the view that schools in all European countries should stress the European idea and predicted that the youth of Europe would play a central role at the next Paneuropean congress. Walter Engesser asserted that German youth would not be outdone by the youth of France in the building of Europe, and when he concluded and stretched out his hand to Luchaire, the congress broke into thunderous applause. Landau, representing student groups in Poland, said that it was a great pity that Germans and Poles were not animated by neighborly feelings but assured the congress that the youth of Poland would work for understanding and peace with Germany. As Landau, Engesser, and Luchaire then embraced, the congress again broke into applause. When the applause subsided, Emil Ludwig, who had himself addressed the congress earlier, arose and said: "The congress has just experienced its most beautiful moment."[19]

During the final hours of the congress, the work committees made their reports. The Main Committee, which had been concerned primarily with the structure and aims of the Paneuropean Union, recommended that the union intensify its efforts to develop strong unions in all European states and assist in every way possible all organizations whose activities were promoting the political and economic integration of Europe. The Economic Committee recommended that the League of Nations be urged to add a special division for European affairs that would work toward a European customs union. The Committee on Intellectual and Cultural Cooperation recommended that a Paneuropean Youth Organization be created and endorsed the Economic Committee's recommendation for a division of European affairs within the framework of the League of Nations.[20]

Then, before adjourning the congress, Coudenhove read messages of encouragement and support from several prominent Europeans, including Benes, Painlevé, and Arthur von Gwinner.[21] He concluded by quoting the celebrated words uttered by Goethe after the battle of Valmy: "From this day and this place begins a new chapter in world history; and we will be able to say that we were there."

The First Paneuropean Congress made a considerable impression on European opinion and received good coverage in both the daily and periodical press. L'Europe Nouvelle saw the congress as fresh evidence of the vitality of the European idea and wondered if Coudenhove's critics were not a bit surprised at what he had been able to accomplish. Yet, the journal continued to worry about the German attitude toward Locarno and to insist that a European community could not take form unless Germany was prepared to come to terms with Poland and the states of central Europe.[22] *La Paix par le droit* called the congress one of the highlights of the year, gave a lengthy summary of its work, and carried the text of Delaisi's address.[23] *Friedenswarte*, though highly critical of Coudenhove, was deeply impressed by the congress and called it a great demonstration for peace which should have been held by the pacifists.[24] The new journal, *L'Esprit international* in its first issue of January 1927, not only described briefly the work of the congress but also carried the text of Politis's address and a long article by Alejandro Alvarez dealing with the league and the European idea. Karl Anton Rohan, in an editorial in *Europäische Revue* (Nov. 1926, pp. 101–2), said that the congress had demonstrated the vitality of the European idea but accused Coudenhove of exaggerating the significance of the congress as well as his role in the European movement. Rohan stated that the European idea was embedded in Europe's history and would go forward with or without Coudenhove-Kalergi. Even the *Manchester Guardian Weekly* was profoundly impressed by the congress, and in its issue of 8 October 1926, said in an editorial entitled "The Oneness of Europe": "The United States of Europe is no longer a dream; it has entered on the world of realities."

Of the journalists who sought to tie the congress in with the other great events of the day and to estimate the impact of the whole cluster of events on the European idea, none did a better job than William Martin, editor of the *Journal de Genève*. Pointing to this stream of events, Martin said that a federated Europe "could be near" and turned to the evolution of the federal system in Switzerland in support of this view. He wrote: "Europe today appears to be at about the same point in its evolution as Switzerland was in 1830. . . . It should not be much more difficult to achieve the unity of Europe today than it was that of Switzerland a century ago."[25] Still, in the final paragraphs of the article, Martin centered on the obstacles to a united Europe and retreated a bit, concluding that it would be unwise, for the time being in any event, for the peoples of Europe to relax their efforts to build a strong League of Nations.

While there were no other events in the late summer and early autumn of 1926 that excited the leaders of the European movement as much as the four that we have described, there were nonetheless a number of developments that caught their attention and helped to raise their hopes. One such event was the Free Trade Manifesto, which was drafted by a group of international bankers and merchants and made public in London on 20 October 1926. Although this document was in no sense a call for a European economic union, it was a blistering attack on trade barriers, and it was signed by representatives of many of Europe's largest banking and business firms, several of whom had spoken in support of a European customs union. It read in part: "There can be no recovery in Europe until politicians in all countries, old and new, learn that trade is not war but a process of exchange; that in time of peace our neighbors are our customers; and that their prosperity is a condition of our well-being."[26] Some immediately linked this manifesto to the new steel agreement and the Paneuropean congress and saw all three as attacks on economic anarchy in Europe, even as evidence of a growing feeling that American economic power represented a real danger to the Old Continent. This evaluation of the manifesto gained strength when Herbert Hoover said in a speech in Chicago that, if the states of Europe should implement the Free Trade Manifesto, they would in reality constitute a United States of Europe in the sense that they would be able to deal with the United States in the same way that the forty-eight American states dealt with Europe. *Le Quotidien* (27 Oct. 1926) commented on Hoover's speech in an editorial entitled "Faites les Etats-Unis d'Europe."

But more exciting to most good Europeans than the Free Trade Manifesto were fresh signs that the German Right, and especially German industrial circles, were supporting more strongly the Weimar system and the ideal of European pacification. For not only was Stresemann assuring Europe that this was so, but some well-known men in German industry, including Paul Silverberg and Walter Greiling, were speaking out in this sense. In a speech on 4 September 1926, before the Federation of German Industry, Silverberg strongly urged the leaders of German industry to support the Weimar regime in good faith and to work with the parties as far to the Left as the Social Democrats to strengthen democratic forces in Germany and to promote economic collaboration at the European level. In an article in *Wirtschaftsdienst* (8 Oct. 1926, pp. 1371–72), Greiling argued that Germany should draw closer to her neighbors in working toward a European economic community and expressed the view that many German industrialists were prepared to do this. In a speech in Cologne on 20 October 1926, Stresemann again stated that many German industrialists were prepared to work more closely with France. On 20 November 1926, *L'Information*, which had shown deep interest in Silverberg's speech, attempted to synthesize all of these signs of growing economic solidarity in Europe and concluded: "An economic United States of Europe is no longer in the realm of dreams; though ills abound on all sides, tenacious hope dwells in Pandora's Box." Two weeks later Count Bernstorff, in an editorial in *Deutsche Einheit* (4 Dec. 1926, p. 1150), said that Briand had inspired this chain of events and had by so doing clearly and courageously established himself as the leader of the movement to organize Europe. Bernstorff added that it was to be hoped that many other statesmen in Europe, including Stresemann, would display the same courage and foresight as Briand had done. In fact, the leaders of the European movement were probably more optimistic in the late autumn of 1926 about the emergence of some sort of a European structure than at any other time between the world wars.

Chapter 10

THE WORLD ECONOMIC

CONFERENCE

By early 1927, it was quite evident that most supporters of the European idea had been too optimistic in the autumn of 1926. The trouble was that they had expected Germany's entrance into the League of Nations, the coming into operation of the Locarno Pact, and the International Steel Agreement to improve the political climate and integrate to some extent the European idea into the context of economic and political events. But as the weeks and months passed, there was no evidence that this was happening, or even that France and Germany were getting any closer to a genuine understanding. On the contrary, there were signs that growing talk about Europe had aroused the forces of economic nationalism and protectionism across most of Europe and Mitteleuropean ambitions in Germany as well.

For in Germany, nationalist circles continued to speak of Geneva and Locarno as massive German sacrifices and to call more intently for the abolition of the military clauses of the treaty of Versailles, the evacuation of the Rhineland, and a free hand to the east. *Kreuzzeitung* explained on 8 February 1927: "The center of German politics is no longer on the Rhine but in Central and Eastern Europe. If Locarno marks an armistice on the Rhine, it frees us for action elsewhere." Even Right wing Socialists and Democrats in Germany were increasingly inclined to say that Geneva and Locarno had cleared the way for a more energetic pursuit of the Anschluss.[1]

On the other hand, most Frenchmen and Belgians continued to talk about security and to insist that the states of Western Europe could not be secure unless the states of Eastern Europe were secure, that there should be no extensive dismantling of Versailles until the Germans settled down and gave evidence of readiness for military compliance, moral disarmament, and parliamentary government. In January 1927, *Le Petit journal*, which was close to Loucheur, carried a series of articles under the caption "Is there a new Germany?" and concluded that proof was yet to come that German opinion had committed itself to Geneva and Locarno. Five days later Loucheur, in a speech in Brussels, said that France could not follow the reasoning of those across the Rhine who talked about Geneva and Locarno in terms of German sacrifices.[2]

In fact, Briand and Stresemann, the two men who had been at the center of the drive for Franco-German rapprochement, were arguing over what had been said at Thoiry, and their exchanges were sometimes sharp and bitter. Stresemann, unwell, needled by German nationalists, and impatient for a major diplomatic victory, was pressing Briand to get along with the dismantling of Versailles. He was saying that Germany had made her decision for Weimar and peace, that Locarno was taking root, and that the occupation of the Rhineland no longer served any legitimate purpose. Briand, who in November of 1926 had stated in the Chamber of Deputies that it might be possible to alter the occupation in "nature and duration" and had taken steps for the formal liquidation of the IMCC, was puzzled and a bit irritated by Stresemann's behavior, and he urged the German foreign minister to show more patience and understanding.[3] For Briand was sure that he could not move any faster toward evacuation unless Stresemann could give him something of a more concrete nature with which to work. What Briand needed to move faster, as Le Temps put it, was "a German republic resolutely oriented to peace."

If the leaders of the movement were disappointed at the course of events, they did not lose heart or have any doubts as to the direction they should work in the weeks ahead. While the approaching World Economic Conference, which was scheduled to open in Geneva on 4 May 1927, was uppermost in their minds, most of them also worked consciously to strengthen proeuropean organizations and to get more press support. This latter effort needs to be treated at least briefly at this point as it was on the whole fruitful, and Briand himself took an active interest in it. The most solid of the organizational gains was scored by the International Committee for a European Customs Union, which had been launched in 1924 by Stern-Rubarth, Ernö Bleier, and Charles Gide. It had developed very slowly at first, but in the autumn of 1926, it gained momentum and by 1927 was probably the most effective and influential of the organizations supporting the European idea, though it was much smaller than even the Paneuropean Union. National committees were functioning in Germany and Hungary and in the process of formation in France, Belgium, Czechoslovakia, and Switzerland. Stern-Rubarth served as chairman of the German committee and was ably assisted by Richard Heilner, president of the European Linoleum Trust: Bernhard Harms, editor of the Weltwirtschaftliches Archiv; Moritz Elsas, well-known statistician; Ludwig Stein, editor of Nord und Süd; and Wilhelm Grotkopp, who was soon to found the journal Europa-Wirtschaft.[4] Stern-Rubarth also said in this connection that Stresemann and several members of the Reichsverband der deutschen Industrie deserved much of the credit for the success of the German committee and that most German businessmen believed Germany's economic strength would enable her to control the policy of a European customs union. The Hungarian committee, though comparatively small, was a very able and de-

voted group. Some of its members, especially former minister and distinguished economist Elemér Hantos, were actually more active than Bleier.
Few men in Europe wrote and spoke so extensively in support of a customs
union during the second half of the twenties as Hantos.

But the emerging French chapter was soon to be the leader of the European
customs union movement. It took shape slowly, mainly because Gide found
himself surrounded by a number of politicians as well as economists who
were clamoring to help but who were already involved in a heated debate over
many points including the name of the committee. Those who gave primary
attention to political considerations and were strongly opposed to limitations
on national sovereignty, insisted that the committee be called Le Comité
Français d'Etudes pour l'Entente Economique Européenne; those who
thought mainly in economic terms, and they were in the majority, preferred
the name Le Comité Français d'Etudes pour l'Union Douanière Européenne.
In the end, those who advocated use of the term "customs union" prevailed,
and on 20 January 1927, the new body was formally launched as the French
Study Committee for a European Customs Union.[5]

The new committee sought to enroll men of varied views, and within a
period of weeks, it attracted to its membership many of the country's most
distinguished political, professional, business, and labor leaders, and its honorary membership included Briand, Herriot, Loucheur, Clémentel, and Paul-
Boncour. Under the direction of Yves Le Trocquer, former minister of public
works, it demonstrated vitality and initiative from the first. In the early spring
of 1927, it founded an official journal, *Europe de demain*, and set up three
work groups. By midspring it was contributing very substantially to the European movement. The international committee tended to look more and more
to the national committees, especially the French committee, to provide initiative and drive. The whole organization concentrated its efforts on a single and
rather concrete aspect of integration, and this helped to keep it coherent and
closely knit. Moreover, it was blessed by the fact that most of its members
believed that a customs union would not only go to the heart of Europe's
economic troubles but would also advance the cause of security and peace.[6]

The newly established League for European Cooperation, which was rather
strongly anchored in parliamentary circles and close to the League of Nations,
was also beginning to move. Borel and Heile, its president and secretary, set
out at once to build an effective organization. After setting up a small secretariat in Paris, they centered their attention on the founding of national committees, and in the autumn of 1926, national committees were established in
France and Germany.[7] Borel selected Max Hermant to give the main address
at the first general meeting of the French group, which was held in the
Luxembourg Palace with Paul Doumer, president of the Senate, presiding.
Hermant spoke out strongly for a European customs union, labeling the network of customs lines in Europe a vestige of medieval life, reminiscent of

customs between French provinces before the time of Turgot and between the
German states before the Zollverein.[8]

Borel and Heile were also hoping to gather into a common front along with
the League for European Cooperation all of the organizations whose central
emphasis was the promotion of peace and European cooperation. In the early
spring of 1927, they sought to arrange joint meetings with several other
groups, and though Borel had measurable success in France, Heile was soon
in open conflict with Coudenhove-Kalergi and the Paneuropean Union.[9]

At the same time, some of the older organizations faced up more squarely
to the European idea. The French section of the League for Peace and Freedom restored the European idea to the center of its program, and at a meeting
on 10 January 1927, the section passed a resolution that called for an all-out
effort to create a European organization within the League of Nations "to
encourage and assist the states of Europe to move as fast as possible to a
United States of Europe."[10] Even the Federation of League of Nations Associations, at its annual congress in Salzburg in October 1926, put the European
idea on its agenda for its next annual congress, which was scheduled for Berlin from 24 to 31 May 1927. But this was apparently done because Alphonse
Aulard, an ardent European, was president of the federation. In any event, the
European idea was not discussed at the Berlin meeting though Aulard did
say in his presidential address that all wars in Europe should be regarded as
civil wars.

A new proeuropean association or group, the New Right (Droite Nouvelle),
was projected by Robert Fabre-Luce in Paris in the early days of 1927.[11] This
French Baron had now come to the view that the states of Europe, since they
were weak in natural resources and were caught between the Russian and
American landmasses, needed to draw together into an economic and spiritual
community resting on the leadership of an enlightened Right. While Fabre-
Luce's New Right bore similarities to Prince Karl Rohan's League for German
Culture (Deutscher Kulturbund), its program was more political and economic
in content and laid more stress on European integration. Although the New
Right attracted considerable attention across Europe and even projected a
periodical, *Vers l'Unité*, it never developed beyond the point of a small, loose
association of Rightist intellectuals.

Moreover, nearly as important to the European movement during these
months as the broadening and strengthening of its organizational base was the
founding of new periodicals that gave the idea careful attention. The most
helpful and devoted of these were: *L'Europe de demain*, *Europäische Wirtschafts-Union*, *L'Esprit international*, *Revue des vivants*, *Notre temps*, *La
Lumière*, *Revue d'Allemagne*, and *Deutsch-Französische Rundschau*. In fact,
the first two named were founded to promote the European idea, and the
following three gave it constant attention as well as full support. For example,
L'Esprit international, which began publication in January 1927 and which

was immediately hailed as one of the leading journals in the field of international politics, carried material on the European idea in every issue for several years. Young Jean Luchaire, who edited *Notre temps*, had attracted the attention of Briand and was soon getting financial assistance from Quai d'Orsay.[12]

But the leaders of the European movement not only worked in the early months of 1927 to strengthen their organizational base and get additional press support, they also sought to make two approaching conferences—the World Economic Conference scheduled to open in Geneva on 4 May 1927 and the Twenty-Fourth Conference of the Interparliamentary Union scheduled for Paris in late August—contribute significantly to their ends. Actually it was the former that really challenged them for that conference sought the causes of Europe's economic ills. While the most optimistic among them did not expect the conference (many of whose delegates would be from non-European countries) to endorse the European idea, many did hope to get it to take notice of that idea and to give full consideration to the growing interdependence of the European states.

Accordingly, their effort was many-sided and included collective appeals to the Preparatory Commission for the approaching World Economic Conference as well as use of the platform and press.[13] The most interesting and unusual of the appeals to the Preparatory Commission were made by the International Committee for a European Customs Union and the International League for Peace and Freedom. The memorandum that the International Customs Union group submitted to the Preparatory Commission was brief but strongly worded. The drafting committee, which was headed by Le Trocquer, put the stress on procedures for arriving at a customs union rather than arguments for such a union. Here are some of the key sentences in the memorandum: "In reality, all Europe is in a state of generalized economic war and the result is permanent economic anarchy among the states. . . . The states should first of all sign a general customs truce. Then they should proceed with the slow and steady suppression of all trade restrictions, including customs duties. . . . An annual reduction in customs of 2½ percent will bring a union in forty years, and should not shock severely the economies of any of the member states."[14]

The International League for Peace and Freedom did not draft a document of its own for submission to the Preparatory Commission but joined the International Peace Office in submitting a memorandum on European economic union which had been drafted at the Twenty-Fifth World Peace Congress. This memorandum, which had been formulated in an effort to crystallize pacifist thinking on the European idea, called on the peoples of the continent to rise above their frontiers and move toward a common market modeled on that of the United States. "The level of life in Europe today and the search for prosperity and peace tomorrow depend on the forging of an economic union."[15]

Moreover, at least one memorandum to the Preparatory Commission was initiated by a regional economic conference. On 18 March 1927, a number of businessmen and economists in the east European area gathered in Vienna and asked Elemér Hantos to draft a memorandum on the economic problems of that area for submission to the Preparatory Commission. Hantos eagerly accepted this assignment and drafted a lengthy document in which he argued that all Europe was suffering from protectionist policies grounded in high customs and other barriers to trade and economic growth. His advice to the coming World Economic Conference was that it underline the need for coordinating and integrating the economies of the states of eastern Europe as the first step toward the shaping of all Europe into an economic community.[16]

Actually, the memorandum concerning customs which had the greatest influence on the Preparatory Commission and the approaching conference was submitted by the International Chamber of Commerce. Modeled on the work of the Economic Committee of the League of Nations and the Manifesto for the Removal of Restrictions on European Trade, which had been drafted in London in October 1926, it urged the conference to work toward a general convention for the removal of prohibitions and restrictions on exports and imports, the free movement of raw materials, maximum application of the most-favored-nation clause, and the simplification and unification of customs nomenclature.[17]

Among those who were to be delegates to the conference who wrote and spoke in these weeks in behalf of the European idea were Loucheur, De Peyerimhoff, and Wilhelm Eggert. Loucheur, who had taken the lead in initiating the conference and who was to serve as its vice president, spent considerable time lecturing to business and professional groups and talking with journalists. If in his lectures and interviews he talked mostly about cartels, he rarely failed to raise at some point the question of a European customs union and even of a United States of Europe. Speaking at the University of Brussels on 22 February 1927, he said that the conference would deal with many matters relevant to a European customs union and that the European delegates to the conference should keep in mind "the possibility of at least the beginnings of a United States of Europe." But the high point of his effort came in Berlin on 8 April when he spoke to a group of German business leaders. Here Loucheur, who in past years had discussed Europe's economic problems with Germans of all ranks and views, from Hugo Stinnes to Konrad Adenauer and Rudolf Breitscheid, and who was still highly respected in German business circles, spoke of Europe's economic fragmentation as a major tragedy and told his German listeners that the time had come for Germany and France to "join hands in organizing Europe." While he concentrated on the virtues of cartelization, he discussed freely and frankly the possibilities of a European customs union and perhaps shocked his audience by raising the question of "a United States of Europe." Loucheur's speech and his interviews with German journalists were rather widely echoed in the German press for a number of days.[18]

De Peyerimhoff, like Loucheur, had much to say about the coming conference, and he gave interviews to German as well as French journalists. On the
eve of the opening of the conference, he told the Paris correspondent of the
Kölnische Zeitung that "France, who has taken the lead in calling the World
Economic Conference, is resolved to play her full part in the creation of a
European economic community." But he hastened to add that such a community could only be built through practical achievements, that there would
have to be a sustained effort and a multitude of small steps relative to the
"facts and realities and the movement of life."[19]

Wilhelm Eggert, an important figure in the German labor movement,
stressed a point that we have not mentioned but was nevertheless receiving
considerable attention at the time. He insisted that the obstacles to any sort of
economic community were so massive that a single conference could not do
much about them and that the most important thing the coming conference
could do would be to insure the creation of a permanent international agency
to work closely with the League of Nations in an effort to erode those obstacles by generating new forces of economic cooperation.[20] In fact, this idea
was to find its way into the recommendations of the conference.

Finally, Briand must be briefly treated in this connection, for few men tried
harder to get the impending conference to strike a real blow for European
economic cooperation and solidarity, even though he had to work at it in a
circuitous fashion. The French foreign minister was now convinced that the
Geneva-Locarno framework would have to be broadened as well as strengthened if Europe was to become reconciled and France secure, and he was
scanning distant horizons as well as reexamining things close at hand. In fact,
in these weeks Briand not only kept in close touch with Loucheur, who was to
serve as vice president of the conference, but he made a series of moves that
bore directly on the European movement.

The first of these moves came on 6 April 1927 in the form of an open letter
to the American people and was to trigger the chain of negotiations that would
lead to the Kellogg-Briand Pact. In this letter the French foreign minister
suggested that the United States join France in some sort of striking and
solemn testimonial for peace, such as "the renunciation of war as an instrument of national policy." While it is obvious that Briand was thinking of
many things when he drafted this letter, including France's war debts and the
approaching economic conference, it seems equally obvious that he was also
trying, as he told Coudenhove-Kalergi at the time, to ease American appre-
hensions about the movement to organize Europe.[21]

Briand's other moves came three weeks later and were even more consciously designed to stimulate the European movement and to bolster the
spirits of its leaders. On 30 April, just five days before the opening of the
World Economic Conference, the second formal session of the Central Council of the Paneuropean Union opened in Paris. Briand, even though he did not

agree with some of the basic tenets in the Paneuropean program, felt that Coudenhove was doing a good job of popularizing the general idea. He decided to utilize the occasion of this session to associate himself more openly with the Paneuropean movement and to encourage other French leaders, including Loucheur, Painlevé, Herriot, Jules Romains, and many others, to do likewise.

On 2 May, Loucheur, whom Briand was now counting on to take the lead in creating an economic climate for the organization of Europe, was elected president of the French Section of the Paneuropean Union, and on 3 May the red carpet was spread before Coudenhove and the other members of the Central Council at both the Ministry of War and the Quai d'Orsay. At the Ministry of War, Painlevé greeted the members of the council, talked with them briefly, and encouraged them in their work. But their reception at the Quai d'Orsay was much more impressive and revealing. Briand seated himself in their midst and called in a photographer; he announced that he was prepared to serve as honorary president of the Paneuropean Union; and finally he chatted with them about the organization of Europe. He told them that he expected to live to see the nucleus of a federal structure and urged them to pay less attention to political events, asking that they center their efforts on the business of generating a powerful current of opinion.[22] Actually there were some who felt that he was now thinking seriously of injecting the question of federal bonds into European politics and that he would almost certainly do this if the movement could muster substantially more strength. For example, L'Ere nouvelle on 2 May, in an editorial entitled "Pour les Etats-Unis d'Europe," interpreted Briand's moves in this sense and called them a landmark on the way to a European community. Paul Hohenau, editor of Das Neue Europa, said repeatedly during the spring and summer of 1927 that Briand was viewing France's mission more and more in terms of European federalism and was obviously thinking along the lines of some positive move in this direction.[23]

But much as good Europeans were elated by Briand's moves, most of them remained, like Briand himself, mildly pessimistic about the conference in Geneva. However, some found new hope in the fact that Georges Theunis, a former Belgian premier and a confirmed apostle of European economic cooperation, was to serve as president and that Daniel Serruys, a key figure in the French Ministry of Commerce and an ardent champion of Franco-German economic collaboration, was to be a delegate. On the day that the conference opened, the Fränkischer Kurier said of this Frenchman: "Serruys believes almost prophetically that Franco-German industrial rapprochement can be realized and that it can provide Europe peace and health." On the same day, The Times (London) reported that Lord Alfred Mond, noted British industrialist who had just returned from the continent, had observed that "the idea of the necessity of forming an Economic Union of Europe to preserve European industry" had made even greater headway than he had supposed.

Although President Theunis's opening address was not quite the sort of speech that Francis Delaisi, who was there with the French delegation, would have made, it was nonetheless a ringing denunciation of economic nationalism and an ardent plea for economic cooperation. Above all, Theunis stressed the fact that the nations of the world, and especially those of Europe, were becoming increasingly interdependent and argued that closer economic cooperation was the only way to greater security and prosperity. In one of his more striking sentences, he said: "Nationally and internationally, politically and economically, but most of all in the economic field, the interdependence of interests is a fact, and it is useless to deny that fact or to fight it."[24]

In the three days of general discussion that followed, forty-two delegates spoke and most of those from European states endorsed rather warmly the views of the president. Several came close to open support of a European customs union, and Madame Emmi Freundlich of Austria compared Europe's customs lines to barbed-wire entanglements "which imprison goods and men . . . and prevent national economic life from developing along natural lines."[25] Though Loucheur injected the idea of "a United States of Europe" into the debate and gave it his blessing, he was cautious and confessed that it was too sharply at variance with national traditions and considerations of national security to be realized in the near future. Lowering his sights, he argued that cartels held the greatest hope for the moment. "I may simply point out that for the moment they [cartels] will help to solve the problem of customs barriers . . . and they will permit the parallel and simultaneous raising of wages necessary to restore to postwar Europe the purchasing power of prewar Europe."[26]

But if the European idea flitted in and out of the general debate, it all but disappeared when the committees of the conference settled down to grapple with the concrete problems of the day. Here hard bargaining was in order and nationalist ideas flamed at times in nearly every committee. The French and German delegations spent much of their time trying to break the deadlock that had recently developed in the protracted negotiations between their governments looking toward a comprehensive commercial treaty.

The conference report was a penetrating and suggestive review of the economic conditions of the time with emphasis on Europe. It was in no sense a Paneuropean document, but it spoke out against economic nationalism, if gently, and asserted that economic conflicts and rivalries constituted the major obstacle to peace as well as to economic health and prosperity. It insisted that trade barriers, especially in Europe, were "highly detrimental to the general welfare" and added: "The Conference declares that the time has come to put an end to the increase in tariffs and to move in the opposite direction." More specifically, the report urged the governments of Europe to begin negotiations aimed at lowering customs duties and at unifying customs nomenclature; and it suggested that the League of Nations should concern itself more actively with economic affairs and set up a permanent organ, similar to the conference's Preparatory Commission, to press for the implementation of the conference's recommendations and to continue the search for a solution to Europe's economic ills.[27]

While the report was not what the leaders of the European movement wanted, it was about what they had come to expect. The more moderate among them would have been reasonably well satisfied had not Anglo-American opposition been so apparent. The reaction of Otto Deutsch, an Austrian economist who wrote regularly on economic matters for *Paneuropa*, was fairly typical of this group. Deutsch admitted that, while he, like most good Europeans, was quite unhappy with the progress that the European idea had made in recent months, he was not too displeased with the report of the conference. The report was, he said, surprisingly favorable to the European idea in view of the fact that several of the non-European delegations, including those of Great Britain and the United States, felt it necessary to "exert pressure against any sort of union."[28] Clearly the World Economic Conference had had a sobering effect on the leaders of the European movement and had even put Coudenhove-Kalergi in a better frame of mind to accept a gradual approach.

When the Geneva Conference adjourned, preparations for the Twenty-Fourth Conference of the Interparliamentary Union, which was scheduled for Paris in late August, were well along, and it had been announced that "A System of European Customs Accords" would be one of the items on the agenda and that a special committee had been set up to direct the gathering of data on this item. Both the International Committee for a European Customs Union and the French Study Committee for a European Customs Union gathered data and prepared lengthy memoranda, both of which concluded that a customs union was the one sure way to put the states of Europe on the road to economic health and prosperity.

On 25 August 1927, eight days after France and Germany signed a general commercial treaty that many hoped would provide the impulse for a sort of economic Locarno,[29] the Twenty-Fourth Conference of the Interparliamentary Union opened in the Luxembourg Palace. Nearly every European delegation numbered at least one parliamentarian who had openly associated himself with the European idea, and there were more than a dozen senators and deputies on the French delegation who had done so. In welcoming the delegates, Premier Poincaré said: "French policy is animated by a passion for peace which equals that of the Interparliamentary Union."[30] Though the general debate was at times tense and punctuated by flashes of national passion, these outbursts were greatly overshadowed by pleas for economic cooperation and peace. On the morning of 27 August, the conference turned to "A System of Customs Accords among the States of Europe," and in the two-day debate that ensued the matter of a European Customs Union got a thorough airing.[31]

Baron Joseph Szterenyi of Hungary and Emile Borel of France spoke in the early hours and set the pattern of the debate. Though they agreed that a customs union would benefit Europe in countless ways, they clashed sharply over the central question as to whether such a union could be realized in the foreseeable future. Szterenyi, after chiding the Allied powers for not revising the postwar treaties, argued that the obstacles to a customs union were for the time being insurmountable and that the greatest hope for the immediate future lay in the pursuit of a network of commercial agreements built around the most-favored-nation principle. Borel agreed that the obstacles were massive, but he argued that it was even possible in the course of time to organize a European market and even to generate a European patriotism. He then informed the delegates that he had a sketch for a European customs union, which the chairman of the customs commission of the Chamber of Deputies had seen, and he proceeded to present the core articles of the plan, expressing the hope that the Interparliamentary Union would sponsor it.

While not all of those who spoke on this item sought to come to grips with the matter of a customs union in the forthright manner in which Szterenyi and Borel had done, several did; some, including Branquart of Belgium and Charles Charbrun of France, pronounced Borel's plan sound and feasible and insisted that the time had come to make a start toward economic integration. Louis Loucheur, who spoke in much the same vein as he had done at the World Economic Conference, said that "a United States of Europe" was his ideal but quickly confessed that it lay in the distance. He said, however, that many Europeans "were thinking seriously of a sort of Paneuropean economic confederation," and he expressed the view that such a structure could be realized if the problem of security could be resolved. Loucheur's advice to the delegates was to think of security and economic union as "two sides of the same coin" and to work simultaneously toward both.[32]

Pierard of Belgium reminded the conference that Europe lay between two economic giants, the United States and the Soviet Union, and argued that its future would be dark as long as it remained fragmented and disunited. He insisted with as much vigor as had Borel that a customs union could be achieved and expressed the view that the best approach would be a customs union between France, Belgium, and Luxembourg with the door left open to all other European states. Edwin Waiss, who headed the Austrian delegation, also spoke briefly and said that he wanted the conference to know that many Austrians were ready to work for both political and economic union in Europe.

When the time allotted for discussion of this item had expired, Treub told the delegates that he had found that the vast majority wished to have Borel's proposal for the progressive elimination of European customs presented in the form of a resolution. After a few minor changes in phraseology, the proposal was presented as a resolution and approved. It was further agreed that the resolution would be submitted to the Assembly of the League of Nations at its approaching session.

While there is no evidence that the Interparliamentary Union's resolution (or Coudenhove-Kalergi's call for a "European Locarno") received any formal attention during the eighth session of the league, the Economic Committee of the league did deal at length with the recommendations of the World Economic Conference, and Daniel Serruys, who was elected chairman of the Economic Committee, said at a press conference that the league was finally realizing that "Europe is nothing more than a single economic unit in the world . . . and that what is now urgently needed is collective action by the governments for the demobilization of customs."[33] Too, Stresemann as well as Briand spoke for Europe in a broad sense. On 9 September, the German foreign minister told the assembly that he agreed the Locarno structure was embedded in the league and that it applied to Eastern as well as Western Europe and added: "There can be no doubt whatsoever that public opinion in Germany supports the fundamental principle of peace and mutual understanding. . . . Accordingly, we [Germans] are anxious not merely to cooperate but to become pioneers in the work of bringing about the universal peace for which the League is striving." Two days later, Briand praised Stresemann's efforts in behalf of peace and told the assembly that all peoples should move forward together to put an end to the scourge of war.

Chapter 11

BRIAND TAKES A

STRONGER STAND

Although by the summer of 1927 nearly all good Europeans, including Coudenhove, were disappointed at the failure of the European idea to enter more significantly into the stream of political and economic events, few of them were really surprised or disposed to relax their efforts. They sensed that the slowdown was mainly a result of the fact that economic nationalism was deeply anchored across Europe and that the struggle for advantage and power was rampant. Too, they were much encouraged by the fact that Briand was speaking out more forcefully, and the feeling was growing among them that the future would prove them right. Friedrich Nelböck spoke for many of them when he said in a speech at Bruun at this time: "The idea of a United States of Europe is so pregnant with good for the whole world . . . that we are morally obligated to work for it with all of our strength."[1] And Nelböck, like Briand, was telling them they should center their efforts on their organizations and the press, especially on the former. While the organizational effort was now fairly impressive, it was still quite limited and it had serious weaknesses, particularly in Germany. There laxness was mounting in many of the Paneuropean groups, and discord was brewing between Coudenhove and Heile, and thus between the German Paneuropean groups and the League for European Cooperation. Heile as well as Löbe, who still directed the German chapter of the Paneuropean Union, shared in a mild way the general German dislike of Coudenhove, and both were pressing him to water down his program and to take a more German view of things.[2]

But Coudenhove, emboldened by Loucheur's promise to help him reschedule a second Paneuropean congress for the autumn of 1928, was determined to make an energetic defense of his whole program. In an address before the German chapter of the Paneuropean Union on 18 December 1927, he said that some German politicians were using "Paneuropean slogans to cloak their nationalist demands for power, freedom, and equality." After underscoring the central points in his program, he said the Anschluss was a Pan-German not a Paneuropean idea and that Europeans should try to blur frontiers instead of sharpening them: "If war is to be averted and Europe truly saved, there must be both a customs union and a federation."[3]

As Coudenhove sharpened his attack so did his opponents. Some attacked him personally and accused him of being anti-German, a tool of Briand and the French. But Heile realized that Coudenhove had done much to extend the idea to the masses, and he was careful to confine his attack to the points in Coudenhove's program that he considered vulnerable. He said the program of the Paneuropean Union was too rigid, too optimistic, and quite wrong in its decision to exclude England from the projected union. He even bid for British support by openly stating that a European federation with England as a member would provide the British people with a new and powerful guarantee of their empire.[4]

Heile's criticisms, however, did not bring any noticeable change in Coudenhove's strategy. After all, the Paneuropean Union was growing in Austria, Czechoslovakia, and Hungary, and in Germany new groups were organized in the autumn of 1927 in Cologne, Düsseldorf, Dresden, Zwickau, Stuttgart, and Hamburg. Even Thomas Mann took a hand in some of this work. So Coudenhove was not too discouraged, and he worked very hard during the last weeks of 1927 and the early weeks of 1928. Among other things, he helped student groups in Austria launch a monthly news bulletin, and he persuaded General Denvignes, who had spent considerable time with the French army of occupation in the Rhineland, and Carl Franz Endres, who had been an officer in the German army at the end of the war, to write articles in support of the Paneuropean program. Denvignes was very outspoken and pleaded with the British to work for a united Europe and to align themselves closely with it.[5] Even more satisfying to Coudenhove was the outcome of the third regular session of the Central Council of the Paneuropean Union that was held in Paris during the second week of January 1928 and over which he presided. The Central Council, which was composed of the presidents of the national unions, agreed to work for the creation of a Paneuropean section within the League of Nations and for the holding of a second Paneuropean congress in Paris in the early autumn of 1928. Even though Coudenhove knew that the Central Council was far from enthusiastic about a second congress within the year and might yet block it, he wanted it very much and was immensely pleased when Loucheur, keeping an earlier promise, agreed to help with preparations for the congress and to serve as its president. Loucheur was respected across the continent, and Coudenhove felt that close association with him would help the Paneuropean Union and might even lessen dissension in the German chapter of the union.

On 14 January 1928, Coudenhove went to Loucheur's office, and the two men began mapping plans for the organization of the congress.[6] Loucheur suggested, and Coudenhove agreed, that the congress should concern itself with "ways and means for realizing a greater measure of economic solidarity among the peoples of Europe." They then decided to set up two committees to assist them. The first of these was to be a type of steering committee (Comité d'Initiative) consisting of the two of them plus three well-known

European industrialists: Mayrisch, Bücher, and Heinemann. Coudenhove was to approach these three men. The second committee, which was to be known as the French Committee, was to be formed by Loucheur, to sit in Paris, and to assume responsibility for the details of organization. In addition, they agreed that a special effort would be made to enlist the support of businessmen. Loucheur was to concentrate on business leaders in France and Coudenhove on those in Germany.

Now that a broad plan of procedure had been developed, Coudenhove was encouraged, and on 3 February, he wrote Loucheur that Mayrisch had agreed to serve on the steering committee and that his contact with Bücher, Silverberg, and Vögler had found them interested in the projected congress. Loucheur, who had asked journalist Marcel Ray to help him with this work, saw Heinemann on 7 February and wrote Coudenhove on the following day that he had found Heinemann hesitant and doubtful but that Heinemann had finally agreed to work with the committee in some capacity. Loucheur also told Coudenhove that it might be possible for all concerned to get together for a planning session on 29 February or 2 March in Brussels.[7] Even though Loucheur obviously felt that the time had not come for the scheduling of a second Paneuropean congress, it appeared at this time that an organizational committee would be set up. But while Coudenhove was trying to find a time when he, Loucheur, Mayrisch, Bücher, and Heinemann could get together, Mayrisch was killed in an automobile accident. Mayrisch's death, coupled with the fact that Loucheur was soon deeply involved in the electoral campaign in France, brought an end to the effort to schedule a second Paneuropean congress. Mayrisch's death was a blow to the entire European movement.

Meantime, the League for European Cooperation, in spite of the crisis in its German sector, had established a chapter in Austria and was having considerable success in France with its drive to coordinate the activities of kindred organizations.[8] Borel, who had taken the initiative in this coordinating endeavor, not only had full cooperation from Loucheur, president of the French Section of the Paneuropean Union, and Yves Le Trocquer, president of the French Study Committee for a European Customs Union, but he also had the support of a host of influential political figures, including Briand, Painlevé, Herriot, and Caillaux. Though Heile's accomplishments were meager in comparison with Borel's, he kept trying and his efforts threw some new light on the German attitude toward the European idea.

Both Borel and Heile made their most dramatic and determined gestures at coordination during the early weeks of 1928. Each scheduled a meeting of his national committee and invited the leaders of the major kindred organizations to participate. Heile moved first and invited Coudenhove-Kalergi, president of the Paneuropean Union; Löbe and Koch-Weser, president and vice-president of the German section of the Paneuropean Union; Stern-Rubarth, president of the German Committee for a European Customs Union;

and Karl Anton Rohan, director of the League for German Culture (Deutscher Kulturbund), to meet with his national committee in the Reichstag on 15 January 1928. The meeting was friendlier than had been expected, partly because Heile sought to avoid a fresh clash with Coudenhove, who had just rubbed elbows with Briand and Loucheur. After an hour of discussion, two agreements were reached, both of which seemed promising to Heile. First, the leaders of all four organizations agreed to set up a joint committee that would undertake to formulate a common program for European understanding; and, secondly, Heile and Coudenhove agreed that the German chapters of the Paneuropean Union would work at the local level to concentrate their efforts on the creation of a mass movement while the German Committee for European Cooperation would work at the national level to concentrate on parliamentary and governmental circles.[9] Encouraged as Heile was by these agreements, neither one worked out as he hoped. The leaders of the various organizations remained jealous and distrustful, and worse still, the German national chapter of the Paneuropean Union remained at odds with the German Committee for European Cooperation and was rocked even further by internal dissension.

Borel's joint meeting, which was held at the Sorbonne on 23 February 1928, was not only much more successful but very different in character and purpose, for Borel, already satisfied with the degree of cooperation that had developed among the French organizations, planned his meeting as a demonstration for the European idea and invited Painlevé, Le Trocquer, Jacques Seydoux, and Arthur Fontaine to prepare papers on different facets of the European movement.[10] After welcoming the delegates, Borel pointed to excessive political and economic fragmentation as the main cause of Europe's troubles. His concluding words were strong: "We do not believe that it is sufficient to say that Europe should be united: we believe that it is necessary to say that Europe must be united if she is to live."[11]

Painlevé, whose paper was rather general, asked his audience to remember: "There is a sort of fraternalism in the European soul. It is this that we must seize upon and build upon. . . . We must work for a European spirit, a European conscience, and a European patriotism." Le Trocquer stressed the problem of American competition and predicted that Europe would soon be inundated by American products unless she struck down her trade barriers and moved by carefully planned stages toward economic union. "The creation of an economic union will be a hard, long road. . . . But it is the only way to achieve durable results and we must pursue it as a progressive evolution." Fontaine, who was president of the Administrative Council of the International Labor Office, called for a European federative structure within the framework of the League of Nations and a European customs union. Seydoux, who was now playing an important role in the formulation of economic policy at Geneva, was a bit more cautious than the others and stressed the need for world solidarity as well as European solidarity. He said that in organizing Europe great care should be taken to avoid the creation of economic barriers, especially with England, the United States, and Russia, and he suggested that it might be wise to encourage the economic organs of the League of Nations to take the lead in the unifying process.[12] Thus, as Borel had hoped, his joint meeting had been a demonstration, however modest, for the European idea.

The smoothest-working and most effective of the new European organizations at this time was the European Customs Union. Though much of its success was certainly due to its limited but clearcut objectives and to the rather homogeneous nature of its membership, good leadership was also a big factor and it was blessed with such leadership at both the international and national levels. The International Committee, to which Yves Le Trocquer and Lucien Coquet had been added in the spring of 1927, was a body of able and devoted Europeans and was remarkably free of personal rivalries and frictions.[13] While it sought to provide effective overall leadership, it concerned itself mainly with the establishment of new national unions and propaganda work at the European level. In the early weeks of 1928, national groups were formed in Austria and Czechoslovakia. The Austrian group was directed by Ernst Geiringer and Ludwig von Mises and the Czech group by Anton Mühlig and Josef Meisl, both of whom were businessmen. At the same time, groups were slowly taking shape in several other states, including Belgium, Greece, Luxembourg, Norway, and Switzerland.[14]

Nor did the fact that the movement became increasingly centered in the national groups noticeably diminish its unity, for the active membership of every national group consisted largely of economists and enlightened business leaders, and these men, wherever they lived, tended to see Europe's basic economic problems in much the same way. There was little disposition among them to gloss over the obstacles, and most of them believed that a large quantity of well-sifted and reliable economic data was needed to begin even the planning of a customs union. In fact, the national chapters, led by the French chapter with its large and distinguished membership, became primarily study groups in these months, gathering and analyzing data on questions that they knew would have to be answered before a customs union could be projected.[15] For example, they not only sought to define the geographical dimensions of such a union but to decide such matters as the allocation of customs revenues among the member states and the sort of political and administrative machinery that would be required to administer the union. They reached a surprising degree of unanimity on most of the questions and even produced a map of the area to be included.[16]

But heavy as was the emphasis on the accumulation and analysis of economic data, the matter of making converts was not neglected. The French group made the same sort of effort to influence the National Congress of French Advisors on Foreign Trade, which was held at Nice from 4 to 8 January 1928, as it had made to influence the Fourth Conference of the Interparliamentary Union. Senator Clémentel, who was a member of the French group, served as president of this congress and saw to it that the documents sent by the French group were put in the hands of the members of the congress. Moreover, scores of the better-known members of the national chapters, including Henri Truchy and Le Trocquer in France, Stern-Rubarth and Stein in Germany, and Bleier and Hantos in Hungary, spoke and wrote frequently.[17]

At the same time, at least four other organizations—the League for Peace through Law, the International League for Peace and Freedom, the League for International Friendship (Association des Amitiés Internationales), and the French chapter of the League of the Rights of Man—made contributions. For example, the League for Peace through Law, which had local groups in many of the cities and towns of France, not only did much to promote the idea at the local level in France but organized and held a joint meeting in Bordeaux on 7 December 1927. The high point of this joint meeting was an address by Regis de Vibraye entitled "The Regionalization of the League and a United States of Europe." De Vibraye, who was a resolute champion of Franco-German understanding, pointed out that large regional groupings, including the Pan-American Union and the Soviet Union, already existed across the world, and he argued that such groups were natural and useful and that the League of Nations would be far more effective if it were organized along regional lines. Europe, he said, was a cultural entity that needed to be organized into a political and economic federation within a regionalized League of Nations.[18]

Meanwhile, in the early weeks of 1928, the leaders of the European movement in France and Germany were giving increasing thought to the parliamentary elections that were scheduled for midspring. While not even the most ardent among them expected the European idea, with its stress on the supranational, to be a major issue in the electoral campaigns, many felt that it was certain to be a matter of some importance because a number of the leading politicians in both countries, many of whom were up for reelection, had taken positions on it.[19] The practical question was whether the European idea as such should be ignored altogether in the campaigns or whether good Europeans should make it clear that they would cast their ballots for those candidates who had demonstrated the greatest interest in the European movement. Though this question was never warmly debated, it appears that the great majority of even the more ardent Europeans decided that it would be a mistake to inject the idea directly into party politics. What the great majority of them did was attempt to prevent appeals to national passions and encourage all candidates and parties to stress the need for European understanding.

There were a few, however, who disagreed with the majority. For example, *Europäische Wirtschafts-Union* (1 Mar. 1928, p. 8) urged the voters of both France and Germany to cast their ballots for those candidates who showed the most enthusiasm for European cooperation and a European customs union. *La Paix par le droit* (March 1928, p. 145) presented a "suggestive" platform for the guidance of both candidates and voters which called for the creation of a European commission to work for the enlistment of all schools in the service of European federalism and world peace.

Actually it is doubtful as to whether the elections had any significant bearing on the European movement as neither election resulted in a major political shift, and Stresemann as well as Briand remained secure. In France the Herriot-Briand policies had taken deep root, and most Frenchmen agreed with *L'Europe nouvelle* when it said editorially on 28 February that, while Germany had failed to respond as had been hoped, France had no choice except to press on with her program of organizing Europe and making the League of Nations an effective instrument of peace. Indeed, Poincaré moved toward the Briand position and stated in key speeches at Bordeaux and Carcassonne in the early weeks of the campaign that France would work toward the progressive establishment of an economic, intellectual, and moral entente with all her neighbors.[20] Moreover, at this time, Poincaré wrote the preface to Gaston Riou's *Europe, ma patrie*, one of the most resounding pleas for European political and economic union to appear in 1928. As expected, the campaign in Germany revolved heavily around Stresemann, who assured the German people that his policies were about to bring the Fatherland enormous gains, including the revision of the Dawes Plan and the Allied evacuation of the Rhineland. Galling as were the Stresemann policies to powerful elements of the population, the majority of the German voters realized their value.

In both countries, the balloting ran fairly true to expectations. The majority of the electorate in France voted for Poincaré's domestic policies and Briand's foreign policies, and René Cassin observed that all of the ardent champions of Geneva and Locarno were reelected and that the new government had "a mandate for the energetic pursuit of the policy of conciliation."[21] In Germany the Social Democrats gained twenty-one seats in the Reichstag, and Hermann Müller became the new chancellor. Most all Europeans felt that Germany with a Socialist chancellor would be more inclined to stress European conciliation and understanding, and no one underscored this feeling more dramatically than Coudenhove-Kalergi. Müller had scarcely completed the selection of his ministry when the young count wrote him an open letter calling his attention to the fact that the German Social Democrats had written European economic union into their platform at the party congress in Heidelberg in 1925. He not only urged the new chancellor to move toward the fulfillment of this party aim but also added an additional challenge by reminding him that for more than three years France's foreign policy had been the responsibility of Aristide Briand, an honorary president of the Paneuropean Union and a devoted apostle of the European idea.

Though Müller failed to reply to the open letter, there was quite a reaction in the European press.[22] In France, for example, the letter not only appeared in several newspapers at the time of its release, but it remained a matter of comment in the press for a period of weeks. Jean Luchaire praised the letter in *L'Homme libre* on 12 July, assured his readers that Briand was indeed giving careful thought to some sort of a European structure, and predicted that the French foreign minister would give the matter open support when he felt the time was right. Raymond Leonard, in a letter to *L'Ere nouvelle* on 21 July, congratulated Coudenhove-Kalergi on the force and clarity of his letter and assured him that many Frenchmen shared his feelings about the need for a federal system.[23]

Literature on the movement had now grown to such a point that it was a matter of comment among friends and foes alike. *Paneuropa* announced in its July-August 1928 issue that it was adding a new section in the journal (Presse Chronik) and prophesied: "The idea of a united Europe has now become such a constant theme in the European press that statesmen will have to face up to it." While this statement was somewhat of an exaggeration, it was not too far from the truth, for by the summer of 1928, the idea was a constant theme in a sizable segment of the periodical press and was showing up with increasing frequency in a wide variety of daily papers. Even the papers that were most hostile to the idea, generally those of extreme nationalist and communist orientation, could not always suppress the urge to denounce it.

A few periodicals made rather striking shifts in their championships of the European idea. For example, *Le Monde nouveau* assumed the role of official organ of the French Committee for European Cooperation and strongly supported Borel's program. Prague's *Wahrheit* became the official organ of the Czechoslovak Committee for a European Customs Union and gave some publicity to the customs union movement in other countries. *De Avondpost*, which had been sympathetic to the European movement all along, stepped up its campaign for an European federation in the early spring of 1928 to the point where it caught the attention of journalists outside the Netherlands. *La Paix par le droit*, which for months had been urging the progressive establishment of a European Customs Union, now began writing about the creation of a European army and the resolution of the Anschluss problem by means of a federalized Europe. *Das neue Europa* not only gave the European movement more attention than ever before but exhibited remarkable skill in getting articles from Europe's leading political figures and in using them in such a way as to make them serve the European movement to the fullest measure.[24]

Books and pamphlets dealing with the idea were also increasing in numbers, and what was nearly as important, many of the books that had appeared earlier, including Demangeon's *Le Déclin de l'Europe* and Heerfordt's *Et Nyt Europa*, were more widely read than ever before. In fact, books on the movement had now accumulated to the point where review articles were beginning to appear. The most ambitious of the review articles in the summer of 1928 came from the pen of Albert Lauterbach, Austrian socialist and journalist, who set out to review the more recent books on the movement for *Der Kampf*.[25] Although Lauterbach omitted too many of the books on the movement for his article to be of any real value to the historian in a bibliographical sense, it is nonetheless a valuable historical document. Lauterbach, despite the fact that he knew little about what had been published in France and Belgium, came upon more books than he had anticipated, and he opened his article with an expression of amazement at the sheer quantity of the material. He then proceeded to assure his readers that the literature on the movement was not only out of proportion to the size and success of the movement but that the greater part of the literature was hostile to the European idea. While a case might be made for the first part of his statement, he was quite wrong in stating that the greater part of the literature was hostile. Had he realized the extent to which the movement for a United Europe had become bound up with the search for a solution to Europe's economic ills and had known a bit more about the volume and nature of the literature across Europe, he probably would not have made either statement. For in addition to the books that made the European idea their central theme, there were hundreds that treated it with increasing frequency in relation to economic and political problems and developments.[26]

Perhaps no book published in these months attracted more attention than a manuscript that Francis Delaisi, fervent apostle of European economic integration, was laboring over. This manuscript, which was to be published in 1929 under the title of *Les Deux Europes*, represented a fresh approach to Europe's economic problems, and Delaisi, who was active as a lecturer as well as a writer, summarized the central ideas of the manuscript in an address before the Polish Section of the League for European Cooperation in July 1928. Delaisi argued that the continent of Europe comprised two distinct economic regions, one of which was basically industrial and the other basically agricultural. Much of Europe's trouble, he said, stemmed from the fact that the two regions were not really integrated economically and that they relied far too little on one another for markets and raw materials and far too much on non-European areas. He urged the peoples of Western and Eastern Europe to get together and predicted that the result would be vast new markets for both regions. He said: "Europe's economic salvation lies in a return to Europe. Its economic vitality and equilibrium can be restored if Europeans will look to Europe. . . . If the 240,000,000 peoples of Europe will quicken their economic relationships and move toward a great common market, their future will be bright."[27]

Chapter 12

THE KELLOGG-BRIAND PACT

In the summer and autumn of 1928 there was a change in the status of the European movement which edged it a bit more onto the fringes of European politics. Although many factors contributed to this change, including the Kellogg-Briand Pact, it stemmed largely from the rapidly rising tide of revisionism in Germany and growing fear across Europe of American economic competition and power. Both of these matters had now become big issues, and many felt that the European idea might contribute to the solution of both. Since German revisionism had a more direct and immediate bearing on the European idea, we shall treat it first.

Although revisionism had many facets, the main stress at this time was on the evacuation of the Rhineland. For not only was Stresemann convinced that a free Rhineland would strengthen Germany's diplomatic position enormously and enable her to pursue more effectively all other revisionist aims, including Mitteleuropa and the Saar, he also knew that the moderate Left in France was all but prepared to accept it. Now with a socialist in the chancellery, Stresemann sought to convince the peoples of Europe that German opinion had accepted the idea of a general pacification and that the Allied occupation of the Rhineland had served its purpose but remained the only serious obstacle to a Franco-German understanding.[1] Thus, he was saying essentially what the powerful moderate Left elements across Europe wanted to hear and believe.

Anxious as Stresemann was to keep Anschluss undercover until evacuation could be achieved, it proved impossible mainly because the Verein für das Deutschtum im Ausland was growing rapidly and the Mitteleuropa and Grossraumwirtschaft concepts and programs were taking on new life. The Anschluss question was set aflame by the Schubert Festival, which was held in Vienna from 19 to 21 July 1928, and Stresemann's embarrassment was all the more acute because Paul Löbe, who was still president of the Reichstag, had attended the festival and made another of his fiery Anschluss speeches.[2] Still not all good Europeans were unhappy because the Anschluss was in the picture. In fact, many of them were now more convinced than ever that the European movement could not break into the open and become a truly vital force unless it proved itself in combat with the harsher issues of the day. Also they felt that the manner in which these complex and explosive issues were resolved could have a heavy bearing on the course of history, and if the Anschluss could be lifted to the European level and settled there, it would give the European idea an enormous boost. So some of them plunged into the discussion of evacuation, and the result was a wide variety of ideas and approaches that had European overtones.

The approach that had the widest support envisioned a Franco-German rapprochement coupled with an energetic campaign to advance the European idea, thus blurring and weakening national frontiers to the point where the Anschluss would lose much of its divisive power. Few expressed this ambitious hope more forcefully than Victor Basch and Georg Bernhard. Basch expressed it many times during the summer but probably put it best in *La Volonté* on 2 October 1928: "If men everywhere . . . will work for a union of the states of Europe, the Anschluss will cease to be a problem. For the real solution to the Anschluss is to make Europe into a great federal state." Bernhard expressed this idea with equal clarity but with less optimism and feeling: "The Anschluss is merely one of the elements in the much greater question of continental unity. Thus, it is not a question of Pan-Germanism but a question of Pan-Europeanism. The moment real progress is made toward Pan-Europe, the French, the Italians, and the Czechs will feel much better about the Anschluss."[3]

This idea of resolving the problems of evacuation and the Anschluss by making "Europe into a great federal union" was, of course, dear to the hearts of all true federalists, and they would not have looked further afield had they known the way to such a union. But most of them, including Basch and Bernhard, realized that the way was uncharted and that the wisest course was to explore all possible approaches, working simultaneously at all those that seemed promising.

As they set about reassessing old approaches and exploring for new ones, many of them lingered over Austria, as Austria, because of her special economic problems and her direct involvement in the Anschluss, continued to be one of the focal points of federalist thinking.[4] Many Germans, including Heile, had come to Europe largely by way of Austria, and Coudenhove-Kalergi had not only established his Paneuropean Union in Vienna but he had said repeatedly that Austria, with her cosmopolitan capital and her long, rich experience in dealing with varied ethnic groups, was singularly qualified to lead the European movement. In fact, long before the summer of 1928, three fairly distinct federalist schemes pivoting on Austria had emerged.

The approach that was most genuinely federalist in nature envisioned Austria as the nucleus for a federalized Europe. More specifically, Austria was to forsake all thought of Anschluss and strive to attach herself to Europe. *La Volonté* (2 Aug. 1928) said: "Let us say to Austria: forget the Anschluss, which will surely lead to a revival of Mitteleuropa, and help us forge a United States of Europe, in whose bosom all Germanic peoples can find union without danger of calling to life a defensive alliance." On the same day, *L'Oeuvre* said: "It is to Europe not to Germany that Austria must unite herself."[5] In a speech before the Chamber of Deputies on 4 December 1928, Briand openly appealed to Austria to renounce the Anschluss and look to Europe.[6] Six days later, when Briand and Stresemann were at Lugano, they discussed the Anschluss quite frankly.[7] Jules Sauerwein reported in *30 Ans à la une* that Briand spoke of Switzerland as a model for Europe as they rode the train to Lugano.

A second approach that pivoted on Austria, and the only one that had real support in Germany, might be called the Anschluss-Mitteleuropean approach. Though it had a number of variations, its central contention was that Europe could only be united and held together by force and that Germany was the only nation that could muster the necessary power. Even Germany could not do so unless she were securely anchored in the central and eastern portions of Europe. Among those who presented this idea most generously were Willy Hellpach, Fritz Nonnenbruch, and Wilhelm Gurge.[8]

The third approach, which hinged to a large extent on Austria, envisaged a federation of the Danubian states. Though Danubian federation had much to recommend it, it never gained real momentum largely because the new states of the region were jealous of their newly won independence and because the powerful Anschluss forces in Austria as well as Germany waged a bitter campaign against it. Among its most active and effective champions were Milan Hodza and Václav Schuster in Czechoslovakia, Elemér Hantos and Ernö Bleier in Hungary, and Barons von Barolin and von Mises in Austria. In numerous articles and books these men, especially Hantos, explored Danubian union from every angle, and most of their arguments proved embarrassing to the Anschluss groups.[9] They not only raised the disturbing question as to whether many Austrian industries could survive in open competition with German industries, but they argued with confidence that Austria would find a readier market for her industrial goods in a Danubian federation and that life in general would be more comfortable. Most of these men also supported the larger European idea, arguing that a Danubian federation would be a step toward a European federation.

There were of course other approaches that pivoted on Austria. Robert Mangin suggested that Vienna and its hinterland be declared a federal territory and designated as the capital for the coming European federation and that the remainder of Austria be encouraged to unite with Germany.[10] Armand Charpentier, a widely recognized French journalist, proposed that the states of Europe instruct the League of Nations to develop and sponsor a plan that would offer the peoples of Germany and Austria union on the condition that they would then work actively and in good faith to make their union the nucleus for a European federal union.[11]

But none of the schemes that saw the Anschluss as a way to unify Europe had much support outside Germany and Austria. Most of the apostles of the European idea had a feeling that Anschluss and European unification were basically incompatible. C. M. Cudenet spoke for many when he wrote in

L'Homme libre (4 Aug. 1928): "We will have to choose between the Anschluss and a united Europe. For the Anschluss will not give us a united
Europe but a greater Germany."

Finally, there were a few good Europeans, mainly in France, who wondered
if the Saar could not be made the nucleus for a federal project. This idea was
perhaps presented most impressively in an unsigned article in *Revue des
vivants*. The author, probably Senator Henri de Jouvenel who was editor of
the journal, argued that the Saar Basin, if formally internationalized and left
permanently under league administration, could start Europe on the road
to federal union. The author concluded: "The government of the Saar is
already intereuropean. Why do we not consolidate this precious European
experience?"[12]

Meantime, concern about American economic competition and power,
which was doubtless aggravated in France by the war debt question, was
slowly mounting over much of Europe, and the nature of America's impact on
the European movement was changing, for, as we have already seen, the
United States with its smoothly functioning federal system, its vast open
market, and its rapidly expanding production, had fascinated and challenged
good Europeans from the first. As they had searched for a possible model for
a federated Europe, nearly all had studied the history and institutions of the
United States about as closely as they had the history and institutions of
Switzerland, and many of them had persisted in the use of the expression
"United States of Europe" when they knew and often said that the term was
misleading. In fact, it seems safe to say that up to the summer of 1928 Europeans had feared Soviet political subversion more than American industrial
and financial power. Even *Revue des vivants*, which by 1929 was crying
aloud about the American peril, had worried much more about the Soviet
danger in 1927. In the June issue of that year, Senator Jouvenel had observed:
"It is quite possible that the follies of Russian communism will give birth to a
European patriotism."[13]

But in the spring of 1928, apprehension about American economic power
began to mount and in some countries, at least, to overshadow concern about
Russian bolshevism.[14] One of the strongest expressions of this apprehension
to appear in the late spring came from the pen of Henri Dubreuil, who had just
returned to Europe from a stay of several weeks in the United States. Dubreuil
told the readers of *Le Peuple* (20 June 1928) that in his judgment greater
industrial and financial pressure from across the Atlantic was close at hand
and warned that the European states might not be able to meet this pressure
unless they formed an economic community. He concluded: "I do not believe
that the United States will take us seriously until we have taken a substantial
step toward unity, and indeed until she has to reckon with a great new reality
—A United States of Europe."

Six weeks later Gustave Rodrigues wrote that American economic power had shown itself to be as full of dangers for the peoples of Europe as was Russian subversion. After briefly picturing the Russian danger, he wrote: "We have equally to fear, even though it appears under a more pacific countenance, America's capacity to deprive us of our economic heritage and to reduce us to a state of virtual slavery. . . . For if Europe persists in its disunity, it will become an easy prey."[15]

If at this time most Europeans were inclined to regard men like Dubreuil and Rodrigues as extremists, they were less inclined to do so by the end of the summer. For the summer brought reports that many American industrial firms, most notably General Motors and Ford Motors, were not only buying stocks in European firms more extensively than ever but were also expanding their productive equipment and sales organizations at an increasingly rapid tempo. Even the Kellogg-Briand Peace Pact tended to augment Europe's concern about American economic penetration. For quite a number of Europeans insisted that American business circles had come to see the pact as a tool for opening up the European market.

Of course the pact also affected the European idea in a positive as well as a negative sense. Most of the men of the moderate Left across Europe, regardless of their attitude toward the United States, had come to feel that the pact would help create a climate more favorable to cooperation in Europe, and some even professed to see the pact itself as a measurable step toward the unity of Europe. Writing in *La Volonté* (16 Aug. 1928), René Marchand predicted that the pact would hasten the evacuation of the Rhineland and "strengthen the forces working for a unified Europe." *Pax* (12 Sept. 1928) declared editorially that the pact demanded spiritual disarmament, which in turn required economic disarmament. "The logical consequence of this pact for Europe is a customs union."

Moreover Briand, though he had not wanted this multilateral pact and had even tried to sidetrack it early in the year, had now adjusted to it and had come to feel that it would cause the United States to take a more benevolent attitude toward French policy and toward the movement to organize Europe—two matters that had been in his mind when he had addressed his open letter to the American people on 6 April 1927. In fact, the foreign minister did two things at the time of the signing of the pact which were significant for the European movement. First, in his speech at the signing ceremony (a speech that contrary to Briand's habit was carefully drafted and read), he was careful to point out that he did not think that the pact had brought peace, but he made it clear that he felt it could be a step on the way toward the organization of peace. Secondly, he told Stresemann that he was prepared to link the problems of evacuation and reparations and that he intended to put the matter of a definitive liquidation of the war before the ninth session of the League Assembly that was about to open in Geneva. In fact, a close examination of Briand's speeches and recorded conversations for these months indicates quite strongly that he feared a situation was building in Europe which would bring another great war before very long. He was talking about war more and more in terms of its human impacts and of the responsibilities of political leaders. This had been noticeable ever since his speech to the delegates of the Interparliamentary Union in Paris on 30 August 1927 when he had speculated on the number of potential statesmen, scientists, scholars, and men of action Europe had lost in the great war and had added: "If we remember that we are accountable to the future, we may find in this moral responsibility the strength to pursue collectively a sacred task which transcends the limits of our individual lives."

Chapter 13

BRIAND ENVISIONS A

FEDERAL PROJECT

The decision that Briand and Stresemann had taken in Paris to step up negotiations looking toward the liquidation of the war was not long in producing results. On 16 September 1928, in the early days of the ninth session of the League Assembly, France, Germany, England, Italy, Belgium, and Japan approved a comprehensive program of negotiations known as the Geneva Protocols for the Liquidation of the War. The core of this program was set out in three protocols. The first of these called for the institution of formal negotiations concerning the evacuation of the Rhineland; the second called for the complete and definitive regulation of German reparations as a condition for this evacuation; and the third provided for the establishment of a Commission of Inquiry and Conciliation, which Briand seemingly hoped would promote the European idea by providing guidance and moral leadership at the European level.

The leaders of the European movement were quite impressed by the Geneva Protocols and had noted with satisfaction that Eduard Beneš had said that the Kellogg-Briand Pact and the Geneva Protocols could bring a significant turn toward economic collaboration across Europe. Too, they strongly suspected that the pact and the new protocols were closely linked to the European idea in Briand's thinking, and a number of the leading figures in the European movement, including Coudenhove-Kalergi, Emile Borel, Jules Sauerwein, Henri de Jouvenel, and Jean Dauriac talked and acted as if they were sure of this. For example, Dauriac, in a series of editorials in *L'Homme libre* said that Briand had become convinced, as he himself had, that the peoples of Europe could not achieve peace and solid prosperity without a federal union grounded in a common market. Dauriac concluded the last editorial in the series with these words: "Without a United States of Europe, unending war and insecurity will be the lot of the states of the Old Continent."[1] Georges Izard professed to see the projected Commission of Inquiry and Conciliation in the protocols as an attempt on Briand's part to found a rudimentary European body.[2]

Indeed, this growing feeling that Briand was thinking more and more in terms of the organization of Europe and was about to make a significant move in that direction seemed to make most good Europeans a bit more cautious, perhaps out of fear of making moves that might embarrass Briand. Perhaps the best way to get at their thoughts, hopes, and fears in the months following the Kellogg-Briand Pact is to examine their behavior in some of the more important private international conferences and their reactions to the growing crisis of the Paneuropean Union in Germany.

Of the many conferences in these months, the ones that touched the European idea most were the Twenty-fifth Conference of the Interparliamentary Union, the International Economic Conference in Prague, the Conference of the League of International Friendship, and the Conference of the National Committees of the League for European Cooperation. Though none of these conferences had the European idea on its agenda, there were many good Europeans at all of them.

The Twenty-fifth Conference of the Interparliamentary Union was held in Berlin just before the signing of the Paris Peace Pact. J. M. Treub, well-known Dutch economist who served as president of the conference, opened the general debate with a blistering attack on economic nationalism and a fervent plea for a program of economic rationalization to lay the groundwork for a "European customs accord."[3] Such an accord would, he argued, satisfy the more urgent demands of technology and interdependence and would "open the door to a general limitation of armaments," which in turn would "strengthen Europe with respect to other regions of the world." To the surprise of many of the delegates, Treub also stated that the parliamentary system was making for superficiality in the realm of economic policy because it was setting the politician above the economic expert.

Those who spoke most strongly for the European idea during the general debate were Fernand Merlin and Emile Borel. Merlin said that the "interdependence and interpenetration of nations" was the dominant economic fact of the day and that Europe's political frontiers had become economically and culturally stifling. He added: "Unity imposes itself like a dogma. Unless Europe is united and a United States of Europe constituted, the Old Continent will become enfeebled and will perish in its eternal struggles."[4]

Borel, obviously feeling that the Germans were in need of some clear and straightforward talk, declared that in some European states military as well as political groups were making unreasonable demands and acting in an irresponsible manner. The League of Nations could not, he said, press the territorial revision of the treaties without risking its own existence and even a general war. But changes could be brought about without the risk of war if men were patient and responsible, and he called on the peoples of Europe to rise above their frontiers and to move progressively toward a United States of Europe. "To achieve a European federation will be difficult. . . . But since it is the only way to save Europe, one should not ask if it is difficult."[5] Karl Drexel of Austria also treated briefly the European idea, stating that he felt he should let the conference know that there were people in Austria who believed the states of Europe would have to draw together if they were to meet British and American competition and hold their own in the world.[6]

The International Economic Conference at Prague ran from 4 to 6 October 1928 and was attended by representatives from some twenty-six economic organizations, and several were members of the International Committee for a European Customs Union or one of its national committees. In fact, a group of the delegates had gotten together before the conference opened and agreed to insist on a full debate on a European customs union and to raise the question of regional customs unions. Some of the leaders in the customs union movement had come to feel that, in view of the rather marked economic and cultural differences across Europe, it might be wise to try for two customs unions at the outset. One would be in western Europe built around France and Germany, and the other in eastern Europe to be composed of Austria, Czechoslovakia, Hungary, Rumania, and Yugoslavia. Proponents of this regional approach argued that it would bring additional support to the movement without in any way ruling out a single union.[7]

As expected, the customs union idea received a thorough and rather sympathetic airing in the conference with Pawlowski, Stern-Rubarth, Hantos, Truchy, and several others taking part.[8] It even became one of the favorite topics of discussion between sessions, and Rennie Smith, a member of the House of Commons and private secretary to Hugh Dalton, treated it at length in an interview with members of the press. To the surprise of many, Smith talked freely about "a positive economic structure stretching from one side of Europe to the other" and did not hesitate to use the term United States of Europe. But the thing that the International Economic Conference did that pleased good Europeans most was to draft a resolution urging the governments of Europe to join hands at Geneva in an effort "to establish a scale for the progressive reduction of customs duties" with a view to their ultimate elimination.[9] Though this resolution was not the ringing call for a European customs union that the more ardent would have liked to have, it was a strong resolution and was often referred to in the months ahead.

Although the European idea received a strong echo in the conferences of the League of International Friendship and the League for European Cooperation, which were held concurrently in Paris in late November 1928, there were signs in the latter conference of increasing apprehensiveness about Anglo-American attitudes toward the European movement. Borel, in his main address, explained that some people in both Britain and the United States were arguing that "a European federation would produce a wave of continental imperialism that might tend to set continent against continent." He admitted that he did not know how serious this was but suggested that it might be wise for the Committees of the League for European Cooperation "to talk less about a United States of Europe and more about continental solidarity."[10]

Nevertheless, Borel spoke in his accustomed manner throughout a good part of his address and at one point said that Europe could and would be made "into a living reality" even if it took two hundred years. Ove Meyer of Denmark told the delegates that cooperation among the peoples of Europe seemed so natural to the Danish people that many were hoping for the emergence of a federal union in the immediate future. Heile, though he admitted that the European idea was not too popular in his own country, concluded his main address with a burst of optimism: "Vive la France, votre patrie! Vive l'Allemagne, ma patrie! Vive l'Europe, notre patrie commune! Vivent les Etats-Unis de l'Europe!"[11]

Moreover, Briand used the occasion of these conferences for another gesture in the direction of a united Europe. He invited both conferences to send delegations to the Quai d'Orsay, and he told these delegations that he believed it possible "for the peoples of Europe to achieve a federal union" in the foreseeable future.[12]

But in the autumn of 1928, few matters worried good Europeans as much as the difficulties that the European idea was encountering in Germany. For many Germans, disturbed by growing rumors that Briand was thinking seriously of sponsoring some sort of project for European union, were stepping up attacks on the European idea. No one took this harder than Coudenhove-Kalergi, who had always felt a special responsibility for the German-speaking areas. The young count, now convinced that Briand was planning to act, tried hard to shore up the German chapter of the Paneuropean Union and to persuade all Germans that they had fully as much to gain from a United Europe as the French.

Turning first to the German Paneuropean Union, Coudenhove told Löbe, who was still its chairman, that the time had come to rid the union of dissenters and troublemakers and to make it into a devoted and disciplined body. Löbe, still an ardent proponent of the Anschluss, argued back, and discord mounted. In late November 1928, the General Assembly of the German Union met, elected Coudenhove as its chairman, named Erich Koch-Weser, Count Harry Kessler, and Joseph Wirth honorary directors, and took steps to revise its charter.[13] At the same time, Coudenhove made other moves. He elaborated on the character and aims of the union in an article that appeared in *Paneuropa* in January 1929; he lectured in Oldenburg, Bremen, and Berlin; he drafted a plan for the creation of a Paneuropean Institute to serve as an information center for the entire European movement; and he wrote Stresemann on 28 January 1929, urging him to call the foreign ministers of the European governments together to discuss a federal project.[14] This time Stresemann himself made a guarded reply to Coudenhove: "You can rest assured that every sincere attempt to promote the peaceful restoration of Europe through the solid cooperation of its peoples will have my full sympathy. I cannot for the moment, however, become engaged in the details of a program such as you suggest."[15]

If Coudenhove had all but failed in his hope of revitalizing the Paneuropean movement in Germany, he had made it possible for good Europeans everywhere to get a clearer picture of the status of the European movement in Germany, and he had impressed and encouraged most of his German followers. The *Sozialistische Monatshefte* continued to urge the Müller government to work for an alignment with France as a basis for a European continental union, and Ludwig Quessel wrote in the January 1929 issue of this journal: "The Anschluss and armaments will take care of themselves in the framework of a united European continent."[16] The *Vossische Zeitung*, though obviously a bit irked at Coudenhove, continued to insist that a European customs union would bring enormous benefits to German industry, especially to her iron and steel industries. *Nord und Süd* continued its policy of publishing articles by prominent Europeans and carried an article by Borel in its October 1928 issue. Professor Erich Obst wrote in the *Hannoverischer Anzeiger* (9 Dec. 1928) "If we fail to create a European federation, we will find ourselves in the tragic predicament foreseen by Spengler in his *Untergang des Abendlandes*." Speaking over the radio in Berlin on 16 December 1928, Dr. Erich Raemisch praised Coudenhove and said: "As long as Russia and the British Empire have their economic interests centered outside Europe, we will stand in need of an economic union. . . . Europe can achieve economic unity if her peoples can make up their minds to it."[17]

At the same time in Austria and France, good Europeans seemed to make conscious efforts to help Coudenhove. Oskar Acht, who was responsible for the Presse-Chronik in *Paneuropa*, wrote: "Though the outlook for the Paneuropean idea is not too bright, Paneuropeans must keep the faith and work harder than ever." *Das neue Europa* weighted its issues in these months with articles and materials favorable to the European idea, and several Austrian journals, including the *Reichspost*, the main organ of the Austrian Christian Socialists, warmly seconded Coudenhove's call for a Paneuropean Institute.[18] In France most good Europeans saluted Stresemann as well as Briand and seemed to work with more purpose. *L'Ere nouvelle* (12 Nov. 1928) told its readers that the League of the Rights of Man in France, with its network of departmental chapters, was speaking more strongly and openly than ever before for a "United Europe." *Le Quotidien* (12 Nov. 1928) called for a "mass campaign" designed to generate a current of opinion strong enough to compel the political leaders of Europe to take the road to federation. *La Volonté* (16 Dec. 1929) said editorially: "So far the effort to achieve a United States of Europe has come mainly from intellectuals. What we need to do now is . . . to get the masses so excited about this idea that they will embrace it."

Few in France spoke out as forcefully for Paneurope as Delaisi and Sauerwein. Delaisi spoke in Stuttgart on 17 January 1929 and in Frankfurt on the following day; on both occasions his subject was "France and Paneurope," and his conclusion was that many in France were prepared to move toward a customs union. Sauerwein said in *Das neue Europa* that he had seen much of Briand over the years and he knew the French Foreign Minister was giving serious thought to some new bold initiative.[19] Indeed, Sauerwein's article turned out to be less sensational than he himself had expected. For even before the article was available to the readers of *Das neue Europa*, there was positive evidence that Briand was on the move. On 3 February 1929, *Le Métropole* reported that Senator Henri Jouvenel had said that Briand had discussed the matter of a European structure with the British and German ambassadors in Paris. Then, in an editorial in the next issue of *Revue des vivants*, Jouvenel himself stated: "On Briand's initiative the question of a European federal union is already a subject of discussion in the chancelleries of Europe."[20]

Meantime, as evidence piled up that Briand was planning to sponsor a project of federal union as soon as the Dawes Plan had been recast and the evacuation of the Rhineland arranged, fear of American economic power was ballooning and becoming a much larger factor in the European movement. Businessmen as well as politicians and journalists were saying with increasing frequency that Washington was about to raise its tariff rates and that Europe was on the point of being inundated by automobiles, trucks, tractors, textiles, and films from across the Atlantic. As Lucien Laurat put it: "Cries of alarm are multiplying all over Europe. In every language one and the same outcry is endlessly repeated, 'the colossus across the Atlantic is menacing us . . . it will soon be a real and serious threat.' Facts to support this view have come fast of late."[21] There was a veritable deluge of articles in the periodical as well as the daily press concerning the "American danger" and considerable speculation about its relation to the European movement. There were those who saw it as a rallying point for a European economic union, and there were those who felt it was being exaggerated and would give the movement too much of an anti-American appearance. Some, including William Martin, editor of the *Journal de Genève*, believed that it had much to do with Briand's growing determination to sponsor a federal project.[22]

There were also developments in the field of journalism at this time that contributed noticeably to the growth of the European idea. The first of these came in March 1929 when Senator Jouvenel announced that *Revue des vivants* would give a prize of 10,000 francs for the best essay on European federation which was sent to the journal by 10 December 1929, and that the journal would publish the essay. The judging, he said, would be done by twenty-five prominent Europeans.[23] The contest turned out better than Jouvenel himself had anticipated. When the deadline for submitting essays arrived, *Revue des vivants* had 502 manuscripts, many of them over 200 pages in length. Then when the judges announced that an amazingly large number of the manuscripts were of excellent quality and worthy of publication, Jouvenel received a letter from French industrialist Paul Rodier offering to add 10,000 francs to the prize sum so that cash prizes could be given to the authors of the six essays that were judged best. The full texts of these six essays were published in *Revue des vivants* during the spring and summer of 1930, and before the end of the year, the six, together with a long interpretative digest of the other 496, were published in a thick volume entitled *La Fédération européenne* (Paris, 1930). In the preface to this volume, which was dedicated to the delegates to the Eleventh Session of the League of Nations, Jouvenel wrote: "We are still amazed at the force of this intellectual current. In view of the particularism and the protectionism that followed the great war, it is astonishing that so many people now regard a European federation as a matter of urgency."

Perhaps the most important development in the field of journalism during these weeks was the appearance of two new journals—*L'Européen* and *La République*. *L'Européen*, a weekly, was founded and edited by André Lamandé and F. H. Turot. As its title implied, it was dedicated wholly to the cause of European federalism. In the prefatory article in the first issue, which appeared on 17 April 1929, Lamandé and Turot told their readers that *L'Européen* would take them on an exciting journey "toward the future and toward the light. . . . It will be a voyage to save our civilization. . . . What we want is Europe, with all its peoples, cities, farms, and gardens, organized and united." Although *L'Européen* never had a large circulation, it numbered among its contributors such well-known Frenchmen as Etienne Fougère, Paul Mantoux, Drieu la Rochelle, René Duchemin, Claude Gignoux, and Gaston Riou. It followed closely the big events of the day, and it laid considerable stress on economic issues and the dangers of American economic power. In its issue of 24 April, it proposed the creation of an Economic League of Nations with delegates chosen by leading businessmen.

La République, which started publication on 10 April 1929, was a daily with a very substantial circulation from the outset.[24] Although it did not profess exclusive devotion to the European idea as did *L'Européen*, its support of the movement was no less wholehearted and certainly few papers in Europe had more to say about the dangers of American economic power. In the first issue, Edouard Daladier, deputy and prominent figure in the Radical Socialist party, wrote of its program: "*La République* will be in the forefront of the crusade for peace. It will struggle for a free federation of the peoples of Europe, which is the only means by which Europe can escape the vassalage which now menaces it."[25] On 13 April, deputy Julien Durand wrote: "How can Europe with its fragmented and competing markets hope to hold its own with the United States, which can in an instant throw its solid, massive weight on the scales? The hour is near when the states of Europe, if they are to survive, must form an economic tariff union as a prelude to a United States of

Europe. . . ." Writing a week later, Jacques Kayser wondered if the creation of the International Bank of Settlement would not spell American financial dominance in Europe and asked: "Is it too late to save Europe from this peril by means of a federation of its states?" He added that in any event it offered "the only real avenue of hope and should be pursued." Thus, from the outset, *La République* entered wholeheartedly in the fight for a federal bond, and by the end of the summer of 1929, it had published more than fifty articles and editorials warmly supporting such a project.

The spring of 1929 also brought a more determined effort from several of the private organizations, especially from the French Study Committee for a European Customs Union and the French Committee for European Cooperation. The two committees, working in close collaboration, decided to try to get all important economic associations in France, including the Chambers of Commerce, to support actively the European movement, and they also agreed to a joint meeting to coincide with that of the Congress of the Union of League of Nations Associations, which was scheduled to open in Madrid in early June. Presidents of the Chambers of Commerce throughout France and representatives of several of the country's economic associations met in Paris from 4 to 8 June to discuss American commercial policies and the possibility of some sort of economic bond.[26] At the same time, the International Committee for European Cooperation and the International Committee for a European Customs Union met in Madrid in conjunction with the annual congress of the Union of League of Nations Associations. This meeting turned out to be a modest demonstration for European federalism as the principal papers were given by Wilhelm Heile, Henri Truchy, and Eduard David. All three men argued strongly for the development of European economic, political, and cultural bonds, and David said that Germany and France should take the lead by working out at once a customs union of their own.[27]

But no private organization showed greater enthusiasm at this time than the French section of the International League for Peace and Freedom, which had written European federation into its program when Briand was a mere boy. In opening the section's spring meeting, President Guébin told the members that it was now obvious that Briand was on the verge of sponsoring a project of federal union and that they, in view of their program and the traditions of their society, should join in the struggle "to crown the Briand venture with success."[28] While most of the members felt that it would be a mistake for the section to press for too much at the outset, some were bold and urged the section to go on record at once in support of a federal structure with extensive powers. Villerelle said: "The time has come to abolish national armies and to institute a genuine European sovereignty," and he called for a federal structure resting on "a European code and a European army."[29]

Meantime, Briand had been watching events with growing interest and had not been too discouraged by the course they had taken. Ernst von Streeruwitz, a member of the Austrian Volksbund, had succeeded Seipel as chancellor of Austria on 4 May 1929, but this did not disturb Briand unduly for Stresemann had told him at Lugano and elsewhere that Anschluss was not urgent and could wait. Indeed, the French foreign minister had all but made up his mind to present some sort of a project for European federation before the summer was over. However, before coming to a firm decision, he wanted to see the report that the Young Committee was writing, and he wanted to talk again with Stresemann. In the early days of June 1929, he was able to do both. The Young Committee completed and signed its report on 7 June, and both he and Stresemann attended the meeting of the Council of the League of Nations in Madrid from 6 to 13 June. On 11 June at a meeting in the Ritz Hotel, he again assured the German foreign minister that he was prepared to tie evacuation of the Rhineland to a new reparation plan based on the Young Report. He said he felt agreement on these two matters should go far to stabilize the European situation and that the next task would be to consolidate and organize European relations in both the political and economic spheres. Stresemann agreed, and Briand then said that he did not believe that the end that they had in mind could be reached without some sort of federal bond or structure in Europe. Such a structure, he said, would give Europe the security it needed and would enable it to deal realistically with American economic power. He made it clear that he was thinking of putting this idea before the governments of Europe and that he wanted Stresemann's thoughts. Although the German foreign minister was a bit noncommittal, he did not discourage Briand and indeed seemed a bit more inclined than formerly to support European economic coordination and integration.[30]

So after the meeting in Madrid, Briand with the help of Alexis Léger began planning his federal initiative. He was sure that it would be best to move slowly and get as much information as possible between steps, and he was especially anxious to get a clearer idea of how the Germans and British would react before he presented anything definite. On 10 July 1929, with the Hague Conference to deal with the Young Committee's Report less than a month away, Briand told a correspondent of L'Oeuvre that he had decided to put the matter of a European federative structure before the governments of Europe in early September at the Tenth Session of the League Assembly. The next day L'Oeuvre carried a front-page article entitled "Un grand project de M. Briand." The article explained that Briand had been giving careful consideration to a federal initiative ever since the signing of the Protocols for the Liquidation of the War and added: "This great project is now ripe in his mind and he has tested it in conversations with key European statesmen. Briand now plans to propose such a project at Geneva in September, and he hopes that a conference can be convened before the end of the year to begin work on a European organization."[31]

For a more formal and official announcement, Briand chose the forum of the Chamber of Deputies, which had just opened debate on the ratification of the Beranger-Mellon debt agreement. On 16 July, after speaking at some length on the debt agreement, the Young Report, and the evacuation of the Rhineland, Briand said that the most urgent and crucial task of the time was to strengthen the foundations of peace but that a durable peace could not be achieved without new measures of a fundamental and positive nature. Briand continued:

> For several years I have personally carried on, among a number of my colleagues representing the European states at Geneva, a propaganda in the sense of an organization of Europe. I have received much encouragement especially in recent months. . . . In fact, I believe that it is necessary to organize Europe, not against any country or any group of countries, but to strengthen the conditions of peace, to put an end to the state of anarchy that will give rise to conflicts as long as actions are not sufficiently coordinated to organize the vital interests of the peoples of the continent. . . . It is in this spirit that I and a number of statesmen who are in accord with me and my government, shall search for a European organization which may become a new page for peace.[32]

Briand had not suggested a blueprint for European unification, but he felt that he had done and said enough to provoke a reaction across Europe which would be of great help to him in deciding on his next move. The reaction centered heavily on Briand's motives and objectives and, broadly speaking, it ranged from rather warm support by a majority of the papers in most countries across Europe, especially in France, Belgium, the Netherlands, and Switzerland, to strong disapproval in a few countries, most notably Germany and Italy.[33] Few papers came closer to summing up the views of the supporting press in France, and indeed of much of the powerful moderate and moderate Left press across Europe, than *L'Information* when it said editorially on 18 July 1929: "The idea of a United States of Europe grows among us. . . . It is a great idea and it can become a great thing. But prudence warns us not to expect too much too soon. . . . Every idea, however seducing, must be weighed at the point where it comes in closest touch with reality. . . . Still, we must seize every opportunity, however modest it may be, that promises to advance the work." *La Dépêche de Toulouse*, with its host of well-known contributors, insisted that Briand had an excellent sense of history and that it was a good thing that "the idea is in the higher sphere of politics and that diplomats and statesmen are having to concern themselves with it. . . . In taking this initiative, Briand has honored France."

While the response in France was on the whole sympathetic and heartening, such was not the case in the other major states. Italian opinion was outwardly quite hostile, and some papers spoke of the project as childish and disgusting. British opinion was decidedly cool, and most papers insisted that England's destiny lay in close union with her dominions and colonies, but it was the German response that Briand watched most anxiously. The German reaction, though generally negative, permeated with mistrust and suspicion, and tied to revisionism, was not without supporting voices. Several papers, mainly Democratic and Socialist papers, held that Paneurope was an emerging fact that would have to be faced, and thus insisted that Briand's federal initiatives should be carefully studied. The *Vossische Zeitung* saluted Briand warmly in its issue of 11 July but urged him to bear in mind that economic union would have to precede political union: "As the German Zollverein preceded the German Reich, so will a European customs union precede a United States of Europe; and a customs union is such a compelling necessity for the states of Europe that a way to it must and will be found in spite of all obstacles."

The *Kölnische Volkzeitung* wrote on 17 July 1929: "The time has come when we must work for cultural, political, and economic understanding among all men. We must draw away from the narrow nationalist and imperialist concepts of the nineteenth century." The *Frankfurter Zeitung* played with the European idea and came close to an open endorsement of Briand's initiative.

But Briand received rough treatment from the powerful Right press, which was heavily influenced by Alfred Hugenberg. The *Berliner Lokal Anzeiger*, in its issue of 12 July 1929, labeled the Briand project "a booby trap pure and simple" fashioned by the Quai d'Orsay "to bury the Anschluss" and "to perpetuate the Versailles settlement." The *Kölnische Zeitung* saw Briand as a shrewd diplomat whose real aim was the consolidation of French hegemony in Europe. "Herr Briand is very clever. Unable to prevent the rise of Germany through his Committee of Conciliation, he now seeks . . . to get all Europe to guarantee the status quo through a United States of Europe."[34] The *Deutsche Tages-Zeitung*, the leading organ of German agrarian interests, also spoke firmly against the Briand initiative: "Such an economic union as Briand envisages. . . . will do enormous damage to German agriculture, especially to that segment devoted to the production of grains."[35] *Der Jungdeutsche*, 26 July 1929, said that German youth would not discuss Briand's proposal until the Versailles diktat had been annulled and Germany restored "to complete sovereignty in all respects." *Germania*, the official organ of the Center party, called Briand's federal initiative unrealistic and expressed the view that it would be pointless if not dangerous to discuss it at the time.[36]

Indeed, the response of the German Right was so unfavorable and so full of mistrust and suspicion that Coudenhove-Kalergi could not control his indignation. In a long letter in the *Neue freie Presse* on 15 July, Coudenhove severely scolded the German papers that had characterized Briand's proposal as a political maneuver to bulwark the Versailles settlement and fasten French hegemony on Europe. He said that he knew the French foreign minister well and that his devotion to peace and to Europe was beyond question. Again, he argued that Germany had much more to gain from a European community than France because such a community would liquidate the postwar settlement and enable Germany to achieve her legitimate revisionist demands without war. He reminded the Germans that the vast segment of the French press that had supported Locarno and the policy of reconciliation was now supporting Briand's proposal. Then dramatically and challengingly, Coudenhove added: "Briand's gesture is not a solution, but it is a question addressed to Europe. The future of our continent depends on the answer that we give to this question."[37]

Some Germans who refused to endorse Briand's initiative, joined Coudenhove in chiding the Nationalist press for its interpretation of Briand's motives. For example, Paul Bloch, Paris correspondent of the *Berliner Tageblatt*, was quite critical of Briand's move, but he nevertheless assured his countrymen that Briand was a man of courage and integrity who felt strongly that the time had come when a step could be taken toward the organization of Europe. "We will be wrong if we do not believe that he is sincere."[38] But Rightist journals on the whole were not impressed by Bloch's plea, and several assaulted Coudenhove as mercilessly as they did Briand, calling him "Briand's stooge" and an enemy of Germany. The substance of what the bulk of the German press was saying was that there could be no serious discussion of the organization of Europe until Germany's military and territorial demands had been met and the Versailles Treaty largely set aside.

Chapter 14

THE HAGUE AND GENEVA

Such in broad outline was the status of the European movement in mid-July as preparations got in full swing for the Hague Conference, which was to shape the Report of the Young Committee into a new reparations plan and link the evacuation of the Rhineland to it.[1] Briand had said in modesty that he would be satisfied if some sort of a European diplomatic conference of a permanent character could be achieved as a first step toward the organization of Europe. But his prestige was great and his announcement that he would have something to say about the Organization of Europe in September at the Tenth Regular Session of the League Assembly made the European idea more of a political issue, intensifying debate on it in the French Chamber of Deputies and the Senate, where the Beranger-Mellon debt agreement was under discussion. In the Chamber of Deputies on 17 July, Edouard Herriot warmly endorsed the foreign minister's move and stated, for foreign as well as domestic consumption, that it should be clear to all that the idea of a European federation had become an important factor in France's foreign policy.[2] On 19 July, Etienne Fougère, who was still president of France's Association for Economic Expansion, told the chamber that the nations of Europe would have to form an economic front if they were to compete on anything like equal terms with the American colossus. Fougère did however express the hope that such a front could be achieved without engendering serious antagonism with the United States, for "antagonism might create a conflict more redoubtable than any we have known."[3]

In the Senate on 24 July, Jouvenel, whose *Revue des vivants* was giving the European movement vigorous support, said: "In this moment when our policies are changing . . . I rejoice in the fact that the Foreign Minister of France has taken the initiative in putting before the world the idea of a European federation."[4] Jean Hennessy, minister of agriculture, followed Jouvenel and, like Fougère, argued that the United States had grown so strong economically that its money and goods were a threat to Europe's markets and even to the independence of its states. He continued: "To create a European union will be difficult, almost impossible, but . . . there can be no doubt that this union, which seems like a dream to us today, will be realized if American economic power presses too heavily on the economic life of Europe."[5] Etienne Clémentel, president of the Senate's commission on finances, also sharply criticized the role of the United States in Europe, observing that the Americans would have to understand that they could not always sell and never buy. "Unless the

United States pursues a different trade policy, the states of Europe may be compelled to move to the verge of a customs union in order to defend themselves." Clémentel had said at the meeting of the International Chambers of Commerce in Amsterdam earlier in the month that the "primary aim of European economic policy should be the creation of a European customs union."[6]

On the following day, Senator Joseph Caillaux applauded Briand's initiative and urged France to hold firmly to her policy of European conciliation, to do all within her power to lay the foundation for a European economic union. "The road will be long and we shall have to work at it from day to day. Nevertheless, I hope and believe with my friend Clémentel that we shall reach this goal."[7]

During the final days of the debate, Briand himself made further comments on his plans for a federal project. On 26 July, just as he was taking over the presidency of the Council of Ministers from the ailing Poincaré, he repeated rather casually in the Senate the substance of what he had said ten days earlier in the Chamber: "It is necessary to organize Europe from an economic point of view, as well as a political point of view. And to do this will be in the interest of the United States itself. To this end, gentlemen, I shall direct much of my remaining strength."[8] Then, on 31 July, on the eve of the opening of the Hague Conference, the European idea received another brief outing in the Chamber of Deputies in which Briand participated. Claude Gignoux, editor of *La Journée industrielle*, stated that he would support the foreign minister's plan to create "a United States of Europe" but would expect a broad approach that envisioned "an international organization of productions" as well as the more familiar idea of a European Customs Union.[9]

Briand then said that Gignoux was correct in stating that the approach would have to be comprehensive and deliberate. He added:

> For the past four years, I have reflected on this vast problem without, however, attaching myself to any formula so pretentious as that suggested by the expression "a United States of Europe." In examining the situation in Europe, I have simply felt . . . that collaboration among the peoples of Europe would have to be closer before a true atmosphere of peace could be created on the continent. The problems are so awesome and so arduous that one is tempted to give up in despair. But such a surrender would be unworthy of a statesman. . . . I have not only encouraged publically committees of propaganda but at Geneva, where I have had the good fortune to be associated with the qualified representatives of all the European states, I have engaged in conversations with some of them about this matter. They have welcomed my suggestions and have shown themselves ready to join me in the near future in examining the great economic and political problems that the organization of Europe will involve. . . . What we want to accomplish is a work

of peace in which the United States is as interested as are the states of
Europe . . . and it is in that spirit that I shall pursue its realization.[10]

The foreign minister concluded by reminding the deputies that he would soon
leave for the Hague Conference, which was scheduled to open on 6 August,
and that the work of that conference with respect to reparations and the
evacuation of the Rhineland would absorb most of his energies for some
weeks.[11]

In fact, speculation about the possible connection between Briand's federal
initiative and the Hague Conference had grown steadily during July, and
Briand himself had observed in the Chamber of Deputies that he did not look
upon the Young Report as merely a blueprint for a new reparation plan but
rather as "a living and creative thing . . . working for the liquidation of the
war and for the organization of Europe." Many papers across Europe, including the *Berliner Tageblatt* (26 July 1929), took note of Briand's observation.
La République put the matter this way: "France wants a European Community, and she wants and expects the conference at The Hague to be a step
toward such a community as well as toward the liquidation of the war."
Moreover, many of those who elaborated on the connection between the
Young Report and Briand's federal initiative found themselves writing about
the projected Bank of International Settlements and arguing that the new
bank could give the European movement a firm monetary dimension, thus
becoming a powerful and manysided instrument for the unity of Europe.[12]

When the Hague Conference opened on 6 August 1929, the delegates felt
that it would be emotional and stormy. Not only was the evacuation of the
Rhineland to be faced, but Philip Snowden, chancellor of the Exchequer in
Britain's new Labour government, had already attacked certain items in the
Young Report and had said that a reparation plan based on that report would
disturb the economic equilibrium of his country. Still the first hours of the
conference were calm enough. Stresemann spoke early and said, to the delight
of good Europeans: "In my mind I envision the convocation of another
general economic conference whose primary aim will be the achievement of a
vast rationalization of production. . . . I hope that the time will come when
the customs barriers that throttle Europe's trade will disappear, and I trust that
our deliberations here will mark a step in this direction."[13] Then, as the first
session neared its end, Snowden launched an attack on the Young Report, and
there were those who wondered if Snowden's attack was not a calculated
effort on the part of the British government to undermine the Briand project.[14]
Briand, anxious to avoid a clash with Britain, instructed Chéron, the French
minister of finance, to reply to Snowden in polite language and to stress the
fact that the Young Report was a product of prolonged negotiations, appearing
to be as good a compromise as could be worked out. Snowden, however, was
not impressed by Chéron's arguments and returned to the attack, calling for a

special committee to rewrite the Young Report in line with the suggestions of his government. Chéron now moved in with sharper words, and the duel was underway between the French and British finance ministers which was to run until the final days of the conference. The Germans, of course, eyed with emotion the opening that Snowden had given them, but they were afraid to strike recklessly for fear they would jeopardize the evacuation of the Rhineland. Though Stresemann raised many points with Briand, he did nothing worse than write him a sharp, emotional letter insisting on a definite and reasonable date for the completion of the evacuation of the Rhineland and for the immediate opening of negotiations concerning the return of the Saar to Germany. Briand, well aware of the dangers at hand, maneuvered carefully and was prepared to give the German foreign minister assurance on both the Rhineland and the Saar.

These were hard and difficult problems for both Briand and Stresemann. They lay near the heart of German revisionism as it looked westward, and they were among the hardest of the problems that Briand had hoped the European movement would help to moderate and resolve. In fact, the members of the Franco-German Committee for Information and Documentation, which had come to grips with these problems in the hope of aiding their governments in arriving at workable solutions, were now wrangling bitterly, and the committee might have broken apart had it not been for the great patience and broadmindedness of Etienne Fougère, Henri Lichtenberger, and D'Ormesson on the French side and Hermann Bücher, E. R. Curtius, and Wilhelm Haas on the German.[15]

Close as the Hague Conference came to a complete rupture, it struggled on, and in late August there was agreement on Britain's reparations claims, and 30 June 1930 was set as the date for the completion of the evacuation of the Rhineland. Even before the exchange of letters between Stresemann and Briand during 29–30 August, there was a burst of speculation on what Briand would propose by way of European union at the Tenth Session of the League Assembly, which was to open on 2 September. *La République*, for example, carried four lengthy editorials on the matter between 28 August and 3 September. In the editorial of 2 September, Jacques Kayser predicted that Briand would try to link his federal project to the question of disarmament and cautioned his readers not to expect a European union over night: "Europe will not be united in a day by a speech, nor in a year by a conference. Europe will be united by stages . . . and the process can be greatly accelerated if we ourselves work hard for peace and understanding."

When Briand boarded the train for Geneva, he was not as optimistic as his more ardent supporters. He was far from sure that even a beginning could be made, but he felt that any sort of federal bond would be a blessing, that even an open and honest discussion of such a bond would facilitate the solution of some difficult problems. He would keep his project within the framework of his broad policy, and seek the help of the statesmen of Europe at every step.

On 5 September, during the general debate at the Tenth Ordinary Session of the League Assembly, Briand made his next move. After calling for a broad and bold approach to the problem of peace, he paused and said:

> I have been associated in recent years with active propaganda in the form of an idea . . . which was conceived many years ago . . . and has been seen at last to supply the answer to a real need. Propagandists have united to spread it abroad, to establish it more firmly in the minds of the nations, and among those propagandists I stand confessed.
>
> At the same time I have never closed my eyes to the difficulties of such an undertaking, nor have I failed to realize the doubtful expediency for a statesman of plunging into what might readily be called an adventure. But all of man's greatest and wisest acts contain, I think, some element of madness or temerity. So I absolved myself in advance and went on; but I proceeded cautiously. . . .
>
> I think that among peoples constituting geographical groups, like the peoples of Europe, there should be some kind of federal bond; it should be possible for them to get in touch at any time to confer about their interests, to agree on joint resolutions and to establish among themselves a bond of solidarity which will enable them to meet any grave emergency that may arise. That is the link that I want to forge.
>
> Obviously, this association will be primarily economic, for that is the most urgent aspect of the question, and I think we may look for success in that direction. Still I am convinced that, politically and socially also, this federal bond might, without affecting the sovereignty of any of the nations belonging to such an association, do useful work, and I intend during this session to ask those of my colleagues here who represent European nations to be good enough to consider this suggestion.[16]

In the interval before the luncheon meeting on 9 September, several of the delegates, including Augustinas Voldemaras of Lithuania, Quinones de Léon of Spain, Stresemann of Germany, Vittorio Scialoja of Italy, and Beneš of Czechoslovakia, took occasion to comment on Briand's project and relate it to the questions that were being debated. On 7 September, Foreign Minister Voldemaras linked the matter of a European bond to the minorities question. "I see a connection between the two problems. If the minority problem develops in accordance with centrifugal principles . . . and if Europe is allowed to go on evolving along these lines, a period of disintegration is bound to ensue. Briand proposes that we should study how best to regroup disintegrated elements, and thus create a stronger centrifugal force. There are great possibilities here."[17]

On the morning of 9 September, Stresemann addressed the Tenth Assembly. Though he was weak and troubled by shortness of breath, the speech was comprehensive and genuine, reflecting both his intense German patriotism and his growing sense of Europe. He spoke of the Saar, of German minorities in eastern Europe, of general disarmament, and he also underlined the need for new economic links and bonds among the states of Europe. He observed that one could not recall without a smile what Germany was like only a short time ago, when each state (*Land*) had its own currency and customs. Europe was now, he said, in much the same condition that Germany was then, and he pictured a train stopped at a frontier, sometimes for hours, for a customs examination. Labeling subdivisions born of national prestige as out of date in Europe and capable of causing immense harm, he called for the rationalization of Europe's economic life and asked: "Where in Europe do we find European currency or European postage stamps?" Finally, he promised that Germany would always be ready to discuss any new proposal for greater economic integration in Europe.[18]

While Scialoja was satisfied with a general reference to Briand's "magnanimous conception" as deserving of close attention and exhaustive consideration, Beneš devoted nearly half of his speech to what he called a "bold conception for a new Europe based on federal principles." The Czechoslovak foreign minister said that Briand's idea was in great part a reflection of the widespread yearning for peace and security in Europe and that it would resolve many problems and difficulties: "When we analyze this idea more closely . . . we cannot but respond to its attraction, we cannot but believe in it and help to bring it about. . . . It will be a long task. It will be worked out gradually, step by step, by all of us, by the efforts of the League, with which this new unit can never conflict in any way. . . . The work will sometimes take a political and sometimes an economic form. It will be the outcome of decades of patient and unremitting labor."

When Beneš finished, it was after midday, and the heads of the delegations of the European states gathered immediately with Briand for what was to be dubbed "The Banquet of Europe." Though journalists were excluded from the meeting, they could see inside, and they were resourceful and many papers on 10 September carried a fairly complete and accurate account of what was said at the luncheon. In opening discussion, Briand, according to *Le Temps* (10 Sept. 1929), told the ministers that he was seeking their advice, and he wanted them to speak freely about his suggestion for federal bonds in Europe. He said he had felt for many years that even the most rudimentary sort of federal structure would undergird peace and security, promote economic coordination and rationalization, and thus provide numerous advantages to all the states.

After Briand had finished, several ministers spoke briefly, among them Henderson and Stresemann who both expressed the view that the idea deserved full and sympathetic consideration, but they insisted that nothing should be undertaken which ran counter to the principle of national sovereignty. Henderson, in addition, insisted that there should not be any move that might weaken the League of Nations or alarm the United States and that all discussions should be in the open. But the ministers of some of the smaller states were much more enthusiastic. For example, Vojislav Marinkovitch, the Yugoslav foreign minister, complimented Briand on his leadership and urged that a detailed plan for political as well as economic organization be drafted to be considered by the governments of Europe before the next session of the assembly.

As the hour for the beginning of the afternoon session drew near, the discussion centered on how the Briand proposal was to be handled. In the end, it was agreed that the Quai d'Orsay would be asked to draft a memorandum on a European federal system; that the governments of the European states would study the memorandum and transmit their views to the Quai d'Orsay; and that the Quai d'Orsay would then draft a report based on these views to be presented to the Eleventh Ordinary Session of the Assembly of the League for discussion and possible action.

While the Briand luncheon all but ended public discussion of a federal project in the Tenth Assembly, the matter of a tariff truce, which was at least indirectly related to the idea of a federal union, did receive some attention in subsequent plenary sessions and in the deliberations of the Second Committee that was concerned with economic problems. Paul Hymans had suggested a tariff truce in his initial speech to the assembly, and William Graham, delegate of the British Empire and president of Britain's Board of Trade, returned to Hyman's proposal just after the Briand luncheon, stating that a customs truce would be in line with Briand's plan and that it might even do much to get the plan going.[19] Then the Second Committee debated the matter at some length and agreed to recommend that the Assembly schedule a Customs Truce Conference for 1930 which would have as its main objective a two-year tariff truce.

Modest and tentative as the moves at Geneva were, they served nonetheless to make the European idea the central theme in a sizable segment of the daily press across much of Europe for a number of days and a more constant theme in the periodical press for many months to come. Although we cannot, for want of space, follow this debate in its full range and depth, we shall take a very brief look at the response of a few of the more important dailies in the key countries of France, Germany, England, Belgium, Switzerland, and Austria.[20] The response in France was so positive that Paul Bloch, Paris correspondent of the *Berliner Tageblatt*, wired his home office: "This time Briand in his speech at Geneva has conquered the whole French press, except for *L'Humanité* and *L'Action française*."[21] Although Bloch's assessment was a bit too favorable, it is true that nearly all of France's best-known dailies warmly applauded Briand and hastened to defend him against charges of idealism, utopianism, and insincerity which they knew would be forthcoming from the extremes of both Right and Left. In fact, a few, including *La République*,

L'Oeuvre, and *Le Soir*, held that Briand should have been bolder in his proposals at Geneva. *La République* (6 Sept. 1929) asserted that Briand had erred on the side of modesty and explained: "Briand says that the main effort will be in the economic domain. Many of us had hoped that it would be in the political domain, and directed at a United States of Europe. . . . What is needed is a broad plan for a European federation."

L'Oeuvre and *Le Soir*, in their issues of 6 September, assured their readers that Briand was not only a statesman of vision and courage but that he also possessed a rare gift for combining idealism and realism. *L'Oeuvre* expressed it most succinctly: "The idealism of a Briand . . . is to foresee and prepare the reality of tomorrow." This journal also suggested that Stresemann's reference to a European currency and a European postage stamp in his speech of 9 September was also evidence of idealism and spoke of the Briand luncheon as the first "Paneuropean banquet," a "historic hour" in the life of Europe.

Le Matin and *Pax* reassured those who were concerned by the fact that Briand had put economic integration ahead of political integration in his 5 September Geneva speech. Both journals believed that Stresemann had pressed for this and that Briand felt it would be a mistake to oppose the German view. On 8 September, Jules Sauerwein, who was rather close to Briand, said in an editorial in *Le Matin* that Briand made no real distinction between political and economic factors, that he would work just as hard for political union as for economic union. He added that Briand was trying above all to create a European consciousness, and he assured his readers that there was no better way to do this than by stressing economic interdependence.

But most important of all, and this was gratifying to Briand, nearly all of the great journals—including *L'Information*, *Le Dépêche de Toulouse*, and *Le Temps*—warmly supported the idea of a federal bond, even though they viewed it cautiously and did not allow their readers to forget that the obstacles to a federal system were enormous. *L'Information* insisted that the main effort at union should be in the economic domain and that everything possible should be done to develop "a loyal and confident collaboration" between Germany and France. It argued editorially that "the best way to league men is to league their interests" and that the best place to start was with small concrete matters. "Many little things are possible which will themselves be useful and which will help to put the European states on the right road. . . . The important thing is to begin, even if with simple digits. But the problem of customs barriers must be included from the first."[22]

Le Dépêche de Toulouse, France's most influential provincial journal, worked hard to promote the Briand project, and said in a lengthy editorial on 15 September: "The United States of Europe are no longer the chimera of a dreamer. They are a necessity if Europe is to live and prosper. . . . And it is to Briand's merit that he saw it at a glance, and it is to his honor that he is trying, day by day, to translate the dream of our greatest poet into living reality."

Few French papers handled the federal project as objectively and realistically as *Le Temps*. This great Paris daily tried to tell its readers exactly what Briand had proposed, how the European foreign ministers reacted, and what the leading papers in France and Europe had to say about it. It also indicated that it was in full sympathy with Briand's proposal and would give it moral support, but it insisted that intensive study and long, delicate negotiations would be required to forge a federal bond. *Le Temps* believed that Briand had acted wisely in merely suggesting an approach and in calling on the governments of Europe to help him devise a plan.[23] The journal said editorially on 7 September: "Europe cannot live much longer floating about, divided and uncoordinated. . . . It must, without delaying too long, proceed to organize its own federation and link its vital forces and common interests as fully as possible."

Perhaps no segment of the moderate Left press in France had as much trouble with Briand's federal initiative as the Socialist papers, for most Socialists continued to insist that federal bonds would weaken the forces of social revolution and bulwark capitalism. Though this feeling of uncertainty about the Briand project was noticeable in *Le Peuple*, the principal organ of the Confédération Générale du Travail, it had less trouble with it than did *Le Populaire*, the central organ of the Socialist party. *Le Peuple* seemed able to salve its conscience by reminding its readers now and then that there was a chance federalism would not make social revolution more difficult. Indeed, this journal, which had been founded in 1921 and was heavily influenced by Francis Delaisi, declared on 6 September that "the time had come for everyone to work for a European federation" and urged that a massive campaign in its behalf be launched through the schools and the press, an approach that it professed to believe could revolutionize mass thinking in a short time.[24]

Le Populaire also gave its support to the federal project, but it was more equivocal and argumentative. The issue of 6 September complimented Briand for formally and prudently launching the idea of a United States of Europe but scolded him sharply for not being able to understand that "the capitalist regime breeds war." In an editorial on 9 September, Léon Blum discussed the federal project at length. Though he spent much time lecturing Briand on the obvious, he agreed that a discussion of the European idea was all to the good because it might curb fascism and would, in any event, promote the spirit of internationalism. He praised Briand for his cautious approach and his stress on the economic side of integration, but he raked the foreign minister for intimating that his project could be realized without any major abridgment of national sovereignties.

As one moves to the Right—to those journals that had been critical of, or hostile to, much of Briand's foreign policy—one encounters a different attitude toward the federal project which was based largely on the fear that the project was strengthening nationalism in Germany and playing into the hands of the Hugenbergs and the Hitlers. *Le Figaro*, like most of the moderately conservative journals, had a great deal of theoretical sympathy for the project but felt that it had little chance of success and would tend to strengthen nationalist forces in Germany. On the extreme Right, *L'Action française* struck hard at Briand's project, labeling it "utopian, meaningless, and dangerous." In stinging editorials, Léon Daudet and Charles Maurras declared that the project was tied up with the dangerous decision to evacuate the Rhineland and that Briand was engaged in the hopeless task of trying to find security for his country in utopian schemes. They declared that Germany had no interest in the project and that Stresemann was giving lip service to it merely to improve his chances of getting the real thing. "If the world were peopled with sheep, something could be said for Briand's project. But in the real world most people believe that they have too little and could defend more. And since this is so, Briand's project is dangerous and even invites attack."[25]

Nor was unyielding opposition to the federal project confined to the extreme Right. *L'Humanité*, official organ of the French Communist party, wrote on 6 September 1929: "Briand's project for a United States of Europe masks the preparations of the capitalist states of Europe for a war of aggression against the Soviet Union."

The response of the German press to the federal initiatives at Geneva was disappointing to good Europeans everywhere. For many were hoping that the Hague Accords, especially the decision to evacuate the third zone of the Rhineland well in advance of the date set in the Versailles Treaty, would moderate the rising tide of nationalism in Germany and strengthen the hands of those working for Franco-German understanding and European solidarity. Now, to the contrary, wide circles in Germany dismissed the decision to evacuate as a thing long overdue, and most German papers proceeded to assess Briand's federal initiative in terms of further German revisionist demands. Actually, the Right wing of the German press, which led the assault on the federal project, was so powerful that it tended to make the press reaction seem even more unfavorable than it was. *Die Münchener neusten Nachrichten* (11 Sept. 1929) did a good job in summing up the central contention when it wrote: "Versailles and Paneuropa are in direct conflict with one another. A European system in the Briand sense is unthinkable until natural frontiers have been restored across Europe." Some of the journals spelled these matters out more positively, stating bluntly that the federal project would dull the dynamism of German policy and weaken its drive for Mitteleuropa, which was, they contended, a German space and a German responsibility.[26]

Moreover, much of the Right press attacked Briand personally, hurling at him such epithets as "phrasemaker" and "puppet of French military circles." *Die Kölnische Zeitung*, though it was much less violent than some papers, called Briand "a good orator but a weak and unsystematic thinker" and asked: "Where is the great project, the great impulsion to federalism, which the French press has been predicting?" *Das Hamburger Fremdenblatt*, and even *Germania*, chided Briand for lack of courage and asked if he had not knuckled under to MacDonald and Henderson.

But unfriendly as this segment of the German press was to the federal project, there were some papers that seemed unsure of the justice of their attacks on Briand and even of the soundness of their main argument. They seemed to suspect that the evidence indicated Briand was doing his best to channel the forces of history toward the pacification and organization of Europe rather than toward the consolidation of the status quo; and it was a well-known fact that French nationalists were attacking the federal project on the grounds that it would undermine, not perpetuate, the Versailles settlement. Too, this feeling that the German attack on Briand was not well grounded seems to have worried many of the liberal and democratic journals, including the *Berliner Tageblatt* and the weekly *Die Hilfe*, and may go far to explain why they had so little to say about the federal project. The *Berliner Tageblatt*, in spite of the exciting reports that its Paris correspondent was sending in, had next to nothing to say about the federal project during these days. Likewise, *Die Hilfe*, which had done much in the early twenties to popularize the European idea in Germany, all but ignored the Briand project.

But the federal project was not without support in the German press. In a long editorial in the *Vossische Zeitung* on 8 September, George Bernhard hailed Briand as a man of great courage and vision, and he argued that Europe's economic position would steadily deteriorate unless the states formed a customs union and created a common market. "What the states and peoples of Europe need to do, above all else, is to form an economic community, and not worry for the moment about the relations of such a community to England and Russia." Two days later this journal treated Stresemann's speech of 9 September at Geneva under the caption: "Stresemann for Paneuropa." In its issue of 10 September, *Acht-Uhr Abendblatt* stated that a Franco-German customs union was within the realm of the possible and declared that such a union would gradually attract all European states to it. *Die Breslauer neuesten Nachrichten* (8 Sept. 1929) complimented Briand on his federal initiative and said that he had acted wisely in placing the emphasis on economic solidarity because such solidarity was not only urgently needed but would help "to stabilize political relations in Europe." *Vorwärts*, though decidedly reserved, said that the federal project should be given careful consideration and urged the German government to work for closer relations with France and for European solidarity.[27]

Moreover, most of Germany's economically oriented journals, except for *Deutsche Tages-Zeitung* and some other agricultural papers, showed interest not only in economic rationalization but also in the idea of a European customs union and a European market. The *Ruhr und Rhein Wirtschaftszeitung* said that it was hard to oppose the federal project on rational grounds and reminded its readers that Briand had the solid and enthusiastic backing of many prominent Frenchmen, including Herriot, Loucheur, Caillaux, Le Trocquer, Clémentel, and Jouvenel.[28] The *Berliner Börsen Courier* also took the federal project seriously and even published in its issue of 14 September 1929 an article by Arnold Rechberg in which the enigmatic industrialist endorsed the project and declared that it was the logical consequence of the chain of industrial accords that had been developing since the middle twenties and had "already ruptured the principle of the Treaty of Versailles."[29]

The reaction of the British press to Briand's federal project was perhaps more uniform and clear cut than that of any of the continental states. This was so in large measure because of certain basic concepts and facts of history and geography. The traditional doctrine of the balance of power was still a factor in British thought and policy. England's economy was a world economy that pivoted heavily on her vast colonial empire, and most Britishers had come to see England's destiny largely in terms of the development and integration of this empire. Also, many felt that, if a European community developed, it would surround itself with "an unscalable tariff wall" and become both hard to deal with and hard to live with.[30] The great conservative dailies, including the *Daily Express*, the *Daily Telegraph*, the *Evening Standard*, and the *Morning Post*, took almost exactly the same position. The *Daily Express* put it this way: "Our people have no more intention of being a part of Europe fiscally than politically. . . . Let us organize the British Empire as a single economic whole. Let us link the boundless productive capacities of the Dominions and Colonies with the pre-eminent manufacturing resources of Great Britain in an impregnable and mutually profitable alliance."[31]

While the Liberal and Labour papers also held that Britain's destiny lay with the dominions and colonies rather than in union with Europe, they said it more gently and were slightly more inclined to see some good even for England in a loose European structure. The liberal *Manchester Guardian* and *The Economist* discussed the project, which they regarded as a possibility at the economic level, without serious alarm, and *The Daily News* and *Daily Herald* said that it was clear that the nations of Europe would have to put an end to their deadly and futile wars or they would perish. Still they felt that the widening of the League of Nations, not a European union, was the true way out.[32]

The three smaller states—Belgium, Switzerland, and Austria—held special significance for the European movement. All of them had common frontiers with Germany, and all except Austria adjoined France. Belgium occupied a strategic geographic position and had close relations with Britain and France. Switzerland was a federal state with German, French, and Italian regions, and most federalists felt that she might serve as a model for a European federation.

Austria was a Germanic state at least linguistically and culturally, and Vienna was regarded by many as the most cosmopolitan city on the Continent.

The response of the Belgian press to the federal project was similar to that of the French press, though it put more stress on the economic aspects of the project. *L'Indépendance belge*, *Le Soir*, and *Le libre Belgique* represented a rather large part of the population and spoke in much the same way. On 11 September 1929, *Le Soir*, Brussels's great Socialist daily, said that a customs union could be worked out within the framework of the League of Nations, that England could be associated with it, and that it would stimulate the growth of the whole European economy. *La libre Belgique* (12 Sept. 1929) put it briefly and simply: "Briand has set in motion a project for an integrated Europe and there should be progressive if slow realization."[33]

The Swiss press, though a little more reserved than the French and Belgian presses, took the federal project seriously and handled it in a natural, matter-of-fact manner. The *Journal de Genève*, the leading French-language journal, and the *Neue Zürcher Zeitung*, the best of the German-language journals, tended to set the tone of the Swiss response, and both were favorable to the federal initiative but cautious, sounding much like *Le Temps*.

The reaction of the Austrian press to the federal project was in some respects more interesting than the press of any other country. Austria was a new, rather weak political entity, and many Austrians toyed much with the idea of union with Germany as well as union with Europe. German pressures were heavy and they were mainly on the side of the Anschluss, and it seems safe to say that there was more support for the federal project in Austria than the press indicates. Even the *Neue freie Presse*, Austria's most influential paper and champion of the Paneuropean movement, was not quite true to its beliefs. Its initial reaction to Briand's European initiative was enthusiastic enough, but it tended to retreat a bit as the German response became clear. Nevertheless, the journal did not shift its position, and in an editorial on 10 September, it concluded that Stresemann's speech, as well as Briand's proposal, was "an event of far reaching significance."[34] Many other Austrian papers, including the *Wiener Allgemeine Zeitung*, said essentially the same thing, and few Austrian papers, except those under Pan-German and Nationalist influence, such as the *Deutsche Österreichische Tageszeitung*, the *Wiener Neueste Nachrichten*, and *Freie Stimme*, rejected the federal project outright.

It is impossible for me to generalize about the Czech press because only one Czech paper, the semi-official *Prager Presse*, was available for examination, but I can say that this journal kept its readers informed of the federal initiatives at Geneva and carried both articles and editorials in support of them.[35]

Chapter 15

THE EFFORT TO ADVANCE

THE FEDERAL PROJECT

Although the sense of elation that had come to good Europeans after the Briand luncheon was dampened by reaction in England, Italy, and Germany, it was in no sense destroyed. To good Europeans the fact of the hour was not the reaction in certain states to the federal project but the fact that there was a federal project. Most of them instinctively felt that whatever might be the fate of such a project, Europe was evolving, and they were working for an idea that had a future. Moreover, most of them noted with satisfaction that the federal project was being taken seriously across the Atlantic by the *Commercial and Financial Chronicle* as well as *The New York Times*, and some were soon to call attention to an article in the *Magazine of Wall Street* in which Theodore Knappen wrote: "It cannot be doubted that the organization of a United States of Europe in an economic sense is now seriously undertaken. With the possibility that the first measure of such a union may be realized by 1931, it behooves Americans to ponder seriously how such a union may affect their interests."[1]

Elated as good Europeans were over Briand's federal initiative, they were not optimistic about their chances of forging a federal bond. The thing, of course, that worried them most was the situation in Germany. Not only had the German reaction to the federal project been disappointing but nationalism was surging. Nationalists and National Socialists were striking ever more savagely at the Young Plan, the Hague Accords, and many of Stresemann's policies. On 11 September, two days after the Briand luncheon and three weeks before Stresemann's death, Adolf Hitler joined with Alfred Hugenberg, chairman of the Nationalist party, Heinrich Class, president of the Pan-German League, and Franz Seldte, director of the *Stahlhelm*, in calling for a plebiscite on a law "against the enslavement of the German people." This strange and fervently nationalist document also called for official repudiation of the "war guilt lie" and stated that any member of the German government who sought to negotiate an agreement with a foreign power should be imprisoned.[2] Then after the death of Stresemann on 3 October 1929, they called more insistently for the rejection of the Young Plan, the return of the Saar, and the energetic pursuit of both Anschluss and Mitteleuropa. Prince Karl Rohan wrote that Germany's primary task for the twentieth century was to organize Mitteleuropa, make it into a solid German space, and that the "Coudenhove-Briand Plan" would have to be rejected because it did not allow for the fulfillment of that task.[3]

Still, millions of Germans, including Chancellor Müller, reacted strongly against the Hugenberg-Hitler-Class-Seldte offensive and many democratic and socialist journals, including *Vorwärts*, presented the Hugenberg venture as an act of desperation that would backfire and bury the Nationalists forever.[4] Max Clauss, though he was not sure the Nationalists were digging their own graves, was sure they were behaving recklessly and irresponsibly. He insisted that Germany had made great gains of late and that she needed above all to exercise self-discipline, continue Stresemann's policies, and grasp the fact that her "European hour" was at hand.[5] And there were many, even in industrial circles, who agreed in general with Max Clauss. At a meeting of the Reichsverband der Deutschen Industrie in Düsseldorf on 20 September 1929, Ludwig Kastl and Richard Heilner gave the principal papers, which stressed the interdependence of the European states and the need for economic bonds. Kastl quoted key sentences from Briand's speech of 5 September and Stresemann's speech of 9 September at Geneva, insisting that Germany would make a grave mistake by refusing to discuss seriously "European economic bonds." Heilner, who had spoken out many times against Europe's custom barriers, said what Germany and Europe needed most of all was a Franco-German understanding and a customs union with its open market. He quoted Franz Oppenheimer to this effect, argued that this was the direction in which Stresemann was working, and indicated that no other course offered Germany so much economically and politically.[6] Even such a confirmed apostle of Anschluss and Mitteleuropa as Gustav Stolper disagreed sharply with the methods, if not the aims, of Hugenberg and his associates. Stolper told them that they were entirely wrong in believing that Germany could regain the freedom to rearm and recover the lost provinces by "catastrophic methods."[7]

Further to the left, *Die Menschheit* labeled the behavior of the Nationalists and Nazis as wanton and senseless and wrote: "We [Germans] should speak sometimes of our obligations to Europe and not always of Europe's obligations to us; we should renounce Pan-Germanism and work to unite rather than divide Eastern and Western Europe; we should offer an Eastern Locarno in exchange for the evacuation of the Rhineland; and we should stop our secret rearmament and work for a federated Europe."[8]

But most good Europeans, pleased and encouraged as they were by the efforts of German moderates, remained very troubled about the situation in Germany. They could see few signs that Germany was moving toward a policy of European pacification—a development that they felt Stresemann had promised and Briand's policies had assumed. Still they believed deeply in their program, were determined to work hard, and hoped that *Vorwärts* was right in asserting that Germany's Social Democrats could take care of the

Nationalists and the National Socialists. *La Paix par le droit* urged its readers to redouble their efforts for peace and for a united Europe and asked them "to hope that Germany will respond to the needs of the hour."[9] Publicist Georges Roux agreed that the situation in Germany was disturbing, but he insisted that German opinion was still "hesitating and oscillating" and advised against any change in French policy as long as there was a reasonable chance for a Franco-German rapprochement. Roux wrote: "The Germans . . . apparently expected Locarno to solve all of their problems. . . . While they are not responding to French advances, no one can as yet say what the orientation of this immense mass of Germans, derobed of their ancient imperial armor, will be."[10] Wladimir d'Ormesson, whose new book, *Confiance en Allemagne?* was being widely read, admitted he was surprised at the nature and force of the Hugenberg assault "on the Weimar system" and at the "undeniable gains" that the National Socialists were making. He did not conceal the fact that he was finding it increasingly difficult to have confidence, and he pleaded with the Germans to discipline themselves, to show a sense of responsibility if not of "penitence."[11]

When good Europeans looked at Europe as a whole, they saw much that encouraged them. Plans for a customs truce conference were going smoothly; the French and Belgians were proceeding with the evacuation of the Second Zone of the Rhineland; the Quai d'Orsay and the Wilhelmstrasse were ready to open talks on the future of the Saar; the British and Americans were drafting plans for a new conference aimed at the further limitation of naval armaments; and they themselves had journals and organizations with which to work. As Borel put it: "We want Europe to live. It can only really live if it is united. When a thing is necessary, it is the duty and task of statesmen to make it possible. . . . If the people of Europe can be made to understand how essential a measure of union is to their future, a formula will be found."[12]

While we cannot explore their resolute and many-sided effort in its entirety, we shall examine briefly the labors of one of their more devoted workers, Edouard Herriot; the initiatives that they launched through both the Twenty-Seventh World Peace Congress and the Collège Libre des Sciences Sociales de Paris; the work of some of the more important private organizations that they controlled or influenced; and finally the Customs Truce Conference, which they tried to bend to their ends.

Although a host of men and women made substantial personal efforts during these weeks in behalf of Briand's federal initiative, it is doubtful that anyone worked harder or more effectively than Edouard Herriot. Just after the Briand luncheon, Coudenhove began urging Herriot to undertake a lecture tour across central and eastern Europe in behalf of the federal project. With Briand's blessing, Herriot agreed to lecture in Vienna, Prague, and Berlin during the second week of October if Coudenhove would help with arrangements. Coudenhove, overjoyed at this opportunity to work with the distinguished Frenchman, asked the leaders of the Paneuropean groups in Vienna, Prague, and Berlin to make ready for Herriot's coming while he sought to persuade top government officials in the three capitals to attend the lectures.

Arriving in Vienna on 8 October, Herriot was met by a delegation from the Austrian government and a group of youths who were wearing the symbol of the Paneuropean Union and chanting "Hoch Europa!" That evening Herriot spoke to an audience that jammed Vienna's Concert Hall and included Chancellor Schober, former chancellors Seipel and Streeruwitz, as well as nearly all high-level government officials. According to the *Neue freie Presse*, Herriot spoke with great earnestness and stated firmly that the states of Europe would have to organize into a federal union if they were to live and prosper. He also expressed the view that Anglo-American opposition to such a structure was greatly exaggerated in certain quarters.[13]

Herriot went to Berlin on 10 October and hastened to lay a wreath on Stresemann's grave, but the warmth and cordiality that he had met with in Vienna was lacking in Berlin. Chancellor Müller did not attend his lecture and only a small portion of the Berlin press played up his presence or gave an analysis of his address.[14] The *Berliner Tageblatt* did little more than announce his arrival, while the *Lokal Anzeiger* (11 Oct. 1929) called his speech "insincere and sonorous," declaring that he had done nothing while he was president of the Council of Ministers "to alleviate the intolerable oppression that lay upon Germany." But the Prussian minister of culture was authorized to give a small luncheon for him, and this gave him an opportunity to speak with a number of Prussian officials and educational leaders.

In Prague on the following day, Herriot received another warm welcome. The *Prager Presse* kept his picture on its front page throughout his stay and said on the day of his arrival that no one embodied the European spirit in a fuller measure or was better qualified to judge the extent to which that spirit could be translated into political and economic realities. Nearly all members of the Czech government were in Radio Hall for his address. In introducing him Foreign Minister Beneš made a confession of faith in the European idea which attracted wide attention and was much quoted or paraphrased in the following months.[15] In his speech Herriot repeated the substance of what he had said in Vienna and Berlin and made a special appeal to the whole Czechoslovak nation to support the European idea. He concluded with a tribute to President Masaryk, calling him a great European, a great Czech, and a living example of the fact that "love of Europe can be combined with love of country."

Herriot was obviously well pleased with his tour, and when he arrived home in Lyon, he told a group of journalists that he had argued in Berlin, as well as Vienna and Prague, for the establishment of a permanent agency to study European problems and to assist with the drafting of a plan for the organization of Europe. While this idea of a formal committee to study European union had long been in the air, Herriot's open support gave it additional impetus.[16] But Herriot's main concern at this time was the Radical Socialist party congress, which he attended at its opening in Reims on 24 October. He knew that many other party leaders, including Daladier and Montigny, were actively working for the federal project and felt that they would approve a strong statement in support of the project. He spoke on the second day and told the delegates his trip to Austria, Germany, and Czechoslovakia had strengthened his feeling "That a union of the states of Europe is possible." He then argued that a program of economic rationalization was feasible, that it would bolster the peace structure, and that the party should say this in its platform. He got something of what he wanted. When the new platform was adopted, it stated that the party would, in its "vigorous pursuit of peace, work for a political and economic rapprochement with Germany, the use of compulsory arbitration in all conflicts, the reduction and control of armaments, and the conclusion of customs accords as the first step toward a federated Europe."[17]

While Herriot had hoped that the party congress would endorse the federal project in a more striking fashion, he was not disheartened and continued to speak and write for the federal project. In the Chamber of Deputies on 26 December 1929, he joined Franklin-Bouillon, Georges Mandel, and others in a discussion of the European idea, and he urged his colleagues to put the matter of the organization of Europe nearer the center of French foreign policy, warning them that a sword would hang over Europe until it organized itself.[18] In the early weeks and months of 1930, Herriot's writings became more important than his speeches. He published, among others, a solid article entitled "Pan-Europe" in *Foreign Affairs* (Feb. 1930), and he pushed to completion the manuscript for *Europe*, which appeared in French, English, and German editions in 1930.

The initiatives taken by the Twenty-Seventh World Peace Congress, which met in Athens, Greece, from 6 to 12 October 1929, were modest but attracted considerable attention. Briand's Geneva moves were discussed in connection with the League of Nations, and in the course of the debate it became clear that many of the delegates from the European states felt that a European structure would strengthen the league. In the end the congress adopted a resolution that, among other things, commended Briand for courage and vision, called for a vigorous effort to create "a European political and economic structure set within the framework of the League of Nations," and urged that "Stresemann's suggestion for a European currency" be made a matter of study at Geneva.[19]

Just after the World Peace Congress adjourned, the Collège Libre des Sciences Sociales in Paris decided to organize a special lecture program in behalf of the federal project. The European idea was to be broken down and presented in its principal parts in accordance with the Cartesian method. A panel of lecturers—including Emile Borel, Henri Truchy, Francis Delaisi, Henri Jouvenel, Arthur Fontaine, Georges Scelle, Charles Brun, and De Peyerimhoff—was quickly lined up. The lectures, which started in early November 1929 and ran into the spring of 1930, touched in depth nearly every question raised by the federal project and echoed far beyond the lecture hall. Not only did many French dailies give lengthy summaries of them but several appeared as articles in a variety of periodicals.[20]

In a brief look at the efforts of the more important of the private organizations, we shall give primary attention to the special emphases and programs that they developed. The Paneuropean Union, still limping from the ordeal that it had gone through in Germany in the preceding year, decided to make a more determined effort to gain mass support, especially in Germany, and to do the ground work for a second Paneuropean congress to be held in the spring of 1930. So during the autumn of 1929 and the winter of 1930, stress was placed on a propaganda campaign, and Coudenhove himself worked with amazing energy.

Not only did he encourage the chairmen of the national and local groups to hold frequent meetings and to wage membership drives, but he also directed the establishment of the Central Pan-european Bureau for Institutions of Higher Learning, drafted and circulated a model statute for a European federation, and wrote numerous articles for *Paneuropa* and other journals. Convinced that the fate of the federal project would be decided in Germany, he called on the members of the Paneuropean Union to think first of Germany and to make a maximum effort "to awaken the Paneuropean soul of the German people."[21] He spoke out repeatedly against the German Nationalists and Nazis and against the Mitteleuropa ideology, which he reluctantly admitted had been given new life by the decision to evacuate the Rhineland and which he believed was a deadly enemy of Paneurope. He told German Democrats and Right-wing Socialists during these months that National Socialism in Germany was a danger to the whole of Europe, and he even predicted that if it was triumphant in Germany it would lead to another war within a decade. But the Paneuropean organizational effort at the local level was not very successful. While *Paneuropa* listed approximately one hundred local Paneuropean meetings between October 1929 and April 1930, it listed few new local groups. Moreover, in Germany where the organizational effort was centered, many of the local groups seemed more wayward than ever, tending to select speakers for their meetings who were known to be cool to the European idea.[22] Coudenhove's influence on the local groups was declining, and he was looking more and more to Briand.

The League for European Cooperation made bold and ambitious plans in support of Briand's initiative. Borel and Heile decided at once on two major moves. First, they would make a strenuous effort to steer the national leagues, especially those of France, Germany, and Britain, toward a substantial common program; and second, they would try to organize a series of spectacular demonstrations in support of the federal project in the capitals of several European states which would be climaxed by a giant demonstration and "work-week" in Berlin. Both men felt the need for face-to-face talks, and Heile agreed to spend several days in Paris in the latter part of October. However, Heile, who was quite shaken by Stresemann's death in more ways than one, decided to inform Chancellor Müller of what was being planned before leaving for Paris. He wrote the chancellor, who was an honorary president of the German union, a long letter and invited him to speak on European federalism during the "work-week" that was being planned for Berlin in December.[23] Although the chancellery promptly acknowledged Heile's communication and thanked him for the information it contained, it did not mention its displeasure with his efforts in behalf of the European idea or that it intended to work in a cautious way to block the "work-week" in Berlin.

Heile went to Paris at the end of the third week of October, and he, Borel, and Jules Rais, executive secretary of the Federal Committee, attempted to coordinate the French, German, and British groups, drafting a questionnaire designed to provide needed data. But after studying the French and German responses to the questionnaire and talking with Rennie Smith, chairman of the British group, they realized that the differences among the national groups were so great that any sort of a common program was out of reach. They felt, nevertheless, that the data they had acquired through the questionnaires would be helpful in carrying out some of the established programs.

On 7 November, shortly after his return to Germany, Heile wrote Chancellor Müller another note dealing with his experiences in France and the impressions that he had formed while there. He told the chancellor something of the Radical Socialist Party Congress that he had attended and addressed, and he hinted that it was to be regretted that the German press did not respond more warmly to the efforts of men like Herriot and Daladier to achieve an understanding with Germany and a general European pacification. He wrote: "On the matter of a general understanding, let me say that the great majority of the French Chamber—and even a larger majority of the French people—are for a European program, and this gratifying fact would stand out much more strikingly were it not for inner political differences."[24]

By mid-November, Heile was beginning to realize that his government was strongly opposed to his plan for a week-long demonstration in Berlin and that Foreign Minister Curtius was not as interested in him or the League for European Cooperation as Stresemann had been. Unable to make a real go of either of their special projects, Borel and Heile turned to more modest goals but did not relax their efforts. Yet both were chastened and realized that there were limits to what they could do.

The organization for a European Customs Union was not affected as much by the steps taken at Geneva as was the League for European Cooperation, largely because its membership was made up mainly of economic experts and businessmen, and it was less sensitive to political developments. Firmly convinced that a customs union should be the starting point for any sort of federal structure, the members of this organization noted with satisfaction that even Herriot was saying: "For the moment the greatest hope lies in the construction of a customs union." They tended to concentrate more wholeheartedly on their own program, and many of them believed that once a customs union was started, it would itself become a powerful integrating force, generating many new impulses to unity.[25] Although the International Committee for a European Customs Union was fairly active, the real response to the federal project was made by the national committees, with the French Study Committee setting the pace. The French group came up with two new projects that were to bear fruit. First, it would endeavor to collect and organize a large body of "precise and usable economic data," and second, it would plan a European-wide customs union congress for the spring of 1930.

After making general plans for the customs union congress, the study group settled down to the business of gathering and processing pertinent economic data. But anxious to get the more salient economic facts before the public as soon as possible, it decided to publish immediately a small economic atlas and then begin the preparation of a comprehensive but attractive European yearbook. The little atlas was soon published in Paris under the title of *Atlas économique de l'Europe*, and one of its more attractive and informative maps appeared regularly in *L'Europe de demain*.

Work on the yearbook went slowly because it was designed as a one volume encyclopedia of the customs union movement in Europe. When the manuscript was finally finished in the late summer of 1930, it ran to over twelve hundred pages and contained short biographical sketches and pictures of some four hundred of the leading personalities in the customs union movement as well as a substantial documentary history of the movement.[26]

In addition to these two major projects, the French Study Committee sponsored numerous lectures; sent a memorandum to the Customs Truce Conference; undertook a thorough assessment of the weaknesses in the customs union movement; and even sponsored a plan for European nationality and thus dual citizenship.[27] In its analysis of the weakness of the customs union movement, the French group came to the conclusion that economic disparities among the states of Europe were a far more serious problem than had been generally realized and that it would be wise for the time being for them to work for a regional customs union to be composed of France, Germany, Belgium, the Netherlands, and Luxembourg—five states that constituted a sort of natural unity, geographically, economically, and culturally. It was felt that a second customs union would gradually emerge among the Danubian states and that the two would then merge into a European union.

Of the older organizations, the International League for Peace and Freedom, the Association for Peace through Law, and the Association for the League of Nations seem most deserving of brief comments, though several others worked actively. When the French section of the International League for Peace and Freedom, which had been proclaiming a united Europe for some sixty years, met for its autumn session on 14 October 1929, it resolved for the immediate future to see if it could find in history an instance of federal organization that might be used as a rough model for a European structure. When President Guebin called for discussion of the first of these questions, three instances of federal organization were immediately suggested: the Swiss Confederation, the American Union, and the German Zollverein. While the members were all but unanimous in the view that the Swiss Confederation had most to offer, they knew so little about the history of the Swiss Confederation that they quickly decided to leave the matter of historical models to a later meeting and to move on immediately to economic bonds.[28] Here they felt more at home, and they stayed with the question of economic organization through the sessions of the winter and spring of 1930. They concluded that the principal cause of Europe's economic ills was political and economic fragmentation, aggravated by insecurity and the fear of war, and that the cure was an extensive program of economic integration grounded in a customs union and a common market. But confident as they were of the accuracy of their diagnosis and prescription, they were far from sure that the patient could be persuaded to take the medicine. But they were quite practical in their outlook, as their discussions had forced them to the conclusion that a customs union and a common market would require enormous changes.

The Association for Peace through Law, with its network of local groups across France and Belgium, hailed the federal project with enthusiasm. The executive committee, which had already scheduled the annual meeting for 2–3 November 1929 in Bordeaux, now decided to put the federal project on its agenda. Théodore Ruyssen urged the chairmen of local groups to discuss the project with their members and to prepare summaries of their views for use by the delegates at the annual meeting. Most of the delegates were lawyers, journalists, and economists, and the debate on European federation though animated was rather realistic. Francis Delaisi read a paper based on his new book *Les Deux Europes* and argued that the projected Bank of International Settlements could be made the cornerstone for a European currency and a great common market resting on Europe's 240,000,000 people.

In the final hours of the meeting, the delegates adopted a resolution that called for a European federation set within the framework of the League of Nations and having "a military establishment sufficient to protect the union."[29] Local chapters in France and Belgium gave the resolution publicity and worked in other ways to promote the federal project, but as the weeks passed they worried increasingly about events in Germany and their hopes for a federal bond slowly ebbed.

The French Association for the League of Nations was unable to restrain itself after Briand used the forum of the League Assembly to launch the federal project. The French Association now decided to put the matter of joint endorsement before the Union of Associations for the League of Nations, which was scheduled to meet in Zurich in late November 1929 and to act alone if its sister associations held back. This course was taken and, when the Union of Associations refused to endorse the federal project, the French group met in Paris on 15 December 1929 and drafted a resolution endorsing the project and calling for the creation of "a special section within the League to study regional problems." It is doubtful that any other endorsement of the federal project underlined so forcefully the strength of the European idea in France. This large organization had links with numerous other private bodies including the French Association for Disabled War Veterans, whose executive council spoke out for the federal project at this time. Apparently it was the effort made by many of the larger private organizations in France that led Senator Frédéric François-Marsal to write at the end of 1929: "If a plebiscite were held today in the countries to the west of the Russian frontier, I believe that the great majority of the peoples would pronounce in favor of a firm and stable union of these states."[30]

Lastly, we come to the effort of the leaders of the European movement to channel political and diplomatic currents behind the federal project. Though they worked across the whole political and diplomatic front and took real interest in both the Second Hague Conference and the London Naval Conference, no official international event intrigued them as much as the Customs Truce Conference, which had been projected at Geneva in association with the Briand project. *La Journée industrielle* (16 Jan. 1930) called it a direct supplement to Briand's Paneuropa plan, and *La République* (13 Jan. 1930) referred to it as a conference for the limitation of commercial armaments. But the point most stressed was that if it could achieve a two-year customs truce, which was its principal immediate goal, it would provide a period for calm deliberation in the highly sensitive areas of trade practices and policies, which might, in the words of the *Vossische Zeitung* (15 Feb. 1930) "lay the basis for the economic reordering of all Europe."

The Truce Conference opened on 17 February 1930 with delegations present from twenty-six European and four non-European states. Immediately following the opening ceremonies, Paul Hymans, one of the original sponsors of the conference, told the group that Europe's greatest need was a vast program of economic rationalization and that a customs truce could provide the security and peace necessary for the achievement of such a program: "In our time economics and politics are interwoven. . . . Peace cannot mature and grow strong in an atmosphere of economic rivalry and war."[31]

While Hyman's plea made a strong impression on the conference, protectionism was still deeply entrenched and as the days passed it became increasingly clear that a two-year customs truce lay well beyond the reach of the conference. In early March, Pierre Flandin, French minister of commerce and industry and head of the French delegation, stated that the conference would have to lower its sights. He made it clear that the French delegation would be satisfied if the participating states would agree to maintain all of their bilateral trade treaties for a full year and to renew negotiations at that time. Several of the other delegations, including those of Belgium and Germany, supported this suggestion, and it became the basis of future discussion. On 24 March 1930, after eleven of the states had signed a Commercial Convention, a Protocol Concerning a Program of Future Negotiations, and a Final Act, the conference adjourned.

The core of the modest achievement of the conference was set out in the first article of the Commercial Convention which read: "The high contracting parties undertake not to avail themselves before 1 April 1931 of the right to denounce the bilateral commercial treaties that any one of them has concluded with any one of the other high contracting parties and that are in force on this day." The document concerning future negotiations listed an array of problems for discussion and promised that another economic conference would be held before 30 April 1931. The Final Act, which was very brief, stated the hope that the Commercial Convention would open the road to economic cooperation in Europe. Many Frenchmen believed that the outcome of this conference served to convince Briand that meaningful economic bonds across Europe were out of the question until political and moral bonds had been strengthened.[32]

But discouraging as the outcome of the Customs Truce Conference was to good Europeans, it was the course of events in Germany that worried them most. The Germans were now sharply divided over the ratification of the Young Plan and were faced with many grave problems of an economic nature, including mounting unemployment and budgetary deficits. The National Socialists, aided both morally and financially by Hitler's association with Hugenberg, Class, and Seldte, had made substantial gains in local elections in many parts of the country and were becoming increasingly militant and violent. In fact, they were doing precisely what many well-known Germans— including Max Scheler, Ernst Troeltsch, Johannes Bell, and even Stresemann —had been saying all along must not be done. They were glorifying blood and authoritarianism. In practicing an arrogant and militant nationalism, they were widening the gulf between German thought and feeling and West European and American thought and feeling. At the same time the Great Coalition was breaking apart, and Chancellor Müller's health was declining. On 11 March 1930, four days after Hjalmar Schacht had resigned from the Reichsbank, President Hindenburg conferred with Hermann Brüning, who was now floor leader of the Center party and was talking in terms of a solid alignment of front-line soldiers in all parties. On 28 March just after the Customs Truce

Conference adjourned, Hindenburg charged Brüning with the formation of a type of presidential cabinet that would be less dependent on the Reichstag. Though Brüning possessed many admirable qualities, he was a conservative nationalist and obviously not the man to push the federal project.

However, there was an element in the German situation that tended in a small way to moderate the attack on the federal project. It was a growing feeling in some governmental circles in Germany that the European idea might be used to advance the Anschluss and Mitteleuropa programs. Some good Europeans, including Hantos, had argued all along that the organization of eastern Europe could facilitate the organization of all Europe. In fact, Austrian Chancellor Johannes Schober and German Foreign Minister Julius Curtius had discussed the European idea and the Briand project in connection with Anschluss when they met in Berlin on 22 February 1930, and they had tentatively agreed to argue that their customs union project would promote Briand's initiative and thus the unification of Europe.[33]

But Curtius and Schober were working in secrecy, and their customs union project would not come to light for more than a year. Meantime, most good Europeans, though deeply worried about events in Germany, continued to work and even managed to keep a bit of hope. They pointed to the Young Plan, the evacuation of the Rhineland, Germany's growing need for loans, and the virtual certainty of higher tariffs in the United States as developments in the making that could yet swing German opinion in the direction that Briand was pointing.[34] A glimmer of the range and character of this hope may be seen in the words of Emile Vandervelde and Richard Riedl, two well-known Europeans. Writing on the eve of the Customs Truce Conference, Vandervelde put it this way: "True, the outlook is not too promising, but it is necessary to hope and to act. Economic nationalism remains powerful, but I do not believe that it can continue to hold the upper hand. . . . If Europe is to survive, it must be truly organized and united and cease to be a powder keg of divided and hostile states." A few weeks later Riedl, a warm champion of the Anschluss, wrote: "What today is attainable, and very necessary, is a sort of economic federation that will provide not only a definite guarantee for the security of Europe but also a foundation for its prosperity. All beyond this belongs to the future, and will have to grow freely and organically, not as a hothouse plant but as a tree."[35]

Chapter 16

THE MEMORANDUM ON A

FEDERAL UNION

By the early spring of 1930, there was growing speculation, especially among good Europeans, as to when the French Foreign Office would release its memorandum on a European federal system. Obviously Briand and his colleagues could not wait much longer, for by the terms of the agreement of 9 September 1929, the European governments were to have the memorandum in time to make formal replies to it some weeks in advance of the opening of the Eleventh Session of the League Assembly.

While Briand realized full well that the chance of getting any sort of European bond was very slight, he was determined to press on and to have a plan for the federal system on time. For not only did he feel that even the most tentative and rudimentary federal bond would help keep the great issues of the hour at the European level, and thus help ward off another bloody and destructive war, but he believed firmly that this was the direction in which the creative forces of history were pointing. So in late April and early May 1930, the men of the Quai d'Orsay led by Alexis Léger, chief of the political section, put the finishing touches on the Memorandum on the Organization of a System of European Federal Union.[1] On 9 May, Briand told Arthur Henderson, British foreign secretary, that the memorandum was in proof form and that it would soon be sent to all European governments and to a few beyond Europe as well.[2]

The day selected for the release of the memorandum was 17 May because that was the day on which the French Foreign Office was to make two important announcements: first, that all conditions had been met for putting the Young Plan and the Bank of International Settlements into full operation; and second, that the evacuation of the Rhineland would be completed by 30 June 1930. It was also the day on which the Second Paneuropean Congress was scheduled to open in Berlin and the day on which Daniel Serruys was to give a paper on the question of a United States of Europe before the eighth session of the Franco-German Committee for Information and Documentation in Heidelberg. Briand and some others at the Quai d'Orsay hoped that this concordance of significant and related events would make a profound impression in Europe and give the memorandum an added boost.

The text of the memorandum produced a double surprise. First, it was much longer than had been expected, and second, it had more to say about political and moral forces and the consolidation of peace than about economic bonds.[3] It reaffirmed the fact that Briand felt strongly that, in the larger sense, economics were at the mercy of politics in Europe and that there was little chance of getting viable economic bonds until there was a decided improvement in the political and moral climate. The memorandum was divided into a preface, four sections, and a conclusion. The preface explained how the memorandum came into being and argued that a European structure could largely eliminate the causes of conflict in Europe and do much "to bring European interests into harmony under the control of, and in conformity with, the League of Nations." The first section stated that one of Europe's greatest needs was a general pact that would "affirm in principle and consecrate in fact the moral union and solidarity of the states." The second section dealt with organs of government, proposing a structure that was much like that of the League of Nations and was to function in close association with the League.[4] There was to be a European Conference, a Permanent Political Committee, and a Secretariat. The European Conference, which was described as the directing body of the union, was a general assembly on which all of the member states were to have representatives. It would meet at regular intervals but could be called into special session if the need arose. The Permanent Political Committee, which was to be composed of representatives of certain member nations to be designated later, was to act both as an executive body and as an organ of research and study. The Secretariat was to work closely with the Secretariat of the League of Nations and was to be enlarged as needed. The specific powers and functions of the European Conference and the Permanent Political Committee were to be decided at the next conference of the European states, to be held just before the Eleventh Regular Session of the league.

The third section of the memorandum attempted to define the broad principles and concepts necessary for the development of a positive European program. It stated that the initial effort at such a European program should be made on the political plane and that the political structure should be a federation founded on the idea of a "union rather than a unity," elastic enough "to respect the sovereignty of each state and firm enough to guarantee the benefits of collective solidarity." On the economic side, the broad objective was an economic pact that would have as its goal the establishment of a common market and the highest possible living standard.

The fourth section indicated in bold strokes nine areas in which programs of cooperation should be initially established. These ranged from laboratories and libraries to highways and railroads. The conclusion urged the European governments to get their comments to the Quai d'Orsay by 15 July and added: "The hour has never been more propitious nor the need more urgent for a constructive effort in Europe. . . . To unite in order to live and prosper; that is the imperious necessity which henceforth confronts the nations of Europe."

The memorandum was a bit bolder and more precise than had been generally expected, and it appears that the Quai d'Orsay had proposed as strong a structure as it felt it could without running the risk of having it rejected out of hand by several governments, including those of Britain and Germany. By the terms of the memorandum, Briand was essentially free to try to create a structure largely independent of the League of Nations. Lucien Coquet said that the memorandum was a logical product of Briand's policies and represented "his philosophy and aspirations more fully both in spirit and substance than any other document of the time, including the Covenant of the League of Nations and the Locarno Pact."[5] It was often said that Briand looked upon the memorandum as a sort of summation and projection of his hopes and dreams for the Europe of the future.

The Germans, the British, and the Italians reacted to the memorandum almost exactly as they had reacted to the Geneva initiatives. As Claude J. Gignoux put it in *Journée industrielle* (20 May 1930): "Last September Briand launched a federal balloon at Geneva. He hoped for favorable winds but the winds have been weak in Germany, England, and Italy. . . . There is no hope for a federal system at the moment."

But most ardent champions of the European idea appeared to get an emotional and moral lift from the memorandum, and many of them insisted that the very fact that it existed and was before the governments of Europe was a historic event fraught with enormous meaning for the future. They showed greater admiration for Briand than ever before and sometimes likened him to a prophet whose day, if not yet at hand, would surely come. J. C. Balet, after confessing that it was all but a certainty that Germany, England, and Italy would wreck the memorandum, wrote in *La République* (22 May 1930): "But we must not lose hope. . . . It is inevitable that the European idea will do much floundering about. But its hour will come, and it will find its way, and it will become a living reality." *Le petit Parisien*, in its issue of 18 May, declared that Briand had shown Europe the road to a better future and that history would not forget his courage and daring no matter what might be the fate of the memorandum. On 24 May, *La libre Belgique* wrote: "Briand's initiative will have a tomorrow; it may be quite distant, but it will come because it is in line with the deepest yearnings of the great mass of the people of Europe. . . ." *L'Indépendance belge* (23 May 1930) said that Briand had demonstrated great courage and generosity in dedicating himself to a task that he knew would be "a slow and painful affair. But he has undertaken it, and he is right." The *Neue Zürcher Zeitung* (20 May 1930) described the memorandum as a remarkable and astonishing document, which in its positive content went much beyond what was generally expected. "Here Briand has sketched the foundations for the organization of Europe. . . . He will go down in history as the great apostle of Europe. No friend of peace can doubt the sincerity or value of his endeavors." The *Neue freie Presse* (18 May 1930) stated that

Briand "with his deep interest in humanity and his finger-tip-feel for the right moment for action . . . has taken the second great step, stronger and more powerful than the first, for the organization of Europe."

The *Vossische Zeitung* (18 May 1930) editorialized: "Briand is not a messiah, but a man of politics. He does not work like Christ, but like the Apostle Paul. . . . A careful examination of the memorandum shows that Briand has fitted his project nicely within the framework of the League of Nations." The *Frankfurter Zeitung* (19 May 1930) said that, while Briand's federal project could not be realized at the moment, he had "made Europe his debtor." *Vorwärts* (18–19 May 1930) wondered if there was any real evidence that the federal project was designed to perpetuate the Versailles settlement and urged the German government to give the memorandum careful consideration and to seize eagerly every opportunity to promote European cooperation.[6] Actually, a few journals that had been staunch supporters of the league, tended to set the projected European structure above the league because they now felt its primary aim would be the elimination of the sources of conflicts rather than a mere attempt to settle conflicts after they arose.[7]

Private groups and organizations also made surprisingly good efforts in view of the fact that nearly everyone expected the memorandum to be politely buried. The Paneuropean Union, the International Judicial Union, and the International Committee for a European Customs Union were the most impressive in their activities. In fact, on the day the memorandum was sent to the governments, the Second Paneuropean Congress opened in Berlin, and the Cobden Club in London was in the midst of a conference on the European idea in which four well-known federalists gave papers. While it was a sheer coincidence that the Cobden Club was so engaged, such was not the case with the Second Paneuropean Congress. In planning this congress, Coudenhove had kept in touch with the Quai d'Orsay at every step, and the congress was thus designed in part as a demonstration in support of the memorandum.[8] Coudenhove knew that the German government did not want the congress in Berlin or even on German soil, but Coudenhove wanted it there, and he had the backing of many good Europeans. On 28 April, Coudenhove had addressed a communication to the Reich Chancellery, stating that many distinguished European politicians and scholars, including Painlevé, Loucheur, and Barthélemy of France, would take part in the Second Paneuropean Congress, and he assumed that the chancellor would want to open the congress and that the Chancellery would want to give a banquet in its honor.[9] The Chancellery, realizing that the German government would have to take note of the congress and face up to the federal project, now asked the Foreign Office for advice on handling the Second Paneuropean Congress and instructed it to begin at once to gather the data that would be needed to draft a reply to the forthcoming French memorandum. The Foreign Office then made two moves. It instructed Blücher to draft a concise history of the Paneuropean movement and make suggestions about the handling of the federal project, and it asked Ambassador Hoesch in Paris for comments on the views of the Frenchmen who were scheduled to address the coming congress.

In a document dated 5 May, Blücher summarized the history of the Paneuropean movement and recommended that the German government continue its policy of "deliberate reservations" toward the Briand project, at least until the Quai d'Orsay released its memorandum. Then, on 9 May, Hoesch informed the Foreign Office that Painlevé had been injured in an automobile accident and would not be able to attend the Second Paneuropean Congress, which meant that Loucheur's address would be most nearly representative of French governmental opinion. The ambassador predicted that Loucheur would be fairly blunt and say that the time had come for action on the economic front in Europe.[10] On 14 May, the Chancellery informed Coudenhove that Joseph Wirth, minister of interior, would be at the opening session to greet the delegates and that the Chancellery would give a breakfast for distinguished guests on 20 May.[11]

The Second Paneuropean Congress opened on 18 May in the Hotel Kaiserhof in Berlin. In a brief greeting to the delegates, Wirth eulogized Erzberger, Rathenau, Ebert, and Stresemann as good Europeans as well as good Germans, and he also expressed the hope that the Young Plan and the Briand Memorandum foreshadowed a better day in Europe.[12] Coudenhove then told the congress that Europe was headed for another war unless the states got on the road to cooperation and union: "We must choose between chaos and order . . . between the ruin and the resurrection of Europe." Ida Roland then read the speech that Victor Hugo had delivered at the opening session of the Peace Congress of Paris in 1849.

For the next two days a succession of distinguished Europeans—Thomas Mann, Barthélemy, Amery, Nincic, and Loucheur—gave papers. Mann, speaking on "Europe as a Cultural Community," urged the peoples of Europe to face up to the fact that Europe was in essence a cultural entity. "As long as the peoples of Europe fear that they will betray their souls by affirming Europe, there will be no Europe," he said.[13] Barthélemy, in a scholarly paper, attacked the concept of absolute sovereignty as a myth that fed the fires of nationalism. He urged the peoples of Europe to renounce this concept and to give Europe a body in order that it could develop a soul: "Our job is to begin the work for unity; to make the soil fine and fertile so the harvest can be rich." Amery, the British colonial secretary, speaking on "Paneurope and the British Empire," explained that he could see real benefits for the peoples of the continent in a federal structure but warned that most of his countrymen were inclined to view a federated Europe as meaning keener competition and a loss of markets for Britain. Still, he assured his hearers that, if a federal system emerged, Britain would endeavor to establish close and friendly relations with it. Nincic, who spoke on "Paneurope and the League of Nations," argued that a European organization would "undergird and buttress the League and enhance its vitality and effectiveness." Loucheur, who was unable to get to Berlin until 19 May, spoke at the final session on "The Economic Organization of Europe." As Hoesch had predicted, Loucheur spoke forcefully, insisting that Europe's most pressing need was a broad program of economic coordination and rationalization and that the time had come for France and Germany to lay aside their quarrels and to join hands in instituting such a program. "France, in a spirit of fraternity, implores the peoples of Europe to unite in order to overcome the common dangers that beset them."[14]

After Loucheur had finished, Coudenhove focused attention on the French Memorandum and called for a strong resolution in support of it. But this was a ticklish matter, especially for those who were members of European governments, and only after much wrangling was a resolution approved. It read: "The Paneuropean Congress greets the Briand Memorandum as the first step toward the fulfillment of its aim, which is an European federation. It urges the interested powers to accept these proposals." Though this congress in Berlin was by far the most spectacular effort that the Paneuropean Union made in behalf of the memorandum, the national and local units of the union remained quite active, and Coudenhove was soon urging the governments of Europe to proclaim 17 May as Paneuropa Day.

While many private organizations across Europe, including the Association of the Peace Societies of France, the General Assembly of the Committee for European Cooperation, and the Paris section of the League for Peace and Freedom, soon endorsed the memorandum,[15] the two endorsements that attracted most attention came at the end of June from the International Judicial Union and the International Committee for a European Customs Union. The former, which had among its members prominent politicians and diplomats as well as jurists, met in Paris on 26 June 1930 and turned immediately to the memorandum. After a lengthy exchange of views, there was a consensus that the federal bonds aimed at in the memorandum would be of great value to Europe and that the International Judicial Union might help matters along by drafting a rather detailed model plan for organs of government in the new structure. Accordingly a drafting committee of twelve was set up under the chairmanship of Alejandro Alvarez, a Spanish jurist and ardent apostle of European federalism.[16]

The committee worked fast and soon presented a document of some two thousand words that described a plan similar to that outlined in the memorandum but more political and precise in emphasis. It stated that the federal system should include all European states; that it should aim at a close and vital moral union capable of harmonizing and coordinating the interests of its members, assuring peace and security among them; and that it should strive for close cooperation with every nation and large regional group across the world.

The machinery it projected was similar to that envisioned in the French Memorandum. There was to be a conference in which all member states would be represented to meet at least once a year to formulate broad policies. There was to be an executive council, with five permanent and three rotating seats, bearing the responsibility for the refinement and execution of programs and policies. There was to be a series of permanent commissions that would, above all, labor to expand intellectual and cultural cooperation and nourish the European spirit. Finally, there was to be a secretariat modeled on that of the League of Nations.[17]

On 30 June 1930, four days after the meeting of the International Judicial Union, the First Congress of the European Customs Union opened in the Ministry of Foreign Affairs in Paris with Yves Le Trocquer presiding. The French Study Committee for a European Customs Union had given much time and thought to the organization of the congress and, indeed, had had encouragement from the French government as well as the active assistance of the thirteen national committees and the international committee. It was a large and imposing gathering. Many of Europe's most distinguished politicians, businessmen, economists, labor leaders, and journalists were present, and more than two hundred business concerns were represented.[18] Premier Tardieu had asked several members of the French government, including Minister of Finance Paul Reynaud, Minister of Agriculture Fernand David, André François-Poncet of the Ministry of Foreign Affairs, and of course Minister of Commerce Flandin, to assist with the work of the congress. Among those who read papers or gave reports were Flandin, Loucheur, Stern-Rubarth, Bleier, Riedl, Coquet, and Lucien Durand. Le Trocquer concluded his address of welcome, which was in great part a summary of the history of the customs union movement, with the words: "Let us go forward to a united Europe; to a Europe scientifically and rationally organized."

Flandin, speaking at the opening session, dealt in a very matter of fact tone with the problems of a European customs union, with special stress on the obstacles to such a union. He said that his experiences as head of the French delegation at the Customs Truce Conference had led him to believe that a large segment of private business was baffled in its attempt to assess the consequences of a customs union and that this had given rise to a powerful fear that such a union would be injurious to them. He said that there were three other major obstacles: (1) the reluctance of governments and their parliaments to surrender the power to levy customs; (2) fear on the part of politicians in some countries that their chances of reelection would be impaired if they took strong stands in support of economic integration; and (3) a vague feeling on the part of many that such a union would damage the economic organs of the League of Nations.

But Flandin was not overly pessimistic. He reminded the congress that he had been studying the matter of a European customs union for many years and believed that such a union could be realized if there were a continuing effort and ample technical preparation. Moreover, he assured the congress that those who were saying that France's pursuit of a European economic community sprang from thoughts of European hegemony were quite wrong, and he received a sharp burst of applause when he said: "Europe needs to be organized. If she fails to attain unity, she will end up in ruin."[19]

Ernö Bleier, who was still an active member of the International Committee for a European Customs Union, described the central objective of the committee as the progressive reduction of customs barriers through collective accords and saw the emergence in the course of time of a great European market: "It is a question, above all, of building a bridge between the near anarchical Europe of today and the organized Europe of tomorrow. We experts can plan the structure, but nothing more can be done until the governments of the more powerful states take a hand." Bleier then paid a warm tribute to Briand and urged the French and German governments to take the initiative in laying the foundations for a customs union.

Stern-Rubarth spoke at length on "The Feasibility of a Preliminary Regional Customs Union." After paying tribute to Briand, Borel, Coquet, and Peyerimhoff as key figures in the movement for an organized Europe, Stern-Rubarth analyzed the more important approaches suggested for arriving at a customs union. He then expressed strong feelings that the most feasible and realistic approach was the one that envisioned a preliminary regional union in western Europe to be composed of France, Germany, Belgium, Luxembourg, and possibly the Netherlands and Switzerland. He said that a number of powerful economic forces were working to link the economies of these nations, and he called on the congress to petition the French and German governments to set up technical committees for the collection of pertinent economic data and preliminary planning. He wondered if the memorandum placed enough emphasis on economic interdependence and solidarity and insisted that it was necessary to subordinate everything to "the creation of a great, free market in Europe." He concluded on an optimistic note, expressing the opinion that protectionist sentiment was waning, that "little by little a European mentality" was developing, and that both Britain and the United States, wishing a stable Europe, would in the end support the customs union effort.[20]

Of the other papers read at the congress, those by Georges Wagner on publicity and propaganda and Lucien Durand on a European postal union seem especially worthy of note. Wagner, who was director of the French Association of Newspaper Editors, said the idea of a common market in

Europe was a powerful and attractive idea and could be made exciting to the masses if mass communication were fully utilized. Wagner then proposed that the customs union groups throughout Europe establish a press service of their own; that they organize frequent conferences for teachers, lawyers, industrialists, and merchants; and that they seek the active support of the directors of cinemas and youth organizations. Lucien Durand, of the Committee of Commerce of the Chamber of Deputies, reminded the congress that Stresemann had called for a European postage stamp and a European postal union in his speech of 9 September 1929 and expressed the view that such a union could be, and should be, created within the framework of the Universal Postal Union.

In the course of its two-day session the First Congress for a European Customs Union made a number of recommendations, some directed to the governments of Europe, some to the League of Nations, and some to the Bureau of the International Committee for a European Customs Union.[21] To the governments of Europe, it recommended that they draft a plan for a European postal union, suppress passports throughout the European community, and examine without delay Europe's agricultural problems. To the governments that had signed the three measures enacted by the Customs Truce Conference, the congress recommended ratification of these measures without delay and the scheduling of another economic conference for the autumn of 1930. To the French and German governments, it recommended that they get together with their neighbors to establish technical committees for planning a customs union in western Europe. To the Bureau of the International Committee for a European Customs Union, the congress recommended the initiation of plans for the construction of a "Maison de l'Europe et les Nations" and the substantial expansion of its press bureau.[22]

Perhaps the most surprising of the collective demonstrations for the memorandum came out of the Twenty-Sixth Conference of the Interparliamentary Union. Although this conference was held in London and the federal project was not even on the agenda, the memorandum received much attention and even loomed large in secretary Lange's general report to the conference.[23] Among those who treated the European idea favorably and at some length were Borel; Heile; Alexander Papanastasiou, former premier of Greece; Cicio Pop, president of the Rumanian chamber of deputies; Senator Fontaine of Belgium; and Senator Merlin of France.[24]

In concluding this chapter, we must once again remind the reader that the picture presented here is sketchy and incomplete in all respects, including the work of the larger organizations. For example, we have not even mentioned the activities of such important groups as the Association of Peace through Law or of the League of the Rights of Man, both of which had networks of local chapters and had given considerable support to the European idea long before the memorandum was published.[25] There is still much work to be done before the history of the movement can be seen in its entirety.

Chapter 17

THE GOVERNMENTS RESPOND

TO THE MEMORANDUM

Meantime, during the late spring and early summer, the governments of the European states formulated their replies to the memorandum. These replies varied greatly in length as well as in content and tone.[1] The Greek reply, which was the shortest, ran to less than two hundred words, while the Danish reply, the longest, ran to over two thousand words. Generally speaking, the replies from the larger and more influential states were more critical in tone and less positive in content than those from the smaller and less influential states. Taken as a whole the replies were, in the words of Joseph Barthélemy, "a bit cool and reserved."[2]

Perhaps the most striking fact about the replies was the way in which the governments reacted to the matter of a general European pact, which lay close to the heart of the memorandum and was, according to that document, "to reaffirm the moral union of Europe" and to provide a European conference "as a living link of solidarity between the European nations." Several of the replies—most notably the British, German, Italian, and Hungarian—failed to make any appreciable response to this idea of Europe as a cultural entity, a thing that Valéry, Painlevé, Mann, and others liked to say was a reality before the nation-state emerged and would be there after the nation-state had passed away.

The Hungarian reply, for example, expressed the keenest satisfaction that the memorandum had expounded the principle, as it put it, "of the absolute sovereignty of states and their equal rights in the proposed union." On the other hand, several of the smaller states, including Finland and Yugoslavia, not only praised the idea of a moral union but made the projected European conference the center of their replies, pointing out that there were all sorts of problems basic to the life of Europe which had little if any interest for non-European peoples.

Almost equally striking and revealing were the differences of opinion as to how the projected European structure would affect the League of Nations. Some of the replies, including those of Britain, Germany, Spain, and Switzerland, expressed the fear that such a union would damage the league, while those of most of the smaller states held that it would supplement and strengthen the league.

Since the British, German, and Italian replies were generally regarded as the most crucial, a brief analysis of each will be helpful. The British seemingly took Briand's federal project seriously, and as soon as the memorandum was available, the government set up a study committee within the Foreign Office to make a thorough analysis of the memorandum in an attempt, among other things, to discover what lay behind Briand's pursuit of a federal structure.[3] On 30 May this committee presented a rather lengthy report to the foreign secretary which probably reflected official British thinking on the federal project more precisely than the finished reply. After identifying the principal elements in the memorandum, the report stated that Briand had seized hold of the European idea for one of two reasons. Either he was convinced that a European organization would be a good thing for both France and Europe, or he was using this idealistic approach in an effort to consolidate and sanctify "the present territorial and political organization of Europe." The authors of the report then made it quite clear that they felt the evidence was overwhelmingly in support of the first alternative. The trouble with the second was, they said, that "it does not fit in with what we know of M. Briand." The report then added that Briand clearly was much concerned about American and Russian competition and power.[4]

Impressed as the framers of the report were with what they believed to be Briand's basic objectives, they professed, nonetheless, to see real dangers to British interests in the federal project and advised that the reply to the memorandum be cordial but very reserved. It should, they said, make clear that His Majesty's government cannot support any continental association that might weaken Britain's ties with the Commonwealth or damage the prestige and authority of the league, "which is the anchor sheet of British policy."

In early June, when the Foreign Office began drafting the British reply, Secretary Henderson and his aides had this report before them and they also knew that the German reply would be loaded with political reservations and that the Italian reply would be essentially negative. Actually the British reply, which ran to just over a thousand words, followed quite closely the suggestions of the study committee. The first half of the document dealt with the objectives of a federal system as defined in the memorandum, and the second half concerned itself with the methods prescribed for the realization of these objectives. It found the objectives commendable and, after a mild warning against any tendency to neglect the economic aspect of European collaboration, endorsed them. But it found the methods faulty and labeled the establishment of a European conference as unnecessary and undesirable, as certain "to diminish both the efficiency and authority of the organs of the League." The document warned that an "independent European Union" of the sort proposed might create intercontinental rivalries and hostilities and ended with the assertion that "the purpose which the French Government have in view can be effectively secured by so adapting the proposals put forward in the memorandum as to bring them fully within the framework of the League of Nations."

The German government, though it had hoped all along to avoid a formal stand on the European idea, worked out its reply with care partly because German leaders felt that the memorandum offered them unusual propaganda opportunities. As we have already noted, the Wilhelmstrasse had begun the collection of data on the federal project before the Second Paneuropean Congress. Then, as soon as the memorandum was in hand, Chancellor Brüning and Foreign Minister Curtius took a number of specific steps to broaden and accelerate the work.[5] They asked each ministry to comb the memorandum for items that related to its area of responsibility; they instructed German ambassadors and ministers across Europe to send all facts and opinions to Berlin they felt would be helpful in drafting the reply; and they made a tactful effort to persuade the moderate left papers, especially *Vorwärts*, to keep in line with governmental policy.[6]

On 19 June, after the various ministries had thoroughly analyzed the memorandum and an effort had been made to ascertain the attitudes of certain European governments, a full-scale ministerial meeting was held with Bernhard von Bülow, state secretary of the Foreign Office, presiding. Bülow opened the meeting by laying down the main lines of the German reply. He said, among other things, that the German government was firmly opposed to an eastern Locarno and that it would oppose any organization tending to sanction the status quo, disturb Germany's relations with Russia or non-European countries, or weaken the minorities program of the League of Nations. Speaking more positively, Bülow said that the German government would make basic changes in the postwar settlement a condition for its participation in a federal system. When Bülow called on the various ministries to report the results of their studies, the most frequent comment was that the Briand project would tend to conceal the minorities in eastern Europe and to hem in the "dynamic forces" that were operating there, thus weakening Germany's Mitteleuropean program.

The German reply that was sent to the Quai d'Orsay on 11 July was essentially a revisionist document, and in the main, it was an elaboration of what Bülow had said in the ministerial meeting of 19 June. It said in essence that the "general political and economic organization of the Continent" was defective and that Germany stood ready to enter into an exhaustive discussion aimed at the removal of these defects and "a bold reform of conditions which are recognized as untenable." It also stated that any new European program must be flexible and should include Turkey and the Soviet Union.[7]

Italy, the other member of the Big Three, took the memorandum rather lightly.[8] Foreign Minister Grandi told the British ambassador in Rome in late May that he had not studied the memorandum thoroughly, but Mussolini had already instructed him to reject it. The Italian reply, sent to Paris on 4 July, was obviously designed to confuse and discourage the French Foreign Office, and many of its comments bordered on mockery. After stating that the Fascist government was ready to cooperate in any procedure that was aimed at peace and both the material and moral reconstruction of Europe, the reply proceeded in a rather clever and argumentative way to find grave defects and dangers in every part of the memorandum. It said among other things that everything possible should be done to bring Russia and Turkey into the organization, and it concluded by chiding Briand for not having put more stress on disarmament.

But if the replies of the so-called Big Three were extremely critical and largely negative, those of most of the smaller states were friendly and positive. Though nearly all of the smaller states had reservations of some sort, only Hungary, Sweden, and Switzerland questioned the need for a European conference or stated reservations in any way comparable to those of the Big Three.[9] The criticisms of the smaller states revolved largely around those parts of the memorandum which dealt with machinery and economic organization. Most of these states, hoping for substantial equality of representation, argued that the projected machinery was too complex and cumbersome, and some of them, most notably Estonia, suggested that it might be best to start with a European conference and add other organs only when experience indicated that they were needed. On the matter of the relation of political and economic factors, a few of the smaller states, including Austria and Latvia, felt that political considerations should come first, but the great majority insisted that the two sets of factors were so interdependent that organization in both areas would have to be pursued simultaneously. The Czechoslovak reply argued that "the two groups of problems stand in a continual relation of interdependence one to the other." The Scandinavian states perhaps placed greater emphasis on economic factors than did any of the others and tended to argue that union in the political sphere would not be possible until there was an effective measure of union in the economic sphere.

The Luxembourg reply accepted the European conference and saw its real objective as being "to prepare and facilitate the coordination of those activities of the League which are essentially European." The Yugoslav reply went even further. It not only welcomed the idea of a European conference to speak for the European community but made this proposed conference the center of its reply, holding that there were all sorts of problems basic to the life of Europe which had little or no interest for non-European peoples.

On the question of the impact of the federal project on the League of Nations, most of the smaller states agreed in substance with the Norwegian government's contention that there were good reasons to believe such a structure would "enhance the League's prestige." The Austrian reply for example argued that the projected European organization would strengthen the league "by placing at its disposal new machinery suitable for its purely European tasks."

Of the replies of the smaller states, the Dutch and Swiss were perhaps the most unusual and the most deserving of special notice. The Dutch reply was not only one of the most favorable but it was unique in asserting that the doctrine of absolute sovereignty was incompatible with "the institution of a system of contractual union aiming at the rational organization of Europe." The Swiss reply was devoted almost entirely to the probable impact of a European organization on its own neutrality and on the League of Nations.[10] In fact, the Swiss government stated rather firmly that it would oppose any European structure that it felt would threaten its neutrality or impair the authority and prestige of the league: "For Switzerland, as for other countries, the League of Nations represents a great achievement of civilization in the cause of peace. . . . A European Union would no longer be desirable if it lessened the possibilities for the development of the League of Nations."

On 6 August, when the Swiss reply reached the Quai d'Orsay, the Eleventh Regular Session of the League Assembly was barely a month away, and Briand and his assistants had no time to waste if they were to have an interpretative summary of these twenty-six replies in readiness for the Geneva meeting. The Foreign Office set to work on the replies but had trouble deciding what sort of digest would be most effective, so a number of rough drafts were made in an effort to hit upon the best pattern. By 20 August the broad pattern of the report had been set, and it was in final form on 1 September though it was not released to the press until the first meeting of the twenty-seven governments at Geneva on 8 September.

The report was, as the press had confidently predicted it would be, a rather concise and objective analysis of the twenty-six replies.[11] It did not modify or reaffirm the original principles of the memorandum, nor did it criticize the replies in any way. Rather, it set out by means of short quotations the measure of agreement and disagreement on the central elements of the memorandum. Only in the conclusion did the French government reveal its hope that the projected organization might be given a measure of independence and not made wholly subservient to the League of Nations. This was done by reminding the governments gently that it had been agreed at the Briand luncheon on 9 September 1929 that there would be "an initial exchange of views and a discussion on questions of principle" before the opening of the Eleventh Session of the Assembly.

On 8 September representatives of all the states that had replied to the French Memorandum gathered in closed session in the council room of the League of Nations. Twenty-three of the twenty-seven were foreign ministers, and ardent federalists took this as a good omen. The crucial question was, as all the delegates knew, whether they would declare themselves a new, self-perpetuating body—a European conference—or whether they would leave the federal project entirely in the hands of the League Assembly. Briand, who was chairman, opened the meeting and directed his remarks mainly to Henderson, Curtius, and Grandi because he was morally certain that if he could win them a European body would be born.[12]

But neither Henderson, Curtius, nor Grandi could be moved, and the moment Briand opened the meeting for discussion, they made it quite clear that they would oppose any sort of European conference unless it emanated from the league and was responsible to the league. Briand had the support of the ministers of several of the smaller states, and he tried to persuade all of the ministers to agree to the drafting of an accord indicating how the federal project should be handled in the League Assembly. Again the ministers of the Big Three objected, and Briand, now feeling that he might make matters worse by persisting, indicated that he would be satisfied with a resolution to the effect that the foreign ministers of the European governments felt that the question of closer European collaboration was a matter of great importance and should be put before the assembly. Such a resolution was presented and unanimously approved, and the conference, after three hours of bitter debate, adjourned.

Briand's only hope now of getting a European conference was to persuade the Assembly of the League of Nations, with its large non-European membership, to authorize it. He realized that his chance of doing this was slender, but he was determined to try. At the morning session of 11 September, just three days before the Reichstag election in Germany in which the Nationalists and National Socialists were to receive nearly 10 million votes, Briand presented the French plan for a European federal system with all the eloquence and logic that he could muster.[13] He said that a rather exhaustive study of such a system had been made since the Tenth Session of the Assembly and that, in spite of determined opposition from many quarters, the idea had made substantial headway. "The idea is deeply rooted in the minds of the peoples; it is a logical idea and does not merely answer the mystic needs of their consciences— though it has a strong hold there—but appeals also to their common sense and their reason." He then made a direct appeal to the delegates from the non-European states, insisting that opposition in the United States had been greatly exaggerated and arguing that every nation in the world would benefit if Europe were organized.

It was one of Briand's better efforts, but the opposition was too strong. Henderson, convinced that he could prevent the French foreign minister from getting what he wanted, did not make a frontal attack on the federal project but treated it briefly and lightly, insisting that if any plan were adopted for the further pursuit of a federated Europe it should meet two conditions. First, it should be drafted by the assembly and should be entirely responsible to the league; and, second, it should be designed to facilitate the league's program of disarmament. The British foreign secretary kept his remarks centered on the league rather than on the federal project, and he pictured the league as the great organ of peace and emphasized that a general reduction of armaments was the great need of the hour. Briand, of course, did not disagree with this, for it was the central aim of his program. He simply said that a federal bond would increase enormously the chances of achieving it.

As the general debate unfolded, Henderson was full of smiles, for nearly all of the speakers from non-European states, after a polite bow to Briand's federal project, concentrated on the work of the league. In fact, long before the general debate was over, the outcome seemed so certain that Curtius, who wanted to postpone his speech until the results of the Reichstag election were in, decided that he could safely do so. Indeed, the German foreign minister did not speak until 16 September after the issue had been settled, and then he referred to the federal plan only briefly and indirectly. With Anschluss in the back of his mind, he talked about the virtues of regional accords and complimented Schober on his advocacy of such accords.[14]

But if the great majority of the speakers from non-European states went with Henderson, most of those from the smaller European states lingered with the federal project, and a few went all out in support of it. Hymans of Belgium, Van Blokland of the Netherlands, Procope of Finland, Motta of Switzerland, Politis of Greece, Marinkovitch of Yugoslavia, and Mironesco of Rumania were among those who showed great sympathy for the federal project but agreed it should be kept in close relation to the League of Nations. In fact, some of these men pleaded for a solid and effective European structure as fervently as had Briand. Politis paid Briand a warm tribute, describing him as a friend of the peoples of Europe and a statesman of great vision.

But on 15 September, when Politis spoke, it was clear to all that the best that could be expected was a study committee on European union. Several delegates had already suggested this course, and it was known that Henderson and Curtius were willing to accept it, provided the league retained strict control of the committee. Accordingly, the French delegation took the lead in drafting a resolution embodying this procedure. The draft resolution was turned over to President Titulesco in the late afternoon of 16 September, and he immediately announced that he would have it printed and distributed to members of the assembly so that they might act on it at the next session.

This resolution, which was adopted on 17 September without opposition, was an unusual document.[15] It invited the European governments who were members of the League of Nations to set up within the framework of the league a commission "to pursue the study already begun" of European federalism and to conduct its study in collaboration with governments throughout the world whether members of the league or not. The failure of the resolution to distinguish between European and non-European states made federalism a secondary matter as Scelle and many others observed at the time. Briand's opponents had done their work well.

On 23 September, while Europe and much of the world was feverishly speculating about the meaning of the heavy gains that the National Socialists had made in the Reichstag election, the heads of the delegations of the twenty-seven states that had participated in the federal project met to organize the new body. Sir Eric Drummond, general secretary of the league, called the meeting to order, and Henderson nominated Briand for the presidency of the new commission. There was a burst of applause, and Drummond quickly declared Briand elected by acclamation. The French foreign minister took the chair, made a brief speech, and asked that Drummond be named secretary. Again, there was a wave of applause, and the president declared Drummond elected by acclamation.

The president then said that before adjourning they should give themselves a name and set the date for their first regular session. After a brief discussion, it was agreed that the new body would bear the name "Commission of Inquiry for European Union" and that it would hold its first regular session in January 1931 to coincide with the next session of the council of the league. It was further agreed that the January meeting would center its attention on the French Memorandum and the responses of the twenty-six states, and the secretary was instructed to begin sifting out league documents that might prove useful to the work of the commission.

Chapter 18

THE COMMISSION OF INQUIRY

FOR EUROPEAN UNION

The marked gains that the German National Socialists scored in the Reichstag election of 14 September 1930 and the creation three days later of the Commission of Inquiry for European Union all but wrecked the European movement. For the creation of the Commission of Inquiry effectively sidetracked Briand's federal project, and the Reichstag election made it clearer than ever that radical nationalism and political recklessness were growing apace in Germany.[1] But many good Europeans, including Briand, continued to hope and to search for grounds on which some sort of a European bond could be built.[2] Thinking first and foremost of a positive Franco-German collaboration, they put the best possible face on the Reichstag election and insisted that the situation in Germany was still fluid and German opinion could yet swing to a European program.

The thing that did most to sustain them in this view, however, was the feeling that there was no acceptable alternative—no other course that had so much to offer in terms of security and a fuller life. Léon Blum, whose influence was considerable in socialist circles across Europe, predicted in *Le Populaire* (17 Sept. 1930) that Hitler, like Boulanger, would fade away if France and her allies continued their pursuit of disarmament, peace, and understanding. The Radical Socialist party, at its congress in Grenoble on 10 November 1930, resolved to continue its effort to organize Europe, and in the same city a few weeks later, the leaders of the large Association of Peace through Law resolved the same. This view was almost as widespread in the ranks of businessmen and labor leaders as it was among writers and academicians. During the last weeks in November 1930, Yves Le Trocquer spoke in these terms in Budapest, Vienna, and Prague, as did Dannie Heinemann in Cologne and Barcelona. On 20 December 1930, Georg Bernhard spoke in Paris to a joint meeting of the leaders of several organizations including the Association of Peace through Law, the French Association for the League of Nations, and the French Committee for European Cooperation, arguing that customs barriers were a tremendous drag on Europe's economic development and that France and Germany should move boldly toward a European customs union.[3]

Even the regional economic conferences that were held in Sinaia, Warsaw, and Bucharest in August and October 1930, stressing the need for expanded trade between the basically industrial states of western Europe and the basically agricultural states of eastern Europe, received much of their inspiration from Briand's federal project and the writings of such good Europeans as Francis Delaisi and Elemér Hantos.[4] Foreign ministers August Zaleski of Poland and Gheorghe Mironescu of Rumania argued that such regional economic agreements as were contemplated in these conferences would not only benefit most of the people of Europe immediately but could also serve as stepping stones to a European customs union. With these conferences in mind, Victor Bovet speculated (*L'Européen*, 3 Dec. 1930) on the possibility of an "inter-European agrarian organism" as a nucleus around which a European community could develop. And Henri Cahen, active in the field of electrical energy, wrote: "At this time when there is much talk of creating a European union, it would appear that nothing could contribute more toward the achievement of such a union in the political domain than the establishment of a European union in the field of electrical energy."[5]

At the same time, good Europeans sought to strengthen the peace movement and played the key role in founding the New School for Peace (La Nouvelle Ecole de la Paix), which was formally established in Paris on 3 November 1930 with Paul Painlevé as president.[6] They were also extremely active throughout 1931 in the campaign to create a climate of opinion highly favorable to the approaching World Disarmament Conference.

Jean Luchaire and Pierre Brossolette were instrumental in bringing together, in Mannheim from 16 to 21 September 1930, a sizable group of democratically inclined French and German students to discuss ways and means of making revisionism serve the ends of an active and creative Franco-German collaboration.[7] This general idea, which was of course a version of Briand's concept of linking Europeanism and revisionism, appeared frequently not only in *Notre temps* but also in *Paneuropa* and a large number of French journals.

So while the European movement was noticeably tapering off in late 1930 and early 1931, there were still those who felt that Briand had some chance of turning the Commission of Inquiry for European Union into some sort of a European bond or structure within the framework of the league. This hope flickered on 30 November 1930 when the Secretariat of the League of Nations sent the governments whose ministers would compose the Commission of Inquiry for European Union a number of documents and asked for suggestions relative to an agenda for the second session of the new body that was now scheduled to open in Geneva on 16 January 1931. The suggestions that attracted most attention were a memorandum from the International Labor Office dealing with the European idea in a general way and a document from the German government relative to the composition of the new body. In the first document, Albert Thomas, director of the Labor Office, made it clear that he had supported Briand's federal initiative from the first and had felt for years that Europe's workers would benefit in various ways from even a modest measure of political and economic integration. The German government in its report again stated that it would press for the participation of Russia and Turkey in the work of the Commission of Inquiry.[8]

But the highlights of the first day of the second session of the Study Commission, which was attended by the foreign ministers of twenty-two of the twenty-seven member states, were Briand's address of welcome and a report on the work of the Second Conference for Concerted European Economic Action by the well-known Dutch economist and statesman Hendrikus Colijn, who had served as president of that conference and who happened to be in Geneva for this day. In opening the session, Briand told the members of the commission that the French government still felt, as it had stated in its memorandum of 17 May 1930, that a measure of unity among the states of Europe was necessary if European civilization was to grow and prosper. He then asked the delegates for their permission to invite Colijn to report at the afternoon session on the conference that had been held in Geneva in November 1930.

Colijn, who had already served as premier of the Netherlands and was destined to serve in that capacity for most of the thirties, stressed the economic interdependence of the European states and argued that a rampant economic nationalism—"a competition in economic armaments"—was the main cause of Europe's economic difficulties. His advice to the Commission of Inquiry was to urge the governments of Europe to move as fast as possible toward a "single vast market" that would enable the forces of production to operate on truly "rational and modern lines." Colijn later said that Briand thanked him warmly for his report and indicated the strong hope that the foreign ministers of Germany, England, and Italy had listened carefully.

After Colijn left the hall, the commission turned to the touchy question of its composition and competence, and soon there was turmoil. Julius Curtius of Germany and Dino Grandi of Italy said that Russia and Turkey should be invited at once to join the commission. Peter Munch of Denmark, Nicolae Titulesco of Rumania, and Mowinckel of Norway protested that any immediate invitation to Moscow and Ankara would be premature and out of line with the resolution of 17 September 1930, which had not authorized invitations to nonmember states unless the commission in pursuit of its inquiry decided that such a move would be useful. At this point the Grandi-Curtius position received an enormous boost when Henderson joined them and asked if they should not "consider at once whether all States, non-European Members and non-Member Governments, should be invited."[9] Marinkovich of Yugoslavia then told Henderson that under the covenant his proposal could only be carried out by the secretariat, and if carried out would have the effect of turning the Commission of Inquiry for European Union into a sort of world conference. But Curtius moved in quickly, saying that he agreed with the British foreign minister and was prepared to extend the scope of his proposal to include all nonleague states beyond the seas as well as in Europe. Briand begged for moderation, pointing out that, if the Commission of Inquiry could do, and should do, what the German and British foreign ministers had proposed, it would have many more members than the League of Nations itself. At this point Giuseppe Motta of Switzerland, who was highly respected in league circles and had always been cool toward a European structure, now moved to Briand's side and made it quite clear that he felt the German, British, and Italian foreign ministers had taken untenable positions. Slightly embarrassed by Motta's plain words, Henderson, Curtius, and Grandi agreed that for the moment invitations to membership should be confined to Russia, Turkey, and Iceland.

During the final four days of the meeting, it was decided that the next session would begin on 15 May 1931; that the governments of Russia, Turkey, and Iceland would be invited to participate; and that the main topic of discussion would be "the world economic crisis in so far as it affected Europe." Also, in the final hours, three committees were established, one to study and report matters of constitution, organization, and procedure, and the others to study agricultural surpluses and credits in central and eastern Europe.[10] Perhaps the most striking fact about this session of the Commission of Inquiry was that the governments of Germany, Italy, and England had made it clear they intended to do everything possible to keep the commission from coming to grips with the European idea. This saddened most good Europeans, but few were surprised.

Meantime, as the new committees came to life and worked on their reports, Chancellors Brüning and Schober moved along in deep secrecy with the plan for an Austro-German customs union, which they had projected at their meeting in Vienna from 22 to 24 February 1930. By early March 1931, they had completed the customs union agreement and, after much bickering, decided to announce it on 21 March 1931, just before Motta's new Committee on Constitution, Organization, and Procedure met, in an effort to relate it to the European idea and keep it within the framework of Paneurope.

But they had bad luck. On 19 March journalists found out about their secret project. Next day the two governments, deeply embarrassed, officially announced the existence of a protocol for a customs union. The protest against the protocol was immediate and sharp, especially in Paris, Prague, Brussels, and Warsaw.[11] Foreign ministers as well as journalists asked Berlin and Vienna why they had moved in secrecy if they were trying to promote European union—an idea that was in the open and formally before the League of Nations. Even Arthur Henderson could not refrain from scolding Berlin and Vienna for moving in secrecy and asked them to put the matter before the league. Briand, who only a few days before had told the Chamber of Deputies that

Austria was becoming "conscious of her nationality" and that the Anschluss was on the wane, was surprised and shaken by the announcement.

The two chancellors, especially Brüning, insisted that the Anschluss was a German-Austrian affair and that Berlin and Vienna intended "to pursue with calm determination the course that they had decided to be the right one." Paris, Prague, Rome, and Warsaw were, however, in a position to apply financial as well as political and moral pressure on Austria, and on 17 April 1931, Schober announced that Austria would not take further steps toward the implementation of the customs union protocol until the League Council had met. But the German government showed no signs of retreating, and it was now certain that the customs union project would be another source of discord at the third session of the Commission of Inquiry for European Union.

The Commission of Inquiry met as scheduled on 15 May 1931 for its third session with representatives from Russia, Turkey, and Iceland present. After the adoption of an agenda and the report of the Committee on Constitution, Organization, and Procedure, the Commission of Inquiry turned to the "World Economic Crisis in so far as it concerned the Community of European States." Curtius was anxious to open the discussion and was given the floor. Though he did not mention the Austro-German customs union project, his whole speech was clearly designed as a defense of it. He declared that the main cause of the economic crisis, as far as Europe was concerned, was "the division of Europe into a legion of small economic units," and he felt that the cure lay in the creation of bilateral or regional customs agreements. Germany was, he said, endeavoring to promote this idea and was prepared "to negotiate immediately with every country, large or small, regarding the feasibility of a customs union."[12]

Briand, speaking as a delegate of France, stated that in his judgment the principal cause of Europe's economic crisis was that the states had acted individually or bilaterally. Such action, he said, could not but produce fear and distrust, aggravating political and economic tensions and augmenting anarchical conditions. What was needed was not bilateral action but concerted action. That had been the central purpose of his project for European federation and it was the purpose, as he understood it, of the Commission of Inquiry for European Union. He urged the German delegate to give "concerted action" a chance and announced that his government would soon present a plan for concerted economic action. After Grandi had reminded Curtius as gently and tactfully as possible that his government was also worried about the Austro-German customs plan, André François-Poncet outlined in some detail the comprehensive plan to which Briand had referred in his initial remarks. The plan embraced four major proposals: a system of preference for European grains created primarily to aid the farmers in central and eastern Europe; a system of international cartels or agreements designed to erode customs barriers; a special European regime for aid to Austria; and a system of agricultural credits intended primarily for the agricultural states of eastern Europe.

Both French and German plans were now before the commission, and discussion for the next three days tended to revolve around these plans. The German plan, with its stress on bilateral agreements, was criticized by nearly all delegates on the grounds that such agreements would aggravate political as well as economic tensions. The French plan, which called for action at the European level, was warmly endorsed by most of the delegates from the states of central and eastern Europe and accepted as a basis for discussion by the delegates from the Low Countries and the Scandinavian states. In endorsing the French plan, Beneš, Marinkovitch, Titulesco, and Zaleski struck hard at the German plan, arguing that it was pointing away from cooperation toward economic nationalism and thus in the wrong direction.

On 21 May, after nearly a week of general and rather uncoordinated discussion, several delegates led by Motta called for the establishment of a Coordination Committee on Economic Relations to be composed largely of economic and technical experts. All member states were to be represented on the new committee, and it was to meet in August so as to have a report on economic problems ready for the Commission of Inquiry when it formally met on 3 September 1931 for its fourth session. Again the Commission of Inquiry had failed to face up to the question of European union largely because the German, British, and Italian representatives had kept it off course. Though Briand was aware of all of this, he closed the session bravely, predicting that the commission would grow in strength and usefulness. He promised with a show of emotion to devote his full strength to this end.

But it was a tempestuous spring and summer, and it witnessed among other things continued tension over the Austro-German customs project, the collapse of the Creditanstalt, Austria's largest banking firm, a severe financial crisis in both Germany and England, and the Hoover Moratorium in the area of reparations. Yet, in spite of much that boded ill, the Commission of Inquiry for European Union made some brave gestures. All of the committees met at least once during the summer, and all had reports ready for the new Coordination Committee on Economic Relations when it met on 31 August 1931, just three days before the fourth session of the Commission of Inquiry was scheduled to open. The new committee quickly put together a report that had substantial and interesting European overtones. It said among other things: "The ultimate goal must be the widest possible collaboration of the nations of Europe in the sense of making Europe a single market for the products of any and every country in it." The report also called on the states of Europe to refrain from groupings inimical to the general interest, and to leave all agreements open to other countries so that markets could be enlarged and the European states could move toward a customs union.

This report was ready for the Commission of Inquiry when it met for its fourth session in Geneva on 3 September 1931. Indeed, it was the first item on the agenda, and most of the brief fourth session was devoted to it and to the question of the renewal of the commission's mandate. Bech of Luxembourg, who had served as chairman of the Coordination Committee, presented the report and ministers from the smaller states dominated the discussion of the report and most of them praised it. Jaan Tonnison of Estonia attacked the concept of "absolute and exclusive sovereignty" as outmoded and called on the Commission of Inquiry to initiate a campaign to put the press, the school, and the cinema in the service of the European idea. The delegates of the Scandinavian states, led by Baron Ramel of Sweden, stressed the need for confidence and cooperation but warned that a special effort should be made to guard "the most-favoured-nation principle" and to restrict tariff preference to a minimum.

On the question of whether the Commission of Inquiry's mandate expired when the League Assembly met, there were differences of opinion. Acting chairman Motta ruled that, since the commission was an advisory committee of the league, the assembly could terminate its proceedings, making it necessary to request continuation. The commission then set up a drafting committee, headed by Motta, to frame the final report to be put before the Twelfth Session of the Assembly of the League of Nations, which was to open on 7 September 1931.

As was expected the Commission of Inquiry for European Union received considerable attention in the Twelfth Session of the Assembly both in the general debate and in the Second and Sixth Committees. In the general debate there were calls for the abolition of the Commission of Inquiry, and there were calls for its continuation and for a more determined effort at European union. For example, Pusta of Estonia charged that the commission had not so far been permitted to pursue its real mission, which was to study the various possible methods for the constitution of a European union. He announced that, on behalf of the Estonian delegation, he was submitting a resolution urging the assembly to promote through the press, the school, and the cinema an active propaganda in support of European union.[13]

The boldness of Pusta's proposal surprised most of the delegates, and while it received warm support from many of the European delegates, it was viciously attacked by delegates from several non-European nations, especially Japan and Persia. Even Lange of Norway said that he was beginning to wonder if a European federation was needed in view of the growing interdependence of the whole world.

Briand, though he had apparently now abandoned all hope of making the Commission of Inquiry independent of the league, much less of making it the nucleus of a European structure, responded gently to his attackers and received staunch support from Pusta, Beneš, and a few others. The French foreign minister told Lange that he was not displeased to hear delegates criticize an organ of the league for "excessive zeal." Motta, chairman of the Sixth

Committee, was not too unhappy with this division of opinion, for he himself wanted the Commission of Inquiry to remain firmly anchored within the framework of the league. He maintained a firm hand over the Sixth Committee and the resolution, which was drafted by that committee on 16 September and later approved by the assembly, that synthesized rather neatly the differing views. The resolution read: "The assembly notes with satisfaction the work of the Commission of Inquiry for European Union. . . . It invites the commission to continue its work in conformity with the principles set out in the resolution of 17 September 1930 and . . . to present a report of its future work at the next session of the assembly." This resolution was approved by the Second Committee and adopted by the assembly on 24 September.

The foreign ministers of the states that made up the commission gathered on 26 September for a final brief meeting. They set up two new committees, reelected Briand president for the coming year and agreed to meet again in January 1932.

But the renewal of the mandate of the Commission of Inquiry for European Union did not create much excitement in the ranks of the proponents of European integration. It was now clear that most good Europeans assumed that the governmental or league phase of the European movement, which Briand had initiated in September 1929, was for all practical purposes at an end. Even the trip to Berlin by Briand and Laval on 27 September 1931, the day after the renewal of the mandate of the Commission of Inquiry, did little to revive the hopes of the apostles of a united Europe, though the trip did result in the creation of the Franco-German Economic Committee, which vaguely resembled the committee of 1908. Briand's health was now breaking fast, and he spent much of his remaining strength trying to prevent the Sino-Japanese crisis from wrecking the League of Nations. After his death on 7 March 1932, Herriot was elected president of the Commission of Inquiry, and he gathered the members of the commission together for the renewal of the commission's mandate during the Twelfth Regular Session of the League Assembly in September 1932, but Herriot made no attempt to schedule another working session of the Commission of Inquiry.

Indeed, by the autumn of 1931 with the National Socialists in Germany moving toward power, the European idea was ebbing fast and was getting only a fraction of the space in the daily press that it had received in 1929 and 1930. Most good Europeans were giving much more attention to the World Disarmament Conference, scheduled to open in Geneva on 2 February 1932, than to the Commission of Inquiry. Not only did they feel that an agreement to limit armaments would bring many benefits to the peoples of Europe, but they also felt that it would advance the cause of European unification.

But the fact that nearly all of the leaders of the European movement had given up hope of a European bond in the immediate future did not mean that they felt the European idea was about to perish. They were deeply impressed with the enormous gains that the idea had made during the 1920s and the enormous body of material it had gathered and stored for the future. Indeed, many if not most of the men and women who had spoken out during the 1920s for a measure of union in Europe not only believed that the European idea had a future but continued to speak out for it during the 1930s, whenever a favorable opportunity arose.[14] For example, the French Study Committee for a European Customs Union, led by Le Trocquer and Coquet, worked on faithfully and almost defiantly long after all hope had gone. Representatives of the Paneuropean Unions in Austria, Czechoslovakia, Hungary, Poland, Rumania, and Yugoslavia met in conference in Budapest on 12 and 13 February 1932 and resolved to continue their efforts to create a European economic union. The Third Paneuropean Congress was held in Basel in mid-October 1932, and the fourth in Vienna in mid-May 1935. Even Léon Blum speculated on the revival of the Commission of Inquiry for European Union in an address before the French Senate on 23 June 1935. Louis Dumont-Wilden wrote near the end of his *L'Evolution de l'esprit européen* (Paris, 1937): "After some convulsions, which may well be rather lengthy, the nations of the old continent will accept the idea of federation as a necessity. They will finally consent to sacrifice a part of their sovereignty to the council (l'Amphictionie) which shall replace the League of Nations." The last issue of Coudenhove-Kalergi's journal *Paneuropa* was dated March 1938 and appeared on the newstands just as Hitler's forces moved into Austria. *Les Etats-Unis d'Europe* also continued to appear up to the eve of World War II.

In fact, it was in large part these staunch apostles who had thought through the pros and cons of the European idea during the 1920s, who reasserted the idea with conviction and hope in the French underground during 1941–42. For it was there in the midst of the second highly destructive and crippling war of the century, which many of them had warned was coming unless the states moved toward union, that the European idea came again to life and moved on with fairly steady strides to the Council of Europe and the European Community with its Common Market.

While it is perhaps much too soon to speculate on how history will finally judge the European movement of the 1920s, it is our belief that it will go down in history as one of the most, if not the most, creative and constructive movement in Europe between the two world wars.

NOTES

CHAPTER 1

1. Some of the most useful of the works dealing with the history of the idea before 1932 which have appeared since Beljaar's *Bibliographie* went to press, are: Foerster, *Europa: Geschichte einer politischen Idee*; Schöndube and Ruppert, *Eine Idee setzt sich durch: Der Weg zum vereinigten Europa*; Rougemont, *The Idea of Europe*; and Brugmans, *L'Idée européenne*.

2. For Dubois's European project, see Voyenne, *Histoire de l'idée européenne*, pp. 53–58. For a list of the major projects from 1306 to 1914, see Foerster, *Europa*, pp. 325–53.

3. For the idea during the Revolution, see Voyenne, "L'Idée fédéraliste sous la révolution française," pp. 815–24.

4. Henri de Saint-Simon and Augustin Thierry, *De la Réorganisation de la société européenne ou de la nécessité et des moyens de rassembler les peuples de l'Europe en un seul corps politique, en conservant à chacun son indépendance nationale* (Paris, 1814); and Maurice Bourquin, *La Sainte Alliance: Un essaie d'organisation européenne* (Leyden, 1955).

5. See Pierre Renouvin, *L'Idée de fédération européenne dans la pensée politique du XIXᵉ siècle*, passim; Foerster, *Europa*, pp. 220–94; Voyenne, *Histoire de l'idée européenne*, pp. 114–55; Rougemont, *The Idea of Europe*, pp. 216–315; and Schöndube and Ruppert, *Eine Idee setzt sich durch*, pp. 82–100. For Mazzini, see G. Bourgin and M. Dell'Isola, *Mazzini, promoteur de la république italienne et pionnier de la fédération européenne* (Paris, 1956), passim.

6. Victor Hugo, *Oeuvres complètes: Actes et paroles*, 42 vols. (Paris, 1937), 1:68–69.

7. This journal was published in Bern most of the time until 1922, and in Paris from 1922 until 1938.

8. On 11 March 1882 in a lecture at the Sorbonne on the nature of the nation, Ernest Renan said: "Les nations ne sont pas quelque chose d'éternel, elles ont commencées, elles finiront. La confédération européenne, probablement, les remplacera." Ernest Renan, *Oeuvres complètes*, 10 vols. (Paris, 1911), 1:905.

9. Leroy-Beaulieu, "La Création d'une union de l'Europe occidentale," pp. 435 ff. and 529 ff.; Leusse, "L'Union douanière européenne," pp. 393–401; Emile Worms, *Une Association douanière franco-allemande avec restitution de l'Alsace-Lorraine* (Paris, 1888); Manuel, *L'Union européenne*, pp. 172–77; and Böhme, *Deutschlands Weg zur Grossmacht*, pp. 595–600.

10. The International Peace Congress in Rome in 1891 approved a resolution urging all of the peace groups in Europe to work for a "United States of Europe."

11. For example, Manuel, *L'Union européenne*, pp. 77–80. Charles Lemmonier, Goblet d'Alvielle, Richard Kaufmann, Eugène Borel, André Godin, Ernest Renan, Emile Zola, Paul Bourget, Ernst Bovet, and Paul d'Estournelles de Constant had much to say about European unity and unification in these years.

12. Stead, *The United States of Europe*, p. 30. The *Review of Reviews* gave attention to the European idea during the coming years. Edwin Hauser published *Die Lösung der Frage unserer volkswirtschaftlichen Existenz* in 1899 arguing that Switzerland could and should become the kernel of an "Europäischer Zollverein."

13. For summaries of these papers, see Manuel, *L'Union européenne*, pp. 85–94. For the work of the congress, see *Publications de la Société des Anciens Elèves de l'Ecole Libre des Sciences Politiques* (Paris, 1901); and Anatole Leroy-Beaulieu et al., *Les Etats-Unis d'Europe* (Paris, 1901). Most of the big arguments for Europe were already there.

14. See Fritz Fischer, "Weltpolitik, Weltmachtstreben und deutsche Kriegsziele," pp. 324–25;

Review of Reviews 39 (Jan.–June 1909): 246, 328, 49 (Mar. 1914): 193–96; and *The Times* (London), 31 Jan. 1914. The whole of p. 6 is devoted to the projected Unity League, which had its headquarters at 39 James Street, London.

15. For the work of these committees, see *Annuaire européen, 1931* (Paris, 1931), pp. 1099–1113; Poidevin, *Les Relations économiques*, pp. 450–57 and passim; and Ajam, *Le Problème économique franco-allemand*, passim.

16. Some periodicals, esp. *La Paix par le droit, Sozialistische Monatshefte,* and *Wissen und Leben* toyed with the idea at this time.

CHAPTER 2

1. Two of the most helpful works are Bonneville, *Prophètes et témoins de l'Europe*, pp. 5–20 and passim; and Grappin, *Der Bund neues Vaterland, 1914–1916*, passim.

2. Charles Gide, "La Guerre pour la paix," pp. 68–75, and *Echo de Paris*, 4 Oct. 1914.

3. See *La Guerre sociale*, 4 Aug. and 28 Oct. 1914, and *Le Bonnet rouge*, 3 Aug. 1914. Several journals across Europe speculated in this sense.

4. Bonneville, *Prophètes et témoins de l'Europe*, pp. 124–52. Also helpful are Ponti, *La Guerra dei popoli e la futura confederazione Europea*, and Wettstein, *La Crise européenne*.

5. The journal *La Paix par le droit* and H. Lepent's *Pour l'abolition des guerres* (Limoges, 1916) are helpful for these study groups. Among the brochures were two by Nico van Suchtelen himself: *Het eenige redmiddel: Een Europeesche Statenbond* (Amsterdam, 1914), and *Europa eendrachtig* (Amsterdam, 1915), and one by D. S. van Nieuwenhoven Helbach, *Een statenbond voor Europa* (Rotterdam, 1916). See also Henri Dunlop's article in *Review of Reviews*, Feb. 1915, pp. 120–21, and Ernst Bovet, "Der Federalismus," *Wissen und Leben* 9 (1 Oct. 1915–15 Sept. 1916): 716–17.

6. For the Bund's program, see *Was will der Bund neues Vaterland?* no. I (Berlin, 1915): passim. Alfred Fried, famous Austro-German pacifist who had joined with Bertha von Suttner in organizing Die deutsche Friedensgesellschaft in 1892, was the central figure in Der Bund neues Vaterland and also editor of *Friedenswarte*, which he moved to Zurich after the outbreak of the war and which appeared for a time under the title of *Blätter für zwischenstaatliche Organisation*.

7. See Romain Rolland, "Adieu au passé," *L'Europe* 26 (15 June 1931): 161–202; and his "Au dessus de la mêlée," *Journal de Genève*, 15 Sept. 1914. Also Marcelle Kempf, *Romain Rolland et l'Allemagne* (Paris, 1962), pp. 127–230.

8. See esp. *The Daily Citizen*, 29 Dec. 1914; *Review of Reviews*, Jan. 1915, pp. 28–31; and Carpenter, "The Healing of Nations," pp. 180–92. In the United States, Nicholas M. Butler and George Kirchway supported the European idea warmly.

9. Others who wrote at length on the European idea during these months and could be added were: Emil Ruegg, Johannes Erni, Auguste Forel, Hermann Fernau, Albert Thierry, Joseph Barthélemy, Ernst Bovet.

10. Curinier, "L'Organisation économique du monde civilisé," pp. 339–44. H. L. Follin, a member of the International Peace Bureau, warmly endorsed Curinier's general idea.

11. Gide's speech followed closely his article cited in the second footnote of this chapter. For an overall view, see Gide's *Les Sociétés coopératives de consommation* (Paris, 1924); and A. Lavondès, *Charles Gide: Un apôtre de la coopération entre les hommes, un précurseur de l'Europe unie et de l'U.N.O.* (Uzès, 1953).

12. See Fried, *Europäische Wiederherstellung*, chaps. 6–7, and Max Scheler's articles in *Die weissen Blätter* 2, nos. 1–3, pp. 124–27, 244–49, and 376–80; August Siemsen, *Anna Siemsen: Leben und Werk*, pp. 90–93.

13. Cornelissen, "Les Etats-Unis d'Europe," pp. 14–18. The pamphlet was entitled *Les Dessous économiques de la guerre*.

14. Hanotaux, "L'Ere nouvelle," pp. 5–52, and esp. 47–52. Alfred Capus reviewed Hanotaux's article in *Le Figaro*, 31 Oct. 1916. See also *La Paix par le droit* 26 (10–25 Nov. 1916): 501.

15. See General Alexandre Percin's article in *L'Humanité*, 14 Oct. 1915.

16. See *La Paix par le droit* 27 (July–Aug. 1917): 320; Franz Blei, *Menschliche Betrachtungen zur Politik*, pp. 253–55; and Rolland, "Un Appel aux Européens par Georg Nicolai," pp. 66–72.

17. *Echo de Paris*, 25 June 1917.

18. See Ruyssen, "Le Mouvement pacifiste," pp. 135, 251–52. Also Hennessy, *L'Organisation fédérale de la Société des Nations*, passim. A collection of Hennessy's articles and speeches without place or date.

19. Agnelli and Cabiati, *Federazione europea o lega delle nazioni?* passim. The book was immediately translated into French under the title of *Fédération européenne ou ligue des nations* with a postscript (pp. 129–34) that compared the programs of Woodrow Wilson and V. I. Lenin and warned that the peoples of Europe would have to save themselves. See also Einaudi, *La Guerra del l'unità europea*, pp. 23–36.

20. *Les Etats-Unis d'Europe* 15 (Apr. 1927): 124–25. Though the vast literature dealing with the problem of peace was centered on a universal league, it was quite varied. See, for example, Paul Otlet, *Les Problèmes internationaux de la guerre* (Geneva, 1917); Percin, *La Guerre et la nation armée*; Mathias Erzberger, *Der Voelkerbund der Weg zum Frieden* (Berlin, 1918); and Pannwitz, *Deutschland und Europa: Grundriss einer deutsch-europäischen Politik*.

21. For literature on central and eastern Europe following publication of Friedrich Naumann's *Mitteleuropa*, see F. Eulenburg, "Literatur über Mitteleuropa," *Weltwirtschaftliches Archiv* 8, no. 1 (1916): 379–94, and vol. 2, pp. 394–420; Paul Sweet, "Recent German Literature on Mitteleuropa," *Journal of Central European Affairs* 3 (April 1943): 1–24. H. C. Meyer, *Mitteleuropa in German Thought and Action, 1815–1945* (The Hague, 1955); and Jacques Droz, *L'Europe centrale* (Paris, 1960), esp. chap. 8.

CHAPTER 3

1. See, for example, Scelle, "Une Ere juridique nouvelle," pp. 297–98; Demangeon, *Le Déclin de l'Europe*, passim; and Christian Lange, *Histoire de l'internationalisme* (Kristiania, 1919), 1: preface.

2. *Vorwärts*, 29 Dec. 1919. See also *La Paix par le droit* 29 (Jan. 1919): 54.

3. U.S. Department of State, *The Paris Peace Conference 1919*, 2:220.

4. Ibid. 12:240–47; and 3:87–90, 146–50.

5. Ruyssen, "La Société des nations devant la conférence de paix," pp. 87–103. Also Scelle, *Le Pacte des nations*, pp. 293–367 and passim.

6. See *La Paix par le droit* 29 (July–Aug. 1919): 357–58.

7. Several journals, including *L'Europe nouvelle*, *Le Monde nouveau*, *Die neue Rundschau*, *Nord und Süd*, and *Revue de Genève*, were using such expressions now and then, and they were also appearing more frequently in books such as Brun, *La Tradition fédéraliste française*; Pasztor, *Europai eggesult Allamok*; Momigliano, *Carlo Cattaneo e gli Stati uniti d'Europa*; Keyserling, *Deutschlands wahre politische Mission*; Ruyssen, *De Force au droit*; Endres, *Vaterland und Menschheit*; Reboux, *Les Drapeaux*; and Rolland, *Les Poètes contre la guerre*.

8. Hennessy, "Si nous ne faisons pas la vraie Société des Nations la France est perdue," pp. 17–20. This journal, which soon claimed a circulation of fifty thousand, probably published more articles in 1919 and 1920 supporting the European idea than any other periodical in Europe. Bovet told the readers of *Wissen und Leben* (15, p. 158) that *Le Progrès civique* was a journal that "must be read."

9. Fischer, "Ein Theoretiker des Föderalismus," pp. 503–9; and Welter, "Weltwirtschaft und

Zollvereinsfragen," pp. 563–73.

10. Premier Clemenceau's letter to Colonel House was published in *La Paix par le droit* 29 (Sept.–Oct. 1919): 424. *Le Temps* (22 Oct.) said that President Wilson should see to it that the initial session of the council coincided with the going into force of the Treaty of Versailles. See also Hennessy, "De la Nécessité d'un nouveau congrès," pp. 7–8.

11. Quessel, "Die kontinentaleuropäische Arbeitsgemeinschaft," pp. 874–75; Koch, "Geistige Bewegung," pp. 924–26. For the slow and painful business of the restoration of contacts across frontiers, see Ruyssen, "Le Renouveau du pacifisme," *La Paix par le droit* 29 (Sept.–Oct. 1919): 403–16; Stein, *Aus dem Leben eines Optimisten*, pp. 260–65; Henri Lichtenberger, *L'Allemagne d'aujourd'hui dans ses relations avec la France* (Paris, 1922); Raphaël, *L'Industrie allemande*, passim; and Troeltsch, *Spektator*, pp. 241–62.

12. See H. W. V. Temperley (ed.), *History of the Peace Conference*, 6 vols. (London, 1920–24), 1:325–38; and Gignoux, "Que faut-il penser des Etats-Unis d'Europe," pp. 10–11; and his *L'Après-guerre*, passim.

13. Fernau, "Frankreichs Politik und Europas Wiederaufbau," p. 138 and passim. For contemporary evaluations of this conference, see *Bulletin de la Société d'Economie Politique*, 5 Jan. 1921, pp. 2–14; and *Die neue Rundschau* 31, no. 2 (1920): 1315–21. Even Hugo Stinnes, who had just put together the Rhein-Siemens-Schuckert-Elbe-Union, had written Maximilian Harden, editor of *Die Zukunft*, of the possibility of "eine Zollunion zwischen Frankreich und Deutschland, möglichst mit sofortiger Anschluss von Holland, Belgien, und Schweiz, vorzubereiten." See Gert von Klass, *Hugo Stinnes* (Tübingen, 1958), p. 312. Klass analyzes several of Stinnes's letters to Harden (pp. 304–41).

14. See esp. Aulard, "Les Etats-Unis d'Europe," pp. 9–10; Hennessy, "De la Nécessité d'un nouveau Congrès," pp. 7–9; Hennessy, "La Paix rendue aux peuples," pp. 18–20; and Hennessy, "Démocrats de tous les pays," pp. 17–19.

15. Bovet, "Die Europäer," p. 552 and passim; Bovet, "Le premier pas à faire," pp. 881–87. See also Voeste, "Von der Idee des Völkerbunds," pp. 477–91; and Reboux, "Le seul Chemin." Reboux also published articles of a like nature in *Paris-Soir*.

16. Demangeon, *Le Déclin de l'Europe*, esp. pp. 21–35, 292–309; and Mauss, "L'Internationalisme," pp. 321–25. Mauss argued that the shift in economic forces would make the states of Europe increasingly interdependent and thus much more in need of a common program.

17. Steinitzer, "Europäisches Zusammenwirken," p. 933. See also Müller, "Europa und die Weltpolitik," pp. 401–18; Georg Bernhard's editorials in *Vossische Zeitung*, 21 and 30 Jan. 1921; Stein, *Aus dem Leben*, pp. 260–65; and Kessler, *Tagebücher, 1918–1937*, pp. 225–36 and passim.

18. For good analyses of Gide's paper, see *La Paix par le droit* 31 (May 1921): 182; and *Bulletin de la Société d'Economie Politique*, 5 Apr. 1921, pp. 52–56.

19. Rivière, "Notes sur un événement politique," pp. 557–70. There is a brief account of Rivière's political activities during 1922–23 in Fernand L'Huillier's *Dialogues franco-allemands*, pp. 16–22; and much general data in the memorial issue of *Nouvelle revue française* in 1925.

20. Rathenau, *Tagebuch, 1907–1922*, 171–87 and Launay, *L. Loucheur: Carnets secrets, 1908–1932*, pp. 84–93. Loucheur stated (p. 88) that Rathenau repeatedly raised the idea of some sort of "Société Internationale de reconstruction." The American Mission in Budapest also reported to the U.S. Dept. of State on 16 June 1921 that Loucheur and Rathenau talked about the possibility of "a Franco-German economic alliance against American competition." See also Erdmann, *Adenauer in der Rheinlandpolitik*, pp. 71–72, 156–62; Hallgarten, *Hitler, Reichswehr, und Industrie*, pp. 12–20; Pinner, *Deutsche Wirtschaftsführer*, pp. 10–31; and Vietsch, *Arnold Rechberg*, pp. 229–43.

21. *Verhandlungen des Deutschen Reichstags, 1920–1932*, 350:4264. See also Steinitzer, "Das Weltproblem Deutschland," pp. 314–20.

22. See, for example, Gide, "Les Rapports intellectuels," pp. 513–17; Klaus Mann, *André Gide*, pp. 280–81 and passim. Thomas Mann, "Das Problem der deutsch-französischen Be-

ziehungen"; Jean Hennessy, "Il faut à la France une politique extérieure," pp. 16–17; and Ribert, "La Reconstruction de l'Europe," pp. 243–46. Ribert said that what was most needed was a European organization resting on the principles of democracy and the solidarity of Europe's workers. He predicted: "De cette société démocratique naîtront les Etats-unis d'Europe."

23. See Launay, L. *Loucheur: Carnets secrets*, pp. 92–102; Pinner, *Deutsche Wirtschaftsführer*, pp. 20–30; and Arnold Rechberg's articles in *Tägliche Rundschau*, 6 and 9 Nov. 1921, and in *Der Tag*, 20 and 30 Dec. 1921. Rechberg was urging his government to work for an economic alliance with France and for the organization of western Europe against Russia.

24. See, for example, Ernest Bovet, "A propos de Gênes," *Wissen und Leben* 15 (1 June 1922): 666–71; Aulard, "Heureux discrédit de la gloire militaire," pp. 7–10; Percin, "Il faut détruire l'esprit de guerre," pp. 15–16; Burgelin, "Le Mouvement pacifiste dans l'Allemagne," pp. 57–88; Schoenaich, *Abrüstung der Kopf*, passim; Rolland, ed., *Les Poètes contre la guerre*, passim; and Lehmann-Russbueldt, *Der Kampf für den Weltfrieden*, passim.

25. *Lyon Républicain*, 30 Dec. 1921; *La Dépêche de Toulouse*, 25 Apr. 1922; *Le Progrès civique*, 25 Feb. 1922, pp. 15–17; *Deutsche Allgemeine Zeitung*, 20 Feb. 1922; and *La Paix par le droit* 32 (Jan. 1922): 43–45 and (Feb. 1922): 90–91. Anatole France, like many other European writers and scholars, was now saying that Europe should be able to achieve a degree of political and economic unity commensurate with its intellectual and cultural unity.

CHAPTER 4

1. Rivière, "Pour une Entente économique avec l'Allemagne," p. 727, "Les Dangers d'une politique conséquente," pp. 5–10. Business contacts were seemingly facilitated by the fact that Leopold von Hoesch, Germany's chargé d'affaires in Paris, was a grandson of the founder of the Hoesch Steel Works in Dortmund and had some sympathy for the European idea.

2. Drieu la Rochelle, *Mesure de la France*, p. 65 and passim. See also his *L'Europe contre les patries*; *Genève ou Moscou*; and *Die deutsche Rundschau* 34, no. 2, pp. 598–99.

3. Joseph Caillaux, *Où va la France?* p. 285 and passim; and "Où va la France?" 19 July 1921, pp. 9–10. Caillaux felt that a large segment of Africa might be integrated into a European community.

4. Two other journals with European tendencies and overtones—*La Revue européenne* and *Europäische Gespräche*—appeared in the spring of 1923. See, for example, *La Revue européenne*, 1 Nov. 1923, pp. 10–24; and *Wissen und Leben* 16 (20 July 1923): 851–2. *La Revue rhénane (Rheinische Blätter)* was also showing an interest in the European idea.

5. See Wilhelm Heile, "Die Vereinigten Staaten von Europa," pp. 274–76. For Heile's political thought in the middle twenties, see his *Nationalstaat und Völkerbund*, and for an excellent treatment of his role in German proeuropean organizations during the 1920s, see Karl Holl, "Europapolitik im Vorfeld der deutschen Regierungspolitik," pp. 33–94.

6. Heinrich Mann, "Der Europäer," *Berliner Tageblatt*, 24 Oct. 1916. At this time Thomas Mann was writing his *Betrachtungen eines Unpolitischen* (Berlin, 1918) in which he made a somewhat troubled defense of German Kultur.

7. Heinrich Mann, "Europa—Reich über den Reichen," 577–602, and "Deutschland und Frankreich," pp. 769–77. For interesting comments on Mann's Europeanism across the twenties, see Banuls, *Heinrich Mann*, pp. 350–60 and passim. Thomas Mann was now moving very slowly toward the political views of Heinrich.

8. The nine-page introduction provides a good summary of Baerwald's view of Europe and of his political philosophy.

9. Malynski, *Pour sauver l'Europe*, esp. pp. 3–40, 201–6. Malynski said the new European community should live on friendly terms with the U.S. and Japan.

10. Riedl's draft of a constitution for a European federation was published in Loesch and Ziegfeld, eds., *Staat und Volkstum*, pp. 51–85. For an excellent analysis of the German govern-

ment's reaction to the European idea from 1923 to 1930, see Lipgens, "Europäische Einigungsidee 1923–1930 und Briands Europaplan," pp. 46–89, 316–83. I have abridged the material that I had in the first draft on the German government's attitude and referred the reader to Lipgens's article.

11. Chancellor Seipel was in Rome in the spring of 1923 and heard both Carlo Schanzer, Italian foreign minister, and Cardinal Gaspari, secretary of state for the Vatican, speak of a Danubian confederation. See Pfeiffer to Stresemann, 15 April 1925, German Foreign Ministry Archives, U.S. National Archives Microfilms T-120, Washington, D.C., H57GH/2344/E171521-7 (hereafter cited as G.F.M. reel and frame number). There is in the Maltzan Papers a memo for Maltzan, 19 April 1923 (G.F.M. 5462/K517536-51), which speculates on a European Zollverein in much the same language that Hugo Stinnes had used with Harden in 1920.

12. For Coudenhove's account of his thoughts and activities at this time, see his *Crusade for Pan-Europe*, pp. 70–78; his *Der Kampf um Europa*, pp. 92–94; and his "Europa und Deutschland" pp. 299–308.

13. For Coudenhove's reasoning on these points, see his *Paneuropa* (1923), 20–50, 81–94. Coudenhove wrote General Hans von Seeckt on 11 Mar. 1923, asking him to comment on the idea of a European army. Seeckt apparently did not reply.

14. For Seipel's views concerning Austria's mission in Europe, see Suval, *The Anschluss Question*, pp. 196–97, 204–9, and passim; Ambassador Hoffmann to the Foreign Office, 16 June 1925, G.F.M. 4576H/2344/E171713; Gessl, *Seipels Reden*, pp. 71–72, and passim; and for a contemporary interpretation of Seipel as a European statesman, Thormann, *Dr. Ignaz Seipel*, passim.

15. Coudenhove-Kalergi, *Der Kampf um Europa*, pp. 98–101. Bankers Max Warburg and Arthur von Gwinner were helping financially.

16. For this youth group and its plans see *La Paix par le droit* 22 (1922): 40–41. Jean Luchaire persisted and in 1927 played the leading role in founding *Notre Temps*. I talked briefly with Luchaire in 1930 but we talked only of *Notre temps* and of Briand's objectives.

17. This manifesto was discussed by the French section of the International League for Peace and Freedom on 7 Dec. 1923, and the composition and program of the new group was treated in *L'Ere nouvelle*, 3 Jan. 1924.

18. See *La Paix par le droit* 32 (1922): 347–54; Noblemaire, "La reconstruction économique de l'Europe," pp. 500–507; and *Vorwärts*, 26 May 1923.

19. Harms, "Die Krisis der Weltwirtschaft," pp. 269–73; Bruins, "Die Bedeutung eines ungehinderten Verkehrs für den Wiederaufbau Europas," pp. 315 ff. (Bruins's call for an "Europäische Völkergemeinschaft" appears on p. 334.) For Harms's view of the overall commercial situation in Europe, see his *Die Zukunft der deutschen Handelspolitik*. Schoenaich argued for a sort of world economic federation in his *Abrüstung der Kopf*; and Nitti stressed much this same idea in his *The Decadence of Europe*.

20. See Saunders, "Stresemann vs. Poincaré," Ph.D. dissertation, University of North Carolina, 1974, passim. See also Pinner, *Deutsche Wirtschaftsführer*, pp. 40–47; Stresemann, *Vermächtnis*, 1:94; Raphaël, *L'Industrie allemande*, pp. 197–98 and passim; Erdmann, *Adenauer in der Rheinlandpolitik*, pp. 156–85.

21. L'Huillier, *Dialogues franco-allemands, 1925–1933*, pp. 20–25.

CHAPTER 5

1. For general works with European overtones, see Seydoux, *De Versailles au plan Young*; Respondek, *Wirtschaftliche Zusammenarbeit zwischen Deutschland und Frankreich*; Montigny and Kayser, *Le Drame financier*; Schmidt, *Das neue Deutschland*; and Hantos, *Die Handelspolitik in Mitteleuropa*.

2. *L'Oeuvre*, 29 Jan. 1924.

3. See *Les Etats-Unis de l'Europe* 15 (Apr. 1924): 52–53.

4. Since the archives of the Paneuropean Union were apparently destroyed by the Germans in 1939, *Paneuropa*, which ran from 1924 to 1938, is the best single source for the activities of the Paneuropean Union.

5. See *L'Europe de demain* 9 (Aug. 1930): 1–3; Stern-Rubarth, *Drei Männer suchen Europa*, pp. 100–102 and passim; Truchy, "La Reconstruction économique de l'Europe," pp. 355–56; and Erkelenz, "Zukunft Aufgaben der Demokratie," p. 172. Erkelenz said that the idea of a customs union was "much in the air." Stern-Rubarth, in a letter to me dated 22 Apr. 1963, said several members of the Reichsverband der Deutschen Industrie, including Richard Heilner and Bernhard Harms, encouraged him in this work.

6. See especially Pirov, "Un Congrès économique d'après-guerre," pp. 274–82.

7. For comprehensive, contemporary accounts, see Georges Lachapelle, *Elections législatives du 11 mai 1924* (Paris, 1924); Louis Marcellin, *Voyage autour de la chambre du 11 mai* (Paris, 1925); and Appay, "Ce que signifient les résultats," pp. 13–14.

8. *L'Europe nouvelle*, 17 May 1924, p. 622. *L'Oeuvre* also speculated about ways and means of turning the Olympic Games, scheduled for Paris in May 1924, into a demonstration for peace and Europe.

9. *Vorwärts*, 13–14 May 1924; *Vossische Zeitung*, 13 May 1924; Rudolf Breitscheid, "La surprise de l'Allemagne devant les élections françaises," *L'Europe nouvelle*, 24 May 1924, pp. 659–60; and Ernst Troeltsch, *Deutscher Geist und Westeuropa*, pp. 4–25.

10. Text is in *Paneuropa* 1, no. 3, pp. 3–13.

11. *L'Ere nouvelle*, 4 Sept. 1924, carried René Cassin's review of Edward Filene's *European Federation and the Peace of Europe*. Other French dailies that were now warmly supporting the European idea were *Le Quotidien*, *La Dépêche de Toulouse*, *L'Information*, and *Le Matin*.

12. See esp. Wehberg, "Eine Umfrage zum Weltfriedenskongress," pp. 206–11; Georg Bernhard, "Völkerfriede and Volksfriede," *Vossische Zeitung*, 5 Oct. 1924; and Stein, *Aus dem Leben eines Optimisten*, pp. 241 ff. Both Bernhard and Stein were working with the International Committee for a European Customs Union, and both belonged to the influential Mittwoch Gesellschaft in Berlin.

13. For Coudenhove-Kalergi's speech and the debate, see *Vossische Zeitung*, 8 Oct. 1924; *Les Etats-Unis d'Europe* 15 (Oct. 1924): 63, and (Jan. 1925): 75–76; and *Sozialistische Monatshefte*, 21 Oct. 1924, pp. 608–10. Ludwig Quessel said the Congress was ruled by the feeling that any show of interest in Paneurope would offend the British.

14. For Coudenhove's estimate of his work in Germany at this time, see his *Crusade for Pan-Europe*, pp. 92–96, and his *Der Kampf um Europa*, pp. 104–6. Georg Bernhard, Julius Wolff, and Albert Einstein were among early members of the German chapter of Paneuropean Union. Stresemann had heard of young Coudenhove and, wanting to size him up, gave him an audience on 11 June 1925. Stresemann's *Vermächtnis*, 2:307.

15. See the letters in *Vossische Zeitung*, 2 Oct., 2 Nov., 2, 3 Dec. 1924. The last two were by Heinrich Mann and were strong pleas for a united Europe.

16. See the editorial "Stresemann und Herriot," *Vossische Zeitung*, 4 Nov. 1924.

17. Koch-Weser, *Deutschlands Aussenpolitik*, pp. 59–60 and 110–20.

18. *Vossische Zeitung*, 14 Nov. 1924.

19. For a typical article, see Kaliski, "Weltsozialismus," pp. 607–11.

20. *Vossische Zeitung*, 14 Nov. 1924.

21. For Germany, see esp. R. J. Haebler, "Organisatorische Aufbau der Deutschen Friedensbewegung," *Friedenswarte* 24 (Sept. 1925): 257–62; Alfred Wolf, "Der Weg zum Frieden," *Die Hilfe*, 15 May 1924, pp. 160–63; the *Vossische Zeitung*, 5 Oct. 1924; and Henri Burgelin, "Le Mouvement pacifiste dans l'Allemagne," pp. 57–88.

22. See, for example, Anton Erkelenz, "Der Zusammenbruch Europas," *Die Hilfe*, 1 Apr. 1924, pp. 121 ff.; Bonnet, "La Baisse de la livre," p. 155; Maier, "Europas weltwirtschaftlicher Niedergang," pp. 759–62; Hauser, "Des Obstacles au retour," p. 737; Vogel, "Erdteilstaaten als

Weltmächte," pp. 55–78; Naudin, *Les Accords commerciaux*, passim.

23. The list of articles on Paneuropa in *Bibliographie der Sozialwissenschaften* (with variant titles) is incomplete even for the German periodical press. The most interesting of the articles to appear in German and Austrian periodicals, other than *Paneuropa*, in 1924 using "Paneuropa" or "United States of Europe" as titles were: Halase, "Zur Frage Paneuropa," pp. 352–60; Gesell, "Die Stauben der Vereinigten Staaten von Europe," pp. 191–98; and Niekisch, "Paneuropa," pp. 1–2.

24. See esp. pp. 21–28. But most socialists continued to struggle with this question. See, for example, Lauterbach, "Um Paneuropa," pp. 280–86; Renner, "Die weltwirtschaftlichen Grundlagen," pp. 397–99; and Léon Blum's numerous editorials on socialist ideology in *Le Populaire* in the late twenties.

CHAPTER 6

1. The year 1925 brought a very substantial increase in books dealing exclusively or mainly with the European idea. Among the best of these books were Maury, *Babel*; Endres, *Vaterland Europa*; Naudeau, *En écoutant parler les allemands*; Schmidt, *Das neue Deutschland in der Weltpolitik und Weltwirtschaft*; Buchholz, *Die Vereinigten Staaten von Europa*; Percin, *Le Désarmement moral*; Nonnenbruch, *Das vereinigte Europa*; Lehrmann-Russbueldt, *Republik Europa*; Delaisi, *Les Contradictions du monde moderne*; Weber, *Die Krise des modernen Staatsgedankens in Europa*; Hantos, *Die Handelspolitik in Mitteleuropa*; Nitti, *La Pace*; Morocutti, *Europa und die völkischen Minderheiten*; and Claparède-Spir, *Pour les Ententes des peuples*.

2. *Journal officiel, Chambre des Députes, débats parlementaries*, Session Ordinaire de 1925, 28 Jan. 1925, p. 371 (hereafter cited as J.O.C. Déb.).

3. Nitti, "Die Vereinigten Staaten von Europa," pp. 24–30. Nitti suggested that an effort should be made to include Russia in such a union.

4. *L'Ere nouvelle*, 2 Feb. 1925. This great peace rally was organized by the new committee to plan a special monument to peace.

5. Borel, "Die deutsch-französischen Beziehungen," pp. 15–16. The appearance of this journal, which was similar to *L'Europe* and *La Revue européenne*, was evidence of the growth of European thought in the German-speaking world.

6. *Les Etats-Unis d'Europe* 15 (Apr. 1925): 78–79. See also Dumont-Wilden, "Européens unissez-vous," p. 485 ff.; and Bec, "Le Peril jaune," pp. 97–104.

7. *L'Ere nouvelle*, 14 July 1925. Rodiques's observation was, of course, true and some Germans admitted it. See, for example, Coerper, *Das wirtschaftliche Europa*, pp. 30–34.

8. Maury, *Babel*, pp. 178–79 and passim.

9. Coudenhove-Kalergi, *Crusade for Pan-Europe*, p. 99. Among the French leaders with whom Coudenhove talked were Herriot, Painlevé, Caillaux, Loucheur, Henri de Jouvenel, and Blum.

10. Endres, *Vaterland Europa*, pp. 28–40, 71–73, 107–11.

11. See esp. Rohan's editorial in *Europäische Revue* 1 (July 1925): 254–55. For Rohan's most important articles and essays during the 1920s, see his *Umbruch der Zeit, 1923–1930*.

12. *Cahiers des droits de l'homme*, 10 Jan. 1926, p. 12.

13. Winifred Katzin, trans. *As They Are: French Political Portraits* (New York, 1923), p. 151. See also Louis Dumont-Wilden, "Le Règlement de la paix et l'esprit européen," p. 585; and Jules Hermans, "L'Evolution de la pensée européenne de Briand," pp. 3–29.

14. Saint-Léger, *Briand*, p. 7. Saint-Léger liked to elaborate on Briand's Europeanism as well as his artistry. Siebert gives careful attention to Briand's European thought in his *Aristide Briand*, esp. pp. 470–530.

15. Göhre, "Die Vereinigten Staaten von Europa," pp. 125–26. See also Endres, *Vaterland*

Europa, pp. 75–118; and Buchholz, *Die Vereinigten Staaten von Europa*, pp. 27–32. The Left wing of the German peace movement, which was dominated by W. F. Foerster and his *Die Menschheit*, strongly supported the European idea.

16. Quessel, "Genf, Heidelberg, und Locarno," pp. 599–600. The doctrine of the balance of power was not, of course, the whole story, for the Left wing disliked England for other reasons.

17. See, for example, Nonnenbruch, *Das vereinigte Europa*, pp. 175–99; and Willi Hellpach's article in *Berliner Tageblatt*, 7 July 1925. Nonnenbruch saw a German-dominated middle Europe as the first step but argued that Africa would be needed to provide an adequate resource base for a united Europe.

18. For the political ideas of the German Right, see Kurt Sontheimer, *Antidemokratisches Denken in der Weimarer Republik* (Munich, 1962), passim.

19. See issues from 27–30 Apr. 1925; also the article by Alfred Fabre-Luce in issue of 3 July 1925; and Holl and Wild, *Ein Demokrat kommentiert Weimar*, p. 142.

20. *Verhandlungen des Reichstags, III. Wahlperiode 1924*, 385:1893–94. See also Breitscheid's "Das aussenpolitische Programm der Sozialdemokratie," pp. 169–75.

21. *Verhandlungen des Reichstags*, 385:1934. Bernstorff was editor of *Die deutsche Einheit* and was constantly writing on political and economic issues.

22. Ibid., pp. 1962–64. See also Bell, "Zentrumsgedanken zur deutschen Aussenpolitik," pp. 175–82.

23. *Verhandlungen des Reichstags*, 385:2040.

24. See, for example, Otto Hoetzsch's article in *Europäische Revue* 1, no. 4 (July, 1925): 213–17; and Hoesch to the Foreign Office, 1 June 1925, G.F.M. 3086/1483/D614074-5.

25. Even *La Paix par le droit* and *L'Europe nouvelle* expressed fear that Stresemann's real purpose was a free hand for Germany in Austria, Czechoslovakia, and Poland.

26. Stresemann to Löbe, 21 Aug. 1925, G.F.M. 4576/2344/E171813-4. The Austrian Section of the Volksbund (Oesterreichisch-deutsches Volksbund) was set up on 4 June 1925. For this demonstration, see *Neue freie Presse*, 30–31 Aug. 1925.

CHAPTER 7

1. For comprehensive contemporary analyses, see Delaisi, *Les Contradictions du monde moderne*; Schmidt, *Das neue Deutschland in der Weltpolitik und Weltwirtschaft*; Seydoux, *De Versailles au plan Young*; Harms, *Die Zukunft der deutschen Handelspolitik*; Montigny and Kayser, *Le Drame financier: Les responsables*; Woytinsky, *Zehn Jahre neues Deutschland*; Cristu, *L'Union douanière européenne*, and Gignoux, *L'Après-guerre et la politique commerciale*.

2. See esp. Thibaudet, "L'Europe de demain," p. 1024. Thibaudet also listed several journals that were giving increasing space to "l'esprit européen."

3. *L'Europe nouvelle*, 26 Sept. 1925, pp. 1263–65. *Vossische Zeitung*, 26 Sept. 1925, commented on the European character of this issue of *L'Europe nouvelle*.

4. See esp. Vandervlugt, "Les Etats-Unis d'Europe," pp. 1061–69; Heile, "Warum ich für Paneuropa bin," pp. 262–64; and Pianos Van Der Elst, "Les Etats-Unis d'Europe," *Pourquoi pas?* p. 1255.

5. Woytinsky, "Neue Weltwirtschaft—neue Weltpolitik," p. 283. Woytinsky was already well along with his *Die Vereinigten Staaten von Europa*. See also Mommsen, "Vereinigte Staaten von Europa?" pp. 1284–90, 1317–20.

6. Lucien Le Foyer, "L'Union de l'Europe et ses sanctions," *L'Ere nouvelle*, 14 Sept. 1925. Le Foyer analyzed both of Painlevé's speeches and said that what the premier was saying was: "If you want peace, decree Europe." *Vossische Zeitung*, 6 Sept. 1925, called Painlevé "Der Europäer."

7. Stresemann, "Deutschlands Stellung im europäischen Wirtschaftssystem," pp. 148–50. Stresemann, like nearly all Germans, thought of European unification largely in economic terms.

See also Stern-Rubarth, *Gustav Stresemann: Patriot und Europäer*.

8. *L'Ere nouvelle*, 23 Sept. 1925. Also the issue of 25 Oct. 1925, for a review of *Désarmement moral*.

9. These resolutions were widely discussed. See *L'Europe nouvelle*, 11 July 1925, pp. 916–19.

10. *Vorwärts*, 18 Sept. 1925 and 20–23 Sept. 1925. Several articles with strong European overtones appeared in *Sozialistische Monatshefte* in Sept., Oct., and Nov. 1925.

11. Louis Loucheur, "Situation de la France," pp. 441–49; and Jacques Kayser et al., *Les Etats-Unis d'Europe*, pp. 196–99.

12. League of Nations, *Official Journal: Special Supplement*, no. 33, 1925, pp. 81–83. Also Louise Sommer, "Die Vorgeschichte der Weltwirtschaftskonferenz," pp. 386 ff.

13. See *L'Information*, 17 and 19 Sept. 1925; and *L'Oeuvre*, 16 Sept. 1925.

14. *The Economist*, 19 Sept. 1925, p. 444. The journal also reminded its readers that one-third of England's foreign trade was with the continent of Europe.

15. The International Chamber of Commerce set up three committees to gather data and to ponder the economic reconstruction of Europe.

16. See *Union interparlementaire: Compte rendu de la XXIIIe Conférence* (Paris, 1926) for the resolution and speeches, and see *Vorwärts* and *Neue freie Presse*, 8 Oct. 1925, for typical press reactions.

17. According to Emile Vandervlugt and several others, Briand's words were: "Les Etats-Unis d'Europe sont nés." See Vandervlugt, "Les Etats-Unis d'Europe," p. 1061; and Henri Hertz, "Natalité du citoyen européen," *Le Monde nouveau*, 15 Feb. 1926, p. 1311. Henry Barde said in *L'Oeuvre* that Briand used the term "United States of Europe" several times while talking with journalists.

18. *L'Ere nouvelle*, 22 Oct. 1925. This journal agreed with Prudhomme's assessment and was now suggesting a revision of history texts with a view to greater objectivity and emphasis on peace and European unity.

19. *Prager Presse*, 18 Oct. 1925, labeled the pact "eine Grosstat der europäischen Politik" and declared Locarno a victory for Europe and for the idea of a European community.

20. See *Berliner Lokal-Anzeiger*, 31 Oct. 1925, for the "Guiding Principles" of the German National People's party. See also *Deutsche allgemeine Zeitung*, 3 Nov. 1925; and Alfred Weber, "Paneuropa," pp. 151–53. German business circles generally felt that the pact would have a wholesome affect on industry and trade.

21. See Robinet de Cléry, "L'Opinion allemande et le traité de Locarno," *Revue politique et parlementaire* 126 (Feb. 1926): 210–23.

22. Max Cohen, "Locarno und Continentaleuropa" pp. 731–36; and Egbert von Frankenberg, "Von Locarno zum Völkerbund," pp. 212–23.

CHAPTER 8

1. See esp. Gutmann, *Um die Welt zu Paneuropa*, pp. 121–35; Vazeille, *Pour les Etats-Unis d'Europe*, pp. 5–10; and Endres, *Vaterland Europa*, pp. 9–40.

2. See *L'Oeuvre*, 22 Nov. 1925; and for texts of lectures Hennessy, ed., *L'Europe fédéraliste aspirations et réalités*.

3. Ibid., pp. 13–14.

4. Ibid., p. 205. See also Rohan, *Heimat Europa*, pp. 119–22; Rameru, *Une Image d'Etats-Unis européens*, passim; and Hagemand, "Paneuropa, Idee und Wirklichkeit," pp. 497–509.

5. *L'Europe fédéraliste*, pp. 205, 230–31. Coudenhove-Kalergi said repeatedly that Switzerland should be the political model and the United States the economic model.

6. Ibid., pp. 106–7. Elemér Hantos generally agreed with Szende. See his *Die Handelspolitik im Mitteleuropa*, passim.

7. Romier, "Europäische Solidarität," pp. 9–10. Also Romier's *Qui sera le maître*, pp. 176–77; and Hauser, "Was ist Europa?" pp. 3–10.

8. Rogge, "Einheit und Hemmungen des europäischen Denkens," p. 386; *L'Ere nouvelle*, 5 Sept. 1925, and *Le Monde nouveau*, 15 Mar. 1928, pp. 64–65. Ignaz Seipel sometimes spoke of Europe as a house of many apartments and many families.

9. See esp. Bonneville, *Prophètes et témoins de l'Europe*, pp. 54–63; and Paul Valéry, *Collected Works* (New York, 1962), 10:321–22.

10. Monzie, "Die Wiederaufnahme der geistigen Beziehungen," pp. 223–30; Müller, "Wege zum europäischen Zollverein," pp. 230–37. For comments by Klemperer and Viénot, see *Europäische Revue* 1 (Jan. 1926): 298–301. See also Viénot, "Réflections sur l'idée d'Europe," 6 Feb. 1926.

11. On 19 Jan. 1926, J. J. Rousseau founded the Bureau International d'Education in Paris to explore the general idea. See *La Paix par le droit*, Apr. 1926, p. 228; and Kayser, Franck, and Lemercier, *Les Etats-Unis d'Europe*, pp. 186–87 and passim.

12. Lanux, "Europäischer Realismus," pp. 56–57; Dankworth, "Zwei europäische Strömungen," pp. 182–83; and Koch-Weser; *Deutschlands Aussenpolitik*, pp. 88–92. Koch-Weser said the conflict was a product of royal dynasties and bad presses.

13. Coerper, "Die innere Macht," p. 225 and passim; also his *Das wirtschaftliche Europa*, pp. 26–34; and Springer, *Das Gesetz der Macht*, passim. For more pointed assertions, see Nonnenbruch, *Das vereinigte Europa*, pp. 170–99; and Poulimenos, *Vereinigte Staaten Europas*, passim.

14. See esp. Teyssare, "Vers un esprit international," pp. 58–60; and Richet, "Vers l'esprit européen," pp. 141–44.

15. For strong expressions of this point, by writers other than Coudenhove-Kalergi, see *L'Information*, 20 Nov. 1926; Vogel, "Nordamerikas Wirtschaftsaufstieg," pp. 104–48; and Kayser, et al., *Les Etats-Unis d'Europe*, pp. 195–96 and passim.

16. For arguments for and against cartels, see Cristu, *L'Union douanière européenne*, pp. 107–23; and Deutsch, "Die Bedeutung der Kartelle," pp. 19–27. For comprehensive analyses, see Conte, *Les Ententes industrielles*; and Grossmann, *Systèmes de rapprochement économique*.

17. Deutsch, "Europäische Wirtschaftspolitik," p. 1904; and Rohan, *Heimat Europa*, p. 179. For recent analysis of the German attitude, see Frommelt, *Paneuropa oder Mitteleuropa*, pp. 52–60.

18. See *Sozialistische Monatshefte*, 16 Jan. 1926, pp. 12–16; and Heiman, *Europäische Zollunion*, pp. 5–7 and passim. This book consists of articles on the customs union idea by twenty-one German and Austrian scholars, politicians, and businessmen. The *Veröffentlichungen des Reichsverbandes der deutschen Industrie* does not indicate as much interest in the custom union idea on the part of German businessmen as Stern-Rubarth believed there was.

19. *L'Europe nouvelle*, 13 Mar. 1926, p. 331; and Woytinsky, *Les Etats-Unis d'Europe*, pp. 129–30.

20. See esp. pp. 105–68 and 467–556.

21. See Delaisi, "Les Contradictions du monde moderne," p. 141. This article is a summary of the main points of his book.

22. Woytinsky, *Vereinigte Staaten von Europa*, pp. 100–126, 129–47, 160–78.

23. Török, *Vom Nationalismus zu den Vereinigten Staaten von Europa*, pp. 71–79, 162–97. Many who tried to face up to a customs union, came to much the same view as Török.

24. Göhre, "Die Vereinigten Staaten von Europa," pp. 113–26. See also Göhre's *Deutschlands weltpolitische Sendung*, passim; Cohen-Reuss, "Die wirtschaftliche Annäherung," pp. 119–37; and Nečas, *Die Vereinigten Staaten von Europa*, passim.

25. See esp. Truchy, "La Reconstruction économique," pp. 358–66; and his "Vers l'entente douanière," pp. 209–21. Lucien Coquet had toyed with a customs union in much the same fashion as Truchy but had embraced it earlier.

26. *Neue freie Presse*, 4 Oct. 1925. Huberman said the Federal Union was the great fact of the system.

27. See pp. 469–70.

28. See Stolper, "Staat-Nation-Wirtschaft," in Hanns Heiman, ed., *Europäische Zollunion*, pp. 45–60. For all the nuances of Stolper's thinking, see the issues of the *Deutscher Volkswirt* for 1926 and 1927.

29. Eulenburg, "Gegen die Idee einer europäischen Zollunion," in Heiman, *Europäische Zollunion*, pp. 109–21. See also Eulenburg's *Probleme der deutschen Handelspolitik*, passim; and his *Aussenhandel und Aussenhandelspolitik*, p. 102 and passim.

30. Coerper, *Das wirtschaftliche Europa*, p. 26 and passim. Some Germans feared that a customs union would severely damage Germany's agriculture. For example, Kalchreuth, "Westeuropäische Zollunion," in Heiman, *Europäische Zollunion*, pp. 83–95.

31. See esp. Hohlfeld's *Zur Frage einer europäischen Zollunion*, pp. 31–38, 60–63.

32. Mayrisch, "Une Opinion luxembourgeoise," pp. 555–56.

33. Layton, "La Politique douanière de l'Europe," pp. 554–55; and *The Economist*, 19 June 1926, pp. 1183–84.

34. For the work of the Third Congress, see *Les Cahiers des droits de l'homme*, 25 Sept. 1926, pp. 418–30; and *Le libre Belgique*, 26–28 June 1926.

35. *Les Cahiers des droits de l'homme*, 25 Sept. 1926, pp. 418–19.

36. Ibid., p. 420.

37. Ibid., p. 426.

38. Ibid., 15 July 1927, p. 360.

CHAPTER 9

1. For recent studies that center on one or more of the organizations, see Holl, "Europapolitik im Vorfeld der deutschen Regierungspolitik," pp. 33–94; L'Huillier, *Dialogues franco-allemands*, pp. 27–40 and passim, and Frommelt, *Paneuropa oder Mitteleuropa*, passim.

2. For the origin of Franco-German committee, see *Echo de Paris* and *Le Figaro*, 1 and 2 June 1926; and L'Huillier, *Dialogues*, pp. 31–48. Louis Marlio and Herbert von Beckerath, both of whom worked for the committee for a time, gave me information concerning its origin and early work.

3. In addition to Holl and Frommelt's works, see Heile, *Europäische Cooperation*, pp. 3–5; *Berliner Tageblatt*, 30 July 1926; *Kölnische Zeitung*, 5 Oct. 1926; *Neue Zürcher Zeitung*, 10 Oct. 1926; and *Friedenswarte* 24 (Nov. 1926): 370–71.

4. *Neue freie Presse*, 5 Sept. 1926. Also *Neue Zürcher Zeitung*, 3 Oct. 1926; and Aulard's article in *Le Quotidien*, 5 Sept. 1926.

5. See *Akten zur deutschen auswärtigen Politik, 1918–1945*, Serie B: 1925–1933, vol. I, no. 2, Docs. 39, 90, 93, 125. (Hereafter cited as *A.D.A.P.*); Hexner, *The International Steel Cartel*, pp. 65–75 and passim; and Naettan-Larrier, *La Production sidérurgique de l'Europe*. Hexner, who had some inside knowledge of the negotiations, said that Benes and T. Masaryk felt that it had real potential for security in Europe.

6. Martin, "Paneuropeanisme ou Société des Nations," pp. 1249–50. See also *L'Ere nouvelle*, 13 Sept. 1926, and *Neue Zürcher Zeitung*, 10 Oct. 1926. German industrialist Arnold Rechberg spoke of the steel agreement as a nucleus for a solid Franco-German economic alliance and even for a military pact. See Rechberg's articles in *Neue Wiener Zeitung*, 6 and 26 Oct. 1926; and Vietsch, *Arnold Rechberg*, pp. 224–42.

7. *L'Oeuvre*, 5 Oct. 1926; and *L'Information*, 7 Oct. 1926.

8. Singer, "Zur Lage," pp. 1369–70; Auboin, "Le Cartel de l'acier," p. 1395.

9. Frederick Sthamer to the Foreign Office, *A.D.A.P.*, I, 2, Doc. 147; and Walter Layton, "Le

Cartel international de l'acier," *L'Europe*, 23 Oct. 1926, pp. 1467–70.

10. *Paneuropa*, 2, nos. 8–9, pp. 2–5. Coudenhove inspired the establishment of the American Committee of the Paneuropean Union in 1926. See *The New York Times*, 9 Jan. 1926; and Weiss, *Mémoires d'une européenne* 2:256–67.

11. Coudenhove got an interview with Loucheur on 13 March 1925. See Louis Loucheur Papers, Hoover War Library, Palo Alto, California, Box 4, Folder 12, Benes to Loucheur, 1 Mar. 1925, and Loucheur to Coudenhove-Kalergi, 11 Mar. 1925.

12. See *Deutsche allgemeine Zeitung*, 3 Oct. 1926; and Lipgens, "Briands Europaplan," pp. 68–69.

13. See Erika Mann, ed., *Thomas Mann: Briefe, 1889–1936*, pp. 257–58, and A. Aulard's article in *Neue Zürcher Zeitung*, 3 Oct. 1926.

14. Two of the best sources for the congress are *Neue freie Presse*, 4–8 Oct. 1926; and *Paneuropa* 2, nos. 13–14, pp. 1–75.

15. *Neue freie Presse*, 4 Oct. 1926. After Seipel spoke, Coudenhove read Briand's greeting to the congress.

16. Politis's speech was widely commented on and was printed in full in *L'Esprit international*, Jan. 1927, pp. 120 ff.

17. Delaisi's paper was published in full in several journals, including *Le Monde nouveau*, 15 Oct. 1926, pp. 973–87.

18. *Neue freie Presse*, 5 Oct. 1926; and *Paneuropa* 2, nos. 13–14, pp. 31–32.

19. Ibid., p. 60 and passim.

20. Ibid., pp. 60–67.

21. "The Koch-Weser Nachlass, Bundesarchiv Koblenz, No. 36," pp. 149–50 tells of Gwinner's financial support of the Paneuropean Union. *Neue freie Presse*, 10 Oct. 1926, made a good assessment of the work of the congress.

22. *L'Europe nouvelle*, 9 Oct. 1926, p. 1392, and 23 Oct. 1926, pp. 1458–59.

23. *La Paix par le droit* 11 (Nov. 1926): 390–420.

24. *Friedenswarte* 24 (Nov. 1926): 367–70.

25. Martin, "Paneuropeanisme ou Société des Nations," p. 1247 and passim.

26. See *The Manchester Guardian Weekly*, 22 and 29 Oct. 1926; and Hobson, "The Economic Union of Europe," pp. 209–97.

CHAPTER 10

1. See, for example, *Deutsche Zeitung* and *Berliner Lokal-Anzeiger*, 4, 8 Feb. 1927; and *Vorwärts* and *Berliner Tageblatt*, 1, 4, 5 Jan. 1927.

2. *Indépendance belge*, 23 Feb. 1927. For assessments by Wladimir d'Ormesson and Jacques Seydoux, see *Le Temps*, 3 Mar. 1927, and *Pax*, 14 June 1927.

3. See Geigenmüller, *Briand*, pp. 148–75; Wirth, "Muss Frankreich einen Krieg mit Deutschland befürchten?" pp. 1–13; Jouvenel, "Il faut voir plus loin que le Rhin," *L'Europe nouvelle* (13 Oct. 1926): 1454 ff.; and *A.D.A.P.*, Serie B, 1925–1933, Bd. IV, Docs. 46, 93, 120.

4. In a letter to this author, dated 22 Apr. 1963, Stern-Rubarth named these men as the most active members of the German committee. See also Stern-Rubarth, *Aus zuverlässiger Quelle verlautet*, pp. 121–23.

5. For a brief analysis of this debate, see *L'Europe de demain*, Pub. 1, pp. 1–4, and Pub. 7, pp. 5–6.

6. See Le Trocquer, *Union douanière européenne*, pp. 78–80; Marchal, *Union douanière*, pp. 214–16, and *Europe de demain*, Pub. 2, pp. 5–7.

7. See Heile, *Europäische Cooperation*, pp. 4–5; *Neue Zürcher Zeitung*, 9 Nov. 1926; *La Paix*

par le droit 37 (Jan. 1927): 35; *L'Europe nouvelle*, 19 Feb. 1927 (Supplement no. 3); and Holl, "Europapolitik im Vorfeld," pp. 55–70.

8. Hermant, "La Coopération européenne," pp. 24–39. For Hermant's views on Germany, see his *Les Paradoxes économiques de l'Allemagne moderne* (Paris, 1931).

9. This idea of coordinating the activities of kindred organizations was widespread in France. See *La Paix par le droit* 36 (Jan. 1926): 39 and passim. Borel and Heile were encouraged by the fact that many were members of several of the major organizations. In Switzerland, Paneuropean student groups and League of Nations student groups held joint meetings fairly often.

10. See *Les Etats-Unis d'Europe* for Oct. 1926, p. 118, and Apr. 1927, pp. 124–25.

11. See, for example, the articles on the New Right in the *Danziger Zeitung*, 27 Jan. 1927, and the *Neue Zürcher Zeitung*, 16 Feb. 1927.

12. The Franco-German Committee for Information and Documentation, which held its first full session in Paris from 14 to 16 June 1927, also had a hand in the founding of these journals. See also L'Huillier, *Dialogues franco-allemands*, pp. 72–73, and *Sozialistische Monatshefte*, Jan. 1928, p. 63.

13. See Bernhard Harms, "Die Weltwirtschaftskonferenz," pp. 211–44; Fernand Maurette, "Avant la conférence économique" *Revue de Genève* (Mar. 1927): 365–80; Louis Loucheur, "La Conférence économique de Genève," pp. 36–43; Hans Beerli, "Wirtschaftliche Organisation," *Neue Schweizer Rundschau* 20, no. 4, pp. 401–8; Cohen, "Der Europaweg der Wirtschaft," pp. 429–33; and Guyot, "La Conférence internationale," pp. 273–300.

14. Truchy, *L'Union douanière européenne*, pp. 17–18; Cristu, *L'Union douanière européenne*, pp. 202–5, 261 ff.; and *Vossische Zeitung*, 26 Feb. 1927.

15. *Les Etats-Unis d'Europe*, July 1927, p. 130.

16. See *Pester Lloyd*, 10 April 1927. Hantos had said this in detail in *Die Handelspolitik in Mitteleuropa*.

17. League of Nations, *Report and Proceedings of the World Economic Conference*, II Economic and Financial (1927), 2:11 and passim. For stronger appeals, see François Crucy's articles in *Le petit Journal*, 14 and 21 Apr. 1927; and Renard, "Vers l'économie internationale," pp. 145–50.

18. See esp. *Vossische Zeitung*, 8, 12, and 16 Apr. 1927; *Berliner Börsenkurier*, 17 Apr. 1927; and Friedrich Nonnenbruch in *Deutsche Zeitung*, 14 Apr. 1927. Nonnenbruch felt that Loucheur was ready to work for a customs union. *Neue Zürcher Zeitung*, 12 Apr. 1927, called Loucheur "a genuine European."

19. See esp. *Kölnische Zeitung*, 30 Apr. 1927; *Le petit Journal*, 21 Apr. 1927; *Berliner Tageblatt*, 29 Apr. 1927; and *Sächsische Staatszeitung*, 7 May 1927.

20. *Vorwärts*, 14 Apr. 1927; and Hantos, "La Conférence économique internationale," pp. 21–43.

21. Coudenhove-Kalergi, *Der Kampf um Europa*, p. 147. Coudenhove said many times that Briand assured him of this on 2 May 1927.

22. At the 2 May meeting of the French section of the Paneuropean Union, Léon Blum and Joseph Barthélemy were elected vice-presidents; Jules Romains, Henri Jouvenel, Marius Moutet, Gaston Moch, Francis Delaisi, and Lucien Romier were participants.

23. See *Neue freie Presse*, 5 May 1927; *Paneuropa* 3, no. 6, pp. 2–3, 24–26; and the issues of *Das neue Europa* for July–Aug. 1927, p. 23, and Sept–Oct. 1927, pp. 6–8.

24. League of Nations, *Report and Proceedings of the World Economic Conference*, II Economic and Financial (1927), 2:64.

25. Others who came close were Von Siemens of Germany, Arthur Fontaine of France, A. R. Zimmermann of the Netherlands, and S. Secerov of Yugoslavia. *Vossische Zeitung*, 6 May 1927, interpreted Zimmermann's speech as a call for a customs union.

26. League of Nations, *Report and Proceedings of the World Economic Conference*, II Economic and Financial (1927), 2:75–76, 132.

27. See ibid., pp. 30–56; and Theunis, "L'Oeuvre économique de la Société des Nations," pp. 3–11.

28. Deutsch, "Wirtschaftsannäherung," pp. 9–11. Max Cohen, and several other writers, charged in *Sozialistische Monatshefte*, Aug. 1927, pp. 624–25 and passim that the British delegation had tried to maneuver the German delegation into an anti-French position. For fuller treatments of the conference, see Moriz Weden, *Die Weltwirtschaft-Konferenz in Genf*, passim; and the special issue of *Europäische Wirtschafts-Union* 1, nos. 6–7 (Sept. 1927).

29. See *Le petit Journal*, 14 June 1927; *L'Europe de demain* 2, no. 2, pp. 599 ff.; and *Europäische Wirtschafts-Union*, 1 Feb. 1928, p. 2; Mertens, "L'Accord commercial franco-allemand," pp. 23–45; and Jean Naudin, *Les Accords commerciaux de la France*, passim.

30. *La Paix par le droit*, Oct. 1927, p. 358, for an assertion that Poincaré was moving toward the Briand policy.

31. *Compte rendu de la XXIVe Conférence* (Paris, 1927), pp. 213–18, 234–35, 308–14, and 326–40.

32. See esp. *Neue freie Presse*, 28 Aug. 1927.

33. *L'Europe de demain* 2, no. 3, pp. 4–5; and League of Nations, *Official Journal: Special Supplement*, no. 54 (1927), pp. 79–82.

CHAPTER 11

1. Nelböck, *Kleine Beiträge zum Kampf um Völkerbund*, pp. 21–22. See also Riou, *Europe ma patrie*, pp. 93–95 and passim; and Freundlich, "Die Arbeit," p. 3. Riou said the initiative for a united Europe would come mainly from the streets, and Freundlich said from communities and towns.

2. See Heile's "Von Versailles über Locarno nach Europa," p. 3; Koch-Weser's Nachlass, Bundesarchiv, Koblenz, no. 36, 2 July 1927, pp. 149 ff.; and Karl Holl, "Europapolitik im Vorfeld," pp. 70–85.

3. See *Neue freie Presse*, 20 Dec. 1927; and *Paneuropa* 4, no. 1, pp. 1–12. Frau Karoline von Kardorff and Ernst Lemmer, a well-known Democratic deputy, also spoke.

4. Esp. Heile's articles in *Europäische Wirtschafts-Union*, 1 Jan., 15 Feb., and 1 Mar. 1928.

5. See *Paneuropa* 4, no. 2, pp. 26–27, no. 3, p. 22; and no. 4, pp. 23–24; *Neue freie Presse*, 26 Feb. 1928; and General Joseph Denvignes, "Krieg oder Frieden," *Paneuropa* 4, no. 1, p. 16.

6. *Neue freie Presse*, 15 Jan. 1928; *Le Temps*, 15 Jan. 1928; and "Conversation entre M. M. Loucheur et de Coudenhove le 14 janvier 1928," Louis Loucheur Papers, box 12, folder 17, Hoover Institution. The items in Loucheur's Papers dealing with this projected congress indicate, as do other sources, that Loucheur was doubtful about the congress from the outset.

7. Loucheur to Coudenhove, 8 Feb. 1928; and Marcel Ray to Coudenhove-Kalergi, 8 Feb. 1928, Louis Loucheur Papers.

8. Luithlen, "Das österreichische Komitee für europäische Cooperation," p. 2. Richard Riedl and Baron Moritz von Auffenberg-Komaron were members of the Executive Committee.

9. See Heile's articles in *Europäische Wirtschafts-Union*, 15 Dec. 1927 and 1 Feb. 1928. Heile said that Löbe and Stern-Rubarth were giving him good assistance.

10. For the papers, see *Le Monde nouveau*, 15 Mar. 1928, pp. 53 ff. Fontaine and Seydoux could not attend the meeting and their papers were read by the secretary.

11. Ibid., p. 53.

12. Ibid., pp. 53–54; and Seydoux, "Etats-Unis d'Europe," pp. 1–2.

13. In 1963 Stern-Rubarth and Ernö Bleier gave me their views of the customs union movement during these months. The *Europäische Wirtschafts-Union*, *Le Monde nouveau*, and *L'Europe de demain* gave attention to the whole movement, but the latter two tended to center on the activities of the French group.

14. See Schuster, "Pioniere der europäischen Wirtschaftsgemeinschaft," pp. 2–3; and the issues of *Europäische Wirtschafts-Union* for 1 Mar., 1 Apr., and 1 May 1928. National customs union groups were ultimately formed in nineteen European states, according to Stern-Rubarth.

15. For the Advisory Committee of the French group, see ibid., 15 Sept. 1927. It contained many of France's most distinguished political and business leaders.

16. For this map, which was informative and a good propaganda device, see *L'Europe de demain* 3 (1928): 23.

17. Ibid., p. 4, and *Le Matin*, 22 Jan. 1928. For a typical article, see Bleier, "Der europäische Zollverein," pp. 2–3. Bleier argued that national protectionism was the main cause of Europe's economic crisis.

18. See *La Paix par le droit* 38 (Feb. 1928): 83–84; Regis de Vibraye, *Allemagne, 1930*, passim; *Europäische Wirtschafts-Union*, 15 Dec. 1927; and *De Telegraaf*, 19 Oct. 1927.

19. Coudenhove-Kalergi "Europäische Parteien," *Paneuropa* 3, no. 3, pp. 1–12, and no. 10, p. 6. A few people, including Jules Romains, had dreamed of a European party over the years.

20. See *Gazette des nations*, 9 Apr. 1928; *L'Oeuvre*, 2–3 Apr. 1928; and *La Paix par le droit*, Apr.–May 1928, pp. 206–7.

21. But the vote in Germany was variously interpreted. For example, *L'Oeuvre*, 23 May 1928; *Sozialistische Monatshefte*, June 1928, pp. 475–76; and Maurice Pernot, "Erreur sur les élections allemandes," *Revue des vivants*, Sept. 1928, pp. 447–59; and René Cassin in ibid., June 1928.

22. For Müller's treatment of the open letter, see Lipgens, "Briands Europaplan," p. 71. Also *La Volonté*, 2 July 1928, and *Vossische Zeitung*, 30 June 1928.

23. See issues of *La Paix par le droit*, June 1928, pp. 237–42; July–Aug. 1928, pp. 338–39; and Sept. 1928, p. 401.

24. *Das neue Europa*, 14, July–Aug. and Sept.–Oct. 1928. Typical, and perhaps most notable, of the periodicals that gave the idea more attention were: *L'Europe nouvelle*, *Die Menschheit*, *L'Esprit international*, *Europäische Revue*, *Revue politique et parlementaire*, *Nord und Süd*, *Revue hebdomadaire*, *Journal des débats*, *Neue Schweizer Rundschau*, *Deutsche Einheit*, *Revue économique internationale*, *Cahiers des droits de l'homme*, and many others.

25. Lauterbach, "Paneuropaliteratur," pp. 93–98. Lauterbach had little sympathy for the European idea.

26. Most of the books published during 1927–28 which bore heavily on the European idea are listed in the bibliography.

27. For the complete text of Delaisi's address see *Paneuropa* 4, no. 8, pp. 12–21.

CHAPTER 12

1. German and Austrian officials had taken a close look at the Anschluss in Nov. 1927 when Stresemann and Marx were in Vienna. See G.F.M., 2346/4576/E173192-7. For an overall view of the Anschluss at this time, see Suval, *The Anschluss Question*, pp. 107–46 and passim.

2. See Köpke Memorandum, 30 July 1928, G.F.M., 2347/4576/E173578-9; also E173585-6; *Neue freie Presse*, 19–23 July 1928; and Räuscher, "Paneuropa und Anschlussfrage," pp. 296–99.

3. *Vossische Zeitung*, 28 July 1928. See also Quessel, "Europa und der Anschluss," pp. 658–63. Quessel was especially hard on Löbe.

4. Szende, "Les Etats danubiens et le fédéralisme," pp. 93–107; and Loesch and Ziegfeld, *Staat und Volkstum*, pp. 116–55.

5. See also *Le Quotidien*, 2 Aug. 1928, and *L'Information*, 5 Aug. 1928.

6. J.O.C. Déb., 4 Dec. 1928, p. 3236 ff. Briand was groping for new avenues. See also Siebert, *Aristide Briand*, pp. 468–72; and *Prager Presse*, 28 Nov. and 5 Dec. 1928.

7. G.F.M., 2347/4576/E173625-7; and Stresemann to the Foreign Office, 10 Dec. 1928,

G.F.M., 1483/3086H/D614417-8.

8. Hellpach, *Politische Prognose für Deutschland*, pp. 272–80; Gürge, *Paneuropa und Mitteleuropa*, pp. 60–70 and passim; and Nonnenbruch, *Das vereinigte Europa*, pp. 170–80 and passim.

9. See esp. Hantos, *Europäischer Zollverein*, pp. 26–66; and Barolin and Scheckner, *Für und wider Donauföderation*, p. 15.

10. Robert Mangin, "Les Etats fédérés d'Europe," *La Fédération européenne*, p. 100. Many federalists felt that Vienna was very cosmopolitan and would be the best site for a European federation.

11. *L'Homme libre*, 1 Aug. 1928 and *La Volonté*, 13 Aug. 1928. Victor Basch, August Gauvain, and others toyed with this general idea.

12. *Revue des vivants*, Feb. 1929, pp. 211–32. See also Robert Raynaud, "La France, en Sarre . . . ," *L'Europe nouvelle*, 29 Oct. 1927, pp. 1455–57; and Klara Fatzbinder, "Französische Stimmen zur Saarfrage," *Die Hilfe*, 15 July 1929, p. 342.

13. Henri de Jouvenel, "La Rupture," *Revue des vivants*, June 1927, p. 810. Also Poulimenos, *Vereinigte Staaten Europas*, pp. 63–106; Luddecke, *Das amerikanische Wirtschaftstempo*, passim; Schulze, *Variationen über das Thema*, pp. 60–70; Vogel, "Nordamerikas Wirtschaftsaufsteig," pp. 104–48; and *Le Temps*, 10 Dec. 1927.

14. For example, Drieu la Rochelle, *Genève ou Moscow*, pp. 110–29; and Dahriman, *Pour les états confédérés d'Europe*, pp. 49–63. Concern about American economic power was reflected in a wide variety of books.

15. *La Volonté*, 27 July 1928.

16. It seems that some good Europeans exaggerated the dangers of American economic competition in the hope of adding momentum to the European movement. Edouard Guyot even argued in *La Volonté* (30 Aug. 1928) that in spite of the pact Washington like Moscow had deserted Europe: "C'est entre européens que nous devons refaire l'Europe."

CHAPTER 13

1. *L'Homme libre*, 21, 25, 26, 27, and 28 Sept. 1928; also *Prager Presse*, 1, 5 Sept. 1928; and *Paneuropa* 4 (Jan. 1930): 2–3.

2. Georges Izard, "Les Etats fédérés d'Europe," *La Fédération européenne*, pp. 381–82.

3. Union Interparlementaire, *Compte rendu de la XXVᵉ Conférence*, pp. 201–2.

4. Ibid., p. 239.

5. Ibid., pp. 271–72. The complete text of the prepared address appeared in *Le Monde nouveau*, Aug.–Sept. 1928, pp. 541–47.

6. *Compte rendu*, pp. 267–70. *Prager Presse*, 2–6 Oct., gave full coverage.

7. The above is based largely on correspondence with Stern-Rubarth in 1963 and on Hantos's *Europäischer Zollverein und mitteleuropäische Wirtschaftsgemeinschaft*.

8. For good summaries of the stronger appeals, see Le Trocquer, *L'Union douanière européenne*, pp. 31–32; *L'Europe de demain* 9 (Aug. 1930): 4–5, and 12 (Apr. 1931): 5–7; and Peyerimhoff de Fontenelle, "La Rationalisation des relations commerciales internationales," pp. 22–36.

9. *Prager Presse*, 7 Oct. 1928; and *L'Europe de demain* 12 (Apr. 1931): 6–7.

10. *Le Temps*, 25 Nov. 1928 and *Le Monde nouveau* 10 (Jan.–Feb. 1928): 861–64. There is evidence that Herbert Hoover's election to the presidency of the United States intensified this fear of American competition. For example, *Prager Presse*, 8 Nov. 1928.

11. *Le Monde nouveau* 10 (Jan.–Feb. 1929): 867–71; and Karl Holl, "Europapolitik im Vorfeld," pp. 83–84.

12. *La Volonté*, 1 Dec. 1928.

13. See *La Volonté*, 5 Dec. 1928, and *Paneuropa* 5 (Jan. 1929): 29–32.

14. For example, *Sudeten-deutsche Tageszeitung*, 10 Feb. 1929; Carl Doka, "Kampf um Paneuropa," *Kampf* 22, no. 6, p. 280 and passim; and *Paneuropa* 5 (Jan. 1929): 3–9, 29–32, and (Feb. 1929): 39.

15. Lipgens, "Briands Europaplan," p. 71.

16. See esp. Ludwig Quessel, "Die Bilanz unserer Aussenpolitik," *Sozialistische Monatshefte* 29 (Jan. 1929): 11–16; and *Vossische Zeitung*, 4 Nov. 1928, and 1 Jan. 1929.

17. Text of speech in *Paneuropa* 5, no. 3, pp. 12–19.

18. Hohenau, "Von kommenden Ereignissen," p. 8; and *Reichspost*, 15 Jan. 1929.

19. Caillaux, "Europa in zehn Jahren," pp. 367–70; and Le Trocquer, "Vereinigte Staaten von Europa," pp. 621–23.

20. Sauerwein, "Der Wiederaufbau Europas," pp. 1–12; *Revue des vivants*, Mar. 1929, p. 442; Sauerwein, *30 ans à la une*, p. 195; and *Paneuropa* 6, no. 3, pp. 1–2.

21. Lauret, "L'Europe devant Les Etats-Unis," pp. 319–29. There were many articles during the spring and summer dealing with the "American danger" in both the periodical and daily press. Several periodicals carried more than a dozen during these weeks. Typical German books were: Wilhelm Grotkopp, *Amerikas Schutzzollpolitik und Europa*; Colin Ross, *Die Welt auf dem Wege*; and Fritz Funk, *Die Vereinigten Staaten von Europa*. Writing in *Le Capital*, 30 May 1929, M. A. Pawlowski spoke of the "avalanche of automobiles, trucks, and tractors" from across the Atlantic and explained: "Le péril jaune est politique et lointain; le danger américain est économique et plus près de nous." This anti-American outburst was intensified by the fact that the Beranger-Mellon Debt Agreement was being debated.

22. For example, *Journal de Genève*, 24 July and 7 Sept. 1929; Gignoux, "Que faut-il penser des Etats-Unis d'Europe?" pp. 5–16; and Caillaux, "Europa in zehn Jahren," pp. 367–70.

23. Among the judges were Beneš, Bernstorff, Sforza, Paul-Boncour, Politis, Seipel, Jules Cambon, René Cassin, Borel, Duhamel, and Heinrich Mann.

24. Emile Roche and Pierre Dominique managed and edited *La République*, and Joseph Caillaux, Anatole de Monzie, Paul Elbel, Marcel Deat, Paul Bastid, Jacques Kayser, and Edouard Daladier were among its collaborators.

25. *La République*, 5 July 1929. Daladier's editorial, which attacked American economic policies, was entitled "Vassalité ou fédération."

26. *Le Monde nouveau* 11 (June 1929): 294–95. See also Le Trocquer, *Union douanière européenne*, pp. 81–92; and Schnitzler, "Europäische Zollunion," pp. 783–85.

27. Heile, ed., *Europäische Cooperation*, p. 13. All three speeches were analyzed in *Le Monde nouveau*, Aug.–Sept. 1929, pp. 459–60.

28. *Les Etats-Unis d'Europe* 61 (July 1929): 181.

29. Ibid., p. 182.

30. René Cassin said in *Revue des vivants*, July 1929, pp. 1103–8 that Stresemann was giving Briand much more encouragement and support than was generally realized. Edgar Stern-Rubarth, who was close to Stresemann at the time, told me the same thing in 1963. See also *Le Matin*, 14, 15, and 29 June 1929, and Hirsch, *Stresemann*, passim.

31. *L'Oeuvre*, 11 July 1929. Briand's initial moves did not receive enough support in Germany and England to enable him to consider such a conference.

32. J.O.C. Déb., 2nd Session, 17 July 1929, no. 72, pp. 2694–95.

33. For example, *Tevere*, 13 July 1929. Many good Europeans felt that there was much sympathy for the idea in Italy and that Mussolini was not nearly as opposed as he pretended. See *L'Oeuvre*, 1 Aug. 1929, and Coudenhove-Kalergi, *Ein Leben für Europa*, pp. 200–206.

34. Issue of 12 July 1929. *Deutsche allgemeine Zeitung* said essentially the same thing and argued that Germany was not sufficiently recovered from the war to join a European federation.

35. Issue of 12 July 1929. The journal asked if an economic union in Europe would not stimulate industrial production in Germany excessively.

36. See esp. the issue of 12 July 1929. For the reaction of the German government, see Lipgens, "Briands Europaplan," pp. 71–76.

37. Coudenhove-Kalergi's "Entscheidung," *Paneuropa* 5, no. 7, pp. 1–5; Edgar Stern-Rubarth, "Europäismus," *Die Wahrheit* (Prague), 1 June 1929, p. 30; and *Vossische Zeitung*, 23 July 1929.

38. *Berliner Tageblatt*, 26 July 1929.

CHAPTER 14

1. The following articles are fairly typical of the many scores that appeared in the periodical press during the summer of 1929: Ormesson, "Une Fédération européenne," pp. 748–70; Martin, "Les Etats-Unis d'Europe," pp. 712–20; Hantos, "Union douanière européenne," pp. 406–11; Seipel, "Der Weg nach Europa," pp. 1–10; Barthélemy, "Etats-Unis d'Europe," pp. 329–45; Serruys, "L'Oeuvre économique," pp. 1206–17; J. A. Hobson, "The United States of Europe," *Contemporary Review*, Nov. 1929, pp. 445–52; and Karl Strupp, "Panismus," *Paneuropa* 5, no. 6, pp. 12–26.

2. J.O.C. Déb., 2nd Session, 17 July 1929, no. 20, p. 2600; and Herriot, "Le Rapprochement intellectuel," pp. 5–8.

3. J.O.C. Déb., 19 July 1929, no. 72, pp. 2694–95. See also Fougère's "Le Devoir de l'Europe," *L'Européen*, 10 July 1929.

4. J.O.C. Déb., 24 July 1929, no. 75, pp. 921–22.

5. Ibid., pp. 924–25.

6. *Ruhr und Rhein, Wirtschaftszeitung*, 16 Aug. 1929, commented favorably on Clémentel's speech in Amsterdam.

7. J.O.C. Déb., 26 July 1929, no. 76, pp. 938–39, and *L'Oeuvre*, 2 July 1929.

8. J.O.C. Déb., 26 July 1929, no. 76, p. 950.

9. J.O.C. Déb., 31 July 1929, no. 78, pp. 2871–72. Gignoux elaborated these ideas in *La Revue hebdomadaire*, 2 Nov. 1929, pp. 5–16.

10. J.O.C. Déb., 31 July 1929, no. 78, p. 2874.

11. See *L'Oeuvre* and *Le Peuple* for 13 July 1929.

12. See Julius Elbau in *Vossische Zeitung*, 7 Apr. 1929; Joseph Caillaux in *Neue Zürcher Zeitung*, 11 Apr. 1929; and Henri Barde in *L'Oeuvre*, 13 Sept. 1929.

13. Several papers in France, including *La Dépêche de Toulouse*, 8 Aug. 1929 and *Le Populaire*, 7 Aug. 1929, said Stresemann had obviously intended to encourage Briand.

14. *La République*, 10–20 Aug. 1929; and *Sozialistische Monatshefte* 35 (Sept. 1929): 773–77.

15. This was the view of Von Beckerath who worked with the committee from time to time. See also L'Huillier, *Dialogues franco-allemands*, pp. 85–93.

16. League of Nations, *Official Journal, 1929, Special Supplement 75*, pp. 51–52.

17. Ibid., p. 64. In the same session, Quinones de Léon congratulated Briand and assured him the Spanish government would support his "work of union and concord."

18. Ibid., pp. 67–71. Also *Frankfurter Zeitung*, 18 Oct. 1929; and Edwin Redslob's observation in *Von Weimar nach Europa* (Berlin, 1972), pp. 197 ff.

19. In the course of the discussion, Langenhove suggested to the members of the committee that they read Arthur Salter's "The United States of Europe Idea" and Stoppani's "The Idea of European Economic Solidarity."

20. One who wants the debate in its range and depth must work extensively in the periodical press. For estimates on the influence of the press, see Claude Bellanger et al., *Histoire générale de la presse française* (Paris, 1972), 3:482–86 and passim.

21. *Berliner Tageblatt*, 6 Sept. 1929. Bloch also told his home office not to doubt Briand's sincerity.

22. See editorials of 10, 11, 12 Sept. 1929. This stress on little things on the economic plane was characteristic of most of the economic journals, and few stressed it as much as Peyerimhoff and the *Journée industrielle*.

23. See the articles and editorials in the issues of 7, 10, and 11 Sept. 1929.

24. See *Le Peuple*, 6, 10, and 20 Sept. 1929; *La Voix du peuple*, C.G.T.'s well-known monthly, took a similar position.

25. Esp. the editorials of 7 and 10 Sept. 1929.

26. See also *Die deutsche Zeitung*, 6 Sept. 1929; *Der Tag*, 6 Sept. 1929; *Jungdeutsche*, 15 Sept. 1929; *Die Augsburger Postzeitung*, 11 Sept. 1929; and K. A. Rohan, "Zukunftsfragen deutscher Aussenpolitik," *Europäische Revue* 5 (Sept. 1929): pp. 369–74. Rohan had predicted early in 1928 that the National Socialists were headed for power because they understood better than any other party the deeper yearnings (*Lebensgefühl*) of the German people.

27. Issues for 6 and 10 Sept. 1929. The *Sozialistische Monatshefte*, called Briand's European initiative at Geneva a "great historic moment."

28. See esp. the issue of 16 Aug. 1929 and *Veröffentlichungen des Reichsverbandes der deutschen Industrie* 48 (Oct. 1929): 36–37, and 49 (Dec. 1929): 11–15.

29. See the letters between Georg Bernhard and Rechberg in Vietsch, *Arnold Rechberg*, pp. 224–42. Socialist Marcel Deat wrote in *Le Populaire* (1 Oct. 1929) that Rechberg's primary aim was a Franco-German economic and military accord that could be used to consolidate capitalism in Europe.

30. See, for example: Churchill, "The United States of Europe," p. 25 and passim; Salter, *The United States of Europe*, pp. 91–92 and passim; L. S. Amery, "The Economic Case for Empire Cooperation," *The National Review* 99 (Dec. 1929): 528 and passim; Dawson, "The Disunited States of Europe," p. 15 and passim; Norman Angell, "The United States of Europe and the Tariff Holiday," *Foreign Affairs* 12 (Oct. 1929): 209 and passim; and "The United States of Europe," *The Round Table* 20 (Dec. 1929): 80 ff.

31. *Daily Express*, 6 Sept. 1929. For a French assessment see Fromont, "La Grande Bretagne et les Etats-Unis d'Europe," pp. 418–44.

32. *Daily News*, 7 Sept. 1929 and *Daily Herald*, 10 Sept. 1929. Also *The Spectator*, 14 Sept. 1929, p. 320; and *The Economist*, 21 Sept. 1929, p. 526.

33. The Dutch reaction was generally similar to the Belgian. See *De Telegraaf*, 10 Sept. 1929, and *Algemeen Handelsblad*, 11 Sept. 1929.

34. Issues of 25 July and 10 Sept. 1929; and *Wiener Allgemeine Zeitung*, 11 Sept. 1929.

35. Issues of 12 and 15 Sept. 1929, and *Die Wahrheit*, 15 Nov. 1929.

CHAPTER 15

1. Theodore M. Knappen, "If Europe Should Unite," *The Magazine of Wall Street*, 2 Nov. 1929, p. 13. Also *The New York Times*, 9 and 15 Sept. 1929; *The New York World*, *Business Week*, and the *Commercial and Financial Chronicle* for 14 Sept. 1929; Jeune, "Le Krach américain," pp. 539–48; Ansel-Mowrer, "Les Etats-Unis d'Amérique et les Etats-Unis d'Europe," pp. 1291–94. The crisis on the American stock market in the autumn of 1929 tended to ease Europe's fear of American economic power.

2. For an attack on Hugenberg and his collaborators, see Max Clauss, "Der Horizont: Unpolitik der nationalen Opposition," *Europäische Revue* 5 (Oct. 1929): 508–11.

3. K. A. Rohan, "Westeuropa," *Europäische Revue* 5, no. 5 (Aug. 1929): 317; also Otto Hoetzsch, "Gesamtaspekt der deutschpolnischen Politik," 6, no. 1 (Apr. 1929): 16–22.

4. *Vorwärts*, 12–20 Sept. 1929; and Ludwig Quessel, "Die nationalsozialistische Welle, woher Die kommt," *Sozialistische Monatshefte*, Nov. 1929, pp. 979–86.

5. Clauss, "Deutschlands europäische Stunde," pp. 81–91. Also Koch-Weser, *Deutschlands Aussenpolitik*," pp. 110–20, and Dewall, *Der Kampf um den Frieden*, passim.

6. See *Veröffentlichungen des Reichsverbandes der deutschen Industrie* 48 (Oct. 1929): 35 ff; and *Paneuropa* 5, no. 8, pp. 8–21. Arnold Rechberg even said it was the attitude of French and German businessmen that persuaded Briand to put the European idea into politics. See *Le Capital*, 16 Oct. 1929; *L'Avenir*, 20 July 1929; and Vietsch, *Arnold Rechberg*, pp. 224 ff., and Frommelt, *Paneuropa oder Mitteleuropa*, p. 80.

7. Stolper, "Messianismus," pp. 267–68.

8. *Die Menschheit*, 2 Sept. 1929, pp. 407–8.

9. *La Paix par le droit*, Oct. 1929, p. 422. The journal estimated there were around 3,000 journals of a political character in Germany and that Hugenberg strongly influenced over half of them.

10. Georges Roux, "L'Allemagne et l'Europe," *Le Monde nouveau* 11 (Oct. 1929): 532–37. There were articles in this number by Robert Sorel, Jean de Pange, and Lucien Bourgues dealing with the European idea, and also a review of Jean Marchal's *L'Union douanière et l'organisation européenne*.

11. See esp. Ormesson's article in *L'Europe nouvelle*, 4 Jan. 1930, pp. 15–19. Ormesson addressed the Institute for Foreign Policy in Hamburg on "The Future of Peace" on 19 Dec. 1929. Also Jean Malge, "L'Allemagne a-t-elle l'esprit européen?" *L'Européen*, 25 Sept. 1929.

12. Borel, "La Coopération européenne," Nov. 1929, p. 756.

13. *Neue freie Presse*, 9 Oct. 1929. Both morning and evening editions gave much space to the meeting and the issue of Oct. 13 reminded its readers that Wilhelm Marx had said that evacuation of the Rhineland would clear the way for serious discussion of a United States of Europe.

14. Coudenhove had sent Chancellor Müller a special invitation. See G.F.M. 3671H/1680/D800780-1.

15. *Prager Presse*, 11–12 Oct. 1929; *Paneuropa* 5 (Nov. 1929): 1–13; and Herriot's *Europe*, pp. 54–55.

16. See *Le Capital*, 15 Oct. 1929; and *La République*, 16 Oct. 1929.

17. *La République*, 26–28 Oct. 1929. The congress ordered Herriot's speech printed and circulated. Wilhelm Heile, who was invited to the congress, was deeply impressed. See Heile to Reichskanzler Müller, 7 Nov. 1929, G.F.M., 3619-H/1680/D800803-10.

18. *La Dépêche de Toulouse*, 26–27 Dec. 1929. Many French papers stressed this point.

19. For a summary of the work of the congress by two of the delegates, see Toureille, "Le Congrès international de la paix d'Athènes," pp. 5–8; and Quidde, "Weltfriedenskongress in Athen," pp. 99–100. Also *Le Monde nouveau*, Oct. 1929, pp. 460–62.

20. For example, Peyerimhoff's lecture appeared in *Revue économique internationale*, Jan. 1930, pp. 22–36; and Scelle's appeared in two parts in *Le Monde nouveau*, Mar. 1930, pp. 18–22 and Apr. 1930, pp. 91–96. See *L'Europe nouvelle*, 2 Nov. 1929, p. 1453.

21. For example, Coudenhove-Kalergi, "Was will Briand?" *Paneuropa* 6, no. 1, pp. 7–8; and "Mitteleuropa," ibid. 6, no. 3, pp. 85–91. Coudenhove also spoke out strongly against *Antieuropa*, a new journal in Italy which fought the European movement.

22. See esp. *Paneuropa* 6, no. 3, pp. 102–4.

23. Heile to Müller, 7 Oct. 1929. G.F.M., 3617H/1680/D800792-5. For Heile's role in the League for European Cooperation in these weeks, see Holl, "Europapolitik im Vorfeld," pp. 76–94. Also Heile, *Das Problem gerechter Grenzen zwischen den Staaten* (Berlin, 1929); Borel, "Les Etats-Unis d'Europe," pp. 3–20; and *L'Europe nouvelle*, 21 Dec. 1929, pp. 1743–45.

24. Heile to Chancellor Müller, 7 Nov. 1929, G.F.M., 3617H/1680/D800803-7. Also Herriot, *Europe*, pp. 58–67.

25. See *L'Homme libre*, 2 Nov. 1929; *La Volonté*, 14 Nov. 1929; Trocquer, "Die Zollpolitik Nordamerikas und die europäischen Staaten," pp. 22–31; his "L'Union douanière européenne," pp. 219–31; Schulze, *Variationen über das Thema*; pp. 28–35 and passim; Török, *Vom Nationalismus zu den Vereinigten Staaten von Europa*, pp. 162 ff.; Marchal, *Union douanière*, passim; Hantos, "Union douanière européenne," pp. 406–11; and Truchy, "La Coopération européenne," pp. 384–97.

26. *L'Europe de demain* 4, no. 7, pp. 1–5. The yearbook, *L'Annuaire européen*, appeared in 1931.

27. See Coquet, "Projet de convention pour l'établissement de la nationalité européenne," pp. 62–64.

28. *Les Etats-Unis d'Europe* 15 (Oct. 1929): 188–89, 211–12.

29. For the text of the resolutions, see *Le Monde nouveau*, Nov. 1929, pp. 764–66. For the debates, see *La Paix par le droit*, Dec. 1929, pp. 449–68; and the issues of *Les Cahiers des droits de l'homme*, Jan. and Feb. 1930.

30. François-Marsal, "Les Etats-Unis d'Europe," pp. 8, 15–20; and Daniel Serruys, "Sur des confins de la politique et de l'économie," *L'Européen*, 11 Sept. 1929. See esp. R. P. Duchemin, "La Trêve douanière," ibid., 13 Nov. 1929; Daniel Serruys, "La Trêve douanière," ibid., 20 Nov. 1929; and C. J. Gignoux, "La Trêve douanière et le Parlement," ibid., 4 Dec. 1929; and R. Moll, "Le Projet de trêve douanière," ibid., pp. 675 ff.

31. Hymans, "L'Union européenne," pp. 8–20. Also Peyerimhoff, "Pour la paix économique de l'Europe," *L'Européen*, 9 Feb. 1930; and Herriot, *Europe*, pp. 82–83.

32. See J. M. Biart, "La Contenu et la portée des documents signés le 24 Mars 1930," *Journal des débats*, 18 Apr. 1930, pp. 615–18; Sorel, "La Trêve douanière," pp. 137–39; Herriot, *Europa*, pp. 103 ff.; and *L'Européen*, 5 Mar. 1930.

33. Gürge, *Paneuropa und Mitteleuropa*, passim; Gerhard Höfers, *Oesterreichs Weg zum Anschluss* (Berlin, 1928), pp. 13 ff.; Brockhausen, "Paneuropa und Mitteleuropa," pp. 140 ff.; Lerchenfeld to Curtius, 25 Dec. 1929, G.F.M., 3036/1484/D614605-611; Schubert to Lerchenfeld, 4 Feb. 1930, ibid., D614644; Curtius, *Bemühung um Österreich*, pp. 12–14.

34. For example, Ormesson, "Rapprochement 1930," pp. 559–60.

35. Emile Vandervelde, "Le Rôle économique de la Belgique," *L'Européen*, 29 Jan. 1930; Riedl, "Die wirtschaftliche Neuorganisation Europas," p. 251; and Ancel, "L'Europe qui naît," p. 620.

CHAPTER 16

1. See Sauerwein, *30 ans à la une*, pp. 195–96; Georges Bonnet, *Dans la tourmente* (Paris, 1971), pp. 19–20; Lucien Luchaire, *Confession d'un français moyen*, 2:239–43. Most Parisiens believed at the time that Léger was largely responsible for the wording of the memorandum.

2. Woodward and Butler, *Documents on British Foreign Policy, 1919–1939*, ser. 2, vol. 1, p. 313. The text of the memorandum appears, along with seventy-seven other relevant documents, in Mirkine-Guetzevitch and Scelle, *L'Union européenne*, pp. 59–70.

3. For representative French and German reactions, see Gauvain, "Le Projet d'union fédérale européenne," pp. 375–86; Scelle, "Le Mémorandum Briand," pp. 269–76; Gygax, "Briands Mémorandum," pp. 556–60; Salomon Grumbach, "L'Acte de naissance d'une Europe unifiée," *La Lumière* 4 (24 May 1930): 12–13; Bilfinger, "Das Briand Mémorandum," pp. 478–86; Rohan, "Deutsche Europapolitik," pp. 486–94; Mendelssohn-Bartholdy, "Mémorandum," pp. 408–24; Siebert, *Aristide Briand*, pp. 542 ff. and Geigenmüller, *Briand*, pp. 585 ff. For the reaction of the German government, see Lipgens, "Briands Europaplan," pp. 316 ff.

4. On this point, see esp. Politis, "Le Projet d'union européenne," pp. 201–11; Wilhelm Heile, "Deutschland und Europa im Völkerbund," *Europa Wirtschaft* 2 (1930): 65–71; and Momtschilo Nintchitch, "Paneuropa und der Völkerbund," *Paneuropa* 6, nos. 6–7, pp. 228–33.

5. *L'Europe de demain* 4 (Oct. 1930): 37.

6. Also Julius Kalinski, "Durch Zusammenfassung zur Wirtschaftsentfaltung," *Sozialistische Monatshefte*, June 1930, pp. 525–30; also R. Kleineibst's article in the August 1930 issue of this journal, pp. 735 ff.

7. For example, Wladimir d'Ormesson, "Pour une Europe fédérée," *L'Europe nouvelle*, 24 May 1930, pp. 783–85.

8. Coudenhove-Kalergi to Louis Loucheur, Loucheur Papers, Box 4, Folder 12. The Franco-German Committee for Information and Documentation and London's Cobden Club were discussing the European idea on this day. See *Le Monde nouveau* 12 (June 1930): 299–305; and Edgar Stern-Rubarth, "Briands Europa-Konzeption," *Europa-Wirtschaft* 1, no. 6 (1930): 239–43.

9. Coudenhove-Kalergi to Chancellor Brüning, 28 Apr. 1930, G.F.M., 1680/D800825 and ibid., D800826-28.

10. Hoesch to the Foreign Office, 9 May 1930, G.F.M., 1680/D800834-35.

11. G.F.M., 1680/D800837-52. Coudenhove had also asked that the president's office send a few words of greeting to the delegates, but this request was rejected.

12. *Paneuropa* 6, nos. 6–7, pp. 201–77 carried the texts of the speeches and summarized the work of the Congress. *Vossische Zeitung* and the *Neue freie Presse* gave good coverage of its daily sessions.

13. *Vossische Zeitung*, 20 May 1930.

14. *Neue freie Presse*, 20 May 1930; and Launay, *Loucheur*, p. 168. Loucheur spent the last days of May in eastern Europe in behalf of the Briand project and addressed the Rumanian Parliament on 28 May.

15. See *Les Etats-Unis d'Europe* 15 (July 1930): 215–16, 219–20; *Le Monde nouveau* 12 (Aug.–Sept., 1930): 466–72; and *L'Esprit international* 4 (Oct. 1930): 580.

16. See Le Fur, "Les Conditions d'existence d'une union européenne," pp. 71–96; and Lapradelle, "L'Union juridique internationale et le projet de M. Briand," pp. 360–63.

17. Text of model plan in *L'Esprit international* 4 (Oct. 1930): 605–12. This document was one of the many from these months that was in the hands of the men who drafted the Statute of the Council of Europe in 1949.

18. See esp. Trocquer, "Le premier Congrès d'union douanière européenne," pp. 317–20; Caillaux, "L'Union européenne," pp. 320–22; Ferrara, "La Crise économique mondiale," pp. 222–27; Kastl, "Le Mouvement européen," pp. 255–60. For the work of the congress, see *L'Europe de demain* 9, 10, and 11 (Aug.–Sept. 1930). *Annuaire européen* contains brief biographical sketches of all the delegates. I followed the congress closely and managed to talk with some of the delegates.

19. *L'Europe de demain* 11 (Oct. 1930): 27; and *Notre temps* 11, 13 July 1930, pp. 198–99.

20. Text of Stern-Rubarth's address is in *L'Europe de demain* 11 (Oct. 1930): 17–23. See also Daniel Serruys, "La Confédération économique des états d'Europe," *L'Européen*, 9 July 1930.

21. See *Annuaire européen, 1931*, pp. 969–83; *L'Europe de demain*, passim; and Andreas Fleissig, *Paneuropa*, passim.

22. The Bureau of the International Committee set up a "Commission for the Realization of the Maison de l'Europe et les Nations," and Henri Chailleux was employed to draft a blueprint. See *Annuaire européen, 1931*, pp. 989–96.

23. See *Compte rendu de la XXVIe Conférence* (Paris, 1931), pp. 55–106. Lange attached a copy of the memorandum to his report.

24. See ibid., pp. 307–12, 262–64, for Papanastasiou's suggestions concerning the Balkans. Heile gave warm support to the memorandum and quoted Breitscheid to the effect that the doctrine of absolute sovereignty belonged in "a museum of patriotic heirlooms." But Heile's influence in Germany was waning and the German Committee for European Cooperation was soon absorbed by the German Committee for the League of Nations.

25. In mid-July 1930, the International Federation of Syndicates met in Stockholm, and the International Diplomatic Academy met in Paris; both debated the memorandum. See *La Paix par le droit*, Oct. 1930, p. 394; and *L'Europe nouvelle*, 26 July 1930, p. 1118.

CHAPTER 17

1. Texts of all replies are in League of Nations, *Documents Relating to a System of Federal Union*, VII Political (Geneva, 15 Sept. 1930), pp. 17–66; Mirkine-Guetzevich and Scelle,

L'Union européenne, pp. 59–70; and in several journals, including *Paneuropa* and *L'Esprit international*.

2. For contemporary analyses, see Barthélemy, "L'Accueil de l'Europe au mémorandum," pp. 421–23; Etienne Fougère, "Le Briand Mémorandum et l'Europe," *L'Européen*, 30 July 1930; Caillaux, "L'Union européenne," pp. 320–22; Montluc, "Les Réponses au mémorandum de M. Briand," pp. 218–20; Pusta, "Vers l'Union européenne," pp. 97–122; and Hennessy, "Le Projet de fédération européenne," pp. 207–12.

3. *Documents on British Foreign Policy, 1919–1939*, ser. 2, vol. 1, pp. 326–33 (hereafter cited as *D.B.F.P.*); Salter, *The United States of Europe*, pp. 105–24; *The Manchester Guardian*, 18 July 1930; *The Times* (London), 19, 21 May and 5 June 1930; *The Economist*, 24 May 1930, p. 1153; *The Spectator*, 24 May 1930; Erdmann, "Der Europaplan Briands," pp. 20 ff.

4. *D.B.F.P.*, ser. 2, vol. 1, pp. 324–29.

5. For key documents dealing with the drafting of the reply, see G.F.M., 3617H/1680/D800873-995. For German reply, see Lipgens, "Briands Europaplan," pp. 329 ff.

6. See Schwarz to Brüning, 11 Aug. 1930, G.F.M., 1680/D800990 and D800914-919.

7. *Der Berliner Börsen-Courier*, 16 July 1930; *Kölnische Zeitung*, 31 Aug. 1930; and *Vossische Zeitung*, 18 July 1930.

8. Louis Schwarz, "L'Italie et le projet de fédération européenne," *La Revue diplomatique, politique coloniale, littéraire, et financière*, July 1930, pp. 3 ff.

9. For the smaller states see Hantos, "L'Organisation économique de la nouvelle Europe centrale," pp. 508–20; Ulitz, "Paneuropa und die Nationalitätenfrage," pp. 10–16; Radu Budisteanu, *Pan-Europa* (Bucharest, 1931); Fernand Baudhum, "La Belgique et les Projets de M. Briand," *L'Européen*, 11 June 1930; and Hymans, "L'Union européenne," pp. 8–20.

10. William Martin, "Les deux Opinions suisses et le Mémorandum Briand," *L'Européen*, 4 June 1930; Maurice de Rameru, *Une Image d'Etats-Unis européens*, passim.

11. See Mirkine-Guetzevitch and Scelle, *L'Union européenne*, pp. 175–94. Curtius, in a note to Chancellor Brüning, expressed surprise at the objectivity of this document. G.F.M., 3617H/1681/D800999-1001.

12. Journalists were excluded, but many watched as best they could through the opaque glass of the council room. Young Jean Luchaire declared in *Notre temps*, 21 Sept. 1930, that the statesmen and journalists were "gathered excitedly around the cradle of the new Europe."

13. The texts of all speeches on European union at the Eleventh Session are in Mirkine-Guetzevitch and Scelle, *L'Union européenne*, pp. 198–319 and *Verbatim Record*, Eleventh Ordinary Session, League of Nations. See also Georges Scelle, "L'Union européenne et la XIe assemblée de la S.D.N.," *Revue politique et parlementaire*, 10 Oct. 1930, pp. 59–70; Zimmern, "L'Idée d'une fédération européenne," pp. 51–60; Gauvain, "La Conférence européenne," pp. 877–78; and M. D. Hage, "De Paneuropeesche Beweging in Nederland," *De Volkenbond*, Apr. 1932, pp. 264–70.

14. Curtius to Brüning, 9 and 11 Sept. 1930, G.F.M., 3617H/1681/D800999-1001.

15. Mirkine-Guetzevitch and Scelle, *L'Union européenne*, pp. 319–20.

CHAPTER 18

1. See Henri Simondet, "Les Elections allemandes," *La Paix par le droit*, Oct. 1930, pp. 376–82; Schmidt, *Statist auf Diplomatischer Bühne*, pp. 195–98 and passim; Eyck, *Geschichte der Weimarer Republik*, 2:350–60 and passim; and *B.D.F.P.*, Ser. 2, vol. 1, pp. 486, 502–5, and passim.

2. The literature is vast, but esp. Jouvenel, "Le Projet de fédération européenne," pp. 483–90; Benda, "Créons des mythes et des héros européens," pp. 157–63; Jean Charles Brun, "A Propos de l'union européenne," *Le Monde nouveau*, Feb. 1931, pp. 797 ff.; Duborq, "Recherche du lien spirituel d'une communauté européenne," pp. 251–62; Yves La Brière, "L'Union continentale européenne," *Revue de droit international et de législation comparée*, 1931, pp. 5–36; Wil-

liam Martin, "Il faut être pour ou contre l'Europe," *Journal de Genève*, 19 Mar. 1931; Georges Scelle, "Les Débuts de l'union européenne," *La Paix par le droit*, Feb. 1931, pp. 89 ff.; L'Huillier, *Dialogues franco-allemands*, pp. 106–20; Aeppli, *Wir fordern Europa*, passim; and Lapradelle, *Union fédérale européenne*, passim.

3. For typical comments see *Le Monde nouveau* 12 (Jan. 1931): 570–74; *L'Europe nouvelle*, 28 June 1930, p. 965; *Le Populaire*, 13 Nov. 1930; *L'Européen*, 8 Oct. 1930; *La République*, 8 Oct. 1930; *La Dépêche de Toulouse*, 2 Oct. 1930; *Neue freie Presse*, 10 Jan. 1931; *Berliner Börsen-Courrier*, 17 and 26 Feb. 1931; and *Vorwärts*, 3 Mar. 1931.

4. *L'Europe nouvelle*, 13 Sept. 1930, p. 1328, and 24 Jan. 1931, pp. 54–56. For comprehensive analyses, see André Tibal, *La Crise des états agricoles européens* (Paris, 1932), and Francis Delaisi et al., *L'Europe centrale et la crise* (Paris, 1933), passim.

5. Henri Cahen, "Une Union européenne électrique," *L'Europe nouvelle*, 28 Feb. 1931, pp. 276–78. Many moderate Left journals, including *Sozialistische Monatshefte*, speculated in this sense.

6. *L'Europe nouvelle*, 8 Nov. 1930, pp. 1600–1601. For a British view, see Wickham Steed, "Peace Research : A Projected European Institute," *Headway*, Feb. 1931, p. 28.

7. Alfred Silvert, "Le Congrès universitaire de Mannheim," *Notre temps* 12, (5 Oct. 1930): 36–39; also the rubrics "La jeune Europe" in this journal for 8, 29 Mar., 13 Dec. 1931, and 24 Jan. 1932.

8. For an overall view, see League of Nations, *Commission of Inquiry for European Union*, VII–Political, 1931. Also Victor Dupuis, "La Commission d'étude pour l'union européenne," *Revue de droit international public*, July–Aug. 1931, pp. 492–99; Paul de La Pradelle, "La Commission d'étude," pp. 617–46; Meurs, "De Europeese Kommissie," pp. 207–11; Montluc, "La Commission d'études," pp. 251–53; C. R. Pusta, "Fonctionnement et travaux de la commission d'études pour l'union européenne," *Revue de droit international* 8, no. 5, 1931; and Ralli, *Essai sur le problème de l'entente européenne*, pp. 159–200.

9. League of Nations, *Commission of Inquiry*, pp. 19 ff.

10. *Paneurope* 7 (Jan. 1931): 1–5; *L'Europe nouvelle* 14 (31 Jan. 1931): 155–56, and (28 Feb. 1931): 259–60; and C. R. Pusta, "Fonctionnement et travaux de la commission d'études pour l'union européenne," *Revue de droit international* 8, no. 4 (1931).

11. Hauser, "Der Plan einer deutsch-oesterreichischen Zollunion," pp. 45 ff.; Pierre Bernus, "Le Projet d'union douanière," *L'Esprit international*, July 1931, pp. 362–86; Norman Johnson, "The Austro-German Customs Union Project in German Diplomacy," Ph.D. dissertation, University of North Carolina, 1974; Krulis-Randa, *Das deutsch-österreichische Zollunionsprojekt von 1931*, pp. 86–150; Curtius, *Bemühungen um Österreich*, pp. 30–41; Curtius to Lerchenfeld, 10 Mar. 1931, and to German ambassadors in Paris and Rome, 18 Mar. 1931, G.F.M., 2520/E284254-59. What Curtius says in *Bemühungen um Österreich* sometimes collides with the documents.

12. League of Nations, *Commission of Inquiry*, pp. 15 and 19–27. See also K. A. Rohan, "Die Zollunion in Genf," *Europäische Revue* 7 (May 1931): 321 ff.; Henri Berenger, "La Question d'Autriche: Du Zollverein au Mittel-Europa," *Revue des deux mondes*, 15 May 1931, pp. 356–72; Cléry de Robinet, "Le Projet d'union douanière austro-allemande," *Revue d'allemagne*, May 1931, pp. 385–402; Georges Marot, "Le Plan austro-allemande et l'Europe centrale," *La Revue de Paris*, 15 May 1931, pp. 376–95; and C. F. Melville, "The European Crucible," *The Fortnightly Review*, July 1931, pp. 46–57.

13. See C. R. Pusta, "Die Europa Kommission," *Paneuropa* 8 (Jan. 1932): 14–26; and *Annuaire européen 1931*, pp. 1105–6 and 1115–17, and passim. After Briand's death on 7 March 1932, Edouard Herriot was elected president, and he presided over a final brief session in September 1932. Although the League Assembly again renewed the commission's mandate, it never met again.

14. One of the quickest ways to get a general idea of this is to read the issues of *Paneuropa* from January 1932 to March 1938.

BIBLIOGRAPHY

Bibliographical Aids

While this selected bibliography is largely a product of my own research, I did get help from some formal bibliographies along the way. In the early stages of my research, I received some help from the *Bibliographie générale des sciences juridiques, politiques, économiques, et sociales*; the *Bibliographie der Sozialwissenschaften* (with its variant titles); and even from the section of the card catalog of the Bibliothèque de Documentation Internationale Contemporaine in Paris (Nanterre) devoted to European unification. Then in 1958, G. A. C. Beljaars's *Bibliographie historique et culturelle de l'intégration européenne* appeared as no. 30 in the voluminous *Bibliographia belgica* with an excellent section concerning the European idea before World War II. Also L. L. Paklons's *Bibliographie européenne*, 1964, had a modest but useful section on the idea before 1945. Unfortunately for students of the history of the idea, nearly all of the many bibliographies that have appeared since 1950, including the voluminous *Recherches: Bulletin d'information et documentaire* and Karl Kujath's 777-page *Bibliographie zur europäischen Integration* (Bonn, 1977), center on the European movement since 1945 and are of slight help for the earlier years.

Documentary Sources

Archives du Bureau International Permanent de la Paix. Manuscript Division, The United Nations Library, Geneva.

Belgium. *Documents diplomatiques belges, 1920–1940*. Vols. 1–2, 1920–1931. Brussels, 1964.

Bulletin du Troisième Congrès International de la Paix. Rome, Novembre 1891. Rome, 1892. This congress adopted a resolution urging all peace societies to work for a European federation.

Cecil, Viscount of Chelwood. *Papers*. British Museum, London.

Europa. *Dokumente zur Frage der europäischen Einigung*. 3 vols. Munich, 1962. Part of vol. 1 is on the 1920s.

France. *Journal officiel de la république française: Débats parlementaires, Chambre des Députés*, 1924–1931.

———. *Journal officiel de la république française: Débats parlementaires, Sénat*, 1924–1931.

———, Ministère des affaires étrangères. *Documents diplomatiques: Conférence économique internationale de Gênes*, 9 Apr.–19 May 1922.

———, Ministère du travail. *Statistique de la France: Annuaire statistique, 1920–1924*. Paris, 1920–24.

Fried, Alfred. Manuscript materials in the Hoover Institution, Stanford University, Palo Alto, Cal.

Germany. *Akten zur deutschen auswärtigen Politik, 1918–1945*. Serie B: 1925–1933. Göttingen, 1967.

———. Foreign Ministry Archives, U.S. National Archives Microfilms T-120. Washington, D.C.

———. *Verhandlungen des Reichstags: Stenographische Berichte, 1924–1930*. Vols. 385–98. Berlin, 1924–30.

Great Britain. *Documents on British Foreign Policy, 1919–1939*. Edited by E. L. Woodward and Rohan Butler. Ser. 2, vols. 1 and 2. His Majesty's Stationery Office. London, 1946–57.

Heile, Wilhelm. Nachlass. Bundesarchiv, Koblenz.

Herriot, Edouard. Papers. Ministère des Affaires Etrangères–Quai d'Orsay, Paris.

Koch-Weser, Erich. *Nachlass* (diary from 1925–1929). Bundesarchiv, Koblenz.

League of Nations. *Commission of Inquiry for European Union*. VII–Political, 1931. Geneva, 1932.

_____. *Documents Relating to the Organization of a System of Federal Union*. VII–Political. Geneva, 15 Sept. 1930.

_____. *Official Journal: Special Supplement*, no. 33, 1926.

_____. *Reports and Proceedings of the World Economic Conference, 1927*. II–Economic and Financial. Geneva, 1928.

Loesch, Karl, and Hillen Ziegfeld, eds. *Staat und Volkstum*. Berlin, 1926.

Loucheur, Louis. Papers. Hoover Institution, Stanford University, Palo Alto, Cal.

Mann, Erika. *Thomas Mann: Briefe, 1889–1936*. Frankfurt a.M., 1961.

Mirkine-Guetzevitch, Boris, and Georges Scelle. *L'Union européenne: Documents de politique contemporaine*. Paris, 1931.

Mommsen, Wilhelm. *Deutsche Parteiprogramme: Eine Auswahl vom Vormärz bis zu Gegenwart*, Munich, 1952.

Painlevé, Paul. Papers. Archives Nationales. Paris.

Paneuropa-Kongress: Mit Beiträgen Coudenhove-Kalergis und führender Politiker und Wirtschaftsführer Europas. Vienna, 1932.

Premiers européens: Annuaire illustré. Paris, 1931.

Proceedings, XXV Universal Peace Congress, London, July 25–29, 1922. London, 1922.

Proceedings, XXVIIᵉ Congrès de la paix tenu à Athènes du 6 au 12 octobre, 1929. Athens, 1930.

Les Projets de fédération européenne, Coopération Européenne et Union Douanière Européenne. Paris, 1930.

Publications de la Société des Anciens Elèves de l'Ecole Libre des Sciences Politiques. Paris, 1901.

Quidde, Ludwig. *Nachlass*. Bundesarchiv. Koblenz.

Union Interparlementaire. *Compte rendu de la XXIIIᵉ Conférence*. Paris, 1926.

_____. *Compte rendu de la XXIVᵉ Conférence*. Paris, 1927.

_____. *Compte rendu de la XXVᵉ Conférence*. Geneva, 1928.

_____. *Compte rendu de la XXVIᵉ Conférence*. Paris, 1931.

United States. Department of State. *Papers Relating to the Foreign Relations of the United States, 1919, 1922, 1925, 1929, 1930*. Washington: The United States Government Printing Office, 1930–46.

_____. *Papers Relating to the Foreign Relations of the United States: The Paris Peace Conference, 1919*. 13 vols. Washington: The United States Government Printing Office, 1942.

Veröffentlichungen des Reichesverbandes der deutschen Industrie. Berlin, 1919–34.

Newspapers Used

L'Avenir; Berliner Tageblatt; Bonnet rouge; Le Capital; Le Correspondant; The Daily Mail; La Dépêche de Toulouse; Deutsche allgemeine Zeitung; Deutsche Tageszeitung; L'Ere nouvelle; L'Etoile belge; L'Europe centrale; Le Figaro; Frankfurter Zeitung; Fränkischer Kurier; Gazette de Lausanne; Germania; Guerre sociale: Hamburger Fremdenblatt; L'Homme libre; L'Indépendance belge; L'Information; Journal de Genève; La Journée industrielle; Kölnische Zeitung; La libre Belgique; Luxemburger Zeitung; The Manchester Guardian; Le Matin; La Métropole; Neue freie Presse; Neue Zürcher Zeitung; L'Oeuvre; Paris-Soir; Le petit Journal; Le petit Parisien; Le Peuple; Le Populaire; Prager presse; Le Progrès du nord; Le Quotidien; La République; Le Soir; Der Tag; Tägliche Rundschau; De Telegraaf; Le Temps; The Times (London); *La Volonté; Vorwärts*; and *Vossische Zeitung*.

Periodicals Used

Arbeit und Wirtschaft; *Cahiers des droits de l'homme*; *The Commercial and Financial Chronicle*; *Contemporary Review*; *Die deutsche Arbeit*; *Deutsche Einheit*; *Deutsch-französische Rundschau*; *Deutsche Politik*; *Der deutsche Volkswirt*; *The Economist*; *The English Review*; *L'Esprit international*; *Les Etats-Unis de l'Europe*; *Europäische Wirtschafts-Union*; *L'Europe*; *L'Européen*; *L'Europe de demain*; *L'Europe nouvelle*; *Firn*; *Le Flambeau*; *Foreign Affairs* (London); *The Fortnightly Review*; *Freiwirtschaft*; *Friedenskämpfer*; *Friedens-Warte*; *Grande revue*; *Die Hilfe*; *Die Hochland*; *Journal des économistes*; *Der Kampf*; *La Lumière*; *Die Menschheit*; *Le Mois*; *Le Monde nouveau*; *The National Review*; *Das neue Reich*; *Die neue Rundschau*; *Neue Schweizer Rundschau*; *Nord und Süd*; *Notre temps*; *Nouvelle revue française*; *La Paix par le droit*; *Paneuropa*; *Le Progrès civique*; *Review of Reviews*; *Revue d'Allemagne*; *Revue d'économie politique*; *La Revue d'évolution*; *Revue de droit international*; *Revue de droit international de sciences diplomatiques et politiques et sociales*; *Revue de Genève*; *La Revue de Paris*; *Revue des deux mondes*; *Revue des vivants*; *Revue économique internationale*; *La Revue européenne*; *Revue générale de droit international public*; *La Revue hebdomadaire*; *Revue nouvelle française*; *Revue politique et littéraire* (Revue bleue); *Revue politique et parlementaire*; *La Revue Rhénanie*; *Der Ring*; *Schriften des Vereins für Sozialpolitik*; *Sozialistische Monatshefte*; *Süddeutsche Monatshefte*; *Die Wahrheit*; *Weltwirtschaftsliches-Archiv*; *Wirtschaftsdienst*; *Wissen und Leben*; *Zeitschrift für Geopolitik*; *Zeitschrift für Politik*.

Contemporary Books, Pamphlets, and Memoirs

Aeppli, Hermann. *Wir fordern Europa*. Basel, 1932.

Agnelli, Giovanni, and Attilio Cabiati. *Federazione europea o lega delle nazioni?* Rome, 1918.

Ajam, Maurice. *Le Problème économique franco-allemand*. Paris, 1914.

Alvarez, Alejandro. *L'Organisation internationale*. Paris, 1931. Various projects from 1915 to 1930.

Ancel, Jacques. *Peuples et nations des Balkans*. Paris, 1926.

André, L. E. *La Paix définitive pour la confédération gallogermanique*. Lyon, 1928.

Annuaire européen. Paris, 1931. Edited by Henri Jouvenel and stressing the customs union movement.

Appelt, Otto. *Ein europäischer Staatenbund*. Leipzig, 1913.

Aron, Robert, and Arnaud Dandieu. *La Révolution nécessaire?* Paris, 1932.

Arrudo, Botelho, and Roberto de Antonio. *Les Etats-Unis d'Europe*. Antwerp, 1930.

Baerwald, Richard. *Ladokka's Malstrom: Visionen des Weges der uns zu den Vereinigten Staaten von Europa führen wird*. Baden, 1923.

Bardoux, Jacques. *L'Ile et l'Europe*. Paris, 1933.

———. *Le Socialisme au pouvoir: L'expérience de 1924*. Paris, 1930.

Barolin, Johannes, and Kurt Scheckner. *Für und wider Donauföderation*. Vienna, 1926.

Barthélemy, Joseph. *Démocratie et politique étrangère*. Paris, 1917.

Barthélemy, Raynaud. *La Vie économique*. Paris, 1926.

Bauer, Heinrich. *Stresemann*. Berlin, 1929.

Bäumer, Gertrud. *Europäische Kulturpolitik*. Berlin, 1927.

Beier, Kurt. *Paneuropa: Ein Querschnitt durch die politisch-ökonomische Struktur des europäischen Staatensystems*. Düsseldorf, 1934.

Benda, Julien. *Discours à la nation européene*. Paris, 1933.

———, ed. *L'Avenir de l'esprit européen*. Paris, 1933.

Benkiser, Nikolaus. *Das Problem der staatlichen Organisation der Weltwirtschaft*. Karlsruhe,

1927. The national state is too powerful for any sort of European union.

Berger, Emil. *Die Organisation der internationalen Friedensliga der Staaten* (Société des Nations) *als Eidgenossenschaft*. Zurich, 1917.

Bernhard, Georg. *Die deutsche Tragödie: Der Selbstmord einer Republik*. Prague, 1933.

Bonnamour, Georges. *Le Rapprochement franco-allemand*. Paris, 1927.

Borgius, Walther. *Der Paneuropa Wahn*. Berlin, 1927.

Bossière, René. *La Crise mondiale: Etude de la cause et d'une projet de solution*. Paris, 1923.

Bourgeois, Nicolas. *Le Fédéralisme et la paix*. Paris, 1927.

Bücher, Hermann. *Finanz und Wirtschaftsentwicklung Deutschlands in den Jahren 1921 bis 1925. Reden*. Berlin, 1925.

Buchholz, Johannes. *Die Vereinigten Staaten von Europa*. Hamburg, 1925.

Budisteanu, Radu. *Pan-Europa*. Bucharest, 1931. Deals with the Briand Memorandum of 17 May 1930.

Caillaux, Joseph. *Où va la France? Où va l'Europe?* Paris, 1922. Economic nationalism has done great damage to Europe; there should be an all-out effort to make Europe an economic entity.

Chair, S. M. *Divided Europe*. London, 1931.

Chaiti, M. B. *Les Ententes industrielles internationales*. Paris, 1928.

Charles-Brun, Jean. *La Tradition fédéraliste française*. Paris, 1919.

Claparède-Spir, Hélène. *Pour les ententes des peuples*. Paris, 1925.

Clémentel, Etienne. *La France et la politique économique interalliée*. New Haven, 1931.

Coerper, Fritz. *Das wirtschaftliche Europa*. . . . Leipzig, 1926.

Cohen-Portheim, Paul. *The Rediscovery of Europe*. London, 1933.

Conte, Roger. *Les Ententes industrielles*. Paris, 1927.

Coquet, Lucien, ed. *Premiers européens et premiers organismes européens*. Paris, 1931.

Cordier, A. W. *European Union and the League of Nations*. Geneva, 1931.

Cornelissen, Christaan. *Les Dessous économiques de la guerre*. Paris, 1915.

Corradin, Enrico. *Die politische Reformation in Europa*. Berlin, 1931.

Coudenhove-Kalergi, Richard Nicolas. *Europa erwacht!* Vienna, 1934.

―――. *Held oder Heiliger*. Leipzig, 1927.

―――. *Kampf um Pan-Europa*. Leipzig, 1925.

―――. *Lös vom Materialismus!* Vienna, 1930.

―――. *Pan-Europa*. Vienna, 1923.

―――. *Paneuropa, A. B. C*. Vienna, 1931.

―――. *Paneuropa, die europäische Seele*. Leipzig, 1928.

―――. *Praktischer Idealismus: Adel, Technik, Pazifismus*. Vienna, 1925.

―――. *Revolution durch Technik*. Vienna, 1932.

Cristu, Jean. *L'union douanière européenne: Ses conditions et ses difficultés*. Paris, 1928.

Curtius, Ernst R. *Französischer Geist im neuen Europa*. Stuttgart, 1926.

Dahriman, Georges. *Pour les Etats confédérés d'Europe*. Paris, 1929.

Daulander, Robert, and Emile Borel. *L'Union européenne*. Paris, 1934.

Daye, Pierre. *L'Europe en morceaux*. Paris, 1932.

Delaisi, Francis. *Les Contradictions du monde moderne*. Paris, 1925.

―――. *Les deux Europes*. Paris, 1929.

―――. *Political Myths and Economic Realities*. London, 1927.

Demangeon, Albert. *Le Déclin de l'Europe*. Paris, 1920. World war shifted the center of economic gravity away from Europe.

Demarquette, J. C. *Pour créer la paix et pacifier des jeunes*. Paris, 1926.

Depuis, Victor. *Vers un fédéralisme européen*. Paris, 1940.

Desart, Jean. *S. O. S.* . . . *Europe*. Brussels, 1931.

Dessauer, Friedrich. *Aus dem Kampf mit der Wirtschaftskrise*. Frankfurt a.M., 1931.

Dewall, Dalf V. *Der Kampf um den Frieden*. Frankfurt a.M., 1929.

Bibliography   195

Dingrave, Leopold. *Wo steht die junge Generation?* Jena, 1929.

Diplomaticus. *Entweder ein europäischer Staatenbund oder.* . . . Vienna, 1914.

Dix, Arthur. *Schluss mit Europa.* Berlin, 1928.

Dood, Caspar de. *Het Plan Briand en de Internationale Arbeidersbeweging.* Amsterdam, 1931.

Dove, K. *Allgemeine Wirtschaftsgeographie.* Berlin, 1921.

Drieu la Rochelle, Pierre. *L'Europe contre ses patries.* Paris, 1931.

————. *Genève ou Moscow.* Paris, 1928.

————. *Le jeune Européen.* Paris, 1927.

————. *Mesure de la France.* Paris, 1922.

Dumon, Roger. *L'Ordre européen vu des bords du Rhin.* Paris, 1928.

Dumont-Wilden, Louis. *L'Esprit européen.* Paris, 1914.

————. *L'Evolution de l'esprit européen.* Paris, 1937.

Dupuis, Charles. *Les Etats-Unis d'Europe.* Paris, 1931.

Dupuis, Renée, and A. Mare. *Jeune Europe.* Paris, 1933.

Durand, Julien. *Les Etats fédéraux.* Paris, 1930.

Echkert, Christian. *Die Neuformung Europas.* Leipzig, 1928.

Endres, Franz Carl. *Vaterland Europa.* Leipzig, 1925.

————. *Vaterland und Menschheit.* Leipzig, 1920.

Erni, Johannes. *Die europäische Union als Bedingung und Grundlage des dauernden Friedens.* Zurich, 1915.

Escholier, Raymond. *Souvenirs parlés de Briand.* Paris, 1932.

Eulenburg, Franz. *Aussenhandel und Aussenhandelspolitik.* Tübingen, 1929.

————. *Probleme der deutschen Handelspolitik.* Jena, 1925.

Eynard, Emilio. *Verso la Federazione europea.* Besson, 1901.

Fabre-Luce, Alfred. *Caillaux.* Paris, 1933.

————. *Locarno sans rêves.* Paris, 1927.

————. *La Victoire.* Paris, 1924.

Faluhelyi, Ferenc. *Paneuropa: Mit Varhatunk töle.* Budapest, 1928.

Feiler, A. *Amerika-Europa.* Frankfurt a.M., 1926.

Ferenci, Imre. *Kontinentale Wanderungen und die Annäherung der Völker.* Jena, 1930.

Ferrero, Guglielmo. *Die Einheit der Welt.* Berlin, 1928.

Filene, Edward. *European Federation and the Peace of Europe.* New York, 1924. Francis Delaisi, tr., *Problème européen et sa solution.* Paris, 1925.

Fimmen, Edo. *Labour's Alternative: The United States of Europe Limited.* London, 1924.

Fischer, Hermann. *Europäische Wirtschaftsfreiheit und Solidarität.* Hague, 1928.

Fischer, J. L. *Über die Zukunft der europäischen Kultur.* Munich, 1928.

Fleissig, Andreas. *Planeuropa: Die soziale und wirtschaftliche Zukunft Europas.* Munich, 1930.

Foerster, F. W. *Mein Kampf gegen das militaristische und nationalistische Deutschland.* Stuttgart, 1920.

Forel, Auguste Henri. *Les Etats-Unis de la terre.* Lausanne, 1915.

Franck, Paul, Jacques Kayser, and Camille Lemercier. *Les Etats-Unis d'Europe.* Paris, 1926.

François-Marsal, Frédéric. *Les Dettes interalliées: La renaissance du livre.* Paris, 1927.

Freimann, Albert. *Die vereinigten freien Staaten von Europa.* Hannover, 1925.

Fried, Alfred H. *Europäische Wiederherstellung.* Zurich, 1915.

Fuchs, Gustav. *Der deutschen Pazifismus im Weltkrieg.* Stuttgart, 1928.

Funk, Fritz. *Die Vereinigten Staaten von Europa.* Aarau, 1929.

Furst, Gaston. *De Versailles aux experts.* Paris, 1927.

Gail, Henri de. *Les Etats à forme fédérative.* Nancy, 1901.

Geissler, Ewald. *Paneuropa in deutscher Dichtung der Gegenwart.* Berlin, 1930.

Gessl, Josef, ed. *Seipels Reden in Österreich und anderwärts.* Vienna, 1925.

Gide, Charles. *Les Sociétés coopératives de consommation.* Paris, 1924.

Gignoux, Claude. *L'Après-guerre et la politique commerciale*. Paris, 1924.

―――. *A la Recherche d'une politique perdue*. Paris, 1926.

Göhre, Paul. *Deutschlands weltpolitische Sendung*. Berlin-Grünewald, 1925.

Goltz, Otto. *Quo vadis Europa?* Berlin, 1924.

Gothein, Georg. *Ist eine paneuropäische Zollunion durchfurhbar?* Berlin, 1925.

Grand, Guy G. *Le Conflit des idées dans la France d'aujourd'hui*. Paris, 1921.

Grossmann, M. E. *Systèmes de rapprochement économique*. Paris, 1928.

Grotkopp, Wilhelm. *Amerikas Schutszollpolitik und Europa*. Leipzig, 1929.

―――. *Europäische Zollunion als Weg aus deutscher Wirtschaftsnot*. Basel, 1931.

―――. *Die Zolle nieder: Wege zu europäischer Wirtschaftseinheit*. Berlin, 1930.

―――, and W. Gurge. *Grossraumwirtschaft, der Weg zur europäischen Einheit*. Berlin, 1931.

Guadalupi, F. de. *Warum Paneuropa?* Leipzig, 1928.

Gualtierotti, F. T. *Europa unita*. Milan, 1930.

Gürge, Wilhelm. *Paneuropa und Mitteleuropa*. Berlin, 1929.

Gutmann, Wilhelm. *Um die Welt zu Paneuropa*. Reichtenberg, 1926.

Guye, Robert. *La Fédération européenne: Vers l'entente politique par l'Organisation économique*. Paris, 1931.

Guyot, Yves. *Les Causes et les conséquences de la guerre*. Paris, 1916.

Haas, Wilhelm. *What Is European Civilisation? What Is Its Future?* London, 1929.

Hagemann, Walter. *L'Allemagne à la croisée des chemins. . . .* Paris, 1930.

Haller, Johannes. *Tausend Jahre deutsch-französischer Beziehungen*. Berlin, 1931.

Hantos, Elemér. *Europäischer Zollverein und mitteleuropäische Wirtschaftsgemeinschaft*. Berlin, 1928.

―――. *Die Handelspolitik in Mitteleuropa*. Jena, 1925.

―――. *Mitteleuropäische Wirtschaftsfragen*. Vienna, 1929.

―――. *Die Wirtschaftskonferenz: Probleme und Ergebnisse*. Leipzig, 1928.

Harms, Bernhard. *Die Zukunft der deutschen Handelspolitik*. Jena, 1925.

Hartmann, Hans. *Die jungen Generationen in Europa*. Berlin, 1930.

Haupt-Buchenrode, Stefan. *Die Zukunft Europas*. Leipzig, 1922.

Hauser, Erwin. *Die Lösung der Frage unserer volkswirtschaftlichen Existenz*. Zurich, 1889.

Heerfordt, C. F. *Et nyt Europa*. Copenhagen, 1924. Translated into several languages.

Heile, Wilhelm, ed. *Europäische Cooperation*. Berlin, 1929.

―――. *Nationalstaat und Völkerbund: Gedanken über Deutschlands europäische Sendung*. Halberstadt, 1926.

Heiman, Hans, ed. *Europäische Zollunion*. Berlin, 1926. Twenty German and Austrian economists and diplomats analyze the question.

Heinemann, Dannie. *Esquisse d'une Europe nouvelle*. (Lectures given at Cologne on 28 Nov. and at Barcelona on 3 Dec. 1930.) Brussels, 1930.

Hellpach, Willy. *Politische Prognose für Deutschland*. Berlin, 1928. Argues that Paneuropa would mean a Europe under French hegemony.

Hennessy, Jean. *L'Organisation fédérale de la Société des Nations*. Paris, 1918.

―――, ed. *L'Europe fédéraliste: Aspirations et réalités*. Paris, 1927.

Herriot, Edouard. *Europe*. Paris, 1930.

―――. *Pourquoi je suis Radical-Socialiste*. Paris, 1928.

Hirsch, Julius. *Das amerikanische Wirtschaftswunder*. Berlin, 1929.

Hobelsperger, Alois. *Europa im Abstieg*. Berlin, 1928.

Hode, J. *L'Idée de fédération internationale dans l'histoire*. Paris, 1921.

Hodza, Milan. *Federation of Central Europe*. London, 1942.

Hohlfeld, Hans Herbert. *Zur Frage einer europäischen Zollunion*. Oblau, 1927.

Holleben-Alzey, Nikolaus von. *Vom Fascismus zu Kleineuropa*. Berlin, 1929.

Horneffer, Ernst. *Drei Wege: Ideen zur deutschen Politik*. Munich, 1924.

Hromadka, J. L. *Masaryk as European*. Prague, 1936.

Hubermann, Bronislaw. *Vaterland Europa*. Berlin, 1932.

Hutcheson, Paul. *The United States of Europe*. New York, 1929.

Isambert, Georges. *Projet d'organisation politique d'une confédération européenne*. Paris, 1904.

Ivanchev, Constantin. *L'Idée des Etats-Unis d'Europe et les projets d'une confédération balkanique*. Paris, 1930.

Jackh, Ernst. *Der Völkerbundsgedanke in Deutschland während des Weltkrieges*. Berlin, 1929.

Jäckh, Robert. *Deutschland: Das Herz Europas*. Stuttgart, 1928.

Jahrreiss, Hermann. *Europa als Rechtseinheit*. Leipzig, 1929.

Johannet, René. *Le Principe des nationalités*. Paris, 1923.

Jouvenel, Bertrand de. *D'une Guerre à l'autre*. 2 vols. Paris, 1940.

————. *Vers les Etats-Unis d'Europe*. Paris, 1930.

Jouvenel, Henri de. *La Paix française: Témoignage d'une génération*. Paris, 1932.

————, ed. *La Fédération européenne*. Paris, 1930. Texts of the six best essays in the contest conducted by *Revue des vivants*, 1929–30.

Jünger, Ernst. *Der Kampf als inneres Erlebnis*. Berlin, 1922.

Kanner, Heinrich. *Der mitteleuropäische Staatenbund: Ein Vorschlag zum Frieden*. Vienna, 1925.

Karl, E. F. *Vereinigte Staaten von Mittel-Europa*. Berlin, 1917.

Kautsky, Karl. *Die Vereinigten Staaten Mitteleuropas*. Stuttgart, 1916.

Kaysenbrecht, Richard. *Das europäische Manifest*. Hague, 1928.

Kayser, Jacques. *Le Paix est en péril*. Paris, 1931.

————, Paul Franck, and C. Lemercier. *Les Etats-Unis d'Europe*. Paris, 1926.

Keller, Rudolf. *Deutschland und Frankreich*. Munich, 1921.

Keyserling, Graf Hermann. *Das Spektrum Europas*. Stuttgart, 1928.

————. *Deutschlands wahre politische Mission*. Darmstadt, 1919.

Kleinwaechter, F. G., and Heinz von Paller. *Die Anschluss-frage in ihrer kulturellen, politischen und wirtschaftlichen Bedeutung*. Vienna, 1930.

Knaus, A. *La Guerre hors la loi*. Paris, 1929. Strong plea for a customs union and federation.

Koch-Weser, Erich. *Deutschlands Aussenpolitik in der Nachkriegszeit, 1919–1929*. Berlin, 1929.

————. *Russland von heute*. Dresden, 1928.

Kolb, Annette. *Versuch über Briand*. Berlin, 1929.

Kranold, Herman. *Vereinigte Staaten von Europa*. Hannover, 1924. A task for the Social Democrats.

Krebs, Hans. *Paneuropa oder Mitteleuropa?* Munich, 1931.

Kühl, Joachim. *Föderationspläne im Donauraum in Ostmitteleuropa*. Vienna, 1958.

La Brière, Yves de. *La Communauté des puissances: D'une communauté inorganique à une communauté organique*. Paris, 1932.

La Mazière, Pierre. *Déshonorons la guerre*. Paris, 1923.

Lange, Christian, et al. *The Interparliamentary Union, 1889–1939*. Paris, 1939.

Lanux, Pierre de. *Eveil d'une éthique internationale*. Paris, 1924.

Lapradella, Albert de. *Union fédérale européenne*. Paris, 1931.

Lazard, Max. *De l'Unification de l'Europe occidentale*. . . . Paris, 1933.

Le Foyer, Lucien. *Rapport sur l'union européenne, présenté au 28e Congrès Universel de la Paix*. Paris, 1931.

Le Gall, Robert. *Le Pacte de Paris*. Paris, 1929.

Lehmann-Russbueldt, Otto. *Der Kampf der deutschen Liga für Menschenrechte und für den Weltfrieden*. Berlin, 1927.

————. *Der Kampf für den Weltfrieden*. Berlin, 1927.

————. *Republik Europa*. Berlin, 1925.

————. *Die Schaffung der vereinigten Staaten von Europa*. Berlin, 1914.

Lelek, Auguste. *La Collaboration économique des nations de l'Europe centrale*. Paris, 1931.

Léonard, Raymond. *Vers une Organisation politique et juridique de l'Europe: Du projet d'union fédérale européenne de 1930 aux pactes de securité*. Paris, 1935.

Leroy-Beaulieu, Anatole. *Les Etats-Unis d'Europe*. Paris, 1901.

Le Trocquer, Yves. *L'Union douanière européenne* (International Conciliation, No. 4). Paris, 1929.

Levy, H. *Die Grundlagen der Weltwirtschaft*. Berlin, 1925.

―――. *Der Weltmarkt 1913 und heute*. Leipzig, 1926.

Lichtenberger, Henri. *L'Allemagne moderne, son évolution*. Paris, 1907. See especially the final pages.

Lop, Ferdinand. *Une Fédération des peuples*. Paris, 1920.

Loucheur, Louis, ed. *Les Réformes politiques de la France: Conférences faites à l'école des hautes études sociales*. Paris, 1924.

Luchaire, Jean. *Vers les états fédérés d'Europe*. Paris, 1929.

Luchaire, Julien. *Le Désarmement moral*. Paris, 1932.

Luddecke, Theodor. *Das amerikanische Wirtschaftstempo als Bedrohung Europas*. Leipzig, 1925.

Luttemer, Georges. *Les Etats-Unis d'Europe*. Paris, 1913.

Malynski, Emmanuel. *Pour sauver l'Europe*. Paris, 1922.

Mann, Heinrich. *Sieben Jahre: Chronik der Gedanken und Vorgänge*. Vienna, 1929.

Mann, Klaus. *Heute und morgen*. Hamburg, 1927.

Mann, Thomas. *Avertissement à l'Europe*. Paris, 1937. Preface is by André Gide.

Manuel, Roger. *L'Union européenne*. Paris, 1932.

Marchal, Jean. *Union douanière et organisation européenne*. Paris, 1929.

Margueritte, Victor. *Briand*. Paris, 1932.

Martello, Tullo. *Lo Zollverein italo-francese e gli stati uniti d'Europa*. Bologna, 1905.

Masaryk, Thomas. *Nová Evropa*. Prague, 1920.

Maury, Lucier. *Babel: L'étranger, la France devant l'étranger, la paix*. Paris, 1925. Argues that a creative balance between the forces of nationalism and internationalism in Europe is possible.

Mayr, Franz. *Ein Weg aus der Not und Friedlosigkeit der Menschen und Völker zum internationalen Wirtschaftsstaat*. Karlsbad, 1927.

Mazière, Pierre La. *Déshonorons la guerre*. Paris, 1923.

Mercator. *Weltfriede nur durch Vereinigte Staaten von Europa*. Duren, 1924.

Meriggi, Lea. *Stati Uniti d'Europa*. Genoa, 1926.

Michels, Robert. *Der Patriotismus*. Munich, 1929.

Mironesco, G. G. *La Politique de la paix*. Bucharest, 1929.

Momigliano, Felice. *Carlo Cattaneo e gli Stati Uniti d'Europa*. Milan, 1919.

Montigny, Jean, and Jacques Kayser. *Le drame financier: Les responsables*. Paris, 1925.

Monzie, Anatole de. *La Reconstruction de l'Europe centrale*. Paris, 1927.

Morocutti, Camillo. *Europa und die völkischen Minderheiten*. Jena, 1925.

Mortane, Jacques. *Le nouvelle Allemagne*. Paris, 1928.

Mouskhaty, Michel. *La Théorie juridique de l'état fédéral*. Paris, 1931.

Mulder, Taco. *De Vereenigde Staten van Europa en de Taak der juridische en economische Wetenschappen*. Haarlem, 1924.

Müller, H. C. *International European Law*. Hague, 1925.

Müller, Joseph. *L'Oeuvre de toutes les confessions chrétiennes (églises) pour la paix internationale*. Paris, 1931.

Mundorf, Michael. *Vorschläge zur wirtschaftlichen Neuorganisation Europas*. Würzburg, 1933.

Murray, Haig. *The Public Finances of Post-War France*. New York, 1929.

Naettan-Larrier, C. *La Production sidérurgique de l'Europe continentale et l'Entente internationale de l'acier*. Paris, 1929.

Naudeau, Ludovic. *En écoutant parler les allemands*. Paris, 1925.

Naudin, Jean. *Les Accords commerciaux de la France depuis la guerre*. Paris, 1928.

Necas, Jaromir. *Die Vereinigten Staaten von Europa*. Prague, 1926.

Nelböck, Friedrich. *Kleine Beiträge zum Kampf um Völkerbund, Paneuropa, Mitteleuropa*. Prague, 1930.

Newfang, Oscar. *The Road to World Peace: A Federation of Nations*. London, 1924.

Nicolai, Georg. *Die Biologie des Krieges: Betrachtungen eines deutschen Naturforschers*. Zurich, 1917.

Nieuwenhoven, Helbach D. van. *Ein Statenbund voor Europa*. Rotterdam, 1916.

Nippold, Otfried. *Deutschland und der Völkerbund*. Zurich, 1919.

Nitti, Francesco. *L'Europa senza pace*. Florence, 1922.

———. *La Pace*. Florence, 1925. Nitti argues that a united Europe is the way to peace.

Nonnenbruch, Fritz. *Das vereinigte Europa*. Leipzig, 1925.

Noussanne, Henri de. *La Fédération de l'Europe*. Paris, 1900.

Novicow, Jacques. *La Fédération de l'Europe*. Paris, 1901.

Nuesch, Arnold. *Souveräner europäischer Staatenbund*. Basel, 1930.

Ormesson, Wladimir d'. *La Confiance en Allemagne?* Paris, 1927.

Otwer, L. Nicolas d'. *Idees i fets entorn de Paneuropa*. Barcelona, 1928.

Paneuropa (Zeitschrift), 1924–38. Devoted to the European idea and the European movement.

Paneuropa, Swiss Section. *Die Vereinigten Staaten von Europa: Die Förderung der Zeit*. Zurich, 1928.

Pannwitz, Rudolf. *Deutschland und Europa: Grundriss einer deutsch-europäischen Politik*. Nürnberg, 1919.

———. *Die deutsche Idée Europa*. Munich, 1931.

Pasztor, Jozsef. *Europai egyesult Allamok*. Budapest, 1919.

Pepper, John. *Les Etats-Unis d'Europe socialiste*. Paris, 1926.

Percin, Général Alexandre. *Le Désarmement moral*. Paris, 1925. This retired general was an active European.

———. *La Guerre et la nation armée*. Paris, 1918.

Pernot, Maurice. *L'Allemagne aujourd'hui*. Paris, 1927.

Petit, Antoine. *Vers l'Union occidentale*. Auxerre, 1917.

Phillips, W. Allison. *The Confederation of Europe*. London, 1920.

Pillavachi, A. *La Politique douanière des trois principaux états européens et celle de la Société des Nations*. Paris, 1928.

Pinner, Felix. *Deutsche Wirtschaftsführer*. Charlottenburg, 1924.

Pinon, René. *La Reconstruction de l'Europe politique*. Paris, 1920.

Pivat, Maurice. *Les Heures d'André Tardieu et la crise des parties*. Paris, 1930.

Planta, Gaudenz. *Europa auf dem Wege zur Einheit*. Basel, 1918.

Ploetzer-Darmstadt, Franz H. *Die Vereinigten Staaten von Europa*. Darmstadt, 1912.

Politis, Nicolas. *Les nouvelles Tendances du droit international*. Paris, 1927.

Pomaret, Lucien. *L'Amérique et la conquête d'Europe*. Paris, 1931.

Ponti, Ettore. *La Guerra dei popoli e la futura confederazione Europea*. Milan, 1914.

Poulimenos, A. *Europäische Politik*. Leipzig, 1929.

———. *Vereinigte Staaten Europas*. Berlin, 1927.

Puech. J. L. *La Tradition socialiste en France et la Société des Nations*. Paris, 1920.

Quartara, Giorgio. *Gli Stati Uniti d'Europa e del mondo*. Turin, 1930.

Raalte, E. van. *De Volkerbond en de Vereenigde Staten van Europa*. Amsterdam, 1931.

Ralli, Georges. *Essai sur le problème de l'entente européenne*. Paris, 1932.

Rameru, Maurice de. *Une Image d'états-unis européens*. Lausanne, 1930.

Raphaël, Gaston. *L'Industrie allemande: Sa récente évolution*. Paris, 1923.

Rathenau, Walther. *Die neue Wirtschaft*. Berlin, 1918.

———. *Was wird werden?* Berlin, 1920.

Reboux, Paul. *Les Drapeaux*. Paris, 1920.

Renatus, Juno. *Die zwölfte Stunde der Weltwirtschaft*. Munich, 1931.

Renouvin, Pierre. *L'Idée de fédération européenne dans la pensée politique du XIXe siècle*. Oxford, 1949.

Respondek, Erwin. *Wirtschaftliche Zusammenarbeit zwischen Deutschland und Frankreich*. Berlin, 1929.

Reynaud, Louis. *Français et Allemands*. Paris, 1931.

Reynold, Gonzague de. *L'Europe tragique*. Paris, 1934.

Richthofen, Wilhelm. *Brito-Germania: Die Erlösung Europas*. Berlin, 1926.

_____. *Brito-Germania: Ein Weg zu Paneuropa?* Berlin, 1930.

Riedl, Richard. *Ausnahmen von der Meistbegründing*. Vienna, 1931.

_____. *Die Vereinigten Staaten von Europa als konstruktives Problem*. Berlin, 1926.

Riou, Gaston. *Europe, ma patrie*. Paris, 1928. Preface is a letter written by Raymond Poincaré.

_____. *S'unir ou mourir*. Paris, 1929.

Rivière, Jacques. *Pour et contre une Société des Nations*. Paris, 1919.

Rohan, Karl Anton. *Schicksalstunde Europas: Erkenntnisse und Bekenntnisse*. Graz, 1937.

_____. *Umbruch der Zeit, 1923–1930*. Berlin, 1930. A collection of articles and speeches.

Rohrbach, Paul. *Amerika und wir: Reisebetrachtungen*. Berlin, 1926.

Rolland, Romain. *Au dessus de la mêlée*. Paris, 1914.

_____, ed. *Les Poètes contre la guerre*. Geneva, 1919.

Romains, Jules. *Problèmes européens*. Paris, 1933.

Romier, Lucien. *Explications de notre temps*. Paris, 1925.

_____. *Nation et civilisation*. Paris, 1927.

_____. *Que sera le maître, Europe ou Amérique?* Paris, 1927.

Ross, Colin. *Die Welt auf der Wege*. Leipzig, 1929. Africa must be closely related to a unified Europe.

Rougemont, Denis de. *Politique de la personne*. Paris, 1934.

Ruegg, Emil. *Die Vereinigten Staaten von Europa und Amerika und der Dauerfrieden*. Zurich, 1916.

Rühlmann, P. *Der Völkerbundsgedanke*. Berlin, 1919.

Ruyssen, Théodore. *De la force au droit*. Paris, 1920.

Salter, Arthur. *The United States of Europe and Other Papers*. London, 1933. With notes by W. Arnold-Forster.

Salvadori, Massimo. *L'Unità del Mediterraneo*. Rome, 1931.

Scelle, Georges. *La Crise de la Société des Nations*. Paris, 1927.

Schavan, August. *Les Bases d'une paix durable*. Paris, 1917.

Scheler, Max. *Die Idee des Friedens und der Pazifismus*. Berlin, 1931.

Schmeidler, Bernhard. *Deutschland und Europa im Mittelalter*. Erlangen, 1929. Insists that Germany has long been the center of Europe.

Schmid, Werner. *Vereinigte Staaten von Europa*. Zurich, 1926.

Schmidt, August. *1929: Das Jahr der weltpolitischen Entscheidungen*. Berlin, 1929.

_____. *Das neue Deutschland in der Weltpolitik und Weltwirtschaft*. Berlin, 1925.

Schmittmann, Benedikt. *Grundkräfte zur Neugestaltung Europas*. Leipzig, 1928.

Schmitz, Otto. *Der österreichische Mensch*. Vienna, 1926.

Schoenaich, Paul Freiherr von. *Abrüstung der Kopf: Ein Weg zum inneren and aüsseren Frieden* (Leipzig, 1923).

_____. *Mein Damaskus: Erlebnisse und Bekenntnisse*. Berlin, 1926. (Especially pp. 200–235.)

Schroeter, Herbert. "Der Briandsche Gedanken eines Paneuropa und die deutsch-österreichische Zollunion." Dissertation, Erlangen, 1932.

Schubert, A. A. *Afrika, die Rettung Europas*. Berlin, 1929.

Schücking, W., and H. Wehberg. *Die Satzung des Völkerbundes*. Berlin, 1931.

Schücking, Walther. *Die Organisation der Welt*. Leipzig, 1909.

Schulze, Georg. *Variationen über das Thema europäische Wirtschaftsunion*. Berlin, 1929.

————. *Was ist, was will Pan-Europa?* Berlin, 1932.

Schwarz, Hans. *Europa im Aufbruch*. Berlin, 1926.

Sée, Henri. *Histoire de la Ligue des Droits d'Homme, 1898–1926*. Paris, 1927.

Seydoux, Jacques. *De Versailles au Plan Young*. Paris, 1932.

Sforza, Carlo. *Les Bâtisseurs de l'Europe*. Paris, 1931.

Siegfried, André. *Das heutige Frankreich*. Stuttgart, n. d.

Siemsen, Anna. *Daheim in Europa*. Jena, 1928. Siemsen worked with Joseph Bloch and the *Sozialistische Monatshefte* before World War I.

Silverberg, Paul. *Reden und Schriften*. Edited by F. Mariaux. Cologne, 1951. Much of it was available in the 1920s.

Spengler, Oswald. *Neubau des deutschen Reiches*. Berlin, 1924.

Springer, J. *Das Gesetz der Macht*. Berlin, 1926.

Stead, William T. *The United States of Europe*. London, 1899.

Stein, Ludwig. *Aus dem Leben eines Optimisten*. Berlin, 1930.

Stein, Robert. *Die Vereinigten Staaten von Europa*. Berlin, 1908.

Sternberg, A. *Das Rebellöse Paneuropa*. Leipzig, 1926.

Stern-Rubarth, Edgar. *Brockdorff-Rantzau: Wanderer zwischen zwei Welten*. Berlin, 1929.

————. *Drei Männer suchen Europa*. Munich, 1938.

————. *Stresemann der Europäer*. Berlin, 1929.

Stolper, Gustav. *Deutsch-Österreich als Sozial- und Wirtschaftsproblem*. Munich, 1921.

Strada, J. *L'Europe sauvée et la fédération*. Paris, 1867.

Suchtelen, Nico van. *Europa eendrachtig*. Amsterdam, 1915.

————. *Het eenige redmiddel: Een Europeesche Statenbond*. Amsterdam, 1914.

Tacomulder, Nico. *De Vereenigde Staten van Europa*. Haarlem, 1924.

Telssonnière, Paul. *Vers d'un soldat, 1914–1918*. Paris, 1919.

Thibaudet, Albert. *La République des professeurs*. Paris, 1927.

Thormann, Werner. *Dr. Ignaz Seipel: Der europäische Staatsmann*. Frankfurt, 1932.

Tibal, Jean. *La Crise des états agricoles européens et l'action internationale*. Paris, 1931.

Török, Arpád. *Vom Nationalismus zu den Vereinigten Staaten von Europa*. Leipzig, 1926.

Trampler, Kurt. *Die Krise des Nationalstaates*. Munich, 1932.

Trax, Robert de. *L'Esprit de Genève*. Paris, 1929.

Troeltsch, Ernest. *Deutscher Geist und Westeuropa*. Tübingen, 1925.

————. *Spektator-Briefe: Aufsätze über die deutsche Revolution und Weltpolitik, 1918–1922*. Tübingen, 1925.

Truchy, Henri, *Cours d'économie politique*. Paris, 1923.

————. *Les Finances de guerre de la France*. Paris, 1926.

————. *L'Union douanière européenne*. Paris, 1935.

Umfrid, Otto. *Europa den Europäern: Nicht Isolierung, sondern Föderation*. Esslingen, 1913.

Unrah, Fritz von. *Europa erwache*. Basel, 1936.

Valéry, Paul. *Notes sur la grandeur et la décadence de l'Europe*. Paris, 1927.

Vandervelde, Emile. *Le Collectivisme et l'évolution industrielle*. Paris, 1921.

Vazeille, Albert. *Pour les Etats-Unis d'Europe*. Paris, 1924.

Vialette, M. A. *Le Monde économique, 1919–1927*. Paris, 1927.

Vibrage, Régis de. *Allemagne 1930*. Bordeaux, 1930.

Viénot, Pierre. *Incertitudes allemandes: La crise de la civilisation en Allemagne*. 1926.

————. *Ungewisses Deutschland*. Frankfurt, n.d.

Waechter, Max. *How to Make War Impossible: The United States of Europe*. London, 1924.

Weber, Alfred. *Die Krise des modernen Staatsgedankens in Europa*. Stuttgart, 1925.

Wechssler, E. *Esprit und Geist*. Leipzig, 1927.

Weden, Moriz. *Die Weltwirtschaftskonferenz in Genf und die landwirtschaftliche Genossenschaftsverbände*. Prague, 1927.

Wehberg, Hans. *Die Führer der deutschen Friedensbewegung, 1890–1923*. Leipzig, 1923.

Weil, Fritz. *Das Werden eines Volkes und der Weg eines Mannes*. Dresden, 1930.

Wettstein, Georges. *La Crise européenne: La guerre, ses résultats, la cour d'arbitrage, l'armistice*. . . . Lausanne, 1914. Appeared in German in 1915 with the title *Europas Einigungskrieg*.

Whyte, Frederic. *The Life of W. T. Stead*. 2 vols. New York, 1925.

Willi, H. *Eurasien*. Bern, n.d. Siberia could become a geopolitical supplement to a United Europe.

Wirsching, Heinz A. *Das Kampf um die handelspolitische Einigung Europas*. Feuchtwangen, 1929.

Wirth, Hermann. *Der Aufgang der Menschheit*. Jena, 1928.

Witte, Erich. *L'Enseignement dans l'esprit de la réconciliation des peuples*. Berlin, 1922.

Woolf, L. S. *International Government*. London, 1916.

Woytinsky, Wladimir. *Vereinigte Staaten von Europa*. Berlin, 1926. A customs union necessary for Europe's economic health.

———. *Zehn Jahre neues Deutschland*. Berlin, 1929.

Ziegler, Leopold. *Der europäische Geist*. Darmstadt, 1929.

Zimmermann, Carl. *Die Vereinigten Staaten von Europa*. Zurich, 1917.

Contemporary Articles

Abendam, S. "La trêve économique à Berlin," *Revue des vivants* 4 (Jan. 1930): 302.

Acht, Oscar. "Europa und Österreich," *Das neue Europa* 15 (Dec. 1979).

Alvarez, Alejandro. "Le Mouvement pour une union européenne et le panaméricainisme," *Le Monde nouveau*, 15 Dec. 1926, p. 1173.

Amery, L. S. "The British Empire and the Pan-European Idea," *Journal of the Royal Institute of International Affairs*, Jan. 1930. Published in other languages and journals.

Ancel, Jacques. "L'Europe qui naît," *L'Europe centrale*, 3 May 1930. Ancel published several articles on the European idea in this journal during 1929–30.

Ancel-Mowrer, Edgar. "Les Etats-Unis d'Amérique et les Etats-Unis d'Europe," *L'Europe nouvelle*, 28 Sept. 1929.

Appay, J. H. "Ce que signifient les Résultats des élections allemandes," *Le Progrès civique*, 17 May 1924.

Arcos, René. "Patrie européenne," *L'Europe*, 15 Feb. 1923, pp. 102–13.

Arnavon, Jacques. "Vers le super-Etat," *Revue des vivants*, June 1929, pp. 928–44 and July 1929, pp. 1093–99.

Auboin, Roger. "Le Cartel de l'acier," *L'Europe nouvelle*, 9 Oct. 1926.

Aulard, Alphonse. "Die deutsch-französische Annäherung," *Neue Zürcher Zeitung*, 1926.

———. "Les Etats-Unis d'Europe servent un premier pas vers la société universelle des nations," *Le Progrès civique*, 20 Apr. 1920.

———. "Heureux discredit de la gloire militaire," *Le Progrès civique*, 14 Feb. 1920.

———. "La Paix par l'école," *L'Ere nouvelle*, 1 Apr. 1927.

———. "Plus que jamais l'Opinion publique doit soutenir la Société des Nations," *Le Quotidien*, 5 Sept. 1926.

Barde, Henri. "La Banque de settlements internationale doit être le premier organisme de la fédération européenne," *L'Oeuvre*, 13 Sept. 1929.

———. "Les Etats-Unis d'Europe inquiéteraient-ils les Etats-Unis d'Amérique?" *L'Oeuvre*, 12 Nov. 1925.

————. "L'Europe, une heure historique," *L'Oeuvre*, 22 July 1929.

Bardoux, Jacques. "Agriculture et fédéralisme," *L'Européen*, no. 45 (5 Nov. 1930).

Barthélemy, Joseph. "L'Accueil de l'Europe au Mémorandum," *Le Monde nouveau* 12 (Aug.-Sept. 1930).

————. "Etats-Unis d'Europe," *Revue politique et Parlementaire* 140 (1929): 329–45.

————. "Le Problème de la souveraineté des états et la coopération européenne," *Revue de droit international*, Apr.–May–June 1930, pp. 420–40.

Basch, Victor. "Remèdes au malaise, fédéralisme et l'Etats-Unis d'Europe," *La Volonté*, 16 Dec. 1928.

Baumont, Maurice. "Le Charbon en Allemagne," *Revue économique internationale*, Nov. 1926, p. 222.

Bec, Lucien. "Le Péril jaune, est-il une mythe?" *Le Monde nouveau*, 15 Apr. 1925.

Becker, C. "L'Esprit international et l'enseignement national," *L'Esprit international*, no. 6 (Apr. 1928).

Bell, Johannes. "Zentrumgedanken zur deutschen Aussenpolitik," *Europäische Gespräche*, Apr. 1926.

Benda, Julien. "Créons des mythes et des héros européens," *L'Europe nouvelle*, 19 Feb. 1933.

Benedek, C. "Die europäische Einheit," *Das neue Europa* 14 (Jan.–Feb. 1928).

————. "Vers l'union européenne," *Neue Schweizer Rundschau* 23 (1930): 100–104.

Bernhard, Georg. "Bolschewismus: Wir brauchen die Zollunion," *Vossische Zeitung*, 23 Mar. 1930.

————. "Die Bürgschaft," *Vossische Zeitung*, 14 July 1929.

————. "Europäischer Zollverein, der einzige Weg," *Vossische Zeitung*, 10 July 1925.

————. "Völkerfriede und Volksfriede," *Vossische Zeitung*, 5 Oct. 1924.

Bernus, Pierre. "Briand et la fédération européenne," *Journal des débats* (Hebd.), 13 Sept. 1929.

Bidart, Albert. "Les Luttes de Victor Hugo pour les Etats-Unis d'Europe," *La Paix par le droit* 39 (June 1929).

————. "Une Motion nouvelle sur la moyens d'empêcher la guerre," *La Paix par le droit* 38 (June 1928). Proposes a European militia.

————. "La Paix par l'armement de l'Europe et le désarmement des Etats européens." *La Paix par le droit*, no. 10 (Oct. 1930).

Bilfinger, Carl. "Das Briand Memorandum," *Europäische Revue* 6 (July 1930).

Binding, Rudolf. "Ecce Europa," *Europäische Revue* 1, no. 8, pp. 73–78.

Bleier, Ernö. "Der europäische Zollverein," *Europäische Wirtschafts-Union*, 1 Jan. 1928.

Block, Paul. "Die Rolle Briands," *Berliner Tageblatt*, 6 Sept. 1929.

Bohet, Robert. "Les Etats-Unis d'Europe," *Flambeau*, 1 Dec. 1929.

Bonnet, Georges. "La Baisse de la livre et la primauté américaine," *L'Europe nouvelle*, 2 Feb. 1924.

Borel, Emile. "Le Congrès de l'Union Interparlementaire," *Le Monde nouveau* 10 (Aug.–Sept. 1928).

————. "La Coopération européenne," *La Dépêche de Toulouse*, 28 May 1930, and *Le Monde nouveau* 11 (Nov. 1929).

————. "Die deutsch-französischen Beziehungen," *Europäische Revue* 1 (Apr. 1925): 15–16.

————. "Les Etats-Unis d'Europe," *L'Esprit international* 4 (Jan. 1930).

————. "Un Questionnaire sur l'organisation de l'Europe," *L'Europe nouvelle*, 21 Dec. 1929.

————. "Die Vereinigten Staaten von Europe," *Nord und Süd*, Oct. 1929.

Boret, Victor. "Les Etats-Unis d'Europe et l'Europe paysanne," *L'Européen* 49 (3 Dec. 1930).

Borguès, Lucien. "Les grand courants de l'opinion," *Le Monde nouveau* 12 (Apr. 1930).

Boris, Georges. "Pour que naisse et vive l'union européenne," *La Lumière* 4 (6 Sept. 1930).

Bovet, Ernst. "Die Europäer," *Wissen und Leben* 14 (Apr. 1921).

_____. "Le premier pas à faire," *Wissen und Leben* 13 (Sept. 1920).

Breitscheid, Rudolf. "Das aussenpolitische Programm der Sozialdemokratie," *Europäische Gespräche* 4 (April 1926).

Brockhausen, Carl. "Paneuropa und Mitteleuropa," *Paneuropa* 4, no. 2.

Bruins, G. W., "Die Bedeutung eines ungehinderten Verkehrs für den Wiederaufbau Europas," *Weltwirtschaftliches Archiv* 18 (1923).

Caillaux, Joseph. "Le Bilan de la guerre," *Cahiers des droits de l'homme* 21 (10 Jan. 1921).

_____. "Europa in zehn Jahren," *Zeitschrift für Geopolitik* 10, no. 5.

_____. "Où va la France? Où va l'Europe?" *Le Progrès civique*, 19 July 1921.

_____. "L'Union européenne," *Le Monde nouveau* 12 (July 1930).

Cambon, Jules. "Le Rapprochement franco-allemand," *Revue des vivants*, Mar. 1927, pp. 191–94.

Cantimovi, Delio, "Italiens Ralli in Europa," *Europäische Revue* 6 (Aug. 1930).

Carpenter, Edward. "The Healing of Nations," *The English Review* 19 (Jan. 1915).

Cassel, Gustav. "Ist eine paneuropäische Währung möglich?" *Wirtschaftsdienst* 2 (1927): 1201 ff.

Cassin, René. "La Vie internationale," *Revue des vivants* 1, pp. 142–48.

Chastanet, J. L. "Les Etats-Unis d'Europe," *Le Peuple*, 17 July 1929.

Churchill, W. S. "The United States of Europe," *The Saturday Evening Post*, 15 Feb. 1930.

Ciccotti, Francesco. "Le Projet de Briand et l'Italie," *Dépêche de Toulouse*, 28 July 1929.

Claingbould, J. E. "Vereenigde Staten van Europa," *Handelsberichten*, 3 July 1930.

Clauss, Max. "Briands Europa Memorandum," *Europäische Revue* 6 (June 1930).

_____. "Deutschlands Europa Stunde," *Europäische Revue* 6 (Feb. 1930).

_____. "Das Rheinland frei," *Europäische Revue* 6 (July 1930).

_____. "Völkerbund wider Willen," *Europäische Revue* 7 (June 1931).

_____. "Wahlfront und Wirklichkeit," *Europäische Revue* 6 (Sept. 1930).

Clemenceau, Georges. "Letter to Colonel House," *La Paix par le droit* 29 (Sept.–Oct. 1919): 424.

Coerper, Fritz. "Die innere Macht Deutschlands in Europa," *Europäische Revue* 2 (July 1926).

Cohen, Max. "Der Europaweg der Wirtschaft," *Sozialistische Monatshefte* 33, no. 6.

_____. "Locarno und Kontinentaleuropa," *Sozialistische Monatshefte*, 10 Dec. 1925.

_____. "Wege nach Kontinentaleuropa," *Sozialistische Monatshefte*, June 1929.

Cohen-Reuss, Max. "Die wirtschaftliche Annäherung der europäischen Völker," *Hamburger Übersee-Jahrbuch*, 1926, pp. 119ff.

Colijn, Hendriks. "Grenzen der Erfüllungspolitik," *Europäische Revue* 6 (Feb. 1930).

Compeyrot, J. "La Finance américaine et l'Europe," *Revue des vivants*, Mar. 1927, pp. 191–94.

Coquet, Lucien. "Bulletin de l'union douanière européenne," *Le Monde nouveau* 11 (May 1929).

_____. "Projet de convention pour l'établissement de la nationalité européenne," *Le Monde nouveau* 12 (Mar. 1930).

_____. "L'Union douanière européenne," *Le Monde nouveau* 11 (June 1929).

Cornelissen, Christiaan. "Les Etats-Unis de l'Europe," *La Paix par le droit* 36 (10–26 Jan. 1916).

Coudenhove-Kalergi, Richard Nicolas. I have in my notes abstracts of upwards of two hundred articles and editorials that Coudenhove-Kalergi wrote about the European idea between 1922 and 1933. Since the great majority of these articles and editorials appeared in the journal *Paneuropa*, I shall only list a few of the ones that appeared in journals other than *Paneuropa*.

Coudenhove-Kalergi, Richard N. "Die europäische Frage," *Friedens-Warte* 23 (Jan.–Feb. 1923).

_____. "Europa und Deutschland," *Die neue Rundschau* 34, no. 1, pp. 299–309.

_____. "Paneuropa und Sozialismus," *Vorwärts*, 28 July 1925.

_____. "The Paneuropean Outlook," *International Affairs*, Sept. 1931, pp. 638–51.

_____. "Vereinigte Staaten von Europa," *Friedens-Warte* 23 (Jan.–Feb. 1923).

Crucy, François. "Tarifs douaniers: Economie douanière: Organisation économique de l'Europe," *Le Petit journal*, 14 Apr. 1927.

Curinier, C. E. "L'Organisation économique du monde civilisé," *La Paix par le droit* 25 (10–25 June 1915).

Daladier, Edouard. "Vassalité ou fédération," *La République*, 5 July 1929.

Dankworth, Herbert. "Zwei europäische Strömungen," *Europäische Revue* 2 (May 1926).

———. "La Jeunesse allemande devant l'Europe," *Notre Temps*, Jan. 1928, p. 23.

Dauda-Bancel, A. "La Paix internationale," *Le Progrès Social*, 2 Jan. 1926.

Dauriac, Jean L. "L'Union des états d'Europe," *L'Homme libre*, 21 Sept. 1928.

Dawson, W. H. "The Disunited States of Europe," *Contemporary Review* 128 (July 1930).

Daye, Pierre. "L'Europe en morceaux," *Le Flambeau* 12 (1 July 1929).

Deak, Francis. "Can Europe Unite?" *Political Science Quarterly* 46 (3 Sept. 1931).

Delaisi, Francis. "Les Bases économique des Etats-Unis d'Europe," *Le Monde nouveau* 8 (15 Jan. 1926): 1151–57.

———. "Les Contradictions du monde moderne," *L'Europe nouvelle*, 10 Jan. 1926.

———. "Les Deux Europes," *L'Européen*, 9 Oct. 1929.

———. "Europa als Wirtschaftseinheit," *Paneuropa* 3, no. 4.

———. "Pour les Abaissements des tarifs douanièrs: Une nouvelle méthode," *Le Monde nouveau* 10 (15 Sept. 1928).

———. "L'Union douanière européenne," *Le Monde nouveau*, 15 Oct. 1926.

———. "L'Union économique Paneuropéenne," *La Paix par le droit* 35 (Nov. 1926).

Destrée, Jules. "Paneuropa und Sozialismus," *Paneuropa* 3 (Mar.–Apr. 1931).

Deutsch, Felix. "Europäische Wirtschaftspolitik," *Wirtschaftsdienst*, 18 Dec. 1925.

Deutsch, Otto. "Die Bedeutung der Kartelle für die Paneuropäische Wirtschaft," *Paneuropa* 3, no. 3.

———. "Wirtschaftsannäherung," *Paneuropa* 3, no. 10.

Dicks, Walter. "Frei zum Werk! Zur Räumung des Rheinlandes," *Friedenskämpfer* 6 (July 1930).

Dix, Arthur. "Kolonialmandate oder Kolonialgemeinschaften," *Weltpolitik*, Nov. 1926.

Doka, Carl. "Kampf um Paneuropa," *Der Kampf* 23, no. 6.

Donatello [pseud.]. "Die europäische Kultur im Rahmen der Paneuropäischen Wirtschaft," *Das neue Europa* 15 (Aug.–Sept. 1929).

———. "Ungarn und Paneuropa," *Das neue Europa* 14 (Jan.–Feb. 1928).

Dortet, Francis. "Dr. Stresemann et le fédéralisme européen," *La Dépêche de Toulouse*, 8 Aug. 1929.

Driesch, Hans. "Einheit in der Mannigfaltigkeit," *Europäische Revue* 1, no. 2 (Apr. 1925).

Drieu la Rochelle, Pierre. "Ni New York ni Moscou," *L'Européen*, 12 June 1929.

Duborq, André. "Recherche du lien spirituel d'une communauté européenne," *Le Correspondant*, 25 July 1931.

Duchemin, R. P. "La Trêve douanière, un débat," *L'Européen*, 13 Nov. 1929.

Dumont-Wilden, Louis. "Les Etats-Unis d'Europe," *Revue Bleue* 67, pp. 508–12.

———. "Européens, unissez-vous," *Revue Politique et Parlementaire* 63 (July 1925).

Durand, Julien. "La Paix," *La République*, 28 July 1929.

Elbau, Julius. "Werdendes Europa," *Vossische Zeitung*, 8 Oct. 1926.

Epprecht, Robert. "Pan-Europa," *Neue Zürcher Zeitung*, 10 Oct. 1926.

Erkelenz, Anton. "Der Kampf gegen Unvernunft," *Die Hilfe*, 1 Mar. 1924.

———. "Zukunft Aufgaben der Demokratie," *Die Hilfe*, 1 June 1924.

Evola, J. "Über die geistigen Voraussetzungen einer europäischen Einheit," *Paneuropa* 8 (Dec. 1932).

Fabre-Luce, Alfred. "Après l'Election d'Hindenburg," *L'Ere nouvelle*, 3 July 1925.

Fabre-Luce, Robert. "Die Droite Nouvelle: Frankreichs und Europas," *Danziger Zeitung*, 27 Jan. 1927.

Fernau, Hermann. "La Faillité allemande," *Cahiers des droits de l'homme*, 25 Sept. 1922.

―――. "Frankreichs Politik und Europas Wiederaufbau," *Wissen und Leben* 14 (15 Nov. 1920).

Ferrara, Oreste. "La Crise économique mondiale et le projet d'union européenne," *Revue de droit international, de sciences diplomatiques, politiques, et sociales*, July–Sept. 1930, pp. 222–27.

Fischer, Hans. "Ein Theoretiker des Föderalismus," *Wissen und Leben* 12, no. 21 (Oct. 1918–Sept. 1919).

Fontaine, Arthur. "Solidarité européenne et organisation internationale," *Politique*, 15 Dec. 1928.

Fougère, Etienne. "Le Briand Mémorandum et l'Europe," *L'Européen*, 30 July 1930.

―――. "Le Devoir de l'Europe," *L'Européen*, 10 July 1929.

―――. "L'Equivoque s'aggrave," *L'Européen*, 1 Oct. 1930.

―――. "Les Etats-Unis d'Europe," *Revue économique internationale* 12 (Jan. 1930).

―――. "L'Organisation de la paix," *L'Européen*, 1 Jan. 1930.

―――. "La Solidarité européenne," *L'Européen*, 28 May 1930.

―――. "L'Union fédérale européenne," *L'Européen*, 21 May 1930.

François, J. P. "Pan-Europa," *Haagsch Maandblad*, Aug. 1927, pp. 185–91.

François-Marsal, Frédéric. "Les Etats-Unis d'Europe." *Revue économique internationale* 12 (Jan. 1930).

François-Poncet, André. "Relations économiques franco-allemands," *Revue des vivants*, Mar. 1927, pp. 230–41.

Frankenberg, Egbert von. "Von Locarno zum Völkerbund," *Deutsche Einheit*, 6 Feb. 1926.

Freundlich, Emmi. "Die Arbeit für den dauernden Frieden," *Europäische Wirtschaft-Union*, 1 Feb. 1928.

Fromont, Pierre. "La Grande Bretagne et les Etats-Unis d'Europe," *Revue politique et parlementaire* 143 (1930): 419–44.

Frontière, Jacques. "Entre Armées européennes," *La Dépêche de Toulouse*, 1 Nov. 1929.

Gauvain, Auguste. "La Conférence européenne et la XIᵉ assemblée de la Société des Nations," *L'Europe centrale*, 13 Sept. 1930.

―――. "Le Projet d'union fédérale européenne de M. Briand," *L'Esprit internationale* 15 (July 1930).

Gerlach, Helmut von. "Die Vereinigten Staaten von Europa," *Die Zeit*, Feb. 1930, p. 100.

Gesell, Silvio. "Die Vereinigten Staaten von Europa," *Freiwirtschaft* 6, no. 7.

Gide, André. "Les rapports intellectuels entre la France et l'Allemagne," *Nouvelle revue française* 17, Nov. 1921.

―――. "Die Zukunft Europas," *Die Neue Rundschau* 32, no. 2, pp. 602–10.

Gide, Charles. "L'Oeuvre économique de la Société des Nations," *La Paix par le droit* 40 (Feb.–Mar. 1930).

―――. "L'Organisation économique de la paix," *L'Ere nouvelle*, 5 Sept. 1925.

Gignaux, Claude J. "L'Entente internationale de l'acier," *Revue économique internationale*, Dec. 1926.

―――. "Que faut-il penser des Etats-Unis d'Europe," *La Revue hebdomadaire*, 2 Nov. 1929.

―――. "La Trêve douanière," *L'Européen*, 30 Oct. 1928.

―――. "La Trêve douanière et le parlement," *L'Européen*, 4 Dec. 1929.

Göhre, Paul. "Die Vereinigten Staaten von Europa," *Die neue Rundschau* 37 (1926).

Gorovetsen, A. "La Société des Nations et les Etats-Unis d'Europe," *La Paix par le droit* 35 (Apr. 1925).

Grabowsky, Adolf. "Das Problem Paneuropa," *Zeitschrift für Politik* 17, pp. 673–74.

Greiling, Walter. "Das Programm der Weltwirtschaftskonferenz," *Wirtschaftsdienst*, 22 Apr. 1927.

Gunther, Christian. "Der positive Weg zur Gesundung Europas," *Europäische Wirtschafts-Union* (Sonderdruck), Sept. 1927.

Guy-Grand, Georges. "Paneuropa, ou la politique des mastodontes," *Grande Revue* 30, pp. 143–51.

Guyon-Cesbron, Jean. "Sur l'Evolution européenne," *Revue des vivants*, May 1927.

Guyot, Edouard. "L'Esprit de la paix et l'enseignement de l'histoire," *La Volonté*, 11 Oct. 1928.

Guyot, Yves. "La Conférence internationale des cartels," *Journal des Economistes*, 15 Mar. 1927.

Gygax, Paul. "Briands Mémorandum," *Neue Schweizer Rundschau* 23 (1930): 556–60. An interview with Briand.

Hagemand, Walter. "Paneuropa Idee und Wirklichkeit," *Hochland*, 27, no. 1.

Halase, A. "Zur Frage Paneuropa," *Der Kampf* 17, no. 9.

Hanotaux, Gabriel. "L'Ere nouvelle: Problème de la guerre et de la paix." *Revue des Deux Mondes* 76, no. 36 (1 Nov. 1916).

Hantos, Elemér. "La Conférence économique internationale," *Journal des economistes*, 15 Apr. 1927, pp. 21–43.

_____. "Der mitteleuropäische Wirtschaftsgedanke," *Europäische Revue* 4 (July, 1928).

_____. "L'Organisation économique de la nouvelle Europe centrale," *L'Esprit internationale* 16 (Oct. 1930).

_____. "La Rationalisation de l'économie européenne," *Revue économique internationale*, Apr. 1930, pp. 8–35.

_____. "La Société économique des nations," *Le Monde nouveau* 11 (Jan. 1930).

_____. "Union douanière européenne," *Le Monde nouveau* 11 (Aug.–Sept. 1929).

Harms, Bernard. "Die Krisis der Weltwirtschaft," *Weltwirtschaftliches Archiv* 18 (1923).

_____. "Die Weltwirtschaftskonferenz," *Weltwirtschaftliches Archiv* 25 (1927).

Hauser, Henri. "Was ist Europa?" *Europäische Revue* 2 (Oct. 1926).

_____. "Des Obstacles au retour à des relations commerciales stables entre peuples," *Revue économique internationale*, 1924, pt. 2.

Haushofer, Karl. "Paneuropa im Lichte der Pan-Asiatischen und Pan-Pazifischen Bewegung," *Paneuropa* 7 (Jan. 1931): 19–32. This is a speech by Haushofer before the Paneuropean Union in Vienna.

Heile, Wilhelm. "Deutschland und Mitteleuropa," *Die Hilfe*, 15 Feb. 1922.

_____. "Europa und der Völkerbund," *Europäische Wirtschafts-Union*, 15 Feb. 1928.

_____. "Frankreich und wir," *Die Hilfe*, 15 Oct. 1922.

_____. "Kleineuropa oder Paneuropa," *Berliner Tageblatt*, 30 Mar. 1926.

_____. "Die Vereinigten Staaten von Europa," *Die Hilfe*, 25 June 1922.

_____. "Von Versailles über Locarno nach Europa," *Europäische Wirtschafts-Union*, 1 June 1927.

_____. "Warum ich für Paneuropa bin," *Friedens-Warte*, Aug. 1925.

Helle, Jules. "Coup d'oeil sur les Etats-Unis d'Europe," *La Paix par le droit* 15 (May 1930).

Hennessy, Jean. "De la nécessité d'un nouveau congrès pour donner au monde une paix durable," *Le Progrès civique* 2 (31 Jan. 1920).

_____. "Démocrates de tous le pays: Unissez-vous," *Le Progrès civique* 4 (15 Apr. 1922).

_____. "La Fédération européenne garantie de la paix du monde," *L'Oeuvre*, 29 Jan. 1924.

_____. "La Paix rendue aux peuples par les fédérations primaires," *Le Progrès civique* 3 (9 Feb. 1921).

_____. "Le Project de fédération européene," *Séances et travaux de l'Academie Diplomatique Internationale* 4 (Oct.–Dec. 1930).

_____. "Si nous ne faisons pas le vraie Société des Nations la France est perdue," *Le Progrès civique* 1 (1 May 1919).

Hermant, Max. "La Coopération européenne dans l'ordre économique," *Revue politique et par-*

lementaire 13 (1927): 24–39.

Herriot, Edouard. "Le Rapprochement intellectuel entre la France et l'Allemagne," *Das Neue Reich* 15 (Aug.–Sept. 1929).

Hertz, Henri. "Locarno, Canossa de l'Europe," *Le Monde nouveau*, 15 Nov. 1925.

Hobson, J. H. "The Economic Union of Europe," *Contemporary Review*, Sept. 1926.

Hodza, D. M. "L'Entente des démocracies agraires en Europe centrale," *Le Monde nouveau* 12 (Nov. 1930).

Hohenau, Paul. "Interessenverbundenheit," *Das neue Europa* 15 (Oct.–Nov. 1929).

———. "Internationale Politik," *Das neue Europa* 13 (May–June, 1927).

———. "Von kommenden Ereignissen," *Das neue Europa* 15 (Jan.–Feb. 1929).

———. "Wirtschaftliche Zukunfts-probleme," *Das neue Europa* 13 (July–Aug. 1927).

Honegger, Hans. "Zur Vorgeschichte der deutsch-französischen geistigen Wiederannäherungs-Bestrebungen," *Das neue Europa* 14 (Sept.–Oct. 1928).

Hubermann, Bronislaw. "Mein Weg zu Paneuropa," *Paneuropa* 2, no. 5.

Human, A. "Wie steht es mit Paneuropa," *Handel und Industrie* 34 (1804): 963–64.

Hymans, Paul. "L'Union européenne," *Flambeau* 13 (Sept.–Oct. 1930).

Jeune, A. L. "Le Krach américain," *Revue des vivants* 3 (Dec. 1929).

Jouhaux, Léon. "Le Mouvement ouvrier et l'union européenne," *La Dépêche de Toulouse*, 21 Aug. 1930.

Jouvenel, Bertrand de. "L'Echec de la Société des Nations: Nécessité de l'état européen," *La République*, 22 Sept. 1929.

Jouvenel, Henri. "Bloc africain et fédération européenne," *Revue des vivants* 4 (Jan. 1930): 1–7. Argues that there should be a common European policy in Africa and Asia.

———. "En Europe ou en décadence," *Revue des vivants* 4 (May 1930).

———. "Locarno . . . suite ou fin?" *Revue des vivants* 1 Feb. 1927.

———. "Le Projet de fédération européenne," *L'Esprit international* 4, no. 16, Oct. 1930.

Junghann, Otto. "Deutschland in der Genfer Europakommission," *Nation und Staat*, Jan. 1931.

Kageneck, Heinrich. "Völkerverständigung," *Das neue Europa* 13 (May–June 1927).

Kaliski, Julius. "Weltsozialismus," *Sozialistische Monatshefte* 30 (Oct. 1924).

Kampffmeyer, Paul. "Deutsche und europäische Konföderation," *Sozialistische Monatshefte* 32 (July 1926).

———. "Zu einer europäische Wirtschafts- und Sozialpolitik," *Sozialistische Monatshefte* 32 (Jan. 1926).

Kastl, Ludwig. "Le Mouvement européen," *L'Economie Internationale*, Aug. 1931, pp. 255–60.

Katscher, Leopold. "Eine europäische Zollunion," *Das neue Europa* 12 (May–June 1927).

———. "Das Problem Paneuropa," *Das neue Europa* 14 (Sept.–Oct. 1928).

Kellersohn, Maurice. "L'Allemagne, la France et l'unité européenne," *L'Information*, 11 Sept. 1929.

———. "L'Europe économique s'organise," *L'Information*, 20 Nov. 1926.

———. "Organisation économique inter-européenne," *L'Information*, 12 Sept. 1929.

Kleineibist, Richard. "Die Entscheidung über Europa," *Sozialistische Monatshefte*, Apr. 1929, pp. 273–77.

———. "Europäisches Zwischenspiel," *Sozialistische Monatshefte* 36 (June 1930): 531–36.

Klesse, Max. "Kontinentaleuropäische Schuldnerfront gegen Amerika," *Sozialistische Monatshefte* 35 (Nov. 1929).

Koch, Walther. "Geistige Bewegung," *Sozialistische Monatshefte* 35 (Sept. 1919).

Kock-Weser, Erich. "Erlebtes und Erreichtes," *Der Demokrat* 24 (Dec. 1925): 536–42.

———. "Die europäischen Krise," *Paneuropa* 9, no. 2.

Kuknert, Herbert. "Geistige Bewegung," *Sozialistische Monatshefte* 33 (Aug. 1927).

La Brière, Yves de. "L'Union continentale européenne," *Revue de droit international et de législation comparée*, 1931, pp. 5–36.

Lacour-Gayet, Jacques. "Fédération européenne et radiodiffusion," *L'Européen* 34 (4 Dec. 1929).

Lamandé, André. "M. Duchemin, président de la Confédération Générale de la Production Française," *L'Européen*, 8 May 1929.

Lambert, Jacques. "Les Etats-Unis d'Europe et l'exemple américain," *Revue générale de droit international* 34, pp. 397–45.

Lange, Christian. "Nationalisme et internationalisme," *Revue des vivants*, Mar. 1929, pp. 444–52.

Lanux, Pierre de, "Europäischer Realismus," *Europäische Revue* 2 (May 1926).

Lapradelle, Albert de. "Les nouvelles tendances du droit international," *L'Esprit International*.

———. "L'Union juridique internationale et le projet de M. Briand," *Revue de droit international*, July–Aug.–Sept. 1930.

La Pradelle, Paul de. "La Commission d'étude pour l'union européenne," *Revue de droit international*, April–May–June 1932, pp. 617–46.

Laskine, Edmond. "La Verité sur les négotiations commerciales," *Revue des vivants*, Nov. 1927, pp. 666–69.

Lauer, Hans. "Paneuropa oder Mitteleuropa," *Individualität* 2, pp. 129–36.

Lauret, Lucien. "L'Europe devant les Etats-Unis," *L'Europe* 21 (Nov. 1929).

Lauterbach, Albert. "Um Paneuropa," *Der Kampf* 22, no. 6.

———. "Paneuropaliteratur," *Der Kampf* 22, no. 2.

Layton, Walter. "La Politique douanière de l'Europe," *L'Europe nouvelle*, 21 Apr. 1926.

Le Foyer, Lucien. "L'Union de l'Europe et ses sanctions," *L'Ere nouvelle*, 14 Sept. 1925.

———. "L'Union fédérale européenne," *La Paix par le droit* 40 (July–Aug. 1930).

Le Fur, Louis. "Les Conditions d'existence d'une union européenne," *Revue de droit international*, July–Aug.–Sept. 1930.

Leroy-Beaulieu, Anatole. "Les Etats-Unis d'Europe," *Revue des revues* 1900, pp. 445–56.

Leroy-Beaulieu, Paul. "La Creation d'une union de l'Europe occidentale," *Economiste française*, 11 Oct. 1879, pp. 435 ff. (cont. in Nov. issue).

Le Trocquer, Yves. "La Politique protectionniste des Etats-Unis," *Le Monde nouveau* 11 (Apr. 1929).

———. "Le premier Congrès d'union douanière européenne," *Le Monde nouveau* 12 (July 1930).

———. "L'Union douanière européenne et l'organisation de la paix," *L'Esprit international* 14 (Apr. 1930).

———. "Vereinigte Staaten von Europa," *Zeitschrift für Geopolitik* 6, no. 8.

———. "Die Zollpolitik Nordamerikas und die europäischen Staaten," *Das neue Europa* 15 (Oct.–Nov. 1929).

Leusse, Paul de. "L'Union douanière européenne," *Revue d'économie politique* 4 (1890): 393–401.

Levy, Roger. "Mosaique d'Europe," *Le Monde nouveau* 12 (Oct. 1930).

Lichtenberger, Henri. "Vers la Rapprochement intellectuel franco-allemand," *L'Esprit international* 2 (April 1928).

Loucheur, Louis. "La Conférence économique de Genève," *Revue économique internationale* 19, no. 2 (1927).

———. "Le Rôle économique de la Société des Nations," *Flambeau*, 1 May 1927.

———. "Situation de la France et de la Belgique dans l'Europe nouvelle d'après-guerre," *Revue économique internationale* 17 (June 1925).

———. "Die weltwirtschaftliche Zukunft in Europa," *Das neue Europa*, Nov. 1926.

Luchaire, Jean. "Aristide Briand: Homme triple," *L'Homme libre*, 17, 18, 19 Aug. 1928.

Luchaire, Jean, and Emile Roche. "Europe: O ma patrie . . . ," *Notre temps* 2 (Feb. 1928).

Ludwig, Emil. "Paneurope the New Fatherland," *Neue freie Presse*, 2 Oct. 1926.

Luithlen, Gert. "Das österreichische Komitee für europäische Cooperation," *Europäische Wirtschafts-Union*, 1 Mar. 1928.

Lyautey, Pierre. "La Législation douanière internationale," *Revue économique internationale*, May 1929.

———. "Zollfriede," *Europäische Revue* 6 (Feb. 1930).

Maier, Karl. "Europas weltwirtschaftlicher Niedergang," *Arbeit und Wirtschaft* 2, no. 8.

Mann, Heinrich. "Die deutsche Entscheidung," *Luxemburger Zeitung*, 13 Dec. 1931.

———. "Europa: Reich über den Reichen," *Die neue Rundschau* 34, no. 2.

———. "Der Europäer," *Berliner Tageblatt*, 24 Oct. 1916.

———. "L'Europe: Etat suprème," *L'Europe*, no. 6 (15 July 1923).

———. "Vereinigte Staaten von Europa," *Vossische Zeitung* 2 (3 Dec. 1924).

Mann, Thomas. "Europa als Kulturgemeinschaft," *Paneuropa* 6 (June–July, 1930).

———. "Das Problem der deutsch-französischen Beziehungen," *Der neue Merkur*, Jan. 1922.

Mantoux, Paul. "Le Protectionisme qui n'ose pas dire son nom," *L'Européen*, no. 4, 8 May 1929.

Martin, William. "Les deux opinions suisses et du Memorandum Briand," *L'Européen*, no. 23 (4 June 1930).

———. "Les Etats-Unis d'Europe," *Neue Schweizer Rundschau* 22 (1929): 712–20.

———. "L'Europe en détresse," *Neue Schweizer Rundschau* 24 (1931): 715–20.

———. "Paneuropeanisme ou Société des Nations," *Neue Schweizer Rundschau* 19 (1926).

———. "L'Union douanière austro-allemande et la Suisse," *Neue Schweizer Rundschau* 24 (1930): 392–400.

Marz, Julius. "Klippen für Paneuropa," *Deutsche Einheit* 10, pp. 319–22.

Mauss, Marcel. "L'Internationalisme," *La Paix par le droit* 30 (Oct. 1920). The war shifted economic forces across the world to Europe's disadvantage and thus made the states of Europe more interdependent and union a greater necessity.

Mayrisch, Emil. "Les Ententes économiques internationales et la paix," *L'Europe nouvelle*, 24 Dec. 1927.

———. "Une Opinion luxembourgeoise sur un projet d'union douanière européenne," *L'Europe nouvelle*, 21 Apr. 1926.

Mendelssohn-Bartholdy, Albrecht. "Memorandum," *Europäische Gespräche*, Aug.–Sept. 1930.

Mertens, A. "L'Accord commercial franco-allemand du Août 17, 1927," *Revue économique internationale*, Oct. 1927.

Meurs, H. J. Van. "De Europeese Kommissie van de Volkenbond," *De Volkenbond*, Apr. 1931, pp. 207–11.

Mirceux, Edouard. "La Vie économique," *Revue des vivants*, Apr. 1929.

Mirgeler, Albert. "Europa," *Europäische Revue*, May 1931, pp. 380–89.

Mirkine-Guetzevitch, B. "Les Tendances internationales des nouvelles constitutions européenne," *L'Esprit international*, no. 8 (Oct. 1928): 531–46.

Moll, R. "Le Projet de trêve douanière," *Le Monde nouveau* 11 (Nov. 1929).

Mommsen, Wilhelm. "Vereinigte Staaten von Europa," *Deutsche Einheit* 7 (14 Nov. 1925).

Montigny, Jean. "La Paneurope?" *L'Information*, 19 Sept. 1925.

Montluc, Leon de. "La Commission d'études pour l'union européenne," *La Paix par le droit*, Apr. 1931, pp. 251–53.

———. "Les Réponses au mémorandum de M. Briand sur le projet de fédération européenne," *Revue de droit international, des sciences diplomatiques, politiques et sociales*, April–June 1930, pp. 114–18.

Monzie, Anatole de. "Die Wiederaufnahme der geistigen Beziehungen zwischen Deutschland und Frankreich," *Europäische Revue* 1 (Jan. 1926).

Müller, August. "Europa und die Weltpolitik," *Die neue Rundschau* 31, pp. 401–18.

————. "Wege zum europäischen Zollverein," *Europäische Revue* 1 (Jan. 1926).

Naphtali, Fritz. "Die Einigung Europas," *Die Gesellschaft* 2 (1926): 334–44.

Nathan, Roger. "Désordre économique et fédération européenne," *L'Europe nouvelle*, 6 Sept. 1930.

Niekisch, Ernst. "Paneuropa," *Firn*, 18 June 1924.

Nitti, Francesco. "Die Vereinigten Staaten von Europa," *Europäische Revue* 1 (Apr. 1925).

Noblemaire, Georges. "La Reconstruction économique de l'Europe," *Revue politique et littéraire (Revue Bleue)* 60 (19 Aug. 1922).

Ormesson, Wladimir d'. "Deutsch-französische Zukunft," *Europäische Revue* 6 (Sept. 1930).

————. "Une Fédération européenne, est-elle possible?", *Revue de Paris*, 15 Oct. 1929, pp. 748–70.

————. "Rapprochement 1930," *L'Europe nouvelle*, 12 Apr. 1930.

————. "Réflections sur la crise allemande," *L'Européen*, no. 33, 13 Aug. 1930.

Paish, Georges. "La Situation," *Le Monde nouveau* 12 (June 1930).

Pange, Jean de. "L'Esprit transnational," *Le Monde nouveau* 12 (Oct. 1929).

Pannwitz, Rudolf. "Internationale und Europäertum," *Die neue Rundschau* 32, no. 1, pp. 449–70.

Percin, Alexandre. "Il faut détruire l'esprit de guerre," *Le Progrès civique*, 11 March 1922.

Pernot, Maurice. "Les Réponses de l'Europe à M. Briand," *L'Europe nouvelle*, 19 July 1930.

Petrie, Charles. "The United States of Europe: Dream or Possibility?" *The Nineteenth Century* 102, Dec. 1927.

Peyerimhoff de Fontenelle. "Pour la paix économique de l'Europe," *L'Européen*, 19 Feb. 1930.

————. "La Rationalisation des relations commerciales internationales," *Revue économique internationale* 22 (Jan. 1930): 22–36.

Piat, Jean. "Belle Occasion de faire d'Europe," *L'Oeuvre*, 1 July 1929.

Pirov, Gaetan. "Un Congrès économique d'après guerre," *Revue politique et parlementaire* 140, May 1924.

Plate, A. "La lutte autour de la frontière," *Le Monde nouveau* 12 (Dec. 1930).

Politis, Nicholas. "Le mouvement Paneuropéen et la Société des Nations," *Le Monde nouveau* 8 (15 Dec. 1926).

————. "Le Projet d'union européenne et la Société des Nations," *Revue de droit international de sciences diplomatiques, politiques et sociales*, June–Sept. 1930, pp. 201–11.

Pommrich, Rudolf. "Paneuropa," *Weltpolitik und Weltwirtschaft* 2, no. 12, pp. 454–58.

Proix, Jean. "La Conférence de Genève en vue d'une action économique concertée," *Revue politique et parlementaire* 143 (Feb. 1930).

Prudhommeaux, J. "La Fédération européenne et le Mémorandum," *Cahiers de droit de l'homme*, 10 Sept. 1930, pp. 507–12.

————. "La quatrième Assemblée générale de coopération européenne," *Le Monde nouveau*, Aug.–Sept. 1930, pp. 466–72.

Pusta, C. R. "L'Union européenne devant la Société des Nations," *Revue de droit international*, Oct.–Dec. 1930.

Quessel, Ludwig. "Europa und der Anschluss," *Sozialistische Monatshefte* 34 (Aug. 1928).

————. "Genf. Heidelberg und Locarno," *Sozialistische Monatshefte* 31 (Oct. 1925).

————. "Kontinentaleuropa im Parteiprogramm," *Sozialistische Monatshefte* 31 (Sept. 1925).

————. "Die Kontinentaleuropäische Arbeitsgemeinschaft," *Sozialistische Monatshefte* 25 (Sept. 1919).

Quidde, Ludwig. "Vereinigte Staaten von Europa," *Berliner Tageblatt*, 22 May 1926.

————. "Weltfriedenkongress in Athen," *Friedens-Warte* 29, pp. 99 ff.

————. "Wie ich zur Demokratie und zum Pazifismus kam," *Frankfurter Zeitung*, 4 Jan. 1928.

Rasson, Peter. "Pan-Europa," *Archiv für Politik und Geschichte* 5, pp. 509–16.

Räuscher, Josef. "Paneuropa und Anschlussfrage," *Hochland* 26, no. 3, Dec. 1928.

Reboux, Paul. "Le seul Chemin," *Revue Mondiale*, 15 Aug. 1920.

Rechberg, Arnold. "Deutsch-französische Beziehungen," *Tägliche Rundschau*, 6, 9 Nov. 1921. Numerous articles across the 1920s urging Franco-German collaboration.

Reinhard, Robert. "Deutschland, Öesterreich, und die Tschechoslowakei," *Das neue Europa* 14 (July–Aug. 1928).

Renard, Georges. "Les Etats-Unis d'Europe," *La Dépêche de Toulouse*, 5 Aug. 1928.

———. "Vers l'économie internationale," *Revue économique internationale* 19, no. 2, pp. 145–50.

Renner, Karl. "Die weltwirtschaftlichen Grundlagen der sozialistischen Politik nach dem Kriege," *Der Kampf* 21, pp. 8–9.

Ribert, M. "La Reconstruction de l'Europe," *Cahiers des droits d'homme*, 25 May 1922. Argues that a democratic Europe will mean a united Europe.

Richet, Charles. "Une Etape vers la paix," *La Paix par le droit* 39, June 1929.

———. "Vers l'esprit européen," *La Paix par le droit* 36, Apr. 1926.

Riedl, Richard. "Die wirtschaftliche Neuorganisation Europas," *Europäische Revue* 6 (Apr. 1930).

———. "Bundespolitik und europäischer Ausgleich," *Europäische Revue* 7 (Apr. 1931).

Riou, Gaston, "S'unir ou périr," *L'Européen*, no. 33, 27 Nov. 1929.

Rivière, Jacques. "Les dangers d'une politique conséquente," *Nouvelle revue française* 19 (July 1922).

———. "Notes sur un événement politique," *Nouvelle revue française* 18 (May 1921).

———. "L'Occupation de la Ruhr," *Luxembourger Zeitung*, 3 Feb. 1923.

———. "Pour une entente économique avec l'Allemagne," *Revue nouvelle française* 20 (May 1923).

Rodrigues, Gustave, "Vers un patriotisme européen," *La Volonté*, 20 July 1928.

Rogge, Heinrich. "Einheit und Hemmungen des europäischen Denkens," *Europäische Revue* 2 (Sept. 1926).

Rohan, Karl Anton. "Deutsche Europapolitik," *Europäische Revue* 6 (July 1930).

———. "Deutschland, Frankreich, Europa," *Europäische Revue* 6 (Oct. 1930).

———. "Europäischer Rundblick," *Europäische Revue* 7 (Apr. 1931).

———. "Österreich," *Europäische Revue* 5 (Sept. 1929). He says perhaps the formula should be "Zusammenschluss" rather than "Anschluss."

Rolland, Romain. "Un Appel aux européens par Georg F. Nicolai," *Wissen und Leben* 12, no. 21, pp. 66–72.

———. "Adieu au passé," *L'Europe* 26, 15 June 1931, pp. 161–202.

Romier, Lucien. "Europäische Solidarität," *Europäische Revue* 2 (Oct. 1926).

Ruyssen, Théodore. "La Xme assemblée de la Société des Nations," *La Paix par le droit* 39 (Nov. 1929).

———. "Le Mouvement pacifiste: Fédération régionaliste et des nations," *La Paix par le droit* 28 (Apr. 1918).

———. "La Société des Nations devant la conférence de la paix," *La Paix par le droit* 29 (Feb.–Mar. 1919).

Sauerwein, Jules. "Europäische Föderation," *Prager Presse*, 15 Sept. 1929.

———. "Fédération européenne," *Le Matin*, 17 July 1929.

———. "La Reorganisation économique de l'Europe," *Le Matin*, 3 Aug. 1929.

———. "Der Wiederaufbau Europas," *Das neue Europa* 15 (Jan.–Feb. 1929).

Saurez, André. "Vues d'Europe," *Revue des vivants*, Aug. 1928, pp. 183–93.

Scelle, Georges. "Une Ère juridique nouvelle," *La Paix par le droit* 29 (July–Aug. 1919).

———. "Essai relatif à l'union européenne," *Revue générale de droit international public*, Sept.–Oct. 1931, pp. 521–62.

———. "Les Etats-Unis d'Europe," *L'Europe nouvelle*, 12 Oct. 1929.

⸻. "La Fédération européenne," *La Dépêche de Toulouse*, 28 May 1930.

⸻. "Le Mémorandum Briand et la fédération européenne," *La Paix par le droit* 40 (July–Aug. 1930).

Schaller, Georg. "Paneuropa," *Preussische Jahrbücher*, Mar. 1925, p. 306.

Schiemann, Paul. "Coudenhove und Rohan," *Nation und Staat*, July–Aug. 1930, pp. 630–36.

Schnitzler, Werner von. "Europäische Zollunion," *Der Deutsche Volkswirt* 4, 14 Mar. 1930.

Schuster, Vàclav. "Pioniere der europäischen Wirtschaftsgemeinschaft," *Europäische Wirtschafts-Union*, 1 Apr. 1928.

Schwartz, Louis. "Les Etats-Unis d'Europe," *Revue diplomatique, politique, coloniale, littéraire et financière*, Sept. 1929, pp. 2 ff.

Scott, James B. "American Background to Briand's Union of a United States of Europe," *American Journal of International Law*, Oct. 1930, pp. 738, 742.

See, Pierre. "Le Passeport européen," *L'Ere nouvelle*, 19 Apr. 1927.

Seipel, Ignaz. "Nationale und internationale Wirtschaft," *Das neue Europa* 14 (Nov.–Dec. 1928).

⸻. "Der Weg nach Europa," *Friedenskämpfer* 5 (Sept.–Oct. 1929).

Serruys, Daniel. "La Confédération économique des états de l'Europe devant l'opinion," *L'Européen*, 9 July 1930.

⸻. "La Coopération internationale au Congrès d'Amsterdam," *L'Européen*, 17 July 1929.

⸻. "L'Oeuvre économique de la Société des Nations," *Revue des vivants*, June–Aug. 1929, pp. 1206–16.

⸻. "Sur des confins de la politique et de l'économie," *L'Européen*, 11 Sept. 1929.

⸻. "La Trêve douanière," *L'Européen*, 20 Nov. 1929.

Seydoux, Jacques. "Les Etats-Unis d'Europe," *Europäische Wirtschafts-Union*, 1 Apr. 1928.

⸻. "Ist eine Verständigung zwischen Frankreich und Deutschland möglich?" *Europäische Gespräche*, Oct. 1927, pp. 517–27.

⸻. "Liquidons la guerre," *Revue des vivants* 28 (Oct. 1928): 597–612.

⸻. "Méthodes de la diplomatique allemande," *Revue des vivants*, Mar. 1927, pp. 205–12.

Sforza, Count Carlo. "Briand," *Nord und Süd*, Oct. 1929.

Sierp, Heinrich. "Vereinigte Staaten von Europa," *Stimmen der Zeit* 61, pp. 241–55.

Silbert, Alfred. "Le Congrès Universitaire de Mannheim, 16–21 Septembre 1930," *Notre Temps* 4 (5 Oct. 1930).

Simondet, Henri. "Le Progrès de l'idée de la paix dans la politique allemande," *La Paix par le droit* 38 (Sept. 1928).

Singer, Kurt. "Zur Lage," *Wirtschaftsdienst* 2 (8 Oct. 1926).

Smedes, E. "De Weg naar de Vereenigde Staten van Europa," *De Ploeg*, 1930, pp. 73–78.

Snell, Victor. "Une Utopie qui devient réalité," *L'Oeuvre*, 25 Feb. 1928.

Sobotka, Rudolf. "Die Vereinigten Staaten von Europa," *Volk und Gemeinde* 3, no. 12.

Soffner, Heinrich. "Die Vereinigten Staaten von Europa," *Arbeit und Wirtschaft* (Vienna) 4, no. 23, pp. 933–38.

Sommer, Louise, "Die Vorgeschichte des Weltwirtschaftskonferenz," *Weltwirtschaftsliches-Archiv* 28, pt. 2 (1928): 340–418.

Sorel, Max. "La Trêve douanière," *Le Monde nouveau* 12 (2 Apr. 1930).

Sorel, Robert. "Les Etats-Unis et l'union économique européenne," *Le Monde nouveau* 11 (Oct. 1929).

Stehli, Robert. "La Politique européenne des industries de la soie," *L'Européen*, 18 Sept. 1929.

Steinitzer, Erwin. "Europäisches Zusammenwirken," *Die neue Rundschau* 31, no. 2.

⸻. "Das Weltproblem Deutschland," *Die neue Rundschau* 32, no. 1.

Stern-Rubarth, Edgar. "Europäismus," *Die Wahrheit* (Prague), 1 June 1929.

⸻. "Pour une Union économique européenne," *Le Monde nouveau* 12 (June 1930).

Stolper, Gustav. "Messianismus," *Der Deutsche Volkswirt* 4 (Nov. 1930).

————. "Wort-Fetisch," *Der Deutsche Volkswirt* 3 (13 Sept. 1929).

Stresemann, Gustav. "Deutschlands Stellung im europäischen Wirtschaftssystem," *Europäische Revue* 1, no. 3 (June 1925).

Strewe, M. T. "Völkerbund und paneuropäische Illusionen," *Deutscher-Spiegel* 3, pp. 537–41.

Szende, Paul. "Les Etats danubiens et le fédéralisme," *L'Europe fédéraliste*, pp. 93–107.

Sztern, M. "Einigung des Abendlandes," *Das neue Europa* 8 (Sept.–Oct. 1927).

Teyssaré, J. E. "Vers un esprit international," *La Paix par le droit* 36 (Feb. 1926).

Théry, René. "Vers l'organisation économique de l'Europe," *Le Monde nouveau* 12 (Feb. 1931).

Theunis, Georges. "L'Oeuvre économique de la Société des Nations," *L'Esprit international*, no. 5 (Jan. 1928).

Thibaudet, Albert. "L'Europe de demain," *L'Europe nouvelle*, 1 Aug. 1925.

Tibal, André. "La Trêve douanière et la crise agricole," *L'Europe centrale*, 15 Mar. 1930.

Tolédano, André. "La Grande-Bretagne et la coopération économique européenne," *Le Monde nouveau* 12 (June 1930).

Török, Arpád. "Die Weltwirtschaftskonferenz und das Europa-Problem," *Zietschrift für Geopolitik* 4, no. 5, pp. 411–19.

Toureille, Pierre. "Le Congrès international de la paix d'Athènes," *La Paix par le droit* 40 (Jan. 1930).

Traz, Robert de. "Briands Vermächtnis," *Paneuropa* 8, no. 4.

Truchy, Henri. "Comment on peut concevoir l'union douanière européenne," *Le Monde nouveau* 12 (June 1930).

————. "La Coopération européenne et la politique douanière," *Revue politique et parlementaire* 140 (1929).

————. "La Reconstruction économique de l'Europe," *Revue politique et parlementaire* 126 (1926). Truchy reported that Edmund Stinnes, son of Hugo, was talking about a European customs union.

————. "Vers l'entente douanière des pays," *Revue économique internationale* 126 (Nov. 1927): 209–21.

Ulitz, Otto. "Paneuropa und die Nationalitätenfrage," *Nation und Staat*, Oct. 1930, pp. 10–16.

Ullman, Hermann. "Berlin und Europa," *Europäische Revue* 7 (June 1931).

Valensi, Georges. "La Téléphonie européenne," *L'Europe nouvelle*, 13 Feb. 1926, pp. 204–9.

Valli, Luigi. "Sinn und Begriff Europas," *Europäische Revue* 4, pp. 161–66.

Valot, Stephen. "L'Ecole européenne," *L'Oeuvre*, 1 Dec. 1929.

Vanderelst, Pianos. "Les Etats-Unis d'Europe," *Pourquoi pas?* 27 Nov. 1925.

Vanderlip, Frank A. "Die Organisation einer Goldreserve-Bank der Vereinigten Staaten von Europa," *Das neue Europa* 15 (Apr.–May 1929).

Vandervelde, Emile. "Le Rôle économique de la Belgique," *L'Européen*, 29 Jan. 1930.

Vandervlugt, Emile. "Les Etats-Unis d'Europe: Utopie ou possibilité?" *Le Monde nouveau* 8 (15 Jan. 1926): 1061–69.

————. "Le Projet Briand et les états-unis économiques d'Europe," *Le Monde nouveau* 11 (Aug.–Sept. 1929).

————. "Vers l'Union économique européenne," *Le Monde nouveau* 8 (15 Apr. 1926).

Vibraye, Regis de. "Bases régionales de la Société des Nations? Etats-Unis d'Europe," *La Paix par le droit* 38 (Feb. 1928).

Viénot, Pierre. "Réflections sur l'idée d'Europe," *La Revue hebdomadaire*, 6 Feb. 1926.

Vloemans, A. "Europeisme, Russicisme, Amerikanisme," *Haagsch Maandblad*, 1927, pp. 618–26.

Vogel, Emanuel. "Nordamerikas Wirtschaftsaufstieg und das paneuropäische Problem," *Weltwirtschaftsliches Archiv* 25 (1927).

Vogel, Walter. "Erdteilstaaten als Weltmacht," *Weltwirtschaftsliches Archiv* 20 (1924): 55–78.

Voeste, Johannes. "Frankreich und Deutschland," *Wissen und Leben* 13 (1 Oct. 1919–15 Sept. 1920).

———. "Von der Idee des Völkerbunds," *Wissen und Leben* 12 (Mar. 1920).

Voyenne, Bernard. "L'Idée fédéraliste sous la Révolution française," *La Fédération*, no. 106 (Nov. 1953): 815–24.

Waechter, Max. "The United States of Europe," *Advocate of Peace*, Nov. 1924, p. 607.

Weber, Alfred. "Paneuropa," *Europäische Revue* 1 (Dec. 1925).

Webster, C. K. "L'Empire britannique et la Société des Nations," *L'Esprit international* 1, no. 2 (Apr. 1927).

Wehberg, Hans. "Briands europäisches Manifest," *Friedens-Warte* 30 (June 1930).

———. "Eine Umfrage zum Weltfriedenskongress," *Friedens-Warte* 24 (Sept. 1924).

Weinberg, Emil. "Europa und die Eisenbahnen," *Das neue Europa* 15 (Apr.–May, 1929).

Weiss, Louise. "Voeux pour la fédération européenne," *L'Europe nouvelle*, 4 Jan. 1930.

Welter, Karl. "Weltwirtschaft und Zollvereinsfragen," *Wissen und Leben* 12 (Oct. 1918 and Sept. 1919).

Wirth, Joseph. "Frankreich und Deutschland," *Deutsche Republik*, 2 Sept. 1927.

———. "Muss Frankreich einen Krieg mit Deutschland befürchten?" *Deutsche Republik*, 14 Jan. 1927.

Wolf, Alfred. "Der Weg zum Frieden," *Die Hilfe*, 5 May 1924.

Woytinsky, Wladimir. "Neue Weltwirtschaft—Neue Weltpolitik," *Die Gesellschaft* 2 (1925).

Zimmern, Alfred. "L'Idée d'une fédération européenne à la dernière assemblée de la Société des Nations," *L'Esprit international* 6 (Jan. 1931).

Some Relevant Later Works

Acker, Detler. *Walther Schücking*. Münster, 1970.

Aron, Robert, Jean Bareth, and Henri Brugmans. *L'Ere des fédérations*. Paris, 1958.

Backhaus, Dorothee. "Die Europabewegung in der Politik nach dem Ersten Weltkrieg und Ihr Widerhall in der Presse von 1918–1933." Dissertation, Munich, 1951.

Banule, André. *Heinrich Mann: Le poète et la politique*. Paris, 1967.

Bariéty, Jacques, and Charles Bloch. "Un Tentative de reconciliation franco-allemande et son échec, 1932–1933," *Revue historique et contemporaine* 15 (1968): 433–65.

Bauer, Hans, and H. G. Ritzel. *Von der eidgenössischen zur europäischen Föderation*. Zurich, 1940.

Bauer, Josef. "Die österreichische Friedensbewegung." Inaugural Dissertation, Vienna, 1949.

Baumont, Maurice. *Aristide Briand: Diplomat und Idealist*. Göttingen, 1966.

Binoux, Paul. *Les Pionniers de l'Europe: L'Europe et le rapprochement franco-allemand*. Paris, 1962.

Böhme, Helmut. *Deutschlands Weg zur Grossmacht*. Berlin, 1967.

Bomback, Gottfried, and Henri Brugmans. *Sciences humaines et l'intégration européenne*. Leyden, 1960. Preface by Robert Schuman.

Bonnefous, Edouard. *L'Europe en face de son destin*. Paris, 1952.

———. *L'Idée européenne et sa réalisation*. Paris, 1950.

Bonnet, Georges. *Vingt ans de vie politique*. Paris, 1969.

Bonneville, Georges. *Prophètes et témoins de l'Europe: Essai sur l'idée d'Europe dans la littérature française de 1914 à nos jours*. Leyden, 1961.

Boulangier, Pierre. *Tocsin de l'ère nouvelle*. Paris, 1948. Argues that the only way to escape chaos is to unite western Europe.

Briantchaninoff, Boris. *Le Problème de l'union fédérale européenne: Ni Europe, ni Asie, la Russie est Russie*. Paris, 1930. The author was a Russian émigré.

Brüning, Heinrich. *Memoiren, 1918–1934*. Stuttgart, 1970.

Brugmans, Henri. *L'Idée européenne, 1918–1965*. Bruges, 1965.

———. *Panorama de la pensée fédéraliste*. Paris, 1956.

_____. *Prophètes et fondateurs de l'Europe*. Bruges, 1974.

Brugmans, Hendryk (Henri). *Skizze eines europäischen Zusammenlebens*. Frankfurt a.M., 1953.

Brunschwigg, Léon. *L'Esprit européen*. Neuchâtel, 1947.

Burgelin, Henri. "Le Mouvement pacifiste dans l'Allemagne de Weimar," *Cahiers de l'Association Interuniversitaire*, Strasbourg, 1961.

Cornebise, Alfred E. "Some Aspects of the German Respone to the Ruhr Occupation, 1923." Ph.D. Dissertation, University of North Carolina, Chapel Hill, 1965.

Cornides, Wilhelm. "Der Strassburger Europarat in der Perspektive der Vorschläge Briands von 1929," *Europa Archiv*, 5 Sept. 1949.

Corrial, Joseph. *La Paix par les Etats-Unis d'Europe*. Avignon, 1939.

Coudenhove-Kalergi, Richard. *Die europäische Nation*. Stuttgart, 1953.

_____. *Europa ohne Elend*. Vienna, 1936.

_____. *Europe Must Unite*. Glarus, 1939.

_____. "Der grösste Europäer," *Paneuropa* 9, no. 3 (Mar. 1935).

_____. *Der Kampf um Europa: Aus meinem Leben*. Zürich, 1949.

Curtius, Ernst R. *Französischer Geist im 20. Jahrhundert*. Bern, 1952.

Curtius, Julius. *Bemühung um Österreich: Das Scheitern des Zollunionplans von 1931*. Heidelberg, 1947.

Deates, Fernand. *La grande Croisade pour la réalisation des véritables Etats-Unis d'Europe*. . . . Paris, 1952.

Dell'Isola, Maria, and Georges Bourgin. *Mazzini, promoteur de la République Italienne et pionnier de la fédération européenne*. Paris, 1956.

Droz, Jacques. *L'Europe centrale*. Paris, 1960.

Duroselle, Jean-Baptiste. *L'Idée d'Europe dans l'histoire*. Paris, 1965.

Einaudi, Luigi. *La guerra e l'unità europea*. Milan, 1948.

Elisha, Achille. *Aristide Briand: Discours et écrits de politique étrangère, la paix, l'union européenne*. . . . Paris, 1965.

Erdmann, Karl D. *Adenauer in der Rheinlandpolitik nach dem Ersten Weltkrieg*. Stuttgart, 1966.

_____. "Der Europaplan Briands im Licht der englischen Akten." *Geschichte in Wissenschaft und Unterricht*, no. 1, 1950.

Europe Unie, 1949-1950: Etudes pour la promotion d'une conscience européenne. Colmar-Strasbourg, 1949.

Ewald, Josef. "Die deutsche Aussenpolitik und der Europaplan Briands." Dissertation, Marburg, 1951.

Fabre-Luce, Alfred. *Caillaux*. Paris, 1933.

_____. *Le Siècle prend figure*. Paris, 1949.

Fodor, Marcus. "Erziehung zum Europäer." *Paneuropa* 11, nos. 6-8, pp. 207 ff.

Foerster, Rolf H., ed. *Die Idee Europa, 1300-1946*. Munich, 1963.

_____. *Europa: Geschichte einer politischen Idee*. Munich, 1967.

Fortuna, Ursula. *Der Völkerbundgedanke in Deutschland während des Ersten Weltkrieges*. Zurich, 1974.

Friedländer, Ernst. *Wie Europa begann: Die geistigen und politischen Wurzeln der europäischen Einigung*. Cologne, 1968.

Frommelt, Reinhard. *Paneuropa oder Mitteleuropa: Einigungsbestrebungen im Kalkül deutscher Wirtschaft und Politik, 1925-1930*. Stuttgart, 1977.

Geigenmüller, Ernst. "Botschafter von Hoesch und der deutsch-österreichische Zollunionplan von 1931." *Historische Zeitschrift* 195 (1962): 581 ff.

_____. *Briand: Tragik des grossen Europäers*. Bonn, 1969.

Gerlach, Helmut von. *Von rechts nach links*. Zurich, 1937.

Gide, André. *Journal, 1889-1939*. Paris, 1948.

Giscard d'Estaing, Edmond. *La France et l'unification économique de l'Europe*. Genin, 1953.